THE NEW URBAN CONDITION

This book explores new architectural and design perspectives on the contemporary urban condition. While architects and urban designers have long maintained that their actions, drawings, and buildings are "post-critical," this book seeks to expand the critical dimension of architecture and urbanism.

In a series of historical and theoretical studies, this book examines how the materialities, forms, and practices of architecture and urban design can act as a critique towards the new urban condition. It proposes not only new concepts and theories but also instruments of analysis and reflection to better understand the current counter-hegemonic tendencies in both disciplinary strategies and appropriation tactics.

The diversely international selection of chapters, from Brazil, Portugal, Spain, Sweden, the United States, and the Netherlands, combine different theoretical and empirical perspectives into a new analysis of the city and architecture. Demonstrating the need for new critical urban and architectural thinking that engages with the challenges and processes of the contemporary urban condition, this volume will be a thought-provoking read for academics and students in architecture, urban design, geography, political science, and more.

Leandro Medrano is Associate Professor in the Faculty of Architecture and Urbanism of the University of São Paulo (FAUUSP). His main work addresses the relationship between social housing and urban development. Theory of urbanism, urban sociology, urban design, and economic development are some of the research fields involved in his research. Medrano has also been involved in partnerships with research groups from other universities, such as GSD Harvard, KTH, UPM, and TUDelft. In addition to teaching and research activities, he has served in many positions at the university, such as Coordinator of the Architecture and Urbanism Course, Board of Directors of the Science Museum of Unicamp, and Executive Committee of the Museum of Visual Arts at Unicamp. He is also Editor-in-Chief of the journal *Pós.Revista FAUUSP* and coordinator of the research group *Critical Thinking and Contemporary City* (PC3). His work has been published in books and academic journals.

Luiz Recaman is Associate Professor in the Faculty of Architecture and Urbanism of the University of São Paulo (FAUUSP). His main work addresses the critique of architecture and aesthetics, and modern Brazilian and contemporary architecture. He is Editor-in-Chief of the journal *Revista ARA FAUUSP* and coordinator of the research group *Critical Thinking and Contemporary City* (PC3). Prof. Recaman is co-author of *Brazil's Modern Architecture* (Phaidon, 2004) and *Vilanova Artigas—Habitação e Cidade na Modernização Brasileira* (Editora da Unicamp, 2014).

Tom Avermaete is Professor for the History and Theory of Urban Design at ETH Zurich. His research focuses on the architecture of the city and the changing roles, approaches, and tools of architects and urban designers from a cross-cultural perspective. Recent book publications include *Architecture of the Welfare State* (with Swenarton and Van Den Heuvel, 2014), *The Balcony* (with Koolhaas, 2014), *Casablanca—Chandigarh* (with Casciato, 2015), *Shopping Towns Europe* (with Gosseye, 2017), and *Acculturating the Shopping Centre* (with Gosseye, 2018). Avermaete curated the exhibitions *In the Desert of Modernity* (Berlin, Casablanca, 2008, 2009), *How architects, experts, politicians, international agencies and citizens negotiate modern planning: Casablanca Chandigarh* (Montreal, 2015), and *Lived-In: The Modern City as Performative Infrastructure* (Antwerp, 2017).

THE NEW URBAN CONDITION

Criticism and Theory from Architecture and Urbanism

Edited by Leandro Medrano, Luiz Recaman, and Tom Avermaete

NEW YORK AND LONDON

First published 2021
by Routledge
52 Vanderbilt Avenue, New York, NY 10017

and by Routledge
2 Park Square, Milton Park, Abingdon, Oxon OX14 4RN

Routledge is an imprint of the Taylor & Francis Group, an informa business

© 2021 selection and editorial matter, Leandro Medrano, Luiz Recaman, and Tom Avermaete; individual chapters, the contributors

The right of Leandro Medrano, Luiz Recaman, and Tom Avermaete to be identified as the authors of the editorial material, and of the authors for their individual chapters, has been asserted in accordance with sections 77 and 78 of the Copyright, Designs and Patents Act 1988.

All rights reserved. No part of this book may be reprinted or reproduced or utilised in any form or by any electronic, mechanical, or other means, now known or hereafter invented, including photocopying and recording, or in any information storage or retrieval system, without permission in writing from the publishers.

Trademark notice: Product or corporate names may be trademarks or registered trademarks, and are used only for identification and explanation without intent to infringe.

British Library Cataloguing-in-Publication Data
A catalogue record for this book is available from the British Library

Library of Congress Cataloging-in-Publication Data
Names: Medrano, Leandro, 1968– editor. | Recamán, Luiz, editor. | Avermaete, Tom, editor.
Title: The new urban condition : criticism and theory from architecture and urbanism / edited by Leandro Medrano, Luiz Recamán and Tom Avermaete.
Description: Abingdon, Oxon ; New York : Routledge, 2021. | Includes bibliographical references and index.
Identifiers: LCCN 2020044771 (print) | LCCN 2020044772 (ebook) | ISBN 9780367607593 (hardback) | ISBN 9780367607609 (paperback) | ISBN 9781003100362 (ebook)
Subjects: LCSH: Architecture—Philosophy. | Space (Architecture)—Philosophy.
Classification: LCC NA2500 .N49 2021 (print) | LCC NA2500 (ebook) | DDC 720.1—dc23
LC record available at https://lccn.loc.gov/2020044771
LC ebook record available at https://lccn.loc.gov/2020044772

ISBN: 978-0-367-60759-3 (hbk)
ISBN: 978-0-367-60760-9 (pbk)
ISBN: 978-1-003-10036-2 (ebk)

Typeset in Bembo
by Apex CoVantage, LLC

CONTENTS

List of Figures — *vii*
List of Contributors — *xi*
Acknowledgments — *xv*

Introduction — 1
Leandro Medrano, Luiz Recaman, and Tom Avermaete

PART I
Theoretical Tenets — 9

1 Remains of Architectural Reason — 11
   Luiz Recaman

2 On Architecture and Urban Space After the Ideological Crisis of Neoliberalism — 32
   Leandro Medrano

3 Constructing the Commons: Towards Another Architectural Theory of the City? — 54
   Tom Avermaete

4 Erving Goffman's Sociology of Physical Space for Architects and Urban Designers — 73
   Fraya Frehse

5 Broken Windows, Revisited — 86
   Reinhold Martin

6 Architecture and the Critical Project — 95
   Sven-Olov Wallenstein

7   Ruins of the Future   106
    Otília Arantes

PART II
Rethinking Spatial Rhythms   **127**

8   Henri Lefebvre and the Morphology of a Spatial Dialectic   129
    César Simoni Santos

9   Anthropophagic Phenomenology: Encounters at Lina Bo's
    SESC Pompeia Cultural and Leisure Center   147
    Natalia Escobar Castrillón

10 Incremental Housing: A Short History of an Idea   160
    Nelson Mota

11 The Bubble, the Arrow, and the Area: Urban Design and
    Diagrammatic Concepts of Human Action   183
    Daniel Koch

PART III
Contemporary Spatial Forms of the City   **209**

12 The Subaltern City: Revisiting the Materialist Critique of Urban Form   211
    Marta Caldeira

13 The Chronicles of Neo   228
    Janina Gosseye

14 The Legitimized Reproduction of a Corporate Typology: Dispositions of
    Architectural Form in the LEED® Rating System   235
    Raphael Grazziano

15 What Ever Happened to Social Housing?   252
    Sergio Martín Blas

16 Five Fronts for One Single Position: Critical Strategies for Contemporary
    Pedagogy in the Subject of Architectural Design   266
    Carmen Espegel Alonso and Daniel Movilla Vega

Image Credits   *285*
Index   *288*

FIGURES

1.1	Residents dive in Praça Mauá in downtown Rio de Janeiro. This location is part of the controversial reform carried out by the Porto Maravilha Urban Operation for the 2016 Olympics. Photo taken in 2015.	13
1.2	The housing complex at Vélizy-Villacoublay, France, built between 1962–1976.	15
1.3	Piscina das Marés de Leça da Palmeira, designed by Álvaro Siza Vieira (1966). Photos taken in 2016.	16
1.4	A bird's-eye view of a community in New Harmony, Indiana, United States, as proposed by Robert Owen. Engraving by F. Bate, London, 1838.	22
1.5	Aerial view of Barcelona in the region of the city's expansion with the morphology defined by Ildefons Cerdá's project (1859). Photo taken in 2007.	23
1.6	São Paulo skyline. At the center of the image is Copan, designed by Oscar Niemeyer (1966). Photo taken in 2011.	24
1.7	A man practices capoeira in an open area of a Brazilian favela, 2017.	29
2.1	Building projection by visual artist Matías Segura displaying "We Will Not Return to Normality Because Normality Was the Problem," Santiago, Chile, 2019.	33
2.2	China Central Television Headquarters, designed by OMA/Rem Koolhaas, Beijing, China, 2012.	36
2.3	Buildings on Paseo de la Reforma, Mexico City, 2013.	39
2.4	Downtown São Paulo, Brazil, 2018.	46
2.5	Interior view of Elza Berquó house, João Batista Vilanova Artigas, São Paulo, Brazil, 1967. Photo taken in 2010.	48
2.6	External view of the Faculty of Architecture and Urbanism of the University of São Paulo (FAUUSP), designed by João Batista Vilanova Artigas and Carlos Cascaldi, São Paulo, Brazil, 1969. Photo taken in 2018.	49
2.7	Internal view of the Faculty of Architecture and Urbanism of the University of São Paulo (FAUUSP), designed by João Batista Vilanova Artigas and Carlos Cascaldi, São Paulo, Brazil, 1969. Photo taken in 2018.	50

Figures

3.1	Christian Remick, *A Prospective View of part of the Commons*, 1902.	57
3.2	Fosse Dione. Tonnerre, France (1758).	58
3.3	Plates from Pierre Le Muet, *Manière de Bien Bastir*, 1647.	60
3.4	Plates from Adolphe Alphand, *Les Promenades De Paris*, 1867.	64
3.5	Patrick Geddes, map of open spaces by Open Space Committee of Citizens, 1910.	66
3.6	A rediscovered backcourt, 1910.	67
3.7	SESC Pompeia, designed by Lina Bo Bardi (1982).	68
3.8	SESC 24 de Maio, designed by Paulo Mendes da Rocha and MMBB Arquitetos (2017).	69
3.9	SESC 24 de Maio, designed by Paulo Mendes da Rocha and MMBB Arquitetos (2017).	70
3.10	SESC Paulista, designed by Königsberger Vannucchi Arquitetos Associados (2018).	71
7.1	Interiors of Moscow's subway stations. Photos taken in 2014 and 2018.	108
7.2	Passage in Galerie Vivienne, Paris, France (1823). Photo taken in 2011.	111
7.3	Demolition of Butte des Moulins for Avenue de l'Opéra, Paris, 1870.	113
7.4	Dreamland Tower, Coney Island, 1906.	115
7.5	Rockefeller Center and RCA Building from 515 Madison Ave, New York, 1933.	118
7.6	Petronas Tower, Kuala Lampur, designed by Cesar Pelli (1998). Photo taken in 2010.	119
7.7	Dubai construction workers. In the background, the tallest building in the world—Burj Dubai, 2008.	121
7.8	World Trade Center, New York, designed by Emery Roth & Sons and Minoru Yamasaki Associates (1976). Aerial view taken in March 2001 and during the attack on September 11, 2001.	122
8.1	According to positions before history.	132
8.2	According to positions before historian thought.	133
8.3	Dialectic between Hegel and Marx.	135
8.4	Lefebvrian dialectic according to the triad of authors.	137
8.5	Developed scheme of the dialectic between formal logic and dialectic.	139
9.1	Aerial view of Lina Bo's SESC Pompeia's Cultural and Leisure Center, São Paulo, Brazil.	150
9.2	Lina Bo's sketch of the SESC Pompeia's collective space conceived as a sensorial landscape.	151
9.3	The decentering chimney and pond at the SESC Pompeia's collective space.	153
9.4	Lina Bo, "View of a Possible Future," sketch of the SESC Pompeia's sport towers.	155
9.5	Material and aesthetic explorations at the SESC Pompeia's workshops and exhibitions space.	156
10.1	Illustration of the "Growing Siedlung," as published in Leberecht Migge's *Die wachsende Siedlung nach biologischen Gesetzen* (1932).	163
10.2	Project submitted by Sau Lai Chan to the International Design Competition for the Urban Environment of Developing Countries (1976).	165
10.3	Axonometric perspective of the typical cluster for low-income families in the Charkop sites-and-services scheme (Kandivali, Mumbai).	168

10.4	Axonometric perspective of the expected stages of growth and change of the dwelling units designed by Aldo van Eyck for the PREVI-Lima competition.	171
10.5	Clustering strategy for typical dwelling plots in Skjetten.	174
10.6	Illustration of the basic design principles of Skjetten Town.	175
10.7	Balance between design and governance in different incremental housing approaches.	179
11.1	Gruen Associates' illustration of the future Fulton Mall.	184
11.2	White Arkitekter AB's winning proposal for Söderstaden-Hovet in Stockholm in 2017.	185
11.3	Kiyoyuki Nishihara's comparisons between the functional approach to spaces in the West and in Japan.	189
11.4	Local, communal, and regional centers in the draft regional plan of Stockholm in 1966 (top) and Granfelt's critical diagram (bottom).	190
11.5	Christine Frederick's illustration of "bad" and "good" kitchen arrangements.	192
11.6	The "Suburban labyrinth" and its cure.	193
11.7	The forecasting model as found in the Chicago Area Transportation Study.	194
11.8	A diagram of the Urban Transport Modeling System and a pedagogical diagram of what the steps entail.	195
11.9	The geographical distribution of income statistics in Gottsunda outside of Uppsala, Sweden. Darker areas for higher income, darker building footprints closer to schools.	197
11.10	Part of the typomorphological map of Stockholm and the 12 types of Stockholm's "Byggnadsordning."	198
12.1	15 Hudson Yards residential tower in New York, by Diller Scofidio + Renfro (2019).	212
12.2	The two separate entrances for condo owners and subsidized renters at 15 Hudson Yards. Although giving access to the same tower, the separate entrance for subsidized units tucked under the High Line has a different legal address, 553 West 30th Street.	213
12.3	Saverio Muratori, morphological study and typological analysis of Venice's quartieri.	217
12.4	Carlo Aymonino, comparative morphological analyses of residential and working sectors in the urban development of London and Glasgow.	218
12.5	Manuel de Solà-Morales, taxonomy of structural typologies of urban growth (left); comparative chart Cuadriculas, Mallas y Reticulas (right).	220
12.6	Pier Luigi Cervellati, morphological analysis of Bologna's urban fabric and "typological structures" of popular housing.	222
12.7	Álvaro Siza, morphological analysis of proletarian islands in S. Victor area in Porto, Portugal (1976).	223
12.8	Joan Busquets, Plan of Areas of New Centrality, Barcelona (1986).	224
14.1	One Bryant Park, designed by COOKFOX Architects (2009).	245
14.2	Eldorado Business Tower, designed by aflalo/gasperini arquitetos (2007).	246
14.3	São Paulo Corporate Towers, designed by Pelli Clarke Pelli and aflalo/gasperini arquitetos (2015).	248
14.4	Facade detail. São Paulo Corporate Towers, designed by Pelli Clarke Pelli and aflalo/gasperini arquitetos (2015).	249

x Figures

15.1	*23 de Enero* housing estate in Caracas (originally *2 de Diciembre*), architects Carlos Raúl Villanueva, José Hoffmann and José Manuel Mijares, 1955–1957.	253
15.2	Aerial view of Caracas in 1958, with Cerro Piloto in the background.	254
15.3	*Cerros de Caracas*. From the series "Caracas una quimera urbana," 1982.	255
15.4	Cerro San Cristóbal in Lima, 2015 (left), and Silodam housing building in Amsterdam, MVRDV, 2003 (right).	259
15.5	Social housing units for EMVS in Vallecas, Madrid, 2011 (left), and plan of Model House for Four Families, London, 1851 (right).	259
15.6	The so-called wall of shame in Lima, defining the border between the informal housing at Pamplona Alta and the affluent neighborhood of Casuarinas, 2015.	263
16.1	Ground floor plan.	275
16.2	First to fifth floors.	276
16.3	View from Embajadores Street.	277
16.4	View of the living room towards Embajadores and Mira el Sol Streets with the expanded metal lattices open.	278
16.5	View of the living room towards Embajadores and Mira el Sol Streets with the expanded metal lattices closed.	278
16.6	Model showing shared collective spaces in red.	279
16.7	View of the gallery with the stairs and the elevator in the background.	279
16.8	Longitudinal section from the courtyard to Embajadores Street.	280
16.9	View of the gallery and stairs from the backyard.	281
16.10	Contextual elevation of Embajadores Street.	282
16.11	View of the residential building in its context from Embajadores Street.	283

CONTRIBUTORS

Carmen Espegel Alonso presents a career linked by three fields: teaching, research, and architectural practice. She is Professor at the School of Architecture of Madrid (Spain) and focuses her research on housing, female architects, and critics in architecture. She is the author of *Women Architects in the Modern Movement* (Routledge 2018), *Collective Housing in Spain 1992–2015* (TC Cuadernos 2016), *Collective Housing in Spain XX Century (1929–1992)* (TC Cuadernos 2013), *Eileen Gray: Objects and Furniture Design* (Polígrafa 2013), and *Aires Modernos: E.1027 by Eileen Gray and Jean Badovici* (Mairea Libros 2010). As an architect with her own office espegel-fisac arquitectos, she participates in many contests and has won awards. Her work has been published in several books and specialized journals.

Otília Arantes is a PhD professor at the University of São Paulo since 1981, giving lectures and supervising students in the Faculty of Philosophy, Literature and Human Sciences and in the Faculty of Architecture and Urbanism. Arantes' PhD was completed at the Université de Paris I (Panthéon-Sorbonne) in 1972. Her essays and books address subjects of modern and contemporary art and architecture, such as *Berlim e Barcelona: Duas Imagens Estratégicas* (Edusp, 2012) and *Chai-na* (2011), about recent developments in the European and Chinese urban planning, or *O Lugar da Arquitetura depois dos Modernos* (Edusp, 1993) and *Urbanismo em Fim de Linha e outros Estudos sobre o Colapso da Modernização Arquitetônica* (Edusp, 1998), dealing with modern and postmodern architecture.

Tom Avermaete is Professor for the History and Theory of Urban Design at ETH Zurich. His research focuses on the architecture of the city and the changing roles, approaches, and tools of architects and urban designers from a cross-cultural perspective. Recent book publications include *Architecture of the Welfare State* (with Swenarton and Van Den Heuvel, 2014), *The Balcony* (with Koolhaas, 2014), *Casablanca—Chandigarh* (with Casciato, 2015), *Shopping Towns Europe* (with Gosseye, 2017), and *Acculturating the Shopping Centre* (with Gosseye, 2018). Avermaete curated the exhibitions *In the Desert of Modernity* (Berlin, Casablanca, 2008, 2009), *How Architects, Experts, Politicians, International Agencies and Citizens Negotiate Modern Planning: Casablanca Chandigarh* (Montreal, 2015), and *Lived-In: The Modern City as Performative Infrastructure* (Antwerp, 2017).

Sergio Martín Blas is an architect, PhD adjunct professor, and researcher on architectural design at ETSAM (Universidad Politécnica de Madrid, Spain). He has also been Academic Secretary of the Advanced Architectural Design PhD Program at UPM since 2016; visiting professor at UNR (Rosario), UCSG (Guayaquil), and La Sapienza (Roma); and visiting researcher at TU Delft, TU Berlin, and Cooper Union (NYC), among other universities. He has served as the coordinator of the NuTAC Research Group and as curator of several international exhibitions on social housing architecture: "I+D+VS: futuros de la vivienda social en 7 ciudades," "A pie de calle: Vivienda Social y Regeneración Urbana," and "Arquitecturas VIS. Vivienda de interés social en seis ciudades iberoamericanas."

Marta Caldeira is an architect, historian, and senior lecturer at the Yale School of Architecture. Her research investigates transnational discourses of architecture and the city, with a particular focus on historical contexts of political transition. Her approach to the history of urban form explores the intersection of architecture and urbanism with politics and social economics in the areas of urban planning, housing, preservation, and urban pedagogy. Her writings on architecture and the city have appeared in international journals and recent anthologies on modern and contemporary architecture. She is currently director of research at the Yale Urban Design Workshop.

Natalia Escobar Castrillón is an assistant professor in Architecture at Carleton University (Ottawa, CA). She holds a PhD degree and her master's in design in critical conservation from Harvard University (Cambridge, US). She received her master's in architecture from the Universidad de Sevilla (Spain) and is a licensed architect. She is the founder and Editor-in-Chief of *Oblique*, a journal on architectural conservation. Dr. Escobar Castrillón has taught at Harvard University and College, at Boston University, at the Pontifica Universidad Catolica de Chile, and was a Visiting Scholar and Researcher at the Faculdade de Arquitetura e Urbanismo da Universidade de São Paulo.

Fraya Frehse is Professor of Sociology at the University of São Paulo (USP), where she coordinates the Centre for Studies and Research on the Sociology of Space and Time (NEPSESTE). She is an alumna of the Alexander von Humboldt Foundation, Productivity Research Fellow of the Brazilian Research Council (CNPq), and Visiting Fellow (2020) and Life Member (from 2020) of Clare Hall College (University of Cambridge).

Her research focuses mainly on urban theory; space, everyday life, and history; space and time in sociology; body, public space, and urbanization (in Brazil); urban mobility; urban inequality/poverty; cultural heritage; urban visual culture; and sociology of everyday knowledge.

Janina Gosseye is Associate Professor at the Delft University of Technology's Faculty of Architecture and the Built Environment. Her research is situated at the nexus of 20th-century architectural and urban history on the one hand, and social and political history on the other. Her most recent book is *Speaking of Buildings: Oral History in Architectural Research* (with Naomi Stead and Deborah van der Plaat, 2019).

Raphael Grazziano holds a PhD degree at the Faculty of Architecture and Urbanism of the University of São Paulo (FAUUSP, 2019). He has a bachelor's in philosophy from the Faculty of Philosophy, Literature and Human Sciences of the University of São Paulo (FFLCH-USP; 2017), and in architecture and urbanism at FAUUSP (2012). He did a stint at École Nationale

Supérieure d'Architecture de Paris La Villette (ENSAPLV; 2010–2011) during undergraduate studies, and was Visiting Assistant in Research at Yale University (2018) during his PhD. He was editor's assistant for *Pós*, the academic journal at FAUUSP (2016–2018).

Daniel Koch is an architect, researcher in urban design, and docent in architecture at the KTH School of Architecture and the Built Environment, whose research investigates spatial configuration, diagrams and abstractions, and processes of subjectification within the larger frame of architectural theory and urban design. Lately his research has focused on the role of memory, projection, and imagination within observation-based research, our understanding of relations between architecture and social structures, and between modelling and analytical concepts of architecture and human behavior. He is also a practicing architect at Patchwork Architecture Laboratory, and has done research and taught at several other universities.

Reinhold Martin is Professor of Architecture in the Graduate School of Architecture, Planning, and Preservation at Columbia University, where he directs the Temple Hoyne Buell Center for the Study of American Architecture, and is a member of the Center for Comparative Media. A founding co-editor of the journal *Grey Room*, Martin's books include *The Organizational Complex: Architecture, Media, and Corporate Space* (MIT, 2003), *Utopia's Ghost: Architecture and Postmodernism, Again* (Minnesota, 2010), and *The Urban Apparatus: Mediapolitics and the City* (Minnesota, 2016). His most recent book is *Knowledge Worlds: Media, Materiality, and the Making of the Modern University* (Columbia University Press, 2021).

Leandro Medrano is Associate Professor in the Faculty of Architecture and Urbanism of the University of São Paulo (FAUUSP). His main work addresses the relationship between social housing and urban development. Theory of urbanism, urban sociology, urban design, and economic development are some of the research fields involved in his research. Medrano has also been involved in partnerships with research groups from other universities, such as GSD Harvard, KTH, UPM, and TUDelft. In addition to teaching and research activities, he has served in many positions at the university, such as Coordinator of the Architecture and Urbanism Course, Board of Directors of the Science Museum of Unicamp, and Executive Committee of the Museum of Visual Arts at Unicamp. He is Editor-in-Chief of the journal *Pós.Revista FAUUSP* and coordinator of the research group *Critical Thinking and Contemporary City* (PC3). His work has been published in books and academic journals.

Nelson Mota is an associate professor at the Department of Architecture of Delft University of Technology, where he coordinates the Global Housing educational program and the Global Housing research group. His current pedagogical and research interests are focused on the relationship between housing design and the reproduction of vernacular social and spatial practices. He is production editor and a member of the editorial board of the journal *Footprint* and the book series *DASH*.

Luiz Recaman is Associate Professor in the Faculty of Architecture and Urbanism of the University of São Paulo (FAUUSP). His main work addresses the critique of architecture and aesthetics, and modern Brazilian and contemporary architecture. He is Editor-in-Chief of the journal *Revista ARA FAUUSP* and coordinator of the research group *Critical Thinking and Contemporary City* (PC3). Prof. Recaman is co-author of *Brazil's Modern Architecture* (Phaidon, 2004) and *Vilanova Artigas—Habitação e Cidade na Modernização Brasileira* (Editora da Unicamp, 2014).

César Simoni Santos is a PhD professor at the Department of Geography of the University of São Paulo. He is a member of the group Urban Geography Radical Critique, researcher in the group Urbanisation and Globalisation, member of the international network Spatial Justice/Justice Spatiale, hosted in France, member of the group Critical Urban Theory at the Institute of Advanced Studies of the University of São Paulo, and coordinator of the academic partnership with the Geographischen Institut of the Christian-Albrechts-Universität zu Kiel, Germany. His writings address the theories of Henri Lefebvre and the contemporary production of space, as in "The geophagic nature of financial dominance in the Brazilian real estate market" (*DIE ERDE*, v. 149, n. 4, 2018).

Daniel Movilla Vega is Associate Professor at Umeå School of Architecture (Sweden), where he leads a studio in the master's program. He holds a PhD in architecture, summa cum laude, from the Polytechnic University of Madrid. His doctoral thesis, *Housing and Revolution*, won the Award for Outstanding Doctorate 2015–2016. Daniel has been Postdoctoral Research Fellow in Architecture at Luleå University of Technology (Sweden). His book, *99 Years of the Housing Question in Sweden* (Studentlitteratur), presents the history of modern architecture in Swedish housing as a spatial, social, and political phenomenon.

Sven-Olov Wallenstein is Professor of Philosophy at Södertörn University, Stockholm. He is the translator of works by Baumgarten, Winckelmann, Lessing, Kant, Hegel, Frege, Husserl, Heidegger, Levinas, Derrida, Deleuze, Foucault, Rancière, and Agamben, as well as the author of numerous books on philosophy, contemporary art, and architecture. Recent publications include *Upplysningens estetik: Nedslag i 1700-talet* (2019), *Spacing Philosophy: Lyotard and the Idea of the Exhibition* (2019, with Daniel Birnbaum), and *Adorno: Negative dialektik och estetisk teori* (2019), as well as translations of Adorno's *Negative Dialektik*, *Ästhetische Theorie*, and *Mahler: Eine musikalische Physiognomie*.

ACKNOWLEDGMENTS

We thank Raphael Grazziano, Mariana Wilderom, and Renata Sanchez for their editorial assistance, and Nelson Kon, Cristiano Mascaro, and Hugo Segawa for kindly granting us the permission to use their photos. We are also grateful to the team of the research group Critical Thinking and Contemporary City (PC3). This book was supported by Conselho Nacional de Desenvolvimento Científico e Tecnológico (CNPq) and São Paulo Research Foundation (FAPESP, grant number 16/22704–8).

Early versions of chapters in this book have appeared in the following publications:

Chapter 3, "Constructing the Commons: Towards Another Architectural Theory of the City?" by Tom Avermaete, was published in 2018 in the journal *Arch+*, 232, pp. 32–43.

Chapter 4, "Erving Goffman's Sociology of Physical Space for Architects and Urban Designers," by Fraya Frehse, is a shorter and modified version of a German article published in 2016, "Erving Goffmans Soziologie des Raums," *Sozialraum.de* (online), *8*, that is a critical review and update of a previous Portuguese article published in 2008, "Erving Goffman, Sociólogo do Espaço," *Revista Brasileira de Ciências Sociais*, *23*(68), pp. 155–166.

Chapter 5, "Broken Windows, Revisited," by Reinhold Martin, was published in 2017 without its preface in *The Urban Apparatus* (2017), Minneapolis, MN: University of Minnesota Press, pp. 120–130.

Chapter 7, "The Ruins of the Future," by Otília Arantes, was first published in 2011, in a Portuguese version, as the preface of *Chai-na*, São Paulo, Brazil: Editora da Universidade de São Paulo, pp. 12–55.

Chapter 8, "Henri Lefebvre and the Morphology of a Spatial Dialectic," by César Simoni Santos, is a modified version of a Portuguese article, first published in 2019 as "Henri Lefebvre e a Morfologia de uma Dialética Espacial," in *GEOUSP Espaço e Tempo (Online)*, *23*(3), pp. 525–550.

INTRODUCTION

Leandro Medrano, Luiz Recaman, and Tom Avermaete

Among the multiple and wide-ranging analyses of the global state of affairs in the past two decades, urban space stands out as a crucial marker of our contemporary modernization processes and their inherent contradictions, tensions, and crises. Time and time again, urban space seems to manifest the most important challenges that our contemporary societies are facing. Let us name a few of these challenges.

First, what we understand as urban space has been radically affected by the exponential dissemination of what geographer Milton Santos defined as the "technical-informational medium" (Santos, 1996/2002). A large part of our social relations has irrevocably migrated into virtual environments, whether geared towards the sphere of production or that of private life. To be more precise, our contemporary urban practices and spaces illustrate that the separation between these spheres seems to increasingly disappear. The new social networks amalgamate work and personal life, dramatically changing the differentiation between public and private domains that underpinned modern revolutions. Our urban spaces illustrate that this redefinition of fundamental categories such as work and personal life, public and private domains, urges us to reconsider what it means to dwell and to appear in the public sphere.

Second, our conceptions of urban space as an artificial and autonomous world are put into crisis by the environmental collapse. The expansion of the "urban fabric"—as Henri Lefebvre characterized the "implosion" and "explosion" of the traditional city since the 19th century—is increasingly confronted with the natural world. The worldwide urban problems with air and water pollution, floods, and extreme weather conditions illustrate that the functional and financial motives that have been driving the development of cities and societies are at odds with our environmental needs and concerns. Our urban space exemplifies how financialization, understood as the increasing dominance of financial logics in all domains of life, has distanced the production of urban space from its everyday reality—at least its environmental reality. This "rift" not only uproots, as Lefebvre maintains, "the organic exchange between society and the earth" (Lefebvre, 1972/2016, p. 121), but also illuminates the necessity to re-establish the ideological primacy of the collective over the individual, and of the public over the private good, in urban and societal matters.

Third, the spatial dimensions of our urban spaces illuminate that our societies are increasingly characterized by a broad spectrum of social segregation processes. Neoliberalism leads to growing social inequality in all countries, mainly by excluding a large share of the population from formal work processes. In contrast to ideological universality, particularly Fordism, neoliberalism as a "new way of the world" drives individuals into a competition for a place within the system. As a result, new ideological places "outside the system" emerge for those who are incapable or unwilling to produce in accordance with the new principles. The many loci "outside the city," including all the manifestations of urban informality which gradually begin to erode the neoliberal urban structure (suburbs, gentrified urban centers, and global commercial districts), are the hallmarks of the inevitability and necessity of a different system. These urban outposts embody the urgent need to conceive different forms of production, not least the production of the city.

From this discussion, it becomes clear that we face today a new juncture in spatial dialectics, propelled by digital modernity, environmental changes, and neoliberal modes of production. Operating in this new urban condition requires the development of new methodologies and theories. The common ground of this book lies precisely in the efforts of the authors to articulate critical methodologies and disciplinary instruments that can respond to these structural changes in contemporary society. Updated concepts or revised methodologies are no longer sufficient to analyze the new urban condition or to intervene in it. We must face the reified space of contemporary capitalism critically, focusing on the very foundations of the "society of the spectacle," as well as on the environmental and social collapse in the era of "planetary urbanization."

This new urban condition will require not only a transformation of the strategies for apprehending and designing individual and collective spaces, but also a reconsideration of the ideological structure of the discipline of modern architecture and urbanism, which is firmly rooted in the principles of progress, universality, and equality—coined by the European enlightenment and the political revolutions following industrialization. The very erosion of these principles, which acted as a global transformational engine throughout the 20th century, while also strongly contributing to the expansion of the structural characteristics of an "uneven and combined" capitalist-industrial development, casts doubt on their critical capacity. Principles such as progress, universality, and equality seem to have been dismissed in the capitalist globalization, breaching the borders between the developed North and the underdeveloped South in unexpected ways. In North and South, the absorbed principles contributed to the widespread emergence of generic urban structures at the detriment of local characteristics, to the emergence of large environmental challenges in cities, and to an increased poverty translated into spatial precariousness.

The critical thinking and the review of the disciplinary foundations of architecture and urbanism that we advocate must be carefully considered from different viewpoints, all of which simultaneously global and local. Though many characteristics of the new urban condition seem to resonate across Northern and Southern hemispheres, their manifestations differ—and so should our reactions. For instance, a discussion regarding the crisis as well as the potential revival of the welfare state must stem from how this political form was made possible, partially possible, or impossible across different latitudes. What may seem like a "challenge" for European welfare states in crisis emerges as a "conflict"—or even a contradiction—in countries with political forms in which the principles of equality and universality were previously not as central. The unique contributions to this book speak of this North-South dynamic.

•

The authors and themes brought together in this book are the result of a years-long process in which researchers from different backgrounds and academic fields contributed their critical perspectives on contemporary urban space. The book is the result of a confluence, enabled through different academic partnerships in the form of seminars, conferences, professor and student exchange programs, and research projects, which encompassed different areas of knowledge such as architecture, urbanism, sociology, anthropology, geography, and philosophy. The resulting diversity seems to us a necessary requirement for the development of a critical perspective on contemporary urban space and has resulted in chapters with diverse styles and methodologies.

All chapters in this book speak of a rising awareness about the ongoing radical urban transformations, but also of the necessity to develop critical foundations to ground and guide our disciplinary action. The contributions reflect the fundamental and paradoxical condition of the disciplines of architecture and urbanism, in which analysis and intervention are intimately and reciprocally connected. For the architect and the urban designer, to reflect and to apprehend critically always implies, simultaneously, to intervene and to propose spatialities—and vice versa. This paradoxical condition is reflected in the composition of this book, as it brings together reflections with an emphasis on theoretical-critical and historical-temporal dimensions as discussions of spatial practices, and understands them all as counter-hegemonic manifestations.

•

The first part of the book, *Theoretical Tenets*, focuses on theoretical and methodological discussions, addressing contemporary issues by way of comprehensive historical-critical perspectives. The use of empirical examples serves to outline a general social framework, which allows us to situate contemporary socio-spatial phenomena within global historical processes. The urgent need to reconsider the disciplinary foundations, dilapidated by the collapse of modernity, and the emerging alternatives attempted in recent decades serve as a rendezvous point for the different researches hereby presented.

The chapter *Remains of Architectural Reason*, by architect Luiz Recaman, historically analyzes the constituent elements of contemporary spatiality, according to a disciplinary perspective from the realms of architecture and urbanism. The author aligns the hegemonic spatial developments in the countries of central capitalism against those implemented in underdeveloped countries, such as Brazil. By understanding modern experiences through the political contradictions of the social state since the interwar period, the author shifts the discussion towards an "architectural ideology," as thought by Manfredo Tafuri as well as Henri Lefebvre, each in their own way. This equation seeks to establish the basis for a critical action amidst the crisis of neoliberalism and the prospects for overcoming it.

In a similar vein, the chapter *On Architecture and Urban Space after the Ideological Crisis of Neoliberalism*, by architect Leandro Medrano, problematizes the pragmatic stances of what became known as the "post-critical" moment of architecture and urbanism, as well as the debate on disciplinary "autonomy." The author looks beyond the horizon to emphasize the need to resume the theoretical-critical disciplinary debate rejected during the decades of an architecture of spectacle and strategic planning. As such, the argument advocates for a further connection between architecture and real urban processes, both socially and spatially, as an alternative to the illusions of architectural autonomy and exceptionality.

One of the most debated themes regarding the possibilities for overcoming the impasses posed by the neoliberal development model is the concept of commons, on the agenda since the 1990s. The chapter *Constructing the Commons: Towards Another Architectural Theory of the City?*, by architect Tom Avermaete, extends this concept to the urban and architectural dimension and brings it closer to emerging social practices. This gulf between the structures of the state and the economy is present in some contemporary and past architectural experiences. A comprehension of their spatial and historical dimensions could become the central theme for the construction of new critical spatialities.

The chapter *Erving Goffman's Sociology of Physical Space for Architects and Urban Designers*, by sociologist Fraya Frehse, directly introduces an issue that permeates the entire structure of the book: space. The centrality of this theme in the second half of the 20th century designated a spatial turn that has since served as a beacon for a particular type of social thought. Goffman expands, as does Henri Lefebvre, the notions of social space towards the practices of everyday life and the scale of intersubjective interactions and the "body." He is a central author for the discussion on architecture and urbanism insofar as he innovates the spatial debate by way of his emphasis on its physical character, which had been somewhat despised by the different conceptions of "social space."

The renewed approach through which we propose to consider space, and particularly urban space, strives to reconcile the experiences of close localities and the totality of social space, according to their representations. This mediation pursues critical alternatives that may resonate in spatial interventions spearheaded by the discipline of Architecture and Urbanism (A&U), building bridges to connect these reflections to urban and architectural processes in the current state of affairs. The chapter *Broken Windows, Revisited*, by architect Reinhold Martin, shines this theoretical focus on an analysis of urban elements and fragments entangled in solidarity experiences in New York City. These practices, however, cannot be understood or even analyzed without problematizing the broader social process from which they are products and producers. Thus, the author unfolds this microcosm towards a criticism of the discretionary—and so-called exception—State and the corresponding economic system: neoliberalism and its current impasse.

Architecture and the Critical Project, by philosopher Sven-Olov Wallenstein, resumes the critical script of the seminal work by Italian architect Manfredo Tafuri, from which he explores the notion of "historical project" as the "project of a crisis." As such, the conventional demarcations between subject and object, language and reality, are problematized in light of architecture and its form. Following a two-decade eclipse, the influence of the Italian critic has recently expanded insofar as the uncritical project of architectural pragmatism, prevalent in the 1990s and 2000s, incited the collapse of the discipline itself as it becomes diluted in its positivity. Criticism, upon lacking objective design solutions, strips away the ideological links that connect architectural design with capitalist development. This critical movement is a spiral and does not allow for a final resolution or synthesis. Wallenstein's text allows us to further understand the difficult task of reflecting upon the possibilities of contemporary architecture, devoid of false illusions, albeit pursuing an *other* inscribed in the dialectic of history.

The possibilities emerging from an alternative understanding of space must evolve alongside a critically renovated stance against the social dynamics subjugated to the global neoliberal rationale. The chapter *Ruins of the Future*, by philosopher Otília Arantes, stems from the perspective of someone who rapidly acknowledged the limits of capitalist modernization on the periphery of the system, as she grasps the radicality "of the extreme urban forms" in the great Chinese global leap. A country which has only recently emerged on the world market shifts from extreme material scarcity to the culture of excess—which, unlike envisioned by Benjamin, turns to the production of glossy architectural structures and entire cities built on emptiness. The relationship between neoliberal economics and cities had already been established in her previous works. Now she favors the Chinese process—and other enclaves in the East—as the historical destiny of the central capitalist modernization, now deprived of their ideological cloud. In other words, the truth of the modernization process reveals itself by way of its most extreme realization: architectural enclaves amid the social ruins of the future.

•

The second part of the book, *Rethinking Spatial Rhythms*, presents a more direct approach to spatialization as conditioned by historicity, temporality, and rhythms. The new social determinations of the *spatial turn* problematize modern historicist perspectives, especially in its teleological radicalism, and rearrange the possibilities for social emancipation amidst totalizing practices (time-space). Hence, possibilities emerge in both theoretical manifestations and in analyses that seek to expand the critical possibilities for understanding architectural and urban space traversed by the different dimensions of time—social, bodily, and the everyday.

The chapter *Henri Lefebvre and the Morphology of a Spatial Dialectic*, by geographer César Simoni Santos, brings to light a theoretical and methodological tool to broaden the meaning of space in modernity by acknowledging dimensions beyond the strict rationality underlying the abstractions in urban and architectural planning. This conception of space opens new possibilities for activating dimensions detracted from modernity, such as the body, pleasure, and everyday life by combining theory and praxis. These reflections confront the hegemonic economic rationality of the modern world, following in the footsteps of the French philosopher, whose ideas echo throughout the entire book.

The same time-body dimension underpins the analysis by architect Natalia Escobar Castrillón in her chapter *Anthropophagic Phenomenology: Encounters at Lina Bo's SESC Pompeia's Cultural and Leisure Center*. Departing from the Brazilian experience, the chapter discusses Lina Bo Bardi's emblematic oeuvre as it relativizes the rational paradigms of modern architecture. Traversing anthropophagy and the work of artist Hélio Oiticica, the author explores space as mediated by the actions of multiple bodies within Brazilian popular culture. This focus on the variety of life in the 1980s provides a vigorous alternative to the reification of popular signs disseminated at the time in postmodernity. The contrast between distinct architectural principles is further reinforced by a methodological choice in which the "anthropophagic movement" becomes closer to Brazilian modernism and phenomenology. By developing the analysis through an architectural oeuvre, the chapter merges a broad critical perspective with the spatial and constructive procedures that directly concern critical interventions within contemporary space.

In *Incremental Housing: A Short History of an Idea*, by architect Nelson Mota, the author turns to the architectural experiences of affordable housing for expanding or modifying standard units. These experiences are analyzed historically and critically, according to their wide-ranging consequences in social, cultural, environmental, and urban practices. The research unfolds the theoretical schemes and practical procedures that equate housing spatial strategies amidst the global urbanization process since the turn of the 21st century. The chapter seeks a mediation between the rationalizing and regulating processes of A&U and the collaborative practices that express the differences and possibilities in contemporary everyday life.

The pursuit for new critical methodologies must consider that the theories of difference, which sought to overcome modern ideologies of homogeneity, reached a somber stalemate with their subsumption to neoliberal reason. If the disciplinary strategies developed since the 1970s opposed modern architecture, why do spaces designed according to this "historical-contextual" logic preserve the segregating and homogenizing schemes of modern cities? The chapter *The Bubble, the Arrow, and the Area: Urban Design and Diagrammatic Concepts of Human Action*, by urbanist Daniel Koch, argues that new assumptions of urban design that incorporate social, environmental, and cultural issues have failed to overcome the limits of social and ecological degradation which, contradictorily, underpin the attempts to overcome them. This ambiguity relates economic valuation and architectural ideologies, which simultaneously result in and produce new productive configurations. Thus, the debate on permanencies—albeit in opposite critical contexts—suggests a march towards abstract and functional space under the dominion of capitalism during the 20th century. The contemporary task of overcoming this scheme requires a radical change in architectural and urban thinking and a reinvention of the city.

•

The third and final section of the book, *Contemporary Spatial Forms of the City*, compiles researches focused on contemporary urban realities from an A&U standpoint. As such, it presents phenomena that portray the production of urban spaces according to the hegemonic logic of neoliberalism, which serve as a motif for exploring practical or theoretical critical possibilities. Spatial and historical issues converge in the evaluation of these phenomena, emphasizing the agonized nature of the discipline against contemporary political-economic models. The analyses suggest a simultaneous movement towards alternatives and the creation of dissent, or at least the conditions for its possibility.

The chapter *The Subaltern City: Revisiting the Materialist Critique of Urban Form*, by architect Marta Caldeira, reflects upon the uncritical condition of contemporary architecture which, as the author argues, accounts for an unprecedented scholarly impasse in the discipline. The subjugation of architectural programs and forms to the ideological and economic determinations of neoliberalism shifted from the "creative" euphoria of the 1990s to a radicalized social segregation design since the 2008 crisis. The new architectural creativity reveals itself through the use of an arsenal of signs that camouflages social cleavages and jeopardizes the very meaning of the urban. A renovating perspective of this subordinate condition, fittingly described by the "poor door" strategy, can, at this moment, be confronted with a critical reflection which, by unveiling the communicative schemes, alludes to a contrary and possible condition.

Another crucial neoliberal strategy for the commodification of urban space is the production of socio-economic enclaves in discontinuity with the existing urban fabric. Such exceptionality and exclusivity are one of the greatest evidences of the "explosion" of the cities, a process analyzed by Lefebvre in *The Right to the City*. Janina Gosseye, in *The Chronicles of Neo*, analyzes one exemplary case of the social and economic fragility found in state-market major enterprises. The *NEO*—an enterprise in Brussels, Belgium—presents itself as a model solution for the development of urban areas (housing, public space, and infrastructure). However, the text argues that this public effort strives to build an environment whose main purpose is to mold everyday life to exacerbate consumption. In other words, in addition to the financial issue where the government contributes with huge investments, we witness the complete surrender of the state logic as it becomes a social and public mediator for augmenting economic rationality.

The public—and state-level—mediation to produce urban space under neoliberalism is further questioned, in its rationality, by introducing a new regulatory agent responsible for converging collective interests and the market. The chapter *The Legitimized Reproduction of a Corporate Typology: Dispositions of Architectural Form in the LEED® Rating System*, by architect Raphael Grazziano, discusses the environmental certificates produced by nongovernmental organizations (NGOs), especially LEED®. These certificates serve to guide and define the best sustainability practices in the design and construction of large-scale buildings and urban areas, serving as a quality and appreciation parameter for the real estate market. This logic, however, is questioned both in terms of what it proposes—sustainability and energy efficiency—as well as its spatial outcome: the corporate glass tower.

The text by architect Sérgio Martín Blas, *What Ever Happened to Social Housing?*, discusses the disciplinary issue from its most prominent topic throughout the 20th century: social housing. Neoliberalism—or in a more wide-ranging sense, the crisis of social democracy since the 1970s—imposed a false polarization on disciplinary strategies: on the one hand, and especially in the European context, a solution through the market production of state-subsidized affordable housing; and on the other hand, as a political reaction to inefficient or lacking state housing programs, especially in Latin America, social movements emerged valuing self-organizing and self-management with a direct democratic participation agenda. This polarity, in addition to the ideological misconceptions that have become clear at the present time, resulted in a radical constraint of A&U insofar as the mediation between the state's infrastructural strategies—urbanism—and the processes and contents of collective life lack critical mediation.

The new determinations for contemporary architectural form are methodologically explored by architects Carmen Espegel Alonso and Daniel Movilla Vega. In *Five Fronts for One Single Position: Critical Strategies for Contemporary Pedagogy in the Subject of Architectural Design*, this myriad of themes that invade the contemporary world, questioning and augmenting traditional architectural schemes, becomes a didactic-project methodology. Emerging themes that shape the transformative possibilities for the city and space are incorporated into research and architectural design processes—a method that implicates the powers of everyday life and architectural rationality in the disturbing panorama of the beginning of the 21st century. The chapter also confronts these ideas with the *Social Housing Lavapiés* project, under the guidance of architect and professor Carmen Espegel Alonso in Madrid (2004).

•

The past few years have accelerated the impasses within architectural and urban theory and practice. The 2020 pandemic catalyzed pre-existing trends across different sectors of society, such as economy, culture, environment, technology, identities, etc. The celerity of these processes imposes challenges for space-related disciplines, constantly delving in permanence and historicity. The researches in this book do not seek an answer to these problems, but rather illustrate that it is possible to distinguish key elements of the contemporary equation and as such lay the foundation for theoretical-critical reflections. Together, the chapters of this book constitute an open work, comprising a diversity of themes, methods, and research objects arising from different perspectives. The authors from various universities and nationalities share a commitment to develop critical stances and to formulate new foundations for spatial thought within architecture and urbanism.

As we already know, critical reflection can lead to stasis, especially given the massive disruptive and destructive forces that condition the present. A similar outlook produced a reaction against the "radical" thinkers of the early 1960s, transforming their critical viewpoints into a pragmatism that was swiftly enraptured by the global economic logic. Aware of this risk of contributing to a renewed inertia, we hope to merge critical thought with disciplinary activity. The ensuing discomfort resulting from this approach lies not in the attempt itself, but is a prerequisite within praxis and the potential transformation of the current state of affairs. In this book we seek neither pragmatism nor totalizing ideologies which strive to reform society. Both succumbed to the determinations of productive irrationality throughout the 20th century. Rather, we suggest that the privileged antagonistic realm for creating new possibilities lies in the new urban condition. Hence, turning towards researchers and those who intervene in urban space seems imperative. Throughout this book the awareness of the limits of this approach is constantly present, just as is the continuous pursuit for critical, transformative tools.

References

Lefebvre, H. (2016). *Marxist Thought and the City*. Minneapolis, MN: The University of Minnesota Press. (Original work published 1972).

Santos, M. (2002). *A Natureza do Espaço: Técnica e Tempo. Razão e Emoção*. São Paulo, Brazil: Edusp. (Original work published 1996).

PART I
Theoretical Tenets

1

REMAINS OF ARCHITECTURAL REASON

Luiz Recaman

In recent years, challenges have appeared regarding architecture and urbanism which require rethinking and overcoming strategies that were conceived of in the 20th century. In the last few decades, throughout the world, large and medium cities have formed, be it through tactics of necessity or the commodification of urban land and constructions, unified by reactive, segregating, frequently hostile infrastructures. The radicality and extent of this process of urban transformation have already been heralded as the end of cities, as a "post-urban" life or as the "post-metropolis" (Habermas, 1981/1998; Choay, 1970, 1992, 1994; Soja, 2000). Or even, in another sense, the complete urbanization of society, as put forth by Henri Lefebvre in the initial moments of this process, in which the possibility of historical realization of the creative, social potentials of the urban was first glimpsed (Lefebvre, 1970/2003, p. 1). The fact is that new technologies modulate global territory in a totalizing functionality, even if it is ultimately perceived as fragmentary, individual, and local. The significations of this new space seem to drift further and further away from the former notions of the city in the West, as explained by Weber (1921/1966). At the same time, collective spatial representations, other than phantasmagoria superimposed onto dystopian scenery, seem impossible.

This late cycle of productive and spatial mutations already suggests, in itself, a possible periodization, beyond the invariable and uninterrupted deterioration of urban life since the beginning of the urban revolution: a moment of celebratory apogee (the "golden years" of neoliberalism), the 2008 financial crisis (a clear inflexion of the collective wagers on space produced by market logic), and the very recent, dramatic sanitary crisis under which these reflections are carried out. The latter brought a significant impact on all of our representations of the urban, of collective life, of proximity and distance. Furthermore, in this social environment of increasing precariousness, the geography of contamination shifts according to its biological dynamics and becomes socially stratified, particularly in countries with increased spatial segregation.[1]

The collective logic of sanitary strategies impinges upon the individual and individualistic strategies cultivated over the last few decades with rare immediateness. Statistic calculations and scientific information are immediately translated into simple operations that, like few other times in the past, directly affect daily life and social interactions. We observe an intensification of practices of sociability which were otherwise only rehearsed or minoritarian, such as telematic calls—intimate or collective—and online commerce. Communication through social networks becomes the exclusive channel of supra-individual expression, amplifying debates, polemics, and new mythologies with great speed. If the robotized distribution of fake news has affected the legitimacy of elections in a number of countries in recent years, it now influences the scientific truth about COVID-19, impacting social-distancing policies, as has occurred in the United States and in Brazil.

We are in the midst of the rapid construction of new social, cultural, and productive strategies that will form global society in the following decades, strategies that start from already existing instruments that will be transformed and enhanced. The newly produced social space shall be progressively dislocated into virtual and immaterial environments. This mental intensification will increasingly trigger an operative rationality in detriment of other dimensions of sensibility, another stage of the "life of the spirit," according to Simmel's arrangement (1903/2010). The productive machine will not relinquish its driving force, but will probably regress it into cheaper, more primitive forms, as we have already observed regarding the circulation of commodities driven, in the pandemic, by basic transport services, such as bicycle-based delivery apps. At the same time, we catch glimpses of intensified tendencies in remotely organized individual labor, rendering centralized spaces of intellectual activity obsolete. The world of information will circulate at novel speed—even in relation to the wagers of the 1990s—territorializing in connected individual or domestic spaces, the physical survival of which will only be possible through the rudimentary flexibility of product delivery.

We can imagine, in a scenario in which this new productive logic is installed without friction, that cities and large urban agglomerations might abandon their last collective meanings, even those that preceded capitalism: the spaces of market and exchanges. Thus, the resulting "urban fabric" would be a hegemony of suburbanization and peripheralization that has already been rehearsed for decades with the aim of intensifying segregation and isolation, given the risks of violence, upheaval, and contamination existing in the traditional urban fabric. Only then would this aseptic idealization of intangible accumulation become possible, the ultimate rationality of the production of value. Physico-spatial activities that maintain life itself would be realized at a degree of extreme inequality and segregation, already well imagined in fictional films. In the space of nature, meditations would also be abbreviated toward the capture of its diversity, even given increasing risks, such as the pandemics of human territory.

This is the opposite scenario in relation to the one thought possible by the Lefebvrian method, based on the new historic centrality that large cities seemed to progressively reclaim given transformations in consumer society (and that were in fact reclaimed under globalization) after over a century of industrial society's anti-urbanity. However, the urban hypothesis, the full realization of urban society, was not an inevitability but a "virtuality," to be constructed theoretically and through *praxis* (Lefebvre, 1970/2003, p. 3). Following his method—that is, seeking out and unravelling the vectors of an ongoing, if not hegemonic, transformation—we must theoretically—and progressively—construct a possibility and, from this concrete-utopian place, focus on the reality in which we find ourselves. From the intellectual perspective, this is the task at hand, even if it seems we have entered into an opaque, incomprehensible, and indeterminate reality.

If we systematically move toward dystopian scenarios, in this moment of opacity, the counter-movements of the reformulation of the role of the state—in great motion during these times that demand universalist logics and financial aids—may pass unnoticed as may new insurgent forms of solidarity, in society and in social movements. In many Brazilian favelas, mechanisms were rapidly and autonomously (without support from public powers) put into action in order to promote social distancing and the distribution of food and hygiene items. In these places, where state presence is feeble and frequently violent, the population resists the advance of the pandemic, even if partially submitted to criminal organizations. In any case, the great

FIGURE 1.1 Residents dive in Praça Mauá in downtown Rio de Janeiro. This location is part of the controversial reform carried out by the Porto Maravilha Urban Operation for the 2016 Olympics. Photo taken in 2015.

rationalizing schemes promoted by the state (in ideological decline since the apex of neoliberalism) and its tactics of appropriating daily life allow us to glimpse new dynamics that might structure the production of space in the near future—as a possibility.

•

This periodization of space under neoliberalism rapidly historicizes the phases of the confrontation between the systemic acceleration of capitalism's financial and global accumulation, on the one hand, and the complex social reality to which it aims to give form and subordinate on the other. This "regressive" vantage point bears special interest for discussing the relations between the schemes of architecture and urbanism and the social production of space—that is, their ideological, utopian, or pragmatic conceptions regarding city space. A further occurrence is added to this recent history with the current conjuncture of the pandemic. Analyses of the fate of cities in the post-pandemic future multiply; only the impact on urban life and its spatial forms is certain: housing units, density, free areas, mobility, etc. A radical present alters the expectations hitherto formulated about the disciplinary possibilities which react to strategic planning, the fetishization of traditional forms of the city and iconic architecture.

Architecture's self-critical reconstruction and socially oriented critiques of recent years now shows two main vectors around which alternative themes and strategies are organized: 1) the character of the orientation of the state's rationalizing action, which is now, during an emergency, required to carry out social and economic roles that have been largely discarded by neoliberal logic; and 2) the new forms of popular organization pressured by the forced conscience of collective (social and biological) meanings of protection and action. The criticisms directed at the minimal state and the wagers on new horizontal tactics of organization around the *commons* (in a more general sense that considers both common goods and common practices) must now be regulated by this rapidly accelerating conjunctural transformation. These poles (the appropriation of the state and of everyday life) can form a nucleus for reorganizing society toward greater autonomy in relation to globalization's economic forces of disintegration. Around these poles turn the "ideologies" of architecture and urbanism. Their referent—the productive reality of late capitalism—will hardly realize systemic, qualitative changes, allowing for any semblance of greater social and environmental balance, as the American left proposes through the popularization of the Green New Deal (Chomsky, Ocasio-Cortez, etc.). A clearer environment of dispute between social forces (civil society and those present or not in the states pressured by the necessity of supra-sectorial productive rationality) and increasingly antisocial productive and financial logics become apparent. *What interests us, at this moment, is only discussing the reorganization conditions for the theoretico-social foundations in the totalizing spatial imagination of a disciplinary field that has as a horizon enlightened, sensory, and programmatic intervention in the social environment—namely, architecture and urbanism.*

Keeping with our disciplinary focus, here the problematic relation between architectural thought, in its hegemonic strategies and processes of urbanization since the Industrial Revolution, are taken up. In this wide cycle, we may observe two great declines: the homogenizing idealism in the age of the machine and the realisms of diversity in the age of consumers. Project strategies were elaborated upon these two socio-productive conditions that are revealed, contrary to the clearly formulated initial hypotheses, as schemes of productive rationalization, be it of territory itself or of its infrastructure; or even the symbolic schemes of the urban in the "society of the spectacle." These formulations gave form to the *two great ideological moments of the 20th century*, that simultaneously reproduced both the systemic logics of industrial capitalism in its late "post-industrial" phase and its contradictions, therefore announcing its critiques as well—which are valid but unconcluded.

Let us see: the "radical architecture" of the 1920s constituted itself according to the standardization principles of ideological Fordism. A mass utopia that dislodged the systemic logic inherent to the production line into a counter-logic that resorts to the state for a social adjustment of this productive potentiality. This contradiction was explored to the limit in the "critique of ideology" that Tafuri directed at the modern movement (Tafuri, 1973/1976). An unfolding, or formalization, of the contradictions in social-democratic administration of the severe conflicts deep inside economic liberalism. Thus, the social dimension of the state—ideological or otherwise—was activated by territorial planning (productive rationality) and the supply of housing (social rationality), based on the technical neutrality of industrial logic. Triggering its emancipatory dimension was a technoscientific issue, dealing with the logical cleansing of the industrial procedures carried out by the artistic-architectural avant-garde.

This ideological critique, widely discussed in the architectural milieu, must be unfolded not only in relation to the "marginal role" or "sublime uselessness"—as Tafuri diagnoses the historical reality of the second post-war period (Tafuri, 1973/1976, p. ix, 161). Added to this "reality of the plan" (Tafuri, 1973/1976, p. 135) is an expansive strategy of productive functionality and colonization of everyday life carried out by architecture and urbanism in the years of planned economic growth in the 1950s and 1960s. Henri Lefebvre's critiques of modern spatiality surpass its ideological character, associated with the "civilization of machines," while simultaneously singling out its anti-urban logic, which implodes the logic of the traditional city form, reinforcing an achronic homogeneity and spatial segregation (explosion) that automate life, actualizing market abstractions and social domination in daily living. We are dealing with an emphasis on the fundamental role of *space* in the mechanisms of *social* reproduction (spatial turn), a displacement of the *productive* emphasis of the Industrial Revolution that accompanies

FIGURE 1.2 The housing complex at Vélizy-Villacoublay, France, built between 1962–1976.

the transformation of capitalism in the 20th century. As much in its fully ideological moment in the period between the two world wars, in the political environment of German social democracy (the *Siedlungen*, Bauhaus), as in its operation and large-scale dissemination in urban planning following World War II, modern architecture can only be understood as an ideology that has its historical place in the environment of the state—whether contradictorily "social" or a contradictory agent of national productive planning.

Over this alienating mediation of territorial order carried out by the planning state are superimposed certain schemes specific to the "bureaucratic society of controlled consumption," as Lefebvre names the most advanced stage of capitalism (Lefebvre, 1971/2017, p. 60). This is the passage from scarcity to abundance: "[s]uch is the predicament in which the ideology of production and the significance of creative activity have become an *ideology of consumption*" (Lefebvre, 1971/2017, p. 56). The new *plan* is now directed at organizing the meanings of the *everyday* and its system of values through communications and advertising. This new debased, pop universe rapidly influences the ideological reversal actualized by the theory of architecture and urbanism from the 1950s onward. Against the idealizing abstractions of the avant-garde, an attention to popular culture and modes of life is proposed. This transition corresponds to the linguistic turn and to the development of language mechanisms that rationalize the symbolic field: in our case that of urban and architectural forms. If, on the one hand, architectural culture investigates the emancipatory potential of new systems of signification, which appear as a critical turning point, on the other it retains management of the mechanisms of systemic rationalization, measuring these against the lifeworld.

We may quickly apprehend this general ideological conjuncture in relation to well-delineated concretions in the history of architecture: 1) an architectural logic that emulates the strategies

(a)   (b)

FIGURE 1.3 Piscina das Marés de Leça da Palmeira, designed by Álvaro Siza Vieira (1966). Photos taken in 2016.

of communication and configures the urban according to vehicular movement and the communication-building perceived in motion (US: Venturi and Scott Brown); 2) a new architecture occupying an intermediate dimension between the building and the urban (clusters) that emulates a fragmented metropolitan style of street, multiplying them in height (streets-in-the-sky) in order to amplify the cultural identity associated with them, in low-income and suburban areas (UK: Alison and Peter Smithson); 3) a systematization, with an accentuated political orientation in the post–World War II context, of the vernacular constructive forms which in the 1960s were guided toward the study of urbanistic or architectural typologies of traditional cities as a basis for "the new" (Italy: Rossi); and 4) some localized experiences—especially in "combined and unequal" contexts—sought design and construction methodologies that would come nearer to popular constructive techniques and "spaces of representation" while reinforcing forms of social organization, seeking to break with the alienation resulting from the on-site division of labor.[2] This last direction is the one most progressively distanced from disciplinary tradition, guided toward participatory political practices (self-management) critical of the state and of the foundational spatial ideologies of architecture and urbanism.

In these four great axes that structure the debate in the last few decades of the 20th century, we encounter the same conceptual displacement, going from the sharpness of the rational object, aesthetically conceived of according to its internal laws, to a conflicting, relational system between architecture (its exchange and use value) and all that involves it, socially. Each cultural conjuncture defined its architectural *other*, all pointing in the direction of the diversity of forms of living, of popular culture, opposed to the abstract forms of modernity's schemes of objective rationality. These abstract forms, professing their own rationality, ended up revealing the abstractions of economic equivalences and their "systemic functionality"—an undue overload, according to Habermas (1981/1998, p. 423), that led to the crisis, or collapse, of architectural modernity in the second half of the 20th century. A perspective directed at "lifeworld" or to "everyday life" intended to revert the framework of totalizing—and totalitarian—abstractions of industrial society, leading humanity and its spaces into unforeseen stages of social alienation.

This disciplinary movement was in tune with the cultural movement forming around new subjective expressions in mass culture, whose main characteristic would be a critique of modernity's institutions, such as the state and politics, the bourgeois family, erudite art, etc. Just as in the case of the historical avant-garde and radical architecture (the experiences with housing and the urban of the late 1920s), the 1960s and 1970s present a theoretical radicalization that sought to institute alternative disciplinary strategies to those disseminated by high modernism.

An eruption of signs communicated strongly with the great urban masses that prefigured changes in social order. Forms of architecture and of the city (gathered in a vast, socially extroverted repertoire) eschewed in a freer, more intense relation between the population and its space, even if this was done through very different strategies, which were sometimes antagonistic (*history* and *consumption*, for example). Their interlocutors would be the memorative-individual, constructor-individual, the imaginative-individual, consumer-individual, and bodily-individual, as opposed to the Corbusian type-individuals. Signs, then, that are clearly attached to well-identified social contents, whose creative manipulation would allow for the genesis of relations and large-scale changes.

However, this linguistic operation, arising from the techniques of the avant-garde, dealt with a supposed double liberation: of the *signified* and of *signifiers*, taking into account the inextricable relation between the two. The displacement toward language and communication that the second post-war period took up was at the same time the negation of contents in a process of commodification that broke with the contours of industrial commodity. In this sense, postmodernity can be understood as the "random play of signifiers ... [that] ceaselessly reshuffles the fragments of pre-existing texts, the building blocks of cultural order and social production," according to Fredric Jameson's synthesis (1991, p. 95). A reifying specialization of social relations would expedite and expand the production of images, whose sense is given by the circulation of the values of global financialization.

The process that led from the more or less engaged research of the 1960s (all of which are certainly critical of high modernism) toward a process of integration into the logics of financial globalization is widely disputed, especially after the 2008 economic crisis, even if it predates it (Jameson, 1991, p. 96).[3] It is, however, more interesting and explanatory to avoid the diagnosis of systemic cooptation of a well-intentioned nucleus of critical propositions about the exterior (whether social, historical, or trivial) determinations of architecture and urbanism, which at another time had imagined itself as functional, technical, and therefore autonomous. Surely there are experimentations and reflections of the 1960s and 1970s, before the generalization of postmodern style, that still await the unravelling of its social and aesthetic radicality. However, the development of the critical dynamics reacting to the normalization of architectural modernism should be considered within an "ideological" dialectics of the modern cultural process, that is, the fact that our antagonistic critical capacity does not escape the permanent capitalist productive revolution in search of new frontiers of value. A *dialectic of architectural reason*, simultaneously involved in actual social (and productive) processes, extracting from them utopian, totalizing perspectives. This dialectical reason was in fact a contradictory unitary movement that required analyses seeking to identify critical edges, in the set of proposals, that could not be smoothed out in the process of actualization or concretization.

Thus, almost all critical content can be incorporated into a new phase of accumulation, given that they single out social impasses that pressure the productive order, and can therefore suggest ways to renovate it. In the specific case of architecture and urbanism, a disposition of important strategies toward forms of life in their variety and historicity, as we have already pointed out, can be identified since at least the 1960s. It is worth noting now that this plethora of signs and forms that mediate social experiences of space, elaborated by architectural culture, have created the urban as images that could be managed in myriad manners by consumer-oriented productive reorganization. This is something quite similar, apparently, to the process described by

Fredric Jameson (1984), with ample validity in his 1960s periodization. In this case, it is better to resort to the author's own words:

> Yet this sense of freedom and possibility-which is for the course of the 60s a momentarily objective reality, as well as (from the hindsight of the 80s) a historical illusion-may perhaps best be explained in terms of the superstructural movement and play enabled by the transition from one infrastructural or systemic stage of capitalism to another.
>
> *(Jameson, 1984, p. 208)*

This "freeing or unbinding of social energies" corresponds to the impulse of globalization. Following a new profusion of images and behaviors came an ordering, mitigation, and accretion of value, reproducing the infinitely varied surface of new cultural commodities counterposed to its essence of abstract, economic equivalence. Architecture, the hollowed-out emblem of content in the process of social modernization, made its powerful communicative apparatus available in order to compose, in a privileged manner, the imaginary of the particular moment. So much so that the historicism and provocative pastiche of the 1980 Venice Biennale ("La Presenza del Passato" and especially the "Strada Novissima" exhibition) went beyond architectural debates and became a mark in the philosophical argument represented by the controversy between Jürgen Habermas and Jean-François Lyotard (Lyotard, 1979/1984; Habermas, 1980/1983).

The confluence between the strategies of architecture and financial globalization, however, became more profound when large cities became not only the *locus* of social production and reproduction but also mechanisms of accumulation in and of themselves. If, in modernity, the metropolis was represented as a "total machine," equating society and industrial production, in the economic order of the *cultural turn* it becomes a corporation-city, as has been widely interpreted by critics and supporters of the current process alike. Managed as an organization, it becomes simultaneously a product to be commercialized, in competition with other cities for a role in globalization.

•

A digression can now be made with the objective of situating with greater precision the movement of privatization in the logic of architecture and urbanism, seeking to historically (and spatially) identify the fundamental elements at play, their systemic relations, and what equations are possible for the coming future. Or, better yet, identify the problems posed by these historical elements, indicating possibilities. Bearing in mind, always, that all of these issues of complex social dimensions are here schematically cut out in order to discuss their relations to the disciplinary field of architecture and urbanism.

The condition that dissipates the complexity of social life and expands its dimension of "exchange value" (resorting to Lefebvre's urban dialectic) reaches a paroxysm in the last two decades of the 20th century and in the first decade of the 21st century, in what we may call the apex of neoliberalism. The twofold determination of cities (the space of second nature) as *oeuvre* and *produit* gives them a dynamic, unstable constitution. The fact is, however, that we may imagine a capitalist historical circuit whose origin point is the city that negates feudal order. Its apex is reached when this phenomenon (the urban) inoculated with new forms of division of labor and intensification of commerce destroys the hegemony of its original pole, the rural. In the budding cities of the late medieval era, the contents in representations of social and community values that were configured in the urban form are unified under the rationalizing impulses of nascent capitalism, under a great social oppression, creator of great *oeuvres*. The extraordinary art of the period was in and for the city, an affirmation of the cultural force of the commercial bourgeoisie.

An unstable equilibrium rapidly played out: to the extent that the network of cities as autonomous political units proved insufficient for the great task of the ongoing productive revolution. A centralizing of power becomes necessary, and the nation state grows stronger in a territory overseen by a *capital*. However, according to Lefebvre's brief and instigating itinerary: "when exploitation replaces oppression, creative capacity disappears" (Lefebvre, 1968/1996, p. 67). Cities thus lose the great representations of "lived space," and a new spatial order is eschewed, in the transition from commercial to industrial capitalism. Philosophy is reencountered in *rationalism* and constitutes the state-individual dichotomy. From its roots in expropriation and violence, the capitalist state acquires a universal dimension and becomes the vanishing point of a rational society. The city and the metropolis lose their leading role in collective representations and become a subsidiary phenomenon of the productive process, a place for consumption. Factories and workers alike are displaced toward the periphery, and the representations of the productive unit that is the large city (production, distribution, consumption) are fragmented and, most of all, reveal their apparent chaos. In this moment, the imploding of the meaning of the city is actualized dialectically in the generalization of the urban, of urban society (Lefebvre, 1996, p. 71).

As we have seen, a resuming of the significations of the city occurred in a moment of productive modifications internal to industrial capitalism, in the 1960s, with movement since the end of World War II. The architectural and urbanistic debate discussed earlier may now acquire a new outline: the centrality of large cities in the new management of globalization. Lefebvre is one of the first to pick up on this change, in its initial stages. This critical moment is at the base of social virtualities and the wager on *the right to the city*. Capitalism repositions large cities as administrative, financial, and consumer centers, while the contradictions arising therefrom eventually explode in the revolts of the late 1960s. An expectation of urban revolution was critically revisited in the preface to the new edition of *The Production of Space*, in 1985 (Lefebvre, 1974/2000, pp. xvi–xxviii), when the political and economic framework allowed for no more great expectations of change and neoliberal globalization became hegemonic.

If the capitalist city has its origins in the intensity of the spatial representations of a developing modern society, in which "exchange value" and "use value" balance each other out in fleeting, mutual enhancement, we are spectators of, at least since the 1980s, an unemancipated return to origins. That is, if financial capitalism returns to cities as the commercial capitalism that originally belonged to them, this globalized return does not reproduce the social expectations that were, and still are, possible in urban environments (*simultaneity and heterogeneity*). However, if the spatial and social constructive aspects of capitalism were annihilated in this process, its negative, destructive dimensions, which were also original, may have prevailed. A sort of dialectics of the urban that, as far as we can tell, stagnates now in the dilution of all preceding socio-spatial forms. The indicated circuit, or short-circuit, closes, perhaps momentarily, in this brutal remission, amplified by apparatuses of control and communication—an oppressive, non-creative exploitation. A remission to the city as simulation, reification, and spectacle. The ideological reunification of the volatile signifiers of the city, operated by the "logic" of financial capitalism, produced, *in extremis*, colossal phantasmagoria, as we may observe in the East Asian frontiers of globalization.[4]

•

The same must have occurred in regard to the state, as the maximal institution of the modern world, to which is assigned fully rational action. This fable, that also has its own dialectic, was already constructed in the 20th century: the irruption of irrationality in the very inside of the ideal form of modern rationality (this Hegelian moment is exactly the dialectical moment as such). The capitalist state also returns to its violent origins, taking its bourgeois universality as exhausted. Or, better yet, operates on two different levels: exercising a universal power in which justice is no longer the rule but the exception to it. This device, as discussed by Agamben (2003/2005), closes out the ideological cycle of the state, at least in the original sense of the term.

It is of interest, however, to draw a specific and fairly schematic relation between this ideological moment and architecture/urbanism. That is, a reconstruction of its set of ideals after the city's loss of "organic quality of form" (Tafuri, 1973/1976, p. 14) that followed the crisis of the *ancien régime*. Not in order to retell it, which seems unnecessary, but in order to emphasize the spatial bases over which architecture and urbanism will develop in industrial society, or better yet, as Lefebvre advises, in urban society.

The absolute state, agent of mercantilism, begins after the bourgeois revolutions to play a leading ideological role, to the extent that the structuring action of industrial society becomes increasingly determined by economic forces. Contradictions arise from this fact, of which the *Communist Manifesto* is the greater symptom. Social division—into classes—demands from this "universal" institution a different sort of reaction: coercion, maintained as the strong arm of the market and its logic; or mediation, creating mechanisms of social protection and politics allowing for economic advances, in a wide sense. It is a *nationally* possible equation, which increasingly creates conflicts, given the unequal condition of international markets. That is, from the second half of the 19th century onwards, capitalism will engender the wars and revolutions of the first decades of the 20th century, the environment of the modern avant-garde (itself a self-proclaimed alternative to capitalist chaos).

It is in this context of modernity—and urban society—that the capitalist state restructures itself in order to (at the same time in which it drives the conditions of production) administer society as a whole, aligning it to this end. We bring up this well-known fact in order to reinforce that the disciplinary reorganization of architecture, as much as the creation of the discipline of urbanism, are both given in this context—reinforcing, then, Tafuri's analysis of the cycle of "architectural ideology," through a different emphasis. This becomes necessary given that, in a different manner than that of the Italian architect, it is important at the moment to bring into focus the contradictions of this ideological state (the political superstructure dealing with the infrastructural conditions of capital's production and reproduction) and the aforementioned disciplinary reorganization. This, considering that the relation between ideological (technoscientific) superstructure and modern art and architecture, in the context of the industrial, Fordist revolution, is already established by the tradition of critical theory, to which Tafuri is indebted at least in part.

Architecture and urbanism accomplished a crucial ideological task: that of giving form to the social in the precise moment that liberalism progressively eliminated the contents of the social sphere, in favor of emphases on the individual and his free market agency. The representation of the spaces of "society" became increasingly abstract, as did the economic forces that began to rule over the bonds between individuals. The same is true of the new discipline, urbanism, and its defining ideological character, of representing unity for the increasingly fragmented reality of the 19th-century industrial metropolis. The life and cities of the past allowed for finite and sensitive knowledge, a world enmeshed in an absolute, unknown infinity; the space of the metropolis, on the other hand, is infinite, and totality (universal knowledge) are now volatile, inapprehensible. Giving social and spatial sense to the industrial world was the primary ideological task of European architecture after the Enlightenment.

The contradictions of industrial society erupt in the space of large cities while a desire for order intensifies. In them, liberal principles encounter their imminent limits: precarious housing, congestion, epidemics, fires, and so many spatially revealed inconveniences that plague early-19th-century metropolises. In his book, itself an inflexion of the gaze directed at the city and its living conditions, Engels writes:

> A town, such as London, where a man may wander for hours together without reaching the beginning of the end, without meeting the slightest hint which could lead to the inference that there is open country within reach, is a strange thing . . . all this is so vast, so impressive, that a man cannot collect himself, but is lost in the marvel of England's greatness before he sets foot upon English soil.
>
> *(Engels, 1845/1993, p. 36)*

Chaos and order compose a binome that runs throughout "urban society" and sits at the base of realist (chaos) and utopian (order) representations of the large city. Social order, in utopian socialism, was imagined outside of the space of the metropolis, in isolated regions such the Saí phalanstère in Santa Catarina, Brazil, and the New Harmony Community, in Indiana, U.S.A.[5] Engels himself analyses these experiences:

> It was necessary, then, to discover a new and more perfect system of social order and to impose this upon society. . . . These new social systems were foredoomed as utopian.
>
> *(Engels, 1878/1987, p. 246)*

This desire for order, however, precedes the eruption of chaos in large cities and initiates an ideological confrontation already present in liberalism's first revolutionary moments. The 18th century then would observe a formal "loss of order" that would guarantee unity between exceptional objects (buildings, squares, gardens, etc.) and the whole of the city. New requirements are presented to architecture: geometric systematization, typologies, constructive rationalities and, most importantly, giving form to the "social" (Tafuri, 1973/1976). With the Enlightenment and with industrial society appear vectors of formal extroversion, regularly multiplying autonomous forms which tended toward pure geometry. This means that new formal and spatial strategies pressure architecture toward the whole of the city (nascent urbanism). The representations of the urban in early liberalism tended to fracture into a unitary totality (which increasingly conflicts with the growing disorder of the industrial city) and a heterogenous whole that acquires its virtue in the free actualization of fragments of space.

We may now see clearly the ideological function of this new "social architecture": to the extent that the urban form fractures and is distended, urbanism and architecture acquire the task of unifying space and giving it meaning (modern society itself). This impulse of spatial organization has, in practice, two main components—namely, the organization of productive territory (pieces of space) and the social utopias which bear a social significance allowed for by new technologies of production (general space). These unfold into *techniques of extensibility*—or, in the 20th century, of reproduction—and *techniques of communication* in the new contents, now no longer self-evident, given that they are jettisoned by the totalizing sense of *tradition*.

Manfredo Tafuri, again, best interprets the crisis of "organicity" in the formal unity of the European Baroque, the world of the *ancien régime*. The Jesuit abbot Laugier suggests, in his 1753 *Essay on Architecture*, regarding "the city like a forest" (Tafuri, 1973/1976, p. 6). He takes

FIGURE 1.4 A bird's-eye view of a community in New Harmony, Indiana, United States, as proposed by Robert Owen. Engraving by F. Bate, London, 1838.

up the idea again in his book *Observations on Architecture*, from 1756, stating that cities must be built with "squares, crossroads, streets. There must be regularity and fantasy, relationships and oppositions, and casual, unexpected elements that vary the scene; great order in the details, confusion, uproar, and tumult in the whole" (Tafuri, 1973/1976, p. 4).

These observations are, for Tafuri, "the acceptance of the anti-perspective character of urban space" (Tafuri, 1973/1976, p. 4). The logical counterpoint to this picturesque aesthetic applied to the spaces of cities ("the tumult in the whole") is the naturalization of *unity*. The well-known fable of the primitive hut as the origin of architecture is also attributed to the abbot. Contrary to Vitruvius, who lived in the last century BC, Laugier describes a primordial scene in which man, alone in nature and in imitation of it, constructs the first house that is the origin of all construction (columns, entablatures, frontispieces, etc.). It precedes the (social) construction of temples, serving otherwise as their model. This elaboration has its origins in the Renaissance interpretations of the Vitruvian Treaty that describes the original house.

This lone man, who ultimately seeks shelter from the elements, deals exclusively with nature. The creative impulse is, therefore, individual. It is not far removed from the solitude of another original being, that possessing something in greater quantity than is needed, exchanges it for something that someone else has left over. In "Origin and Use of Money" in his 1776 *The Wealth of Nations*, Adam Smith (1776/2000) similarly seeks out the creative impulse underlying the complex mercantile operations of the modern world. Accordingly, an "invisible hand" allows for the transformation of individual action into collective virtues: a heterogenous whole resulting from the isolated actions of individual exchanges and their objective of maximizing profit.

The liberal city, however, will announce its limits early on. Individualized action, at least in its relations to the spaces of cities, did not reach collective virtue. Macro-interventions, following Haussmann's Paris model, spread throughout Europe. As the opposing pole to liberal beliefs, these interventions were conceived of by centralizing states, who ripped the traditional urban fabric imposing new typologies for new centers of consumption.

Thus, in most cases, rigorous design and control of the collective dimensions of cities was guaranteed, through typologies inherited from traditional cities, from the Middle Ages through the Baroque period. In the exemplary case of the Cerdá plan in Barcelona (1860), the expansion of the urban grid (*ensanche*) freed up the overpopulated and unhealthy old city (which, nonetheless, kept existing). Ensured by royal power, these transformations guaranteed the profit interests of the local bourgeoisie, who rapidly built homes in newly urbanized areas. The plan composed a rigorous general structure that created the characteristic *manzanas* (quadrate blocks with beveled corners), later subdivided into private lots. This was a result of liberal capitalism. That is, of its incapacity to propose general urban hypotheses resulting from the entrepreneurial impulses of the individual capitalist alone. Private exploitation of land required certain formal or legal parameters in order to function, even if this was never quite understood on these terms.

A pragmatic, less inspired, albeit more economically successful version of this was the tracing of the New York grid in the early 19th century, the basic arrangement of which guaranteed functional aspects of circulation (large streets and orthogonal avenues) and allowed for maximal occupation of the lots composing each block, impelled even further through widespread use of the elevator from the late 19th century onward. This simple, constructively permissive urban arrangement allowed for the creation of a new constructive typology, the multifunctional skyscraper.

FIGURE 1.5 Aerial view of Barcelona in the region of the city's expansion with the morphology defined by Ildefons Cerdá's project (1859). Photo taken in 2007.

The New York scheme applies simple, clear rules, with minimal interference, in order to guarantee that individual agents create their best possible business opportunities. This "whole," contrary to Laugier's, no longer seeks spontaneous variety but programmed regularity. Variety is restricted to lots and their implausible skyscrapers, especially between the late 19th century and the Great Depression in the 1930s. Beyond this restriction to lots, variety can be counterproductive and must be controlled, even if it runs contrary to the autonomous impulses of capital. The public virtues of private action, that dictum of revolutionary liberalism, were no longer a guarantee nor even a necessity, given the acceleration of monopolist accumulation.

The "European" arrangement, still tied to certain emblems of civilization and to a supposedly universalist rationality, bore the increasingly heavy load of being the regulating force of nation states. This presence is related to the efforts of late industrialization in continental Europe, the very condition of unequal capitalist modernization. Rationalizing productive stimuli hovered ideologically above the immediate profit evaluations of private capitalists. This rationality was increasingly required, especially given the most evident conflict: metropolitan chaos in conflict with the remaining historical city (order).

The growing political influence of the working class in this context of metropolization—be it in revolutionary struggle or the rise of worker's parties—incited directly on schemes of spatial representation. Thus, the failure of the metropolis would also be superseded by a spatiality understood as proletarian. Berlage, in the early 20th century, defined the "residential block" in opposition to the "degeneration of form he saw being applied by architects to each house separately" (Grinberg, 1982, p. 44). This situation of spatial—and social—unravelling could be overcome by a new formation: "standardized, repeated dwelling units would be a valid and representative aesthetic of the working class" (Grinberg, 1982, p. 48). This new rationalized urban order, in which traditional urban structures still remain (streets, squares, blocks, etc.), organizes

FIGURE 1.6 São Paulo skyline. At the center of the image is Copan, designed by Oscar Niemeyer (1966). Photo taken in 2011.

the variety and homogeneity of the city of the future, the socialist city. Thus, economic chaos (liberalism), social chaos (class struggle), and spatial chaos (metropolis) funnel social imagination toward a rationality already far removed from the *real city*. The *rupture*, in a general sense, depersonalized social agents around the absolute homogenization of *types* which, contradictorily, deepened the domination of mental schemes of economic value. Proletarian and industrial aesthetics—both imaginary—became fused *pari passu* with the radicality of the social process.

The convergence of the principles, strategies, and solutions devised by the historical avant-garde in the second half of the 1920s culminates in a radical synthesis carried out by architecture. These radical vectors were mostly concentrated in central Europe and in the experiences of a roaming Le Corbusier. Germany and Austria host the most advanced processes, regarding the great problem, generalized after the first World War, of workers' housing. To configure this type of housing became modern architects' main urbanistic strategy, as we may observe in the German hegemony at the second CIAM (*Congrès Internationaux d'Architecture Moderne*), the object of which was the minimum housing unit, in 1929.

The advance of the crises of liberalism, felt most of all in Europe because of the war effort, began to set off "desires for order," which were repressed by liberal ideologies. Tafuri then defines the daring urban and architectural (in this case there is no difference between the terms) projects of the late 1920s: *the ideology of the Plan*. The productive and social disorganization of liberal capitalism was reaching its limit, and prefigurations of the programmed rationality were constructed mainly through a functional architecture.

This contradiction between the rational order of the factory and the social disorder of the city was confronted most immediately by social democracy (both German and Austrian). The consolidation of German industry was a well-articulated state strategy for overcoming the structural deficiencies of its late industrialization. This strategy involved developing and teaching industrial design, which culminated in the foundation of the Bauhaus in 1919. During the Weimar Republic (1919–1933), architects participated intensely in public administration, developing admirable housing policies. Various housing complexes—*Siedlungen*—were rapidly built through the development of the civil construction industry.

Located in the unoccupied outskirts of large German cities, these complexes were, according to Tafuri, an "oasis of order," of spatial and social rationality (Tafuri, 1973/1976, p. 119). They could be counterposed, without interference, in metropolitan "disorganicity," for which radical architecture had found no answer. The empty lots of the outskirts provided no resistance to the new plan, contrary to cities, those spaces governed by the most direct productive logic of industrial capital. This contradiction reproduces that of social democracy, responsible for administering the social unbalance generated by an unaltered productive process.

This culminates in the radical proposals of Ludwig Hilberseimer, a teacher at the Bauhaus before its deactivation by the Nazi government. In his book *Metropolisarchitecture* (1927/2014), he proposed the quintessential ideology of the Plan, of the Fordist-Taylorist logic which drove architectural rationality. The housing unit is built through components that form cells, which in turn form buildings, which then form the *totality of the territory* made available through a rational (industrial) imperative.

At that moment, the ideological formulation of state-sponsored planning, as much as the actual political struggle between the Weimar Republic and the National Socialist party, arrived at a final confrontation. From then on, coinciding with the general crisis of the early 1930s, planning was actualized, as always, as its very opposite: the economic and military planning that ushered in a new stage of capitalism, the first chapter of which was global totalitarianism and authoritarianism.

The economic planning that characterized the hegemonic social state in Europe after World War II also involved constructing collective housing solutions for workers on a massive scale.

However, the large-scale housing projects built after 1945 created working-class ghettoes that had little in common with the original schemes of modern architecture, universals. During those years, Fordism was effectively applied to industry, leaving behind the mass utopias that inspired architects in the interwar period. Translated into mass housing, road-based transportation, and zoning, modern architecture and urbanism began to play the role of vehicles in capitalism's global expansion.

The spaces reserved for the working classes were based, in these European experiences of the 1950s and 1960s, on the homogenous, regular extensibility associated with a life-flattening functionality. In the cities, however, these vectors of extensibility were constricted by the limits of the lot. In this operative moment of modern ideology, freed from social utopias, vectors of formal extroversion crash against those of formal introversion. The glass tower, proposed by the so-called international style, which eventually became the symbol of big corporations, combines the centripetal rotation of skyscrapers with the requirements of reproducibility and expansion that erupt within the formal, constructive logic of the building itself. An analysis of the Seagram Building, completed in 1958 in New York, allows us to understand the sophisticated aesthetic strategies in which this contradictory unification (of universality and particularity) was formally resolved. The same tower was, incidentally, designed by a great master of modern architecture, Mies van der Rohe, the Bauhaus's final director before its deactivation in 1933.

This is a well-known contradiction between technical advances, allowing for large-scale reproduction and multiple social restrictions, such as property relations. The Seagram Building achieves a complex formal synthesis, becoming the symbolic and constructive paradigm for capitalism's new phase of planetary expansion. To do this, the building required the potential representations of modern space, as both homogeneous and infinite, even if it was in part restricted to the unit of a lot on the New York grid.

This particular example, with its promising future as corporate architecture-image, serves to mark the end, in big cities, of the distinction between building form and exterior form (block, city, or plan). Not even the pragmatism of the New York grid can condition the internal constitutive vectors of the building as a unit. The recent constructive boom in supertall skyscrapers already confuses the Manhattan skyline with that of any other postmodern city built anywhere else: random units are juxtaposed according to random urbanism, acquiring meaning that directly associates the image of financial capitalism with a hallucinatory sensibility.

According to our argument, the fragile structures of urban form vanish. Specifically, those that had conditioned a mediating social arrangement, between abstract rationality and the intimate life of everyday, producing the meaning of "society" ("there's no such thing as society," said Margaret Thatcher). Contemporary big cities offer, in place of this mediation, a planned, alienating estrangement. This process occurs according to the movement of fragilization of the political ideologies of the state, which became accentuated and globalized (save for some well-known exceptions) in the 1980s. If neoliberalism is the "new way of the world," as Dardot and Laval (2009/2013) argue, it is not enough to identify the economic processes behind the buildings and the spectacular urban interventions of private initiatives (mainly through corporation-states) but rather to identify the extensive production of new subjectivities. With this in mind, the schizophrenic space that Jameson (1991, p. 25) writes of becomes the fundamental *inductor/induced* (Lefebvre, 1968/1996, p. 65) of this process.

We identify, thus, political ideologies (the state) with the structuring forces of urban form that would order and direct the economic processes of industrial capitalism. Therefore, subordinated to autonomous economic processes and subject to cyclical crises, urban ideologies maintain the twofold character of ideology: making the expansion of accumulation viable while attributing to it a universal meaning. That is to say, the internal laws of liberal economy (competing individuals) possess social value and form both society and the city. The greater the crisis and economic uncertainty (crises of liberal ideologies), the greater the representations of order and spatial rationality of architecture and urbanism become. In these moments the state becomes reinforced, as does (spatial, economic, military, sanitary) planning.

The neoliberal assault on states and planning is, therefore, much more of an attack on their political ideologies, to the extent to which the various state functions and capacities are summoned for an economic project, such as military power and investment in communication infrastructures. Urban planning has been all but eliminated from the state's collection of social strategies, and urban space is now managed and appropriated by corporate logic or precarious occupation. If, at the height of social democracy, the block and planning carried out the mediation between profit and general urban logic, in the last few decades this state-sponsored mediation resides in its financial, bureaucratic corporatization, which allows for the attribution of value. The spatial dimension becomes de-territorialized, and urban territory becomes the representation of an other (spectacular) order, not a mirage of the social.

•

This somewhat erratic itinerary had as its objective the establishment, as we said, of beacons and conditioning principles for rethinking the disciplinary strategies of architecture and urbanism. We know this discipline is historically constituted in vast theoretical formulations (treaties, manifestos, theories, etc.), which in turn are incessantly confronted with social and constructive practices. It cannot remain in the field of conceptual constructs, isolated or ignorant of a perspective of spatial intervention. This is its specificity among fields of knowledge. Only the permanent critique of its underlying principles and actualizations can promote socially desirable transformations. A first task consists in comprehending the historical processes leading to a systemic crisis in a determined time and place, identifying the structuring elements of a phenomenon and projecting, through rearrangement, new possibilities. In other words, as Lefebvre says, scientific truth is conditioned by the projection of a concrete utopia, a virtuality within reality (Lefebvre, 1970/2003, p. 5).

The crisis of neoliberalism, the historical mark of which takes us back to 2008, is currently undergoing its paroxysm. We stand before terrifying possibilities. However, the radical nature of the process set off by the ongoing global pandemic allows for values which had been submerged in the "new way of the world" to rise to the surface. In keeping with the interests of this discussion, we observe a double signification: the urgency of the everyday, with its practice and vital necessities and scientific/rational knowledge, universal and socially constructed (the *latu sensu* modern). Modernity was an attempt to unify these poles of social existence, an integral functional rationalization of life, which encountered limits and provoked regressions and dehumanization.

All of a sudden, in a few weeks, the global world began to depend on this polarity of existence, faced with the risk of immeasurable tragedy. This critical conscience of neoliberal undoing (of individual and collective life) is an unquestionable social energy of the moment, which is not to say that positive transformations will necessarily derive from it. However, we are dealing with an unexpected conjuncture as well as a rare reaction of self-preservation that actually gets the prognostic right (society and collaboration). Scientific knowledge and daily practices become realigned as survival strategies, whether individual or collective. Of course this energy does not necessarily have political form, to the extent that, in this logic of social management, these no longer have sense or effectiveness. The question is: what form will it assume? Will it dissipate?

These answers cannot be given through a partial strategy, as is the case with what we discuss here. However, the emergence of this resignified polarity (between the state/society and everyday life) puts into question the foundations of disciplines that have the city (the mediation of these poles) as its main object of knowledge and transformation. The modern disciplinary formation of architecture and urbanism can be directly associated with liberal ideology, as Manfredo Tafuri realized, or with political ideology (*qua* instrument of the state) as our own argument suggests. Thus, we can imagine that little remains of it under this perspective, especially after being at the front of the spatial hallucinations of economic financialization. A problem considered here in a restricted manner, but which serves as a counterpoint to a crucial social question, is the role of the state in the next cycle. To it is attached the possibility of disciplinary reorganization, to the extent that the socially required rationalizing mechanisms have, in our case, a fundamental role to carry out. Thus, we depend also on the meaning of this necessary rationalization: a less economic, more creative appropriation of the city or the deepening of the cybernetic panopticon already under way.

The proposed debate should consider, however, a modification that is as important as it is problematic: a reorientation toward daily life, which has been severely impacted and transformed by the current moment. Initially identified with "hard" superstructures—a "systemic functionality," which for Habermas meant a "categorial error" (Habermas, 1981/1998, p. 423)—architecture and urbanism rehearsed a number of possible approaches to this subjective, bodily aspect of space: from vernacular research and tradition to the dimension of labor and material production of low-income housing (which was believed to bear emancipatory qualities). A considerable amount of these approaches ended up contributing to disciplinary dilution, which, in the terms of our argument, implies the negation of state ideologies and, therefore, of the more general possible representations of urban space in a rationalized society. At least in regards to the social potentials of urban life, which are historically constituted through continuities and ruptures. The political conjuncture of the 1960s allowed for wagers on self-management as the advanced social form of the social state and its achievements, which seemed irreversible. In central countries, this meant the possible changes in the democratic, advanced social organization of some or all of state functions, *in a consolidated urban environment*. In peripheral countries, however, experiences in self-management remained in many cases closer to survival tactics or to an administration of precariousness. One question remained unanswered: what to do with territory, collective spaces, infrastructure, or the right to the city, especially in places with no assistance from these dimensions, precisely because of the absence of the social state (and the presence of the political state).

The suggestion is that there exists, underway, in the best possible hypothesis concerning the immediate future, a reconfiguring of social life which might require a new order of relations between the social state and the processes of popular antinomy. Since the mediation between abstract social structures and daily life was historically actualized by the city and urban experience, a critical reformulation of architecture and urbanism as disciplines must follow and explore this possibility. What urban spaces catalyze this new configuration? It is no longer about the fact that this shift should be preceded by another, broader one, but about helping to create the spaces in which these shifts, constant and always humanizing, may appear. Homogeneity and segregation, two favorite topics of modern strategies, led society to unforeseen levels of alienation and individualism. Counter-hegemonic spaces, however, do not appear outside of a direct, intense relationship with the processes and initiatives of automatization that exist and may be manipulated in the coming years. Therefore, it is a synthesis between disciplinary strategies and popular tactics that does not consider these polarities in a positive way, but as contradictory, fluent realities.

The state, doubtless the most problematic dimension of this configuration, should not be considered a unified monolith, with unidirectional actions. The "state-finance" nexus, deepened in

FIGURE 1.7 A man practices capoeira in an open area of a Brazilian favela, 2017.

recent years by these states becoming indebted (Harvey, 2014, p. 46), determines all other functions that are under the controlled budget of the economic nucleus. This does not occur, however, without conflicts and instability between the different parts and activities that form what we call "government." This is the sense behind our insistence on the ideological dimension of architectural action; let it be in this environment that we might produce friction between those actions, those unkept promises. In them are the representations of a rational, human society, that can serve as a basis, for lack of a better one, for reorganizing everyone's efforts. This was a difficult horizon to glimpse in recent years. An actual possibility opens up, at the moment when rational and human procedures flow into each other, even if these conflict with an also-dominant irrationality. There is no doubt that irrational processes of the instrumentalization of life around economically destructive objectives is hegemonic. We must think of possible schemes for confronting them.

Notes

1. Class and race trace the dissemination of the virus. Black people are four times more likely to be contaminated than whites, followed by Pakistanis, Indians, Chinese, etc. (see Booth & Barr, 2020, May 7). In Brazil, the pandemic started in the upper classes and in the Southeast. Its development, however, soon shifted to the peripheries and to more unequal states and cities. Seeking to calm investors by saying that the pandemic in the country "is fine," the president of a major bank said that "The peak of the disease [of COVID-19] is over when we look at the middle class or upper middle class. The challenge is that Brazil

is a country with a lot of poor communities, a lot of slums, which ends up making the whole process difficult" (see Mendonça, 2020, May 7).
2. The work of architect Hassan Fathy on Gourna, in Egypt, was published in 1969 with the title *Gourna: A Tale of Two Villages*. It became known throughout the world with a new American edition (Fathy, 1973). Architect John Turner's research about social housing and community participation began between 1957 and 1965 in Peru. This experience with precarious settlements led him to develop and publish theories about housing quality and popular participation in the project (Turner, 1972, 1976).

   The most eminent Brazilian case is the work of architect Sérgio Ferro. His studies on the civil construction industry led him to a critique of site organization and division of labor. The proposal for reorganizing housing construction work, with its autonomy as an objective, was the theoretical basis for most of the task forces constructing housing in São Paulo since the 1970s (Ferro, 1969/2006, 1976/2006).
3. In Brazil, the most prominent case is the work of Otília Arantes, who, since the 1990s, has been analyzing both urban and architectural processes, identifying the regressive forces present in the most celebrated works of the late 20th and early 21st centuries, a dissonant voice at a time when most critics were excited about the partnerships between the market and the state (Arantes, 1998, 2000, 2011).
4. See chapter in this book by Otília Arantes, "Ruins of the Future."
5. The Saí phanalstère was built in the state of Santa Catarina, in the southern region of Brazil, by 100 French families in 1841, according to the theories of Charles Fourier (1772–1837). New Harmony, in the state of Louisiana, in the USA, was built by Robert Owen (1771–1858) in 1824.

References

Agamben, G. (2005). *State of Exception* (K. Attell, Trans.). Chicago, IL; London, UK: Stanford University Press. (Original work published 2003).

Arantes, O. (1998). *Urbanismo em Fim de Linha e Outros Estudos sobre o Colapso da Modernização Arquitetônica*. São Paulo, Brazil: Editora da Universidade de São Paulo.

Arantes, O. (2000). Uma Estratégia Fatal: A Cultura nas Novas Gestões Urbanas. In O. Arantes, E. Maricato, & C. Vainer (Eds.), *A Cidade do Pensamento Único: Desmanchando Consensos* (pp. 11–74). Rio de Janeiro, Brazil: Vozes.

Arantes, O. (2011). *Chai-na*. São Paulo, Brazil: Editora da Universidade de São Paulo.

Booth, R., & Barr, C. (2020, May 7). Black People Four Times More Likely to Die from Covid-19, ONS Finds. *The Guardian*, Health. Retrieved from www.theguardian.com/world/2020/may/07/black-people-four-times-more-likely-to-die-from-covid-19-ons-finds

Choay, F. (1970). L'Histoire et la Méthode en Urbanisme. *Annales, 25*(4), 1143–1154. Retrieved from www.persee.fr/doc/ahess_0395-2649_1970_num_25_4_422350

Choay, F. (1992). *L'Orizzonte del Post-urbano*. Rome, Italy: Officina Edizioni.

Choay, F. (1994). Le Règne de l'Urbain et la Mort de la Ville. In J. Dethier & A. Guiheux (Eds.), *La Ville, Art et Architecture en Europe, 1870–1993* (pp. 26–35). Paris, France: Éditions du Centre Pompidou.

Dardot, P., & Laval, C. (2013). *The New Way of the World: On Neo-liberal Society*. London, UK; New York, NY: Verso. (Original work published 2009).

Engels, F. (1987). Anti-Dühring. In *Karl Marx-Friedrich Engels Collected Works* (Vol. 25, pp. 1–309). Oxford, UK; New York, NY: Oxford University Press. (Original work published 1878).

Engels, F. (1993). *The Condition of the Working Class in England*. Oxford, UK; New York, NY: Oxford University Press. (Original work published 1845).

Fathy, H. (1973). *Architecture for the Poor: An Experiment in Rural Egypt*. Chicago, IL: The University of Chicago Press.

Ferro, S. (2006). A Produção da Casa no Brasil. In P.F. Arantes (Ed.), *Arquitetura e Trabalho Livre* (pp. 61–101). São Paulo, Brazil: CosacNaify. (Reprinted from *A Casa Popular*, 1969, GFAU).

Ferro, S. (2006). O canteiro e o desenho. In P.F. Arantes (Ed.), *Arquitetura e Trabalho Livre* (pp. 105–200). São Paulo, Brazil: CosacNaify. (Reprinted from "A Forma da Arquitetura e o Desenho da Mercadoria", *Almanaque, 1976*(2), and "O Desenho", *Almanaque, 1976*(3)).

Grinberg, D. (1982). *Housing in the Netherlands—1900/1940*. Delft, The Netherlands: Delft University Press.

Habermas, J. (1983). Modernity—An Incomplete Project. In H. Foster (Ed.), *The Anti-Aesthetic: Essays on Postmodern Culture* (pp. 3–15). Port Townsend, WA: Bay Press. (Original work presented 1980).

Habermas, J. (1998). Modern and Post-Modern Architecture. In K.M. Hays (Ed.), *Architecture Theory since 1968* (pp. 416–426). Cambridge, MA; London, UK: The MIT Press. (Original work presented 1981).

Harvey, D. (2014). *Seventeen Contradictions and the End of Capitalism*. New York, NY: Oxford University Press.

Hilberseimer, L. (2014). *Metropolisarchitecture*. New York, NY: Columbia University Press. (Original work published 1927).

Jameson, F. (1984). Periodizing the 60s. *Social Text, 9/10*, 178–209. https://doi.org/10.2307/466541

Jameson, F. (1991). *Postmodernism, or, The Cultural Logic of Late Capitalism*. Durham, NC: Duke University Press.

Lefebvre, H. (1996). Right to the City. In E. Kofman & E. Lebas (Eds.), *Writings on Cities* (pp. 63–181). Oxford, UK; Malden, MA: Blackwell Publishers Ltd. (Original work published 1968).

Lefebvre, H. (2000). *La Production de l'Espace* (4th ed.). Paris, France: Anthropos. (Original work published 1974).

Lefebvre, H. (2003). *The Urban Revolution*. Minneapolis, MN: The University of Minnesota Press. (Original work published 1970).

Lefebvre, H. (2017). *Everyday Life in the Modern World*. New York, NY: Routledge. (Original work published 1971).

Lyotard, J.-F. (1984). *The Postmodern Condition: A Report on Knowledge*. Minneapolis, MN: University of Minnesota Press. (Original work published 1979).

Mendonça, H. (2020, May 7). Pandemia expõe "necropolítica à brasileira" e uma certa elite que não vê além do umbigo. *El País*, Economia. Retrieved from https://brasil.elpais.com/economia/2020-05-08/pandemia-expoe-necropolitica-a-brasileira-e-uma-certa-elite-que-nao-ve-alem-do-umbigo.html

Simmel, G. (2010). The Metropolis and Mental Life. In G. Bridge & S. Whatson (Eds.), *The Blackwell City Reader* (2nd ed., pp. 103–110). Malden, MA; Oxford, UK; West Sussex, UK: Blackwell Publishing. (Original work published 1903).

Smith, A. (1776/2000). *An Inquiry into the Nature and Causes of the Wealth of the Nations*. New York, NY: The Modern Library.

Soja, E. (2000). *Postmetropolis: Critical Studies of Cities and Regions*. Oxford, UK: Blackwell Publishing.

Tafuri, M. (1976). *Architecture and Utopia: Design and Capitalist Development*. Cambridge, MA; London, UK: The MIT Press. (Original work published 1973).

Turner, J. (1972). *Freedom to Build: Dweller Control of the Housing Process*. New York, NY: Macmillan.

Turner, J. (1976). *Housing by People: Towards Autonomy in Building Environments, Ideas in Progress*. London, UK: Marion Boyars.

Weber, M. (1966). *The City*. New York, NY: The Free Press. (Original work published 1921).

2
ON ARCHITECTURE AND URBAN SPACE AFTER THE IDEOLOGICAL CRISIS OF NEOLIBERALISM

Leandro Medrano

The spatial relations that have since emerged as a result of neoliberal policies have been harshly criticized in the first decades of the 21st century, the outcome of an ideological crisis, which escalated especially after the burst of the *Internet bubble* in 2000, the terrorist attacks on the Twin Towers on September 11, 2001, and the *housing crash* of 2008. Currently, the toughest challenge amidst this crisis has been the COVID-19 pandemic, whose consequences remain uncertain. While some predict chaos in light of a general system collapse, others wage on a reorganization of the world order towards solutions for pressing global problems, such as the environmental issue, political systems, and social inequality. In this regard, architecture and urbanism seem to regain a *critical* meaning which had been subdued in the heydays of the economic, political, and cultural program that defined late capitalism. This recovery is far from a nostalgic return to 19th-century utopias or to the vanguards of the first decades of the 20th century, but rather the pursuit of a disciplinary stance capable of resisting dominant orders and, as much as possible, proposing better alternatives. Taking as a starting point the rise and crisis of the neoliberal model developed since the 1970s, this chapter promotes a dialogue between the theoretical-critical issues related to the spatial realities of the so-called peripheral countries and the topics under debate in core countries. To this end, we seek evidence within the realities of the largest metropolis in South America that the *crisis of the city*[1] arising from the Industrial Revolution has not only been preserved, but further radicalized: the partial arrangements that led to the creation of appeasing islands in the Global North and South no longer sustain themselves against the advance of chronic problems in the urbanization processes, such as global warming, the scarcity of natural resources, and extreme poverty. The humanitarian refugee crisis in Europe, alarming pollution levels in the megacities, growing deforestation of the Amazon rainforest, and the rise of nationalisms and the far right are some of the symptoms that endanger the civilizing project of Enlightenment origin. Within the current context, this means putting the future of the entire planet at risk, as intellectuals from different ideological backgrounds, such as Bruno Latour, Noam Chomsky, or Ailton Krenak, have warned.

This perception about the socio-spatial reality, which may now seem evident, was not prevalent within the *high architecture* circles during the apparent triumph of the neoliberal strategies adopted in the 1980s and 1990s, sustained by the virtuous results of the accumulation system via financialization in times of globalization. At the height of what David Harvey called the "postmodern condition," the new logic of transnational capital relied on deterritorialization as

FIGURE 2.1 Building projection by visual artist Matías Segura displaying "We Will Not Return to Normality Because Normality Was the Problem," Santiago, Chile, 2019.

a premise for both its real and virtual expansion. The borders, walls, and barriers would dissolve themselves in the face of the then-new possibilities that the communication and information technologies presented to the flexible accumulation regime.[2] On the other hand, the fall of the Berlin Wall in 1989 symbolically underlines the lack of alternatives to the strategies of Western capitalism, given that the polarization of the Cold War years would lose sense with the dissolution of the Socialist Bloc. There would be no room, therefore, for architecture or urbanism *critical to* the (neoliberal) capitalist system in times of "single thought." Within these intellectual disciplines, the role of *criticism*, which had been largely instructed by Manfredo Tafuri's version of neo-Marxist concepts devised by the Frankfurt School, would make no sense in a world that flattened its own contradictions. Even Tafuri distanced himself from the spatial problematics posed at the time, as if conformed to the "end of history" imposed by the new world order.

Distant from the demands for social housing as well as from the utopian ideals of the Modern Movement, architecture and urbanism have treaded a recalcitrant course since the mid-1960s. Nonetheless, a certain critical activism gained traction in the following decades, and whose examples are still referenced to this day, as in the "war machines" of Archigram, Superstudio, or Buckminster Fuller, in the hippie provocation of Ant Farm, in Gordon Matta-Clark's radical denouncement, or in the Marxist-inspired engagement proposed by the Arquitetura Nova group and in the "penetrables" of artist Hélio Oiticica (to cite some examples of the so-called Global South). On the other hand, in the 1980s, although historians such as Anatole Kopp published manifestos longing for the heroic times when architecture and urbanism were engaged in the social causes of the Modern Movement, the role played by disciplinary criticism acquires novel and diverse outlines. Instead of proposing alternatives to the spatial conditions of industrial society, it now seeks consonance with the plurality of postmodern artistic and cultural expressions, as well as academic studies devoted to the new condition of late capitalism. In this regard, the fragile convergence between the Euro-American "great narrative" and the peripheral countries—which had become acceptable since "Brazil Builds"—practically disappears. Without the ideological ballast of a social function, or even a modernizing techno-scientific (or techno-utopian) narrative, architecture and urbanism in peripheral countries loses visibility and relevance in wide-reaching disciplinary subjects. One rare exception were specific studies that sought, through their own condition of alterity, the oppositional forces to the conservatism of the dominant hegemonic system, as in the case of the "post-colonial studies" disseminated through American academia by neo-Marxist intellectuals, such as Terry Eagleton. After all, the technological progress of materials and programs, not to mention the billionaire budgets that abounded in those virtuous times of commodity-architecture and enterprise-cities, found no place in countries removed from the new world economic order—often grappling with internal political problems, State debt, and hyperinflation. Museums, cultural centers, and corporate buildings—technologically sophisticated and extremely expensive—set the tone for the "aesthetic" debate within the field of capital-produced architecture in times of globalization and disseminated in international specialized journals. As for the urban projects, in the 1980s and 1990s, the emphasis was on the emblematic examples of "strategic urbanism," which through public-private partnerships and the logic of the commodity-city, sought instruments to circumvent the ruin of the State or its inefficiency for addressing urban issues in post-industrial cities. Political engagement—so crucial for the precursors of New Architecture—lost ground to an uncompromised version of *disciplinary autonomy* and regionalisms of all kinds. A dangerous wager towards the seductive allure of images and spectacle, which seemed to have no end in times of easy money, and the configuration of social sensitivities that concealed the contradictions of the so-called culture industry.

Post-Critical (?)

Within this context, theory, and particularly critical theory, lost ground in the architectural debate in countries that spearheaded the implementation of neoliberal policies and, consequently, the cultural logic of postmodernity. The ultra-pragmatism of free market strategies would no longer face resistance as the plight of the welfare state dissolved itself in the general crisis of the State, expedited by the 1973 oil shock. Within the field of architecture and urbanism, criticism, meant to unravel the contradictions within the modernization process and especially the contradictions of its rationality, was thus deemed obsolete since its abstractions and subjectivities, regarded as utopian, would have little use for the emerging lucrative markets in the field of arts, architecture, and urban development. For authors such as Michael Speaks, considered one of the first to oppose *critical architecture*, not only would there be no use to theory, but it would also hinder the pursuit for "alternative ways of thinking."[3] In other words, reactions to conflicts arising from the capitalist neoliberal model would exist in everyday practices aligned with the demands of capital itself. Similarly, Stan Allen, Carol Burns, Robert Taylor, Sylvia Lavin, Jeffrey Kipnis, Robert Somol, and Sarah Whiting sought alternatives to the theoretical stalemates posed by Marxist and neo-Marxist-inspired critics associated with the ideas of Manfredo or the Frankfurt School. While they were not an institutionalized or intellectually coherent group, authors such as George Baird situated them among the so-called post-critics (or post-theorists), a term which would later be used to label several cultural and artistic works in the final decades of the 20th century.[4] Baird sees in the post-critics a unity in their pursuit for overcoming the stalemates posed by the critics of the previous generation (Baird, 2004). After all, progressive critical thought in the vigorous epoch of neoliberalism had become an aporia, and would run against a discipline shaped by practice—through a concrete dialogue with the world and its daily realities. A dialogue synthesized in the famous essay "Notes Around the Doppler Effect and Other Moods of Modernism" by Robert Somol and Sarah Whiting (2002), whose heated repercussion in the Anglo-Saxon academic milieu would come to affirm not only a way of thinking about architecture, but above all, to produce it—a kind of project methodology within the field of theory, which had outlined the debate of the previous decades regarding "post-critical" or "projective" architecture. It is no accident that the article gained traction within the same environments in which "the design methods movement" was prominent. In this scenario, architecture and urbanism should act proficiently to solve the spatial problems that emerge in each social context, and the method should assist the conjunction between disciplinary historical knowledge and the new techniques and tools of the project. Good architecture and good urbanism would operate in a kind of perfect algorithm, shaped by the needs of the program, while excellence would come from the professional virtues of those skilled enough to surpass the expectations placed by the demands of users, society, and the market—the solutions would be in the project itself, in praxis, and not necessarily through a dialogue with criticism or theory. Architects such as Rem Koolhaas and Bernard Tschumi would be the most sophisticated representatives of this approach, whose *leitmotiv* involves the pursuit for new spatial content by using market strategies and the cultural plurality of late capitalism.

Yet it is precisely in the alleged absence of contradictions among the individual, society, and the market from which emerges the leading criticisms to post-critical pragmatism and neoliberalism in general. In North America, Michael Hays, a professor of history and architectural theory, formulated the most daring hypotheses on the critical possibilities of architecture. In his 1984 groundbreaking article, "Critical Architecture: Between Culture and Form," Hays calls for a critical architecture, resistant to conciliatory tendencies against the dominant culture, and in constant dialogue with both architectural criticism and critical historiography, as well as with

FIGURE 2.2 China Central Television Headquarters, designed by OMA/Rem Koolhaas, Beijing, China, 2012.

the dialectical process amidst the contingencies of place and time and formal autonomy. In his best-known book, *Architecture's Desire: Reading the Late Avant-Garde*, Hays refers to the Lacanian triad (the Imaginary, the Symbolic, and the Real) to analyze the works of Rossi, Eisenman, Hejduk, and Tschumi. In his view, the critical potential found in these works emerges from how these architects established connections among the Imaginary, the Symbolic, and the Real to contrive an "autonomous architecture" against the historical condition conveyed by postmodernity. Over the course of his writings and intellectual career, Michael Hays was notoriously close to the ideas and concepts of Manfredo Tafuri and, consequently, to the Frankfurt School's variant of Marxism. However, we can only understand his particular version, devised for the postmodern North American context, in contrast to the neoliberal expansion movement in developed countries, especially in the Anglo-Saxon world. It is no surprise, therefore, that urban themes or city issues are not a priority for Hays. After all, the North American model of the city is structured by the logic of individual rights and private property, hence the associations between urban, urban life, and architecture are not as directly interconnected as in societies whose spatial dynamics are intrinsically linked to the spatial conditions of public and collective spheres.

The opposite occurs in European contexts, especially in southern Europe, where a spectacular postmodernity contrasts with the resistance mechanisms of the cities, their places, their culture, and their history. Critics and designers such as Josep Quetglas, Ignasi de Solà-Morales, Vittorio Gregotti, Carlo Aymonino, and Bernard Huet, among others, made use of the critical wealth devised by Tafuri to confront the consequences and legacies of the International Style as a capitalist planification strategy. Furthermore, they turned to the Venice School for the concepts and elements to claim an architecture of the place, of temporalities, and of permanencies as a reaction project to the generic models adopted on a large scale in times of globalization. Understanding the historical singularities and the everyday spatial dynamics of cities and places seemed like an alternative to the totalizing schemes abandoned by the financial system, the real estate market, and the major transnational corporations. Their inspiration in phenomenology and their dialogue with the new French philosophy (particularly Jacques Derrida and Gilles Deleuze) brought a striking originality to this generation eager for alternatives to a discipline in crisis. Not surprisingly, these authors often devised spatial and formal hypotheses independent of ad hoc disciplinary practices—a direct consequence of their sophisticated theoretical foundations—which would go on to influence the most vibrant schools and the most original architects of those times.

Excluded from the economic affluence experienced by the Western democracies of the Global North in the 1980s and 1990s, most Latin America countries, and especially Brazil, remained relatively distant from the post-critical debate. There are several reasons for this disparity, but two hypotheses are particularly noteworthy when it comes to the relationship between architecture and urban space. The first refers to the long-standing tradition of the local Modern Architecture, whose innovative works by architects belonging to the generation of Oscar Niemeyer and Lúcio Costa gained prominence in the international architectural debate, especially after the art exhibition "Brazil Builds," held at the Museum of Modern Art (MoMA) in New York City in 1943.[5] The notion of an architecture designed to engender a new—modern—spatiality would thus become a structural part of cultural, political, and economic movements that sought to overcome a local agrarian and archaic past and promote the modernization of the country and its society. In the words of one of the most renowned intellectuals of the period, Mario Pedrosa, "Brazil is condemned to be modern," as this would be the only possible artistic and cultural expression capable of synthesizing and aggregating the diversity and complexity of its territory under a common goal: modernization and "independence." The second hypothesis concerns the economic, social, and political crises that have plagued Brazil—as well as Latin America in general—over the course of the re-democratization process following the end of the military dictatorship. The high debts contracted in previous decades and the inflation resulting from the bankruptcy of the State did not ensure the same economic robustness to this region that late capitalism provided to many countries in the Global North. The result of this process exacerbated an "uneven and combined development," since the possibilities for a definitive emancipation were contained by pre-existing conditions incapable of reversing the local dependence process.

Thus, the dialogue between the artistic and cultural production with the logic of the globalized market, with the "culture industry," or with the consumer society would not acquire the same meaning or same potency in regions that were still recalcitrant in their industrialization processes. Within this context, the debate on postmodernity becomes undermined both by the absence of an economic backdrop able to sustain the abundance and festive frivolity of the liveliest cultural forms of late capitalism, and by the resistance of "high culture" to distance itself from the so-called local modern tradition. The modern project laid out in Jürgen Habermas's "Modernity—An Incomplete Project" (1980/1983), or even the ideas for preserving the Enlightenment principles proposed by Sérgio Paulo Rouanet in *As Razões do Iluminismo* (1987), had a far-reaching impact among local architects, especially those associated with the FAUUSP (Faculty of Architecture and Urbanism of the University of São Paulo). In this context, the essays by philosopher Otília Arantes, compiled in the books *O Lugar da Arquitetura depois dos Modernos*, from 1992, and *Urbanismo em Fim de Linha*, from 1998, were pivotal for understanding the complex and peculiar local reality. The initial focus was on the singularity of the Modern

Project developed in Brazil, considered by the author as a fully realized project precisely for not having faced the contradictions of the modernization process in Brazilian society. In the author's words:

> There were many incongruities and disparities (registered from early on by visiting foreigners), and yet we cannot deny that the Modern Project reencountered its truth in the ancient colonial fringe of the system, thanks to the entrepreneurial power of the ruling classes organized by way of strong and modernizing States. One could say that, among formalistic involutions and private architectural rationality with social implications, the utopian spirit of the Plan developed itself verbatim.
>
> *(Arantes, 1998 p. 31)*

The particularity and significance of her work lies in the novel way through which she situates architectural and urban issues that were relevant in Brazil in the late 20th century in relation to the neo-Marxist international debate—a debate in those years mediated by authors such as David Harvey, Fredric Jameson, Mike Featherstone, and Andreas Huyssen, among others. Furthermore, the so-called new French philosophy, particularly in the works of Foucault, Lyotard, Baudrillard, and Lipovetsky, was also central for her understanding of the cultural order amidst postmodern times. The critical content devised by Otília Arantes is, in a way, devastating. Her interpretation of the Brazilian reality extends to the world, in those years engulfed by the neoliberal logic of late capitalism. The contradictions among art, culture, and a world ruled by commodity fetishism could lead to no other outcome than the general collapse that we face today. Neither architectures nor cities would survive this accelerated and irresponsible model of capital expansion based on aggressive free market strategies, the absence of the State, and the destitution of the idea of society.[6] Many considered her ideas, when published in the 1980s and 1990s, excessively pessimistic and aporetic in their connection to unorthodox Marxist concepts distant from the Brazilian academic tradition or for disregarding the artistic virtues of Brazilian modern architecture. Nowadays, not so much.

Another important Latin American author of that period was Argentine architect and historian Marina Waisman, whose work stands out in its approach to Latin American architectural and urban production away from schematic syntheses, or distorted analyses, derived from thought schemes originating from "core" countries (Waisman, 1988). As she would often state, "Aim at yourself with your own eyes." Her critique, akin to other local intellectuals such as Francisco Liernur and Graciela Silvestri, sought to acknowledge the independence and originality of Latin American production, albeit in constant dialogue with the conceptual and analytical tools derived from the so-called dominant cultures (Waisman, 1998). In this regard, the city becomes a dissonant note in the scholarly production of peripheral countries. For as much as one acknowledges the virtues and singularities of Latin American architecture during those years, represented by architects such as González de León, Abraham Zabludovsky, Clorindo Testa, Enrique Browne, Rogelio Salmona, and Vilanova Artigas, these architectures had little or no influence on the chaotic and problematic urban fabric of its cities—or its everyday life spaces. Waisman calls this result "collage cities," appropriating a term coined by Colin Rowe and Fred Koetter, in which disconnected and often conflicting fragments are accommodated without forming any possibility of a coherent urban reading, whatever it may be. This is not, as the author herself underlines, a secondary problem:

> For we should not forget that the main sphere of life of architectural products is the city, and that the development and evolution of cities, and the history of architectural forms,

are deeply and intimately linked together. However, most Latin American cities suffered during this period of excessive growth, and even worse, growths that were not produced by their own expansion, but by the confused aggregate of multitudes of inhabitants expelled from their environment due to economic, political, and social circumstances.

(Waisman, 1988, p. 37)

Unlike the pragmatism that had settled within the cultural environment of developed countries, something of the utopias still remained in Latin American countries. After all, as Waisman wrote: "to build in a world dedicated to destruction; to believe in a disbelieving world; to trust in the future of the South, yet condemned by the North to destitution. Such is the modern Latin American utopia" (Waisman, 1988, p. 41).

Under a different context—within the neoliberal epicenter—Fredric Jameson was one of the most influential voices of the neo-Marxist tradition, critical of the social conditions of late capitalism. His essays, with far-reaching repercussions in the field of cultural studies (including in Latin America), strayed away from the conformist pragmatism that pervaded the post-critical environment of those years. Jameson was also one of the first authors to understand architecture as one of the most thorough manifestations of the cultural logic of postmodernity. In "Spatial Equivalents in the World System" (Jameson, 1992), for example, he mentions the house that architect Frank Gehry built for himself in Santa Monica, California, to problematize the condition of spatial isolation conveyed by American postmodern suburban mass culture. According to the author, Gehry's interventions in the transitional spaces between the public and the private, using oddly arranged ordinary industrial materials (in post-industrial contexts), suggest that the innovative spatial dynamics of that anti-urban society would exist within the dividing

FIGURE 2.3 Buildings on Paseo de la Reforma, Mexico City, 2013.

membrane between the domestic interior (private) and the urban exterior (public)—bearing in mind that the vocation for the public sphere, which in theory lies at the heart of modern spatial thought, inverts itself in the social and cultural practices of postmodernity. The other, the public, the urban, the social, the city, were to be avoided by the instruments of architectural design. This insight seems very contemporary nowadays when compared to the strategies of neoliberal biopolitics, geared towards the spatial segregation desired by the "urban enclosures,"[7] as seen in the following excerpt:

> The other is, on the face of it, unrelated to this, for it seems to imply a positive principle of relationship rather than this centrifugal movement, and rather suggests the way in which organisms react to foreign bodies and seek to surround and neutralize them in a kind of spatial quarantine or cordon sanitaire.
>
> *(Jameson, 1992, p. 101)*

In "The Constraints of Postmodernism" (1994), Jameson emphasizes how the seemingly postmodern plurality tends to convert into a marketing strategy for late capitalism, since appeals to the local or regional would not suffice for a *critical architecture* against the dominant cultural systems. In the same essay, he explores the tensions between public and private spaces through an analysis of Dutch architect Rem Koolhaas's earliest large-scale projects. Through an attempt to integrate the *totality* of urban issues into the building, Koolhaas ultimately incorporated public spaces into the private domain, now "replicated" within a geometric image of major proportions—the "block." Heterogeneity, now simulated within this "new individual building" displaced from the urban tissue, would be consistent with the freedom and flexibility desired by the market—a *replica* of the surrounding chaos. Such a resource would also result in depoliticization and alienation from everyday life, since by consenting to the logic of corporate power, its pragmatism and opportunism would operate to reduce social awareness (Jameson, 1994).

Jameson, as well as Hays, Arantes, Waisman, Quetglas, and Morales, among others, were dissonant voices amidst the most virtuous times of neoliberalism and the cultural logic of late capitalism. Whereas dedicated to the typological dialogue with history or the possibilities of innovation via technological advances, formal experiences prevailed. Jameson prescribed that by renouncing its utopian or anticipatory possibilities against dominant values, architecture became an accomplice to such values—its spatial variant (Jameson, 1992). After all, it was in the interest of the globalized capitalist market to create symbolic landmarks on a global scale, capable of heightening the virtues of the commodity-city and the individual against the State and society. The billion-dollar financial operation that resulted in the construction of the Guggenheim Museum Bilbao, known as "the Bilbao Effect," is perhaps the most emblematic example of the status enjoyed by architecture in those years, especially as it occurred in a country with a singular tradition in the field of architecture and urbanism, both in professional practice and in the development of theoretical-critical systems. The eccentricity of the Guggenheim Bilbao brand-image, which spread throughout the world, concealed the spatial, economic, and social contradictions that would later emerge in the first decades of the 21st century. This would ultimately assist to erode the image of the architectural form as a producer of broader meanings and sensitivities, since analogies to "spectacle-images" and commodity fetishism would diminish any other cultural or artistic meaning.

In recent decades, several authors, specialized journals, and academic events have dedicated themselves to post-criticism within the field of architecture and urbanism. Most of them emphasize the return of criticism as a fundamental instrument to the disciplinary practices in the early 21st century. This could happen from a closer alignment to the material conditions of the production of space or by way of a systematic isolation towards an alternative—or opposing—spatial logic against the realities of the world. In both cases, if the contradictions inherent in spatial relations are neglected, the discipline's fields of activity would be limited or non-existent.

Contradictions of Space

What would be the possibilities for a critical architecture and urbanism in this early 21st century? Aesthetic autonomy or political and social engagement? In this regard, the debate has been somewhat similar within the field of architecture and urbanism as in other areas of culture, such as visual arts, cinema, and theater.

The question of autonomy has been approached both in an historical or philosophical perspective, with a view to understanding its meaning in relation to cultural dynamics arising from modernity, as for the methodological possibilities of establishing autonomous practices in societies increasingly dependent on the economic and political strategies of late capitalism. If, on the one hand, critics such as Manfredo Tafuri sought to demonstrate the ideological nature of the emancipation hypotheses posed by the Modern Movement, given their alignment with instrumental reason and with the strategies of industrial capital, on the other hand, the postmodern (post-critical) mainstream failed to even consider the role of architecture as a discipline of resistance or opposition against dominant social forces. The debate on autonomy, in this context, would be focused on the articulation of its forms with the historical narratives, in order to operate within a phenomenology of space;[8] or towards the deconstruction of its self-referential language in search of new meanings;[9] or, more recently, in the pursuit of a vision of autonomy away from an apolitical condition, in which the architectural form would be confronted with the urban and its social reality.[10]

In contrast to these versions of autonomy, an engaged discipline, especially when addressing everyday urban and social issues, would reject any "formalist" appeal or even major aesthetic theories dedicated to the fields of culture and art. In this regard, they would act directly on the mechanisms of production, both material and symbolic, in an attempt to overcome capitalism's structural and hegemonic strategies of domination. The "aesthetic" outcome would be a consequence of the techniques, management forms, and cooperation systems fostered during the process.

In this context, the debate concerning philosophers Georg Lukács and Ernst Bloch and their stances on the clash between Realism and Modernism could help us to understand autonomy-related issues within the scholarly disciplines addressing space—especially in the so-called post-critical period. The theme was the subject of an important essay by Rodney Livingstone, Perry Anderson, and Francis Mulhern in 1977.[11] Regarding the issue of autonomy, our interest in this essay lies in the debate on the political role of art, in this case centered on literature. Georg Lukács favored the classically inherited modernity of the Enlightenment and rejected any contamination from irrationalism—as found in Expressionism—which he considered bordering fascism for obscuring a critical perception of society. Lukács, deemed as one of the most renowned exponents of 20th-century Marxism, believed in the aesthetic potential of form and its subsequent capacity to synthesize political, economic, and ideological positions. And *realism*, as glorified by a late Hegel, would be the most promising artistic expression of this model. Ernst Bloch, however, like Bertolt Brecht, valued artistic movements akin to the cultural sphere of the societies in which they sought to intervene. According to Bloch, straying away from historically structured cultural schemes would hinder an alternative becoming to the schemes instituted by the dominant classes, thus being an obstacle for overcoming the strategies of the conservative classes. Livingstone, Anderson, and Mulhern underline Lukács' oversight when failing to consider the contradictory dimension in his critical scheme of Expressionism, equally valid for art-related issues in general. Bloch, in turn, resorted to "popular" practices that were not always convincing in their aesthetic or political content—which could conceal the innovative, transformative, and critical role of art.

Similarly, in the post-critical period, resistance movements against a complete submission to the cultural forms of late capitalism would sometimes promote an agenda for the autonomy of form and space towards an absolute internal spatial logic (the *telos* of the new sublime or historical ideal), and in some cases propose to dissolve the ad hoc disciplinary models to approach the everyday demands of social classes oppressed or ignored by the dominant market forces. We are not short of recent historical examples regarding these two forms of critical action against the hegemonic cultural expressions of late capitalism. Architects Mies Van der Rohe and John Hejduk are perhaps the most sophisticated proponents of the autonomy of the field through the protection of its forms and spatialities against the fragilities of ordinary spatial production (the *oeuvre* versus the *world*). As for those who sought to operate directly within the forces that determine the production of space, their representativeness is diffuse and commonly related to state management bodies, nongovernmental organizations (NGOs), "tactical urbanism," spontaneous activism, or even in specific fields of art. Furthermore, precisely because they strove to operate through non-hegemonic forms, architects and urban planners who sought direct social and political engagement generally denied the discipline's canonical or iconic formal solutions—as these would allegedly carry the vices of the dominant systems, either in the scale of the social order of a given region or in the neocolonial cultural assimilation processes in developing countries. Such examples are plenty in the works of architects Ralph Erskine, Nicolaas John Habraken, the Uruguayan Housing Cooperatives, and *Grupo Arquitetura Nova*. A critical stance, in this case, meant criticizing historically consolidated disciplinary strata, both with regard to formal results (typological or aesthetic) as well as in the design and production processes.

While the limit of *autonomy* occurred within the *architecture of spectacle*, and therefore in connivance with the spatial model of late capitalism, *engagement* became practically unfeasible within a context dominated by the economic regulation of neoliberal policies, centered on profit and the private sector.

Hence, the recent reunion of theory and criticism with the disciplinary perspectives of architecture and urbanism has led to reassessments of their relationships with the State. The European welfare state, for example, has been the subject of several academic studies that underline its consequences in the everyday life of the working class, deemed incomparable with the policies aimed at privatizations and the minimum State,[12] especially in the social housing sector, which, when privatized, did not evolve its technical-spatial attributes or its financial management mechanisms.[13] Hence, the autonomy advocated by art, which freed it from its direct social functions and from its representational obligations (whether theological, political, or social), could not be directly applied to disciplines concerned with the urban space and its contradictions. After all, between the project and its implementation, the various agents involved would ensure the heteronomy of the process, at least from a methodological standpoint. Against this backdrop, the hypothesis of a hedonistic and *radically autonomous* architecture becomes unfeasible—regardless of the productive systems and urban dynamics—as in Georg Lukács' version of realism or in Niklas Luhmann's principle of autopoiesis. Its material, historical, heterological, and dialectical nature leads us to pursue other critical evaluation methods and theorical formulations.

It is no coincidence that one of the most recurring authors in contemporary studies related to architecture or urbanism has been French philosopher Henri Lefebvre. His interpretations and theories on urban space and urban life, discussed in the volumes of *Critique of Everyday Life* (1947/1991) and further developed in the emblematic *Right to the City* (1968/1996), *The Urban Revolution* (1970/2003), and *The Production of Space* (1974/1991), among others, have been fundamental for understanding the urban and social dynamics emerging from modernity.

Like so many other critics of the 1960s and 1970s, Lefebvre understands that the Modern city has failed to create spaces fully dedicated to the public life, to the contradictory, to uncompromised interactions, to cultural and artistic activation, to party, to pleasure, to enjoyment. Behind an apparent socializing and egalitarian ordering, as found in the Modern housing complex or in the urban system of the isolated suburban houses, the rationalization of everyday life would serve the authoritarian logic of industrial capitalism. This other order, imposed by technicians and technocrats, would affect both the dynamics of everyday life as well as the spatial and political segregation of those excluded or secondary to the "system" (Lefebvre, 1969). Undoubtedly, themes such as the expansion of global capitalism, the decline of the welfare state, global warming, racial and ethnic conflicts, and refugees, among others in our everyday life, are very distant from the world in which Lefebvre debated. And they are above all distant from the concept of city in the molds of the ancient boroughs of medieval Europe—a reference point for the French philosopher—often understood as romanticized or anachronic. However, his complex and sometimes paradoxical theoretical legacy has acquired a new meaning in recent decades, as his criticism of the modern capitalist city (the city of *use value*) can now be regarded as a premonition to the urban conflicts of our planet. When Lefebvre claims the City as the fundamental spatial unit for the "socialization of society," he is not referring to a nostalgic return to the "liberating" urban agglomerations of European historical tradition, such as the medieval city described by Weber in *The City*. What Lefebvre seeks to develop is an understanding of the urban phenomenon that considers the contradictions and the confluences between space and society. In this regard, the City is the result of collective desires mediated by its objectivities and subjectivities, both historical and virtual. As he writes: "The prescription is: there cannot be a going back (towards the traditional city), nor a head long flight, towards a colossal and shapeless agglomeration" (Lefebvre, 1968/1996, p. 148).

As Lefebvre would argue, to make progress in this complex task it would be insufficient to use fragmented sciences and knowledge, such as architecture, engineering, sociology, and geography. In order to understand and intervene in the urban dynamics, we must develop new theoretical and methodological tools that systematically integrate material production, society, and space. Among them, I believe that Lefebvrian *trialectics* could contribute to the debate on *autonomy* since its capacity to respond simultaneously to the various spatial scales of urban everyday life emphasizes, within the theoretical field, the contradictions of the term *germane* to contemporary architectural and urban practices. Such contradictions, as we shall see, are more glaring in the accelerated modalities of late capitalism in developing countries, where the urban crisis unfolds without the effective historical experience of the City. After all, the classic notion of autonomy—centered on the possibility that the oeuvre is *critical* against the dominant structures of the world precisely because it does not belong to this same world—has proven ineffective to the themes of architecture and urbanism. When we consider architecture to be "oeuvre," and the world to be the city (material and social), an internal fissure fractures the symbolic and phenomenological instruments of both architecture and the city. Both fail to be realized by operating *partially* in their spatial conditions. Such is the case of urban territories conceived according to their exchange-value, validated within the logic of the market, consumption, the commodity-city—the everyday nature of late capitalism, currently enduring an unprecedented crisis.

Conversely, when we consider Lefebvrian spatial *trialectics* as an instrument for disciplinary understanding, whether by architecture or urbanism, *city and space* become integrated around a single and comprehensive social theory, which allows for a multi-level analysis (Schmid, 2012). For (social) space is considered a (social) product, which does not exist *in* itself as an independent category—space is produced by the forces of a given social reality. In this sense, the production of space must consider the forces determined by space as well as (historical) time. For space represents the *synchronic* order of a social reality, while time represents its *diachronic* order—the historical process of social production (Schmid, 2012, p. 91). In other words, for Lefebvre, space and time are not independent or pure material factors, and thus must be understood as integrated with social practices. Therefore, they can only be understood in their specific social context, which makes them essentially historical. This suggests that the appreciation of the contradictions of social reality must occur through its spatial issues, which, according to Lefebvre, would be determined both by the triad of "spatial practice," "representations of space," and "representational spaces" as well as the conditions of the "perceived," "conceived," and "lived" space. The broad understanding of these terms has been the subject of several Lefebvrian studies, which are not always convergent. What interests us, however, are its foundations directly related to the issues of cities and urban space, in which the interdependence of its spatial triad seems fundamental. In this sense, broadly speaking, an understanding of the relations between space and society would occur through the simultaneous understanding of these three categories, that is: the ways through which they are "materially" apprehended through the sense, their everyday dialectical interactions of spatial practices (*perceived space*), the forms of material production of spaces and their representations (*conceived space*), and the way in which the spaces of representation (and their subjectivities) manifest themselves in the everyday lives of the inhabitants, as mediation and dialogue between the perceived and the conceived (*lived space*).

Thus, considering the dependence of the architectural object—and urban themes—upon the contradictions of the material and symbolic realities of societies, the problem of *autonomy* set forth by critical or post-critical authors emerges as incomplete—or even obsolete. Accepting urban conditions as purely determined by market forces, or by the demands of a dominant culture, indicates that the critical task of an *autonomous* architecture would be to oppose these forces towards better and more promising spatial proposals, whether utopian or otherwise. A mistake if we consider the Lefebvrian theses on the production of space. Likewise, it would not be possible to surmise the urban as the space in which social expressions exist authentically, even if mediated by interests and contradictions, in relation to an architecture always subjected to the interests of private capital or State strategies.

What we do find, in the conditions presented in these first decades of the 21st century, is that a critical perspective for architecture or urbanism must consider the contradictions and forces that determine the production of space. After all, given our current conditions, the prospects for a general crisis in the system, whether due to social chaos or environmental collapse, seem to be inevitable.

Urban Virtualities

One of the most discerning characteristics of the Lefebvrian approach lies in his intent to go beyond philosophy and theory to address the actions of everyday life (Schmid, 2012). Hence the connection between his theories and the practices of different fields of study dedicated to space and society.

This connection would also become fundamental for the authors behind the so-called *spatial turn*, a term ascribed to the perception that social change cannot be fully understood without the conceptualization of the spatial categories of social life. Under the influence of Lefebvre, as well as Foucault, Certeau, and Virilio, authors such as Edward Soja, David Harvey, and Dorey Massey, among others, sought to consider the spatial contradictions of late capitalism in times when the fragilities of the neoliberal model were not yet self-evident, especially in core countries. The critical legacy of these authors helped to reveal new contradictions in *post-critical architecture*. In addition to the condition of product—or spectacle—such architectures, under the logic of late capitalism, would account for the spatial strategies of biopolitical control. Perhaps therein resided the mutually fueled distrust between those who dealt with urban themes (the spaces of the city) and those who addressed architecture (the space of the building), or even between urbanists and architects.

One example is the essay "What Ever Happened to Urbanism?" first presented in 1994 by Rem Koolhaas (Koolhaas et al., 1998). As in several of his manifesto-essays, Koolhaas attacks the normative ideals behind some practices of urbanism and urban planning and claims for architecture the role of operating complex spatial issues, with strategies and meanings that could interact with everyday dynamics. His goal is not merely to ignore the city, the urban, and its material and symbolic conditions, as one could deduce from his famous diatribe "fuck context." The point is to enhance human relations through the interrelationships of the program, architecture, and the pragmatic nature of late capitalism. We see this in his major "absolute-scale" works, as well as in the China Central Television (CCTV) complex built in Beijing, as in the sophisticated small-scale interventions, as in the Prada store in Soho, New York. In these emblematic examples, the *Generic Cities* (to use a term coined by Koolhaas) would be the natural result of individual values and market forces, their planning being both obsolete as a disciplinary technique as well as ideological as a theoretical-conceptual foundation. Thus, the CCTV headquarters building finds, through a sophisticated vertical geometric variation of the traditional perimeter occupation common to 19th-century European cities, the solution for its complex program distributed across 473,000 m^2 and 44 floors. The ultimate independent, patented form—a postmodern version of the *Grossform* proposed by Oswald Mathias Ungers in the 1970s—thus becomes the possible urban response to the cultural, social, and economic dynamics of global neoliberalism. The same occurs in the simple scale of the Prada store in Soho, whose articulation among the streets serves merely as a pretext to locate the visitor/consumer in a de-territorialized reality, shaped by images and shapes arranged as if at random, in subtle reference to the Venturian Las Vegas Strip, now inverted into a private territory associated with the symbol-brand of yuppie consumerism and the aesthetic glamor of the billionaire market of the "fashion world." It is no accident, therefore, that Paul Valery's aphorism "What is deeper in a man is the skin" (via Nietzsche) would be widely used by postmodern architects who trailed the adventure of Robert Venturi and Denise Scott Brown towards the reorganization of the discipline against the logic of consumer society and late capitalism. Valery's poetic phrase did not always have, in its architectural and urban interpretations, the same ambiguous effect as the original meaning. After all, Valery questioned the viability of a universal human condition for the simple fact that, as Foucault stated in "The order of things" (Foucault, 1966), man does not exist. The only thing to exist is the being. Or, more precisely, the "being-there" (*Dasein*), in the terms of Martin Heidegger, another highly influential philosopher for these architects who tried to situate themselves amid the dilemmas of postmodernity. Koolhaas established his dialogue both with the opening provided by Venturi in relation to consumer society, and with the discursive possibilities and the diversity of narratives offered by the new French philosophy. In this context, the role of the discipline would not be to associate itself to broad social or ideological issues, but to use the structural mechanisms of the system to allow for *multiple possibilities of the being* to manifest themselves freely.

The mere existence (its viability) of architecture would suffice, in its practical and pragmatic clashes with the realities with which it dialogued. As we have seen, theory and criticism could be dismissed since its engagement would take place through the project, and its methods and techniques.

The ideological obsolescence of this type of "autonomous" architecture gains consistency from some of the traumatic events of the first decade of the 21st century, as mentioned early in this chapter. Such events, on the one hand, call into question the values associated with the so-called architecture of spectacle, destined to represent the power of major transnational corporations and of the countries associated with the economic strength of the private sector and the financial market. On the other hand, they deeply affect the neoliberal economic system based on global financial flows, practically independent from the State-controlled regulatory instruments. Especially after 2008, the implications became drastic for architecture and urbanism, since housing production, responsible for most of the demands in the field, was one of the most deeply affected sectors. Presently, another event underpins the critical arguments against the neoliberal model—the pandemic resulting from the COVID-19 virus. While it is too early to speculate about its economic, social, political, and urban consequences, the debates have been unanimous as to the need to re-discuss the role of the State amidst the major global problems.[14] Such problems—universal access to the health system, *minimum income*, preservation of the environment, minimum housing conditions—are commonly ignored or systematically poorly managed by the private sector.

In the major cities of the so-called Global South, such as São Paulo, there is ample evidence of the need for a critical architecture and urbanism—and therefore for updating the discipline's theoretical-critical thought.

FIGURE 2.4 Downtown São Paulo, Brazil, 2018.

From the 1970s onwards, the architecture and urbanism produced in the city of São Paulo developed its own internal dynamics, whose most renowned variant became known as the *Escola Paulista*—a peculiar version of autonomy, with a double meaning. The first sought to consolidate the efforts of the first generations of Brazilian modern architects in their pursuit for their own language and identity, intensified during those years of post-colonial debates in vogue in the field of cultural studies. The second, with a more complex design and not always intentional to architects, sought a movement towards urban and spatial introspection, as it sought to create a self-referential spatiality away from the problems experienced by the major capitalist city in those years. In other words, given the impossibility of dialogue or intervention in an uneven and predatory structure in which a *bulldozer-like* urbanism transformed the historical and social fabric of the city, the *critical option* would be for a kind of "testudo formation"—in which the limits of the lot or architecture is akin to the demarcation between the real city and the possible (utopian) city (Medrano & Recaman, 2013). The most virtuous exponent within this architecture was the architect and professor João Vilanova Artigas, one of the founders of the Faculty of Architecture and Urbanism of the University of São Paulo (FAUUSP). Author of several projects, still relatively unknown in the international context, Artigas was a member and activist for the Brazilian Communist Party, an experience that continuously influenced both his professional performance and his pursuit for an architecture focused on the architect's social role amidst an unequal society. His most renowned residences, schools, and public buildings stood out in their sophisticated and original formal repertoire, whose greatest virtue was to delve into the technical possibilities of concrete to devise a spatial proposal away from the commonly accepted demands of the local bourgeoisie. However, if on the one hand, isolation enabled him to create unique and emblematic spaces, such as those of the FAUUSP building and the Elza Berquó House,[15] on the other hand the scheme authorized a certain distancing of architectural issues from city issues. The consequences of this *anti-urban* choice are still felt today. And what emerges as a critique of the capitalist modes of production ultimately becomes a model for the capitalist market itself. After all, free of the symbolic, utilitarian, and aesthetic urban implications, the territorial occupation strategies could follow the flow of profit and the patrimonial dynamics that characterized a large part of the growth of the city of São Paulo. The alleged autonomy, understood as a legitimate critical resource in opposition to the dominant conservative forces in the city, failed to present consistent or viable urban solutions generalized at the city scale. The *anti-urban* model (utopian or otherwise) was only possible in the lot, and could only become critical if the real urban model served as an opposition.

Nonetheless, if the *Paulista Architecture* failed to produce enough instruments to operate in the urban field, then urbanism and urban planning were equally unable to ensure a more just and democratic spatial organization to São Paulo—albeit not for the lack of efforts in the academic and professional field addressing the problems of the metropolis. But the political and economic forces, which prevailed in the city during its rapid expansion period, were guided by the interests of large construction companies and the real estate market, in line with the developmental policies of the military dictatorship. The result was a city with a social geography marked by inequality and a spatial organization without any connection to structured formal or typological models.

Throughout this period, much of the efforts of the FAUUSP teachers and students turned towards political activism against the military regime. Their activism was ideologically inspired by progressive Marxist doctrines, whose practical actions and theoretical foundations were diverse and ranged from radical revolutionary variants to reformist stances. Regarding the urban theory in vogue at the time, the concepts elaborated by Manuel Castells in the book

FIGURE 2.5 Interior view of Elza Berquó house, João Batista Vilanova Artigas, São Paulo, Brazil, 1967. Photo taken in 2010.

The Urban Question of 1972[16] were particularly influential. Not to mention, of course, the theoretical-critical repertoire devised by intellectuals belonging to the Faculty of Philosophy, Languages, and Human Sciences of the University of São Paulo (FFLCH-USP), such as Chico de Oliveira, Milton Santos, and Lúcio Kowarick, among others. Although we find diverse theoretical and practical responses among them, urban activism associated with political instruments for territorial transformation had the most promising consequences. Urban space as the result of social and political forces, along the lines developed by Castells, seemed to be a very adequate hypothesis for understanding a local reality undergoing transformations from the development imposed by the military regime, which were drastically reshaping the local landscape—accentuating the spatial contrasts between rich and poor. In this particular case, the contrasts are between neighborhoods that followed the normative instruments of urban planning and those that followed their own rules guided by basic needs and assorted internal dynamics (as in the precarious settlements of the peripheries or in the slums). Issues related to urban spatiality, to the urban form, to the relationship between alienation and the city, in the terms laid out by Henri Lefebvre in *Right to the City* (1968/1996), had little impact on the local intellectual production of those years, even though the first translation into Portuguese was published as early as 1969. After all, the political and spatial issues that emerged from areas of extreme poverty, as one would expect, seemed to demand more urgent and pragmatic solutions than those resulting from the subjectivities proposed by certain aesthetic-spatial configurations and the desire for a *oeuvre* city, as posed in a pretentious and complex manner by the French philosopher.

The architects were also influenced by neo-Marxist movements in those difficult years during the dictatorship. The most prolific and well-known comprised the *Grupo Arquitetura Nova*, founded by architects Flávio Império, Rodrigo Lefèvre, and Sérgio Ferro.[17] According to

FIGURE 2.6 External view of the Faculty of Architecture and Urbanism of the University of São Paulo (FAUUSP), designed by João Batista Vilanova Artigas and Carlos Cascaldi, São Paulo, Brazil, 1969. Photo taken in 2018.

the group, active since the early 1960s, the alienation resulting from the relationship between production and consumption in the capitalist system would be one of the main challenges posed to architecture. Hence, they sought in their methods and concepts an approach to the working-class conditions of the construction site by way of political and aesthetic instruments. From a political standpoint, they would act in opposition to the capitalist logic imposed by the dictatorship, partaking in progressive movements. From an aesthetic standpoint, they would seek a language that represents the contradictions of the material conditions of the working class, emphasizing formal issues pertaining to the construction site, technical precariousness, lack of resources, etc. Through their works, *Grupo Arquitetura Nova* seeks to express the results of a productive process that truly results from popular participation in the broadest sense of the word (aesthetic, technique, and productive).

Over the course of the following decades, both the idealism proposed by Artigas' architecture (close to Lukács' "formalist" aesthetic conceptions, for example) as well as the engagement proposed by *Grupo Arquitetura Nova* (close to Bloch's activism or the organic forces of Gramscian intellectual production) would represent the impasses of the national issues, equally embodied in other cultural or artistic expressions. Both cases, when faced with the intensification of the military regime, saw their instruments of action and their reproducibility or evolution capabilities become unfeasible. Furthermore, apart from local political issues, their conceptual arguments would lose ground in the theoretical-critical field, in symmetry with other progressive manifestations devised in core countries. The last disciplinary *utopian* impulses of architecture and urbanism towards the modernization of society would thus become overshadowed by the new liberal order that dominated Western capitalism.[18]

FIGURE 2.7 Internal view of the Faculty of Architecture and Urbanism of the University of São Paulo (FAUUSP), designed by João Batista Vilanova Artigas and Carlos Cascaldi, São Paulo, Brazil, 1969. Photo taken in 2018.

In both the Brazilian and Latin American context, as well as in developed countries, perhaps the biggest mistake of specialized criticism has been to underestimate the implications of the desire for the city or, in Lefebvrian terms, the desire for *the right to the city*. Calling for *autonomy* without considering the urban inferences of architecture, or advocating for changes in the structural logic of urban society without regard for the social consequences of form proved to be strategies incapable of resisting the overwhelming methods of late capitalism. Therefore, the City depends on the simultaneous actions of its constituent parts and its projecting mechanisms—its expectation as to the future, its *urban virtuality*. Thus, a *disciplinary critical-theoretical perspective* should consider the possibilities of architecture and urbanism to distance themselves from the instruments of social domination operating in the different forms and scales in the production of space. This would allow for a closer approach to spaces suitable to different forms of social manifestations capable of problematizing their internal contradictions while seeking alternatives to these contradictions—in a continuous process that is both constituent and fundamental to urban society. These spaces would not result solely from delimited uses, bureaucratic land regularization processes, the dualism between public and private, the organization of functional orders, or the creation of new programs—or even from the preservation of unconscious and deeply rooted schemes that reinforce historical conditions for maintaining dominant orders, in relation to their class, gender, race, etc. These spaces should understand the importance of the *spatial conditions* that determine the public and private spheres, as well as their multiple social, symbolic, historical, and political interrelations—informed, perhaps, by new relations of solidarity, and no longer by competitiveness and individualism, typical to neoliberal ideologies. This situation is not at all novel to progressive political or ideological premises focused on the issue of urban space—the expanded concept of the City. What is novel, as we have seen, are the material and symbolic conditions that the current widespread crisis of the neoliberal models demand both from the field of theory and criticism, as well as from the different forms of practical or political action.

Notes

1. For example, Massimo Cacciari, in the book *La Città* (2004), updated for the 21st century the questions posed to the urbanization processes of industrial cities, in accelerated course since the 19th century.
2. Paul Virilio's book *L'Espace Critique* (1993) establishes an important dialogue between the spatial dynamics of urbanism and the transformations resulting from the new information and communication technologies.
3. Although we find "post-critical practices" in the field of architecture and urbanism since the 1980s, it is from the beginning of the 21st century that these practices are identified as belonging to the same theoretical and methodological pattern, as found, for example, in the essays "Design Intelligence and the New Economy" and "After theory: debate in architectural schools rages about the value of theory and its effect on innovation in design" by Speaks (2002, 2005).
4. Hungarian scientist-philosopher Michael Polanyi used the term "post-critical" to indicate the *fiduciary* nature of knowledge. When appropriated in the field of architecture and urbanism, the term is used in reference to a so-called pragmatic production—without any commitment to go against the dominant cultural, economic, or political systems by way of theoretical foundations. Several authors refer to the term when addressing the disciplinary production in the final decades of the 20th century and the first years of the 21st century (e.g., Foster, 2012; Mallgrave & Goodman, 2011; Montaner, 2011; Saunders, 2007; Sykes, 2010).
5. The exhibition, which consisted of photographs, drawings, and audiovisual material, had enormous repercussions in the US as well as in the various countries where it was held. Modern Brazilian Architecture presented itself to the world as the most original and promising version of the New Architecture with Central-European origins. It also spawned the book *Brazil Builds: architecture new and old 1652–1942*, by Philip Goodwin and G.E. Kidder Smith (Goodwin & Smith, 1943).
6. On this subject, see the essay/review "Nem Arquitetura nem Cidades," by Luiz Recaman, originally published in the *Praga* journal (Recaman, 1999) and republished as an "afterword" in the second edition of the book *O Lugar da Arquitetura depois dos Modernos*, by Otília Arantes (1992).
7. See, for example, the article "The New Urban Enclosures" (Hodkinson, 2012).
8. For example, Michael Hays in *Architecture's Desire: Reading the Late Avant-Garde* (2008).
9. North American architect Peter Eisenman is perhaps the most influential example of this variant, commonly called "deconstructivist."
10. The issue of autonomy gains traction in the field of architecture mainly through the initiatives and texts of Joan Ockman and Pier Vittorio Aureli, e.g., Aureli (2008, 2011).
11. The publishing house Verso Books reissued the essay in 2007 in the book *Aesthetics and Politics* (Adorno et al., 2007).
12. For example, Tony Judt in *Ill Fares the Land* formulates an interesting critical reflection on the privatization processes that have occurred in the past 40 years, especially in Europe (Judt, 2011).
13. In recent years, several books, conferences, and academic articles have delved into the relationship between social housing, the State, and the financial market. Some examples are the books *Urban Warfare: Housing Under the Empire of Finance* by Raquel Rolnik (2019) and *Architecture and the Welfare State*, edited by Mark Swenarton and Tom Avermaete (Swenarton, Avermaete, & Heuvel, 2014).
14. The debate about a post-COVID-19 world has brought together intellectuals from all over the world. I emphasize here, for example, the recent contributions by Bruno Latour, Slavoj Zizek, Giorgio Agamben, José Luís Fiori, and Laura Carvalho.
15. The Elza Berquó House, from 1967, is one of the most enigmatic works by Vilanova Artigas. In this mature work by the architect, its pillars made of raw tree trunks, in contrast to the reinforced concrete, perhaps signal the hardships encountered by local modernity. The technological advances, so overwhelming to Modern Architecture, were not symmetrical to the structural social changes in Brazilian society. This mismatch thus began to inform the local production, both as a criticism and as a strategy for eccentric and original spatial solutions.
16. Regarding this topic, see Pedro Fiori Arantes in the article "Em busca do urbano: marxistas e a cidade de São Paulo nos anos de 1970" (2009).
17. Three seminal articles lay out the principles of Arquitetura Nova: "Proposta Inicial para um Debate: Possibilidades de Atuação" (1963/2006), by Rodrigo Lefèvre and Sérgio Ferro, "Uma Crise em Desenvolvimento" (1966), by Lefèvre, and "Arquitetura Nova" (1967/2006), by Sérgio Ferro.

18. Among the authors who have faced this debate, which emerged from the original issues posed by Manfredo Tafuri, we find Reinhold Martin, Felicity Scott, and Sven-Olov Wallenstein. In Brazil, philosopher Otília Arantes was the most important representative of this theoretical-critical posture in recent decades.

References

Adorno, T.W., Benjamin, W., Bloch, E., Brecht, B., & Lukács, G. (2007). *Aesthetics and Politics*. London, UK: Verso Books.
Arantes, O.B.F. (1992). *O Lugar da Arquitetura depois dos Modernos*. São Paulo, Brazil: Editora da Universidade de São Paulo.
Arantes, O.B.F. (1998). *Urbanismo em Fim de Linha: e outros Estudos sobre o Colapso da Modernização Arquitetônica*. São Paulo, Brazil: Editora da Universidade de São Paulo.
Arantes, P.F. (2009). Em busca do urbano: Marxistas e a cidade de São Paulo nos anos de 1970. *Novos Estudos CEBRAP, 83*, 103–127. https://doi.org/10.1590/S0101-33002009000100007
Aureli, P.V. (2008). *The Project of Autonomy: Politics and Architecture Within and Against Capitalism*. Princeton, NJ: Princeton Architectural Press.
Aureli, P.V. (2011). *The Possibility of an Absolute Architecture*. Cambridge, MA: The MIT Press.
Baird, G. (2004). "Criticality" and Its Discontents. *Harvard Design Magazine, 21*. Retrieved from www.harvarddesignmagazine.org/issues/21/criticality-and-its-discontents
Cacciari, M. (2004). *La città* (5th ed.). Rimini, Italy: Pazzini.
Ferro, S. (2006). Arquitetura Nova. In P.F. Arantes (Ed.), *Arquitetura e Trabalho Livre* (pp. 47–58). São Paulo, Brazil: CosacNaify. (Reprinted from *Teoria e Prática* (1967), *1*, 3–15).
Ferro, S., & Lefèvre, R. (2006). Proposta Inicial para um Debate: Possibilidades de Atuação. In P.F. Arantes (Ed.), *Arquitetura e Trabalho Livre* (pp. 33–36). São Paulo, Brazil: CosacNaify. (Reprinted from *Caderno Encontros*, 1963).
Foster, H. (2012). Post-Critical. *October, 139*, 3–8. https://doi.org/10.1162/OCTO_a_00076
Foucault, M. (1966). *Les Mots et les Choses*. Paris, France: Gallimard.
Goodwin, P.L., & Smith, G.E.K. (1943). *Brazil Builds: Architecture New and Old 1652–1942 / Construção Brasileira: Arquitetura Moderna e Antiga 1652–1942*. New York, NY: The Museum of Modern Art.
Habermas, J. (1983). Modernity—An Incomplete Project. In H. Foster (Ed.), *The Anti-Aesthetic: Essays on Postmodern Culture* (pp. 3–15). Port Townsend, WA: Bay Press. (Original work presented 1980).
Hays, K.M. (1984). Critical Architecture: Between Culture and Form. *Perspecta, 21*, 15–29. https://doi.org/10.2307/1567078
Hays, K.M. (2009). *Architecture's Desire: Reading the Late Avant-Garde*. Cambridge, MA: The MIT Press.
Hodkinson, S. (2012). The New Urban Enclosures. *City, 16*(5), 500–518. https://doi.org/10.1080/13604813.2012.709403
Jameson, F. (1992). *Postmodernism, or, The Cultural Logic of Late Capitalism*. Durham, NC: Duke University Press. https://doi.org/10.1215/9780822378419
Jameson, F. (1994). The Constraints of Postmodernism. In *The Seeds of Time* (pp. 129–205). New York, NY: Columbia University Press.
Judt, T. (2011). *Ill Fares the Land*. London, UK: Penguin Books.
Koolhaas, R., Mau, B., Sigler, J., Werlemann, H., & Office for Metropolitan Architecture. (1998). *Small, Medium, Large, Extra-Large: Office for Metropolitan Architecture, Rem Koolhaas, and Bruce Mau*. New York, NY: Monacelli Press.
Lefebvre, H. (1969). *Introdução à Modernidade*. Rio de Janeiro, Brazil: Paz e Terra.
Lefebvre, H. (1991). *Critique of Everyday Life (Vol. 1: Introduction)*. London, UK; New York, NY: Verso. (Original work published 1947).
Lefebvre, H. (1991). *The Production of Space*. Oxford, UK: Blackwell. (Original work published 1974).
Lefebvre, H. (1996). Right to the City. In E. Kofman & E. Lebas (Eds.), *Writings on Cities* (pp. 63–181). Oxford, UK; Malden, MA: Blackwell Publishers Ltd. (Original work published 1968).
Lefebvre, H. (2003). *The Urban Revolution*. Minneapolis, MN: The University of Minnesota Press. (Original work published 1970).

Lefèvre, R. (1966). Uma Crise em Desenvolvimento. *Acrópole, 333*, 22–23.

Mallgrave, H.F., & Goodman, D.J. (2011). *An Introduction to Architectural Theory: 1968 to the Present*. New York, NY: Wiley-Blackwell.

Medrano, L., & Recaman, L. (2013). *Vilanova Artigas. Habitação e Cidade na Modernização Brasileira*. Campinas, Brazil: Editora da Unicamp.

Montaner, J.M. (2011). *Arquitectura y Política: Ensayos para Mundos Alternativos*. Barcelona, Spain: Gustavo Gili.

Recaman, L. (1999). Nem arquitetura nem cidades. *Praga, 8*, 143–150.

Rolnik, R. (2019). *Urban Warfare: Housing under the Empire of Finance* (G. Hirschhorn, Trans.). London, UK, New York, NY: Verso.

Rouanet, S.P. (1987). *As Razões do Iluminismo*. São Paulo, Brazil: Companhia das Letras.

Saunders, W.S. (Ed.). (2007). *The New Architectural Pragmatism: A Harvard Design Magazine Reader*. Minnesota, MN: University of Minnesota Press.

Schmid, C. (2012). A Teoria da Produção do Espaço de Henri Lefebvre: Em Direção a uma Dialética Tridimensional. *GEOUSP Espaço e Tempo (Online), 16*(3), 89–109. https://doi.org/10.11606/issn.2179-0892.geousp.2012.74284

Somol, R., & Whiting, S. (2002). Notes around the Doppler Effect and Other Moods of Modernism. *Perspecta, 33*, 72–77. https://doi.org/10.2307/1567298

Speaks, M. (2002). Design Intelligence and the New Economy. *Architectural Record, 190*(1), 72–79.

Speaks, M. (2005). After Theory: Debate in Architectural Schools Rages about the Value of Theory and Its Effect on Innovation in Design. *Architectural Record, 193*(6), 72–75.

Swenarton, M., Avermaete, T., & Heuvel, D. (Eds.). (2014). *Architecture and the Welfare State*. New York, NY: Routledge.

Sykes, A.K. (Ed.). (2010). *Constructing a New Agenda: Architectural Theory, 1993–2009*. Princeton, NY: Princeton University Press.

Virilio, P. (1993). *L'Espace Critique: Essai*. Paris, France: C. Bourgois.

Waisman, M. (1988). Paradojas de la Utopía. Las Dos Últimas Décadas. *A&V Monografías, 13*, 13–41.

Waisman, M. (1998). Autocrítica II.1994. *DANA, 39/40*.

3

CONSTRUCTING THE COMMONS

Towards Another Architectural Theory of the City?

Tom Avermaete

This text starts from a certain unease. Over the past few years, a panoply of innovative activism, scholarship, and projects that focus on "the commons" have gained momentum. In many fields of thinking and practice—ranging from ecology to geography and media studies—the theme of the commons has become an important point of reference. This rapidly growing movement is based on new thinking in the domains of economy, political science, and social science, suggesting radically different ways to organize our societies. Inspired by the seminal publication *Governing the Commons* (1990) by Nobel prize-winner Elinor Ostrom, these theories focus on "common pool resources" as a way to think about our everyday assets beyond the dominant discourses of market economy and state intervention (Ostrom, 1990). Thinkers like Silke Helfrich and David Bollier have in *Die Welt der Commons* (2015) argued that this requires new "practices of communing" that challenge our conventional understanding of politics, economy, and culture (Helfrich, 2015).

In these general theories of the commons, however, there seems to be little attention for the value of the city as a shared resource and as one of the main tangible forms in which the commons exist in society. Architectural and urban theorists have started to explore the question of the "urban commons," but have mainly conceived it as a matter of collective practices in the built environment, referring alternatively to processes of participation, joint construction initiatives, and collective management. Obviously, these perspectives are important, but they refer mainly to the commons as a matter of what Richard Sennett has called "the rituals, pleasures and politics of cooperation" and are silent about all other aspects of the urban commons (Sennett, 2013). As a result, the aptitude of the concept of the commons for conceiving a new perspective on the architecture of the city has not been fully explored; it has remained a theoretical *terrain vague*.

This blind spot is in my opinion the result of a generalization in how we understand the growth and transformation of cities. We have learned to think about urban development as firmly embedded in the matrix of the state (explicated for instance in various studies on the relationship between urban development and the welfare state) and the market (as represented amongst others in the numerous investigations that link urban form to neoliberal market logics). This conception of the city as driven by state and market has not only become intrinsic to our contemporary thinking about the city, but it has also entered our critical studies and historiographies that have been firmly narrated along these lines.

In this text, I want to open a different theoretical and historiographic perspective that does not neglect the state and the market, but rather focuses a complementary set of actors and values that have profoundly influenced the architecture of the city. The concept of the commons will be the crowbar that opens this new historiography on the architecture of the city. In other words, I want to explore how conceptions of the commons have relentlessly been part and parcel of the development of the architecture of the city. This will require that we go beyond the well-established understanding of the commons as collective ephemeral practices and that we move into a more profound investigation of its other dimensions. In this text, I want to investigate what the fundamental definitions and principles of the commons have to offer to our understanding of the development of the architecture of the city. In order to do so, I propose to explore the commons from three angles, which I coin respectively "res communis," "lex communis," and "praxis communis." These three angles are strongly intertwined and refer to some primary aspects of the commons.

Res Communis: Common-Pool Resources in Architecture and Urban Design

My exploration of the commons starts by necessity with its most basic definition: the idea of collective resources. As Elinor Ostrom claims, thinking about the commons always start from the idea of shared assets, of so-called common-pool resources. Ostrom maintains that these common-pool resources can be found in all instances of our environment and always consist of a "resource system," which can be "fishing grounds, groundwater basins, grazing areas, irrigation canals, bridges, parking garages," and the "resource units," which entail the "fish harvested from a fishing ground, water withdrawn from a groundwater basin or an irrigation canal, the tons of fodder consumed by animals from a grazing area" (Ostrom, 1990). The common-pool resource system and unit maintain a reciprocal relationship that needs to be governed and regulated, Ostrom claims.

Silke Helfrich has pointed out that it is paramount to understand that "a common-pool resource is not yet a commons. Instead, it has to be turned into a commons by its users. One cannot talk about the commons without talking about the communities that use and sustain it" (Helfrich, 2011). Helfrich points out that we are constantly surrounded by natural and human-made common-pool resources and that the very question we have to answer is:

> What do we want to do with them? Do we want to produce commodities and convert everything—our collective knowledge, our genes, solar energy, public arenas and spaces, water, beaches, social care etc.—into commodities? Or do we want to sustain and reproduce them as commons? It's our choice.
>
> *(Helfrich, 2011)*

This idea of a resource being managed beyond private interest is also central in the definition by Austrian philosopher Ivan Illich:

> People called commons that part of the environment which lay beyond their own thresholds and outside of their own possessions, to which, however, they had recognized claims of usage, not to produce commodities but to provide for the subsistence of their households.
>
> *(Illich, 1983)*

Illich also argues that in the most robust commons, the resource system plays multiple roles and engages with different groups of citizens:

> An oak tree might be in the commons. Its shade, in summer, is reserved for the shepherd and his flock; its acorns are reserved for the pigs of the neighbouring peasants; its dry branches serve as fuel for the widows of the village; some of its fresh twigs in springtime are cut as ornaments for the church—and at sunset it might be the place for the village assembly.
>
> *(Illich, 1983)*

The Belgian political theorist Michel Bauwens offers a more nuanced way of understanding the nature of common-pool resources that we encounter in urban territories. Bauwens differentiates between three categories of common-pool resources (Parker et al., 2014, p. 288). The first category is "inherited commons," which he links to resources such as earth, water, and forests. These common-pool resources are inherited by different generations of citizens just by the sheer fact that they live on earth. Besides these natural common resources, Bauwens recognizes "immaterial commons," which encompass the cultural and intellectual knowledge, as well as the craft skills that exist in a certain place. Indeed, an important resource of cities resides in the knowledgeable and skillful practices that are held by the citizens. As a last category, Bauwens identifies "material commons," which he relates to the large human-made and human-handled reserves of materials that we find in our environments. Indeed, cities can be looked upon as a stock of materials that is constantly been used and re-used as the urban condition evolves, which is nowadays prevalent with professionals engaging with reuse and sustainability. With his tripartite division of inherited, immaterial, and material commons, Bauwens points to the varied character of common-pool resources in urban territories.

Unlocking Common-Pool Resources: The "Meent," the Common, the Lavoir

When looking upon the history of the city from this perspective, we find that there is a long and rich tradition of looking upon our urban territories as a matter of common-pool resources. A good example can be found in the territorial figure of the so-called *meent*, which emerged as a way to deal with the inherited common-pool resource of fertile ground as towns and cities were expanding in the Low Countries.[1] The concept of the *meent*, which translates to English as the "commons," was since the late Middle Ages in the Netherlands and Belgium a prevalent way of managing the agricultural land in the vicinity of towns and villages. It mediated between a medieval system of castle lords leasing lands and a more modern system based on private landownership. Season after season, the common use of the agricultural land was renegotiated by the farmers, called *erfgooiers* (*erf* literally means "inherit"). During a yearly meeting they renegotiated collectively the use of the common agricultural resource. Minimal architectural elements played a central role in unlocking the common-pool resources for common use. Through a system of permanent dirt roads and flexible simple fencing, the land was continuously redefined, and the negotiated division of the land was articulated. These simple architectural elements provided the possibility for the land to be disposed, managed, and unlocked as a common resource.

Another example of an inherited common-pool resource in relation to the city is the "Boston common."[2] Still existing until today, the common in the city of Boston was, like the *meent*, a green and open space on which individual and collective interests were mediated (Figure 3.1). Also in

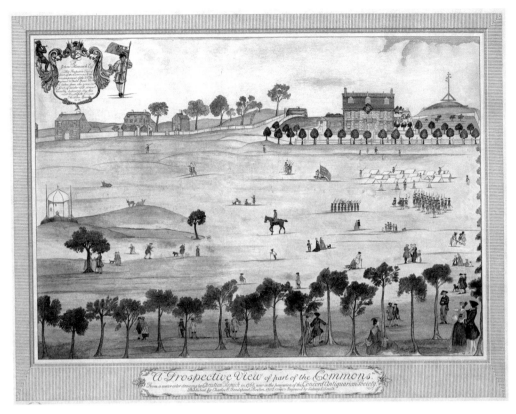

FIGURE 3.1 Christian Remick, *A Prospective View of part of the Commons*, 1902.

this case, architecture played an important role in unlocking and maintaining the common-pool resource. As the urbanization of Boston proceeded, the particular location and form of the common in the urban landscape was maintained by the buildings along its perimeter, combined with a very simple system of paths and fences. The very interrelationship between the open space of the commons and the monumental fronts of the public buildings along it acted as a protecting belt for the intra-urban common-pool resource. At the same time, the programmatic variety of the buildings around the commons, ranging from governmental buildings to a courthouse and a masonic lodge, set the basis for the common-pool resource to play multiple collective roles. Hence, the Boston commons was a place where activities for various groups of citizens coexisted; from more private purposes, such as farming and military training, to public purposes, such as leisurely strolling, festivals, manifestations, and at some points even executions. The Boston common unlocked the land as a productive resource—with cows grazing and providing milk and meat to the city until 1830, as well as a political resource where meetings and executions could take place and a leisurely resource where citizens could come for a picnic, a stroll, or to play sports.

While in the case of the *meent* and the Boston common, large territorial resources were turned into commons, it is also possible to think about the unlocking of inherited common-pool resources through smaller architectural interventions. In the history of the city we find condensed architectural projects that provide access to common-pool resources. The washing house or *lavoir*, which can be found in Southern European cities, illustrates this logic.[3] Commonly found in France, *lavoirs* are generally very small architectural structures that unlock the resource of water by providing a set of minimal architectural definitions; they consist of a solid material

FIGURE 3.2 Fosse Dione. Tonnerre, France (1758).

base to perform the washing activities and a roof for protection from the elements, and are either situated along or on rivers. Initially, *lavoirs* emerged in small towns and villages and were simple utilitarian, often jointly created, structures that offered the much-needed access to the resource of water. Gradually *lavoirs* became more sophisticated and fully integrated into the urban setting, where they started to play a role as places of social gathering and interaction. The 18th-century *lavoir* of Brienon-sur-Armançon in Yonne, situated at the source of a small river, the so-called fosse de Dionne, is a prime example. Its intricate architectural typology of several concentric spaces articulates the productive, functional, and social understanding of how the resource of water enters the city.

When we approach the city through the lens of common-pool resources, we discover that in many instances of the city, architecture has repeatedly played an important role in unlocking and maintaining the commons. The strategies applied to obtain this unlocking can differ, from the introduction of very minimal and basic territorial definitions in the *meent* to monumental composition in the Boston common and sophisticated typology in the *lavoir*. Nevertheless, this short exploration illustrates that unlocking common-pool resources as commons has throughout the history of the city been at least as an important task for architecture as articulating them as fully public goods for the state or as commodities for the market.

Lex Communis: The Commonality of the Discipline and the Discipline of the Common Place

A second primary aspect of the commons refers to the common codes and conventions of the city. In his inaugural lecture at the College de France, the French philosopher Michel Foucault indirectly referred to this important dimension of the commons, by positioning the common organization of a discipline as opposed to the notion of individual authorship. Foucault claims that

> a discipline is defined by a domain of objects, a set of methods, a corpus of propositions considered to be true, a play of rules and definitions, of techniques and instruments: all of this constitutes a sort of anonymous system at the disposal of anyone who wants to or is able to use it, without their meaning being linked to the one who happened to be their inventor.
>
> *(Foucault et al., 2013)*

Unlike an individual artist, architects can—following Foucault—rely on the already shared rules of the city and architecture. They do not have to invent a unique and new piece of art. Architecture, as discipline, can pose a set of common codes and norms, which together form an anonymous system that does not belong to the single architect but rather to the broader collective of professionals. Out of such a perspective, the architecture becomes a common. Though in times in which individual signature in architecture remains to be celebrated, such a common and anonymous approach to architecture might seem to be strange, we can find in the history of architecture multiple instances that illustrate the force of such a commons attitude toward architectural design.

The Common Codes of the Corps des Ponts et Chaussées

A good example is the approach of the so-called *Corps des Ponts et Chaussées* [Corps of Bridges and Roads], a French public body that was initiated in 1716 and designed virtually all of the public spaces and buildings in the French territory (Picon & Thom, 2009). Typical for the *Ponts et Chaussées* is that their design approach often did not entail a full-fledged project but rather the definitions of a set of principles for the public spaces and buildings that they were planning. Hence, when Jean-Charles Adolphe Alphand as a director of public works of Paris was planning important public spaces such as the Parc Monceau or main streets such as the Boulevard Richard-Lenoir, he did not rely on a full design. In his publication *Les Promenades de Paris*, Alphand explains how he rather defined common principles of urban design. He defined a set of codes that comprised urban elements such as different trees, benches, city lights, and possibilities to combine them to define the streets of Paris (Figure 3.3). His colleague Louis Bruyère explains in his *Études a l'Art de Construction* that the conception of indoor public spaces such as storage-houses and market-buildings was also based on the definition of certain architectural elements and the principles to combine them. The principles of the *Corps des Ponts et Chaussées* were published in books, but more importantly also in the *Annales des Ponts et Chaussées*, a low-cost publication that was distributed across the French territory to all the engineers and designers of the *Ponts et Chaussées*. In their turn these local engineers and designers were reporting in the *Annales* how they had been applying the norms and principles in their local situations, assuring not only that the norms and forms of the discipline developed but also that they belonged to all; that they were what I call a *lex communis*.

Next to the understanding of "the commonality of the discipline" by the engineers of the *Ponts et Chaussées*, we find almost simultaneously different attempts to describe what we could call "the discipline of the commonplace." A notable example is the study that the French architect Pierre le Muet made in the 17th century (Le Muet, 1730). Muet was looking at the houses in cities like Paris and illustrated how the disposition of the spaces and circulation of row-houses depended on the plot size (width, depth, orientation) on which they were erected (Figure 3.4). In his book *Maniere de bien bastir*, he illustrates how the way that the rooms are articulated in terms of size and relation

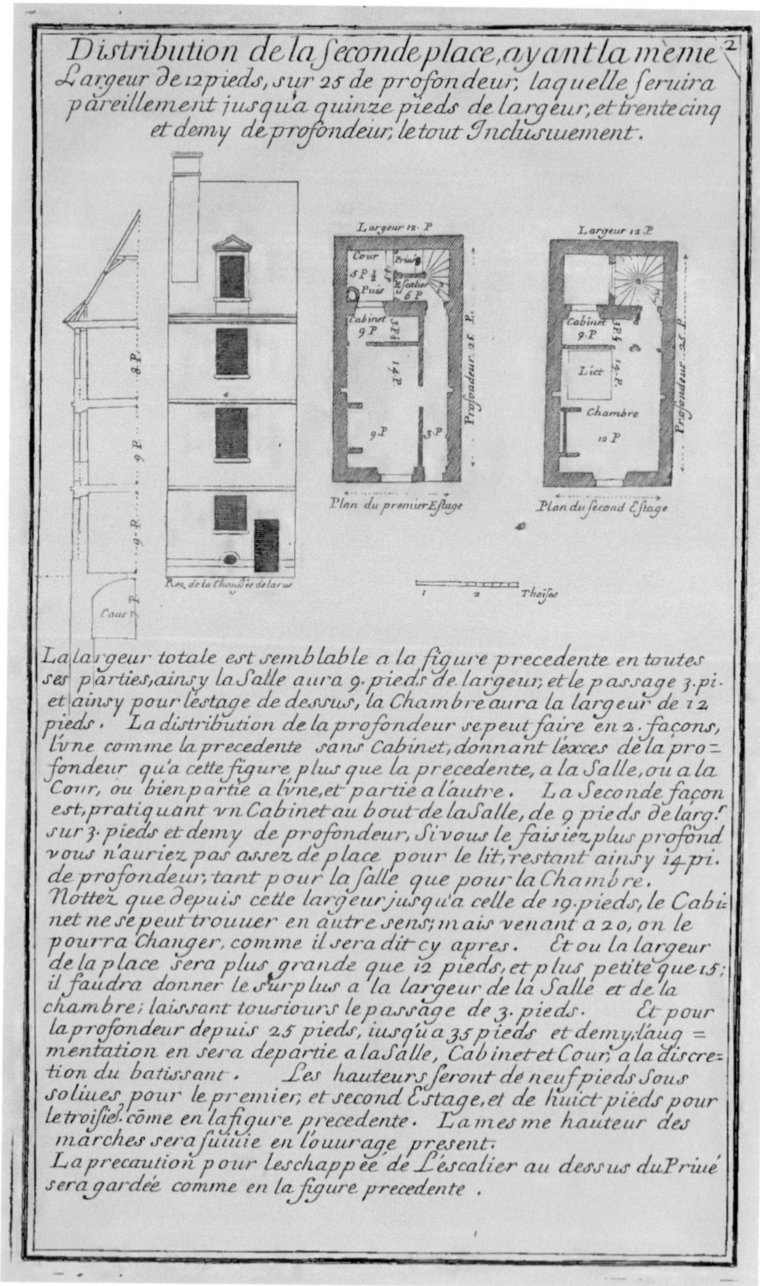

FIGURE 3.3 Plates from Pierre Le Muet, *Manière de Bien Bastir*, 1647.

to one another, as well as the positions of the stairs, depends strongly on the form and largeness of the parcel and its relation to the street. Muet illustrates convincingly that independent of the approach of architects or of architectural style, the city of Paris can be read as a series of common codes of how to link the typology of the house to the size and position of the parcel.

The perspective of *lex communis* illustrates that there is a long pedigree of conceiving the architecture of the city not as a juxtaposition of private approaches nor as a response to public

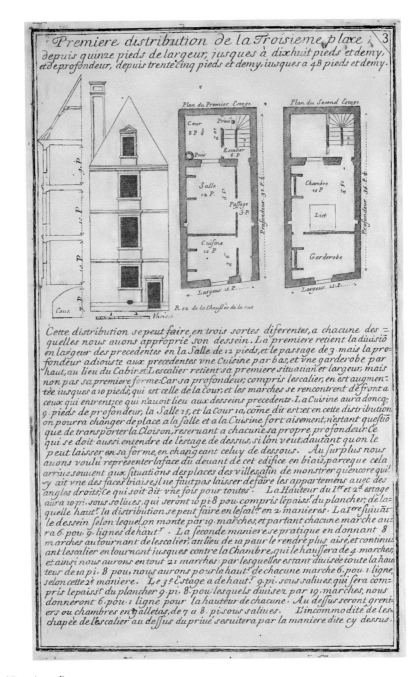

FIGURE 3.3 (Continued)

laws, norms or programs, but rather as a matter of common codes and conventions. These can concern as well the materiality, the architectural elements, the typologies, and the composition of the city. Sometimes these codes and conventions are made explicit and become an overt part of a design approach, such as with the *Ponts et Chaussées*, whereas in other cases they remain tacit and are silently but not less powerfully embedded in the urban fabric of the city, as Pierre le Muet illustrated. However, throughout the history of the city we see that architects have

62 Tom Avermaete

(c)

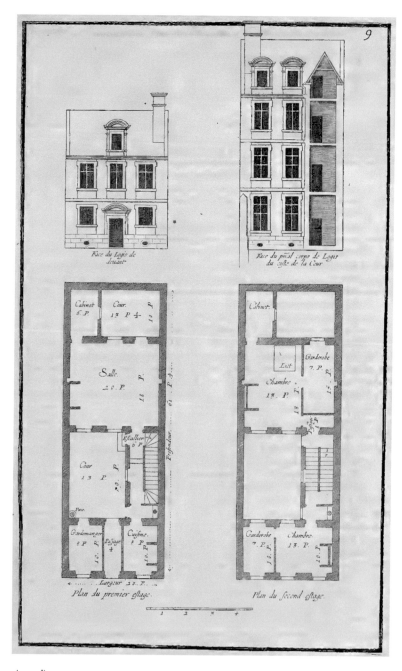

FIGURE 3.3 (Continued)

engaged with these common codes in various ways and have in that sense understood their role and projects as contributing to the commonality of the city and the discipline.

Praxis Communis: The Rituals, Pleasures and Politics of Cooperation

A third aspect of the commons that I want to touch upon is *praxis communis*. As many thinkers about the commons have argued, the commons also depend upon social practices of *commoning*—acts

(d)

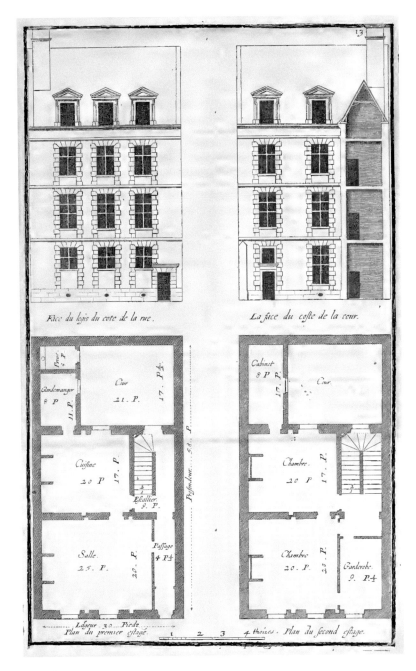

FIGURE 3.3 (Continued)

of mutual support, negotiation, collaboration and communication, and experimentation that are needed to create systems to manage common-pool resources and to engage with common codes and conventions. Ivan Illich has qualified these acts as processes of "conviviality" and has defined them as the "autonomous and creative intercourse among persons, and the intercourse of persons with their environment" (Illich, 2009).

Illich has pointed out that these convivial processes have the capacity to enhance "the contribution of autonomous individuals and primary groups to the total effectiveness of a new system

64 Tom Avermaete

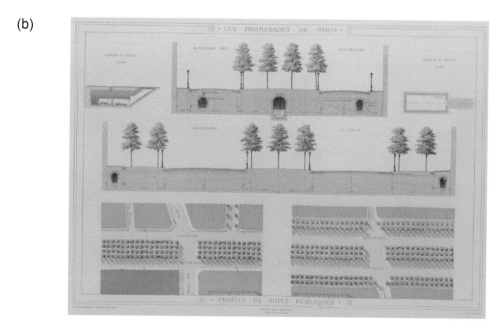

FIGURE 3.4 Plates from Adolphe Alphand, *Les Promenades De Paris*, 1867.

of production, designed to satisfy the human needs which it also determines" (Illich, 2009). He continues to state that "people . . . need above all the freedom to make things among which they can live, or give shape to them according to their own tastes, and to put them to use in caring for and about others" (Illich, 2009). More recent thinkers about the commons such as David Bollier have seconded this perspective and maintained that "rather than look to state authorities as guarantors or administrators of their interests, commoners generally prefer to seek direct sovereignty and control over spheres of life that matter to them: their cities, neighborhoods, food, water, land, information, infrastructure" (Bollier, 2015).

Jane Bennett is one of the thinkers who helps us to conceive of the very character of the processes of commoning. In her seminal book *Vibrant Matter*, she argues that "in a commons, 'care work' . . . is primary. By contrast, capitalist markets and economics routinely ignore the 'care economy'—the world of household life and social conviviality that is essential for a stable, sane, rewarding life" (Bennett, 2010). Indeed, while in market systems labor is motivated by monetary rewards, it seems that processes of commoning are instead characterized by "affective labor."[4] Out of such a perspective, people's sense of self and subjectivity becomes intertwined with the resources that they are dealing with: "They take pride and pleasure in becoming stewards of resources that matter to them and their community" (Bennett, 2010).

Civic Survey and Civic Action

The power of care work and of processes of commoning is not a new phenomenon in the history of the city. This becomes clear when we look at the urban practice of biologist and planner Patrick Geddes, who worked in the late 1860s in the city of Edinburgh in Scotland.[5] The historical center of Edinburgh was at the time generally considered a decayed area, following industrialization and the rapid emergence of a very large working class. The standard procedure was that town planners, following the 1867 Chambers Improvement Act, demolished "unhealthy buildings" and replaced them with new ones. Consequently, the citizens of Edinburgh were pushed away, as every demolished house was replaced with a modern and expensive one, an early example of gentrification.

Geddes employed a totally different method than his contemporaries, by relying strongly on the immaterial common-pool resource of the citizens' knowledge of Edinburgh and by actively collaborating with them in what he called the "civic survey." This would involve groups of citizens exploring together with Geddes the possible qualities of the existing city. By walking in the city and by talking to its inhabitants, citizen committees collectively charted the spatial qualities and social practices of Edinburgh. The result was stunning: spaces such as backyards, left-over terrains, and small alleys that had been previously qualified by urban planners and architects as worthless were now mapped by the so-called Open Space Committee of citizens as potentially valuable urban resources. Relying on their own knowledge of the city, but also by tapping into the acquaintance of their fellow inhabitants, the citizens' committees redraw the map of historical Edinburgh as a juxtaposition of valuable spatial resources.

The civic survey was only one aspect of Geddes' approach. The discovered urban common-pool resources had to be unlocked, so that they could become a commons, and this required "civic action." Indeed, Geddes invited groups of citizens to elaborate small interventions such as stairs and gates that could offer access for larger groups of citizens to the newly discovered areas. These small, often self-constructed urban elements unlocked the previously undiscovered resources for common use. In addition, Geddes assisted the citizens to "take care" of the newly discovered resources by offering proposals to cultivate plants in the new areas that would enhance their leisurely or productive use.

The perspective of *praxis communis* problematizes the question of agency in the development of the architecture of the city. While our historical studies have often maintained that strong state administrations or initiative-rich private developers have been propelling the development of the city, the perspective of *praxis communis* points us to the different agency of "communing." It requires that we recognize that the intellectual, political, practical, and financial actions of citizens have proven to have the capacity to change cities, and that we reconsider our

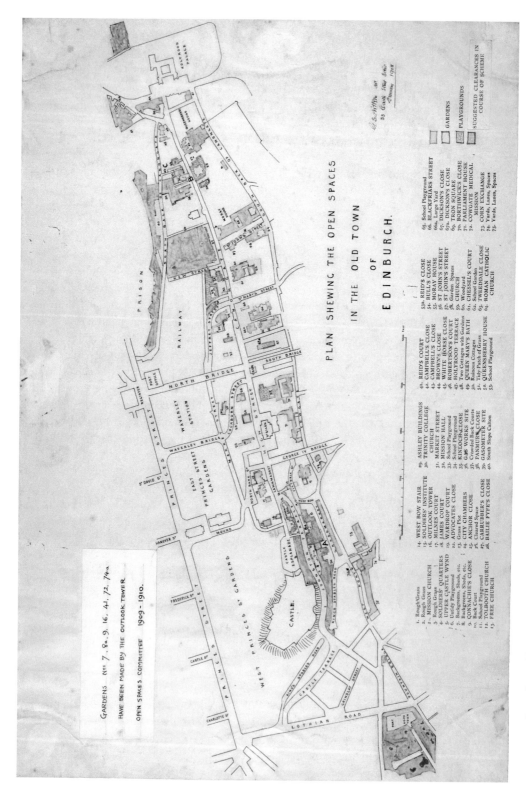

FIGURE 3.5 Patrick Geddes, map of open spaces by Open Space Committee of Citizens, 1910.

FIGURE 3.6 A rediscovered backcourt, 1910.

understanding of the agency of so-called professionals, including architects and urban designers. The example of the civic survey and civic action by Patrick Geddes illustrates that as well on the level of the analysis, as concerning the initiation, the development, and the maintenance of new projects, the agency of citizens can play a crucial role in the development of cities—and has the capacity to establish a new relationship between citizens and the common-pool resources of the city.

A New Path for Contemporary Logos and Praxis?

As the short introductions on res communis, lex communis, and praxis communis illustrate, the concept of the commons has the potential to offer us a new perspective on the architecture of the city. When we look at our cities from the viewpoint of the commons, we realize that we have been conditioned to understand the built environment as the outcome of processes and values that are related to the state and the market. Market and state are nowadays understood as the main propellers of urban development. My concise exploration of the commons illustrates that another perspective can be opened and another story can be told. Within the long history of architecture, we find ample examples of projects and neighborhoods that were constructed on the basis of common resources, codes, and practices.

Such an assertion is not without implication for our understanding of the history of architecture. We are in urgent need of new histories of architecture that can account for logics and processes that go beyond the state and the market. I believe that contemporary historians have a moral obligation to start constructing narratives in which the care for the common-pool resources by common codes and common practices is at the core of the argument. Such an approach would not only introduce new processes and values into the history of architecture, but also shed light on new categories of actors that have been central in the development of our urban environments. I am committed to contribute to such a new historiography of the modern architecture of the city in which the common-pool resources, common codes, and common practices are at center stage.

The perspective of the commons also offers a great basis to construct a new theory of the architecture of the city. Out of a perspective of res communis, such a theory might invite us to think about the character and role of common-pool resources in our contemporary city. In our present-day society, we talk amply about resources—discussing for instance their scarcity, their renewal, etc.—but the same questions should be asked concerning the inherited, the material, and immaterial resources of our cities. In other words, we should start to define what in the 21st century can be identified as common resources around which citizens can gather and construct the city. I am convinced that such a focus on common resources will lead to different urban projects. In Brazil the impressive initiatives by the not-for-profit organization SESC (Serviço Social do Comércio) illustrate the prospect of such a new production of the city.

The viewpoint of lex communis challenges us to think about the common codes and conventions through which we want to construct our cities. What are, in other words, the general principles that organize the architecture of the city, and how do these relate to the common

FIGURE 3.7 SESC Pompeia, designed by Lina Bo Bardi (1982).

FIGURE 3.8 SESC 24 de Maio, designed by Paulo Mendes da Rocha and MMBB Arquitetos (2017).

resources? Beyond stylistic questions, I believe that the discipline of architecture, especially when performing in the city, can formulate common principles which allow each intervention in the built environment to reach beyond its own confines. Re-identifying the role of codes and conventions in our contemporary architectural practice for the city seems to be an important challenge.

The praxis communis perspective offers us the opportunity to rethink what agency means in the built environment, but also how this agency relates to the question of the care for common

FIGURE 3.9 SESC 24 de Maio, designed by Paulo Mendes da Rocha and MMBB Arquitetos (2017).

resources. It implies that we are invited to think about the architecture of the city much more as a matter of collaborative practices among so-called professionals such as designers, craftspeople, and engineers but also among so-called laypeople who also hold important knowledge about the city. Understanding the complex character of the interactions among these different actors as matters of care, affective labor, and negotiation might bring us to different design approaches of the city.

FIGURE 3.10 SESC Paulista, designed by Königsberger Vannucchi Arquitetos Associados (2018).

From these reflections on res communis, lex communis, and praxis communis emerge a set of questions concerning the role of the architect as well as the approaches and tools of architecture. Indeed, thinking about an architecture of the commons will require that we start to conceive of the architect no longer as a solo-player but rather as a commoner; an urban agent who explicitly situates her/his agency in relation to other urban actors. This will also require that we need to rethink our tools. Drawings and models might become less the media of seduction that they often are nowadays and more a matter of negotiation, but it also could imply that our discipline needs to think about new tools that are more fitting to the role of the commoner.

"Constructing the commons" could in such a way become not only a new lens for architectural historiography but also a new leitmotiv for architectural thinking and practice. If the city is the ultimate common—a collective social, cultural, and material construct that is composed by and for its inhabitants—would it then not be propitious to understand the interventions of architects and urban designers as the caretaking and unlocking of these common resources?

Notes

1. For an introduction to the figure of the *meent*, see: Anton Kos, *Van Meenten tot markten* (2010).
2. For an introduction, see: Douglass Shand-Tucci, *Built in Boston: City and Suburb, 1800–1950* (1988).
3. This figure is well introduced in Mireille Roddier, *Lavoirs. Washhouses of Rural France* (2003).
4. This concept is coined by Indian geographer Neera Singh (2013).
5. Geddes' work as city planner is well discussed by Helen Meller, *Patrick Geddes: Social Evolutionist and City Planner* (1993).

References

Bennett, J. (2010). *Vibrant Matter: A Political Ecology of Things*. Durham, NC: Duke University Press.
Bollier, D. (2015). *Commoning as a Transformative Social Paradigm*. Retrieved on April 1, 2018 from https://thenextsystem.org/commoning-as-a-transformative-social-paradigm.
Foucault, M., Defert, D., Ewald, F., Fontana, A., & Burchell, G. (2013). *Lectures on the Will to Know: Lectures at the Collège De France, 1970–1971 with Oedipal Knowledge*. New York, NY: Palgrave Macmillan.
Helfrich, S. (2011). *The Commons: Marginalized but Rediscovered, Year One of the Global Commons Movement*. Retrieved on April 1, 2018 from https://commons.blog/2011/01/29/the-commons-year-one-of-the-global-commons-movement/
Helfrich, S. (2015). *Die Welt Der Commons: Muster Gemeinsamen Handelns*. Bielefeld, Germany: Transcript.
Illich, I. (1983). Silence is a Commons. *The CoEvolution Quarterly* (Winter 1983), 1–6.
Illich, I. (2009). *Tools for Conviviality*. London, UK: Marion Boyars Publishers.
Kos, A. (2010). *Van Meenten tot markten*. Hilversum, The Netherlands: Verloren.
Le Muet, P. (1730). *Maniere de Bastir: Pour Touttes Sortes de Personnes*. Paris, France: Claude Jombert, Jean et Joseph Barbou Frères.
Meller, H.E. (1993). *Patrick Geddes: Social Evolutionist and City Planner*. London, UK: Routledge.
Ostrom, E. (1990). *Governing the Commons: The Evolution of Institutions for Collective Action*. Cambridge, MA: Cambridge University Press.
Parker, M, Cheney, G., Fourier, V., & Land, C. (Eds.). (2014). *The Routledge Companion to Alternative Organization*. London, UK: Routledge.
Picon, A., & Thom, M. (2009). *French Architects and Engineers in the Age of Enlightenment*. Cambridge, MA: Cambridge University Press.
Roddier, M. (2003). *Lavoirs: Washhouses of Rural France*. New York, NY: Princeton Architectural Press.
Sennett, R. (2013). *Together: The Rituals, Pleasures and Politics of Co-Operation*. London, UK: Penguin.
Shand-Tucci, D. (1988). *Built in Boston: City and Suburb, 1800–1950*. Amherst, MA: University of Massachusetts Press.
Singh, N.M. (2013). The Affective Labor of Growing Forests and the Becoming of Environmental Subjects: Rethinking Environmentality in Odisha, India. *Geoforum*, 47, 189–198.

4

ERVING GOFFMAN'S SOCIOLOGY OF PHYSICAL SPACE FOR ARCHITECTS AND URBAN DESIGNERS[1]

Fraya Frehse

Preface

Given the objective of this book to promote an architectural critique of the spatial challenges that the contemporary "urban condition" imposes on architects and urban designers, the conceptual and methodological interchange with sociology is more than welcome. The presence of philosopher and sociologist Henri Lefebvre (1900–1991) in the former chapters is clear-cut evidence of the fact that sociology offers the architectural discipline a uniquely wide array of approaches to address the production of space, whether in conceptual, methodological, or practical terms. In fact, Lefebvre was a pioneer in sensitizing not only sociology, but also every other human science (which in my view includes architecture and urban design) to the status of macro- and microsocial processes involved in (re-)generating space as a set of bodily and materially mediated social relations (for an overview on this sociological debate, see Frehse, 2020, pp. 3–4).

As I argued elsewhere (Frehse, 2020, passim), during the second half of the 20th century, Lefebvre was not alone in his endeavor of exploring in sociological terms the empirically given social elements and processes involved in the spatialization of bodily and materially mediated social relations and interactions. Since the 1950s, Canadian sociologist Erving Goffman (1922–1982) published on the same issue, albeit from a wholly different theoretical and methodological standpoint. With the life-long aim of conceptualizing the microsocial dynamics involved in face-to-face interaction, Goffman developed a particularly broad analytical toolkit for researchers interested in the subtle social mechanics involved in the relations that human beings (re) establish with the so-called physical space within a peculiar *temporal-spatial scale*: the immediacy of situations of social interaction (Frehse, 2020, pp. 6, 10–15).

By taking into consideration that the immediacy of situations is precisely the temporal-spatial realm within which the practice of architecture and urban design takes place on a daily basis—in the framework of the various social contacts involved in projecting, planning, and designing urban elements from scratch—I demonstrate in the next pages that Erving Goffman's work bears two conceptual contributions particularly for the purposes of this book. These inputs underlie the argumentative structure of a former critical review of mine about Goffman's sociology of space originally conceived for social-scientific debate (Frehse, 2016).

Indeed, when recently updating my previous (Frehse, 2016, pp. 1–3) bibliographic inquiry into studies that simultaneously focus on "Goffman" and "space," I found that 1) the hitherto identified trend towards an operational mobilization of fragmentary spatial concepts by

Goffman (Frehse, 2016, pp. 2–3) remains; and 2) Goffman's thought on space is widely unexplored in architecture (for an exception, see Jensen, 2010, 2013).[2] Both findings suggest that the statement of my previous review of Goffman's sociology of space (Frehse, 2016) remains up-to-date regarding the (sociological) scholarship on both the production of space and Goffman's work: rather than being fragmentary, Goffman's spatial concepts are part of a wider sociological rationale about the spatial dimension of social interaction. It is a conceptually and methodologically sensitizing sociology of physical space.

By unfolding Goffman's approach to physical space, we will engage with a multi-dimensional sociological conception of space that is two-fold inspiring for contemporary sociology. These two contributions will make it possible to bring to the conceptual forefront both aforementioned inputs that Goffman's sociology of physical space offers particularly to present-day architects and urban designers.

Introduction

Stemming from Goffman's generally fragmented presence within the sociological debate about space (see Frehse, 2016, pp. 1–2), my interest here lies in outlining the contours of his *sociology of space*, not to be confused with "spatial sociology" (Raumsoziologie), a more recent proposal for a sociological subdiscipline focused on a relational analysis of the "constitution of spaces" (Löw, 2001, p. 57).[3] When I refer to a sociology of space, I think of the plethora of sociological approaches that are concerned with the physical-material dimension of social life and refer, conceptually, to the role of space in social relationships and interactions. Perhaps the first demonstration of this investigative variant in the history of sociological thought is one in a more than a centenary-old essay by Georg Simmel (Simmel, 1903/1995a, pp. 132–183). Nonetheless, the "sociology of space" remains as contemporary as ever (for an overview, see for example, Schroer, 2006, pp. 174–181).

My argument here is that Goffman's work from the 1950s, 1960s, and early 1970s brings to light a hexa-dimensional and therefore sociologically unique conception of space that offers two contributions to architects and urban designers. Therefore, we must tackle chronologically how Goffman addressed an issue that is unavoidable for those concerned with the theoretical framework of space within both the fields of sociology and architecture: physical space. Based on a long-standing sociological debate on the issue (Frehse, 2016, p. 2), I here heuristically define physical space as *the physical-material environment of the social life among human beings* in order to inquire into how Goffman developed his conceptual approach to this phenomenon during his lifetime.

This fascinating and multi-faceted dimension of his oeuvre has remained largely unexplored (Frehse, 2016, pp. 2–3). Differently, my long-standing sociological and anthropological interest in the spatial dimension of social life within the immediacy of the everyday instantaneously drove me towards Goffman's words about "space." By taking as my reference corpus articles and books from the 1950s to the 1980s (Goffman, 1951, 1959, 1961a, 1961b, 1963a, 1963b, 1967, 1971, 1974, 1979, 1981, 1983a, 1983b), I found that within a defined set of writings originally published in the 1950s, 1960s, and early 1970s, the lack of an explicit definition of physical space coexists with numerous spatial references—although many of which are about vague "places" (Goffman, 1951, 1959, 1961a, 1961b, 1963a, 1967, 1971).

By way of this finding, I propose that all of these allusions play not only a descriptive but also an interpretive role in Goffman's work.[4] Primarily these spatial mentions refer to conceptions about the physical environment of social life that carry a significant theoretical importance in the sociologist's conceptual scheme for apprehending the normative structure of face-to-face interactions that are not strictly conversational—what he throughout his life called the "public order" or "life" and, in his last (and posthumous) text on this topic (Goffman, 1983b), "the interaction order."

But precisely due to their interpretative role in Goffman's work, the spatial conceptions at stake also transcend the author's sociology of interaction. They disclose a hexa-dimensional sociology of physical space that is above all conceptually exciting to sociology, and hence also to architects and urban designers in this early 21st century.

In Search of Physical Space, Two Spatial Premises

When we review the Goffman of the interaction order in search of spatial allusions, we stumble upon a Simmelian concern as early as in his first academic article (Goffman, 1951, p. 292): individual behaviors are "signs of social positions," which, in turn, constitute "status symbols" when employed as "resources" to locate individuals socially. The approach stems from a translation of Simmel's essay about fashion (Simmel, 1895/1904) and is one of the two mentions to the German thinker in Goffman's early writings (Gerhardt, 2003, p. 146).

This aspect indicates the relevance that Goffman assigned to a specific dimension of Simmel's work. I am referring to the social distances that permeate the "forms of sociation," which comprise the forms taken by the process of reciprocal influences and determinations between individuals (Simmel, 1917/2006, p. 17; Waizbort, 2001, p. 100).

If there are distances at play, implicitly there is also space at stake. However, at this moment of Goffman's oeuvre, space is conceived rather as a configuration of interacting interactions. Space is a theoretical-methodological abstraction, a conceptual construction that has usually helped sociologists to understand what separates and socially unites individuals into groups.[5] To put it briefly, a first conception of space that underpins Goffman's work is *social* space.

In the earliest days of the Goffmanian oeuvre, this representation coexisted with a second one, which the author explored much more intensely during his lifetime: *interactional* space. It comes to the conceptual forefront when we consider Goffman's approach to "interaction rituals" (1967).

By establishing a dialogue not only with Émile Durkheim's proposition that collective rituals aimed at the individual celebrate the sacredness of social life (Durkheim, 1912/1994), but also with Alfred R. Radcliffe-Brown's argument regarding the ritual as an act of respect for an object that is socially imposed upon its members (Radcliffe-Brown, 1939/1952), Goffman pairs the rules of conduct that underpin face-to-face interactions with avoidance and presentational rituals (Goffman, 1967, pp. 70–71). Both types of rituals are "forms" of the ceremonial activity of deference, which, according to the author, is an important ritual obeisance by one individual to another that takes place during the everyday face-to-face interaction (Goffman, 1967, pp. 47–63). The crucial aspect for the purposes of this chapter is that the aforementioned approach implies a distinction between "positive" and "negative rites," which delimit the "ceremonial distances" between individuals. Goffman grounds his perspective in the North American translation of Simmel's essay on discretion (Simmel, 1908/1950, pp. 320–324): to adopt avoidance rituals is to use a form of deference that keeps the "ideal sphere" around every individual intact, and which, once penetrated, would destroy the "personality value of the individual" (Goffman, 1967, p. 62).

And hence space returns to Goffman's conceptual stage, only now it is interactional, configured symbolically by the rules of conduct that "guide" individuals in symbolic terms when they are in physical co-presence. If such a space is traversed by relations of "symmetrical familiarity" or "asymmetry," depending on the respective "sociological distance" at stake (Goffman, 1967, p. 64), it does not coincide with social space—although it reveals it.

In light of both conceptions of space, we realize that Goffman's dialogue with Simmel and Durkheim is grounded on a reflection on the—abstract—space that social interactions stretch over the—also abstract—social structure. Analogous references to both scholars reappear in the definitive version of Goffman's first book (Goffman, 1959, p. 69).[6] The same applies to the aforementioned two spaces: while the "stimuli" that compose the "appearance" of an "actor" during the interaction reveal this actor's "social status," those referring to the "manner" would inform the "interaction role" that the actor hopes to perform within the situations of face-to-face contact (Goffman, 1959, p. 24).

Even though Simmel and Durkheim are not explicitly referenced in Goffman's subsequent texts, both aforementioned conceptions of space pervade the author's entire oeuvre. In 1961, Goffman further develops the notion of "role distance" as a counterpoint to the classic sociological debate about social roles (Goffman, 1961b, pp. 83–152). He includes in the analysis the possibility that individuals performing in situations of interaction may stray away from the set of rights and duties implicit in their social role. This presupposes the conception of an interactional space within which individuals move when in physical co-presence. Goffman explicitly proposes this referential space when remarking that face-to-face interactions are "ideal projective *fields*," which the participating individuals inevitably help to structure (Goffman, 1961b, p. 102; emphasis added). Being a spatial abstraction, the interaction has a "boundary" which, due to its metaphorical "membrane," "filters" events external to it (Goffman, 1961b, pp. 25–34, 65–66).

Two years later, the metaphors change, new concepts are tested, but the reflection remains pervaded by conceptualizations about, for instance, the role that the rule of conduct to "fit in" in situations plays in the North American context: its spatial connotation indicates the importance of inserting oneself normatively, through behavior, within the abstract space of interaction (Goffman, 1963a, p. 11). An important analytical counterpoint to the normative relevance of this kind of situational rule is the influence of "situational improprieties" on the delimitation of interactional and social distances (Goffman, 1963a, pp. 225, 229).

In the early 1970s, in turn, Goffman underlines how power and social position interfere with the "territories of the self"—that is, with the physical or situational demarcations alongside objects, which are operated by individuals in social interaction to preserve their visions of themselves (in short, their selves) when interacting with others (Goffman, 1971, p. 41). Furthermore, within the framework of a "sociology of place," the author argues that the attribute of a deviant behavior applies to everyone who does not maintain their "place" in the group to which they belong (Goffman, 1971, p. 343). This statement points to the existence of a direct relationship between the self and the individual's normatively defined position within the group; that is, their "social place" (Goffman, 1971, p. 354)—and, thus, to the theoretical relevance that Goffman assigns to the location of the individual within what I am calling interactional and social spaces.

These remarks suggest that, as Goffman's reflection on social interaction unfolds, the social space demarcated by positions is increasingly overwhelmed, theoretically speaking, by the interactional space encompassed by "gatherings." What may be said about social distances seems to increasingly depend on what may be said about interactional distances. The latter reveal the former, challenging classic sociological distinctions.[7]

In light of these aspects, one could imagine that, for Goffman, space is essentially a metaphor for theoretical abstractions with methodological implications that stem from the also essentially theoretical conceptions of social interaction and structure. These conceptual constructs are common to sociology since its inception—with Simmel and Durkheim being pioneers in this regard.

Nevertheless, there is much more space at stake. Goffman's studies on non-conversational interactions suggest that the interactional and social spaces are, in fact, two powerful *premises* of the interpretive scheme developed by the author to unravel the normative structure of social interaction. If individuals, upon interacting, express themselves and manage their interlocutors' impressions about themselves to preserve a certain self, then such expressions and impressions locate the individual within the social interaction and social structure given that they locate them within the interactional and social spaces.

Nevertheless, the crucial point here is that this localization process takes place within the restricted space-time of social interaction by way of communicative resources. And hence I arrive at the physical space.

Four Conceptions of Physical Space Within the Interactional Space

Goffman's interest in physical space comes as no surprise when we bear in mind that he concluded his graduate studies at the University of Chicago and had the esteemed Everett Hughes—who was a student of the prominent Chicago sociologist Robert Park with a keen ethnographic sensitivity for urban research—as his most important teacher (Smith, 2006, p. 31). During the 1990s, one researcher on the so-called Chicago School even regarded the emphasis on "time and place" as a particularity of the Chicagoan social scientists from the years 1910 to 1930: conversely, "contemporary sociology" would find it "strange" that social facts are "*located facts*" (Abbott, 1997, p. 1153; original emphasis).

In Brazil the most immediate spatial association with Goffman's oeuvre is the concept of "total institution," especially clinical centers and psychiatric hospitals, which were the chief empirical references in his first book published in Brazil, in 1974 (Goffman, 1961a). Such institutions are instances of what the sociologist had previously called (Goffman, 1959, p. xi) a "concrete social establishment" in order to summarize his research object: the type of social life that unfolds within the physical boundaries of a building or factory or domestic, industrial, and commercial establishments. The formulation allows us to infer a wide range of physical-material environments of social life or, in my terms here, a wide-ranging scope of physical spaces.

Whether or not directly referenced as "places," these physical spaces go hand in hand with Goffman's rationale about his research activity: he considered himself "a Hughesian urban ethnographer."[8] The author delved into urban contexts after 18 months of a doctoral research in a "community" in one of the Shetland Islands (Winkin, 1988, pp. 66–70). After this ethnographic experience, he spent three years conducting participant observation in the pharmacological and schizophrenia research wards of the National Institutes of Health Clinical Center and in the St. Elizabeths Psychiatric Hospital. Subsequently, he observed "other people and places" (Treviño, 2003, pp. 31–32): surgical staff inside the operating rooms of Herrick Memorial Hospital, gamblers and dealers in the Las Vegas and Nevada casinos, and a disc-jockey on a Philadelphia radio station.

Hence emerged a simultaneously encompassing and thoroughly detailed ethnography of the social interactions and relationships in different physical spaces of "Western society." After all, Goffman analyzed social life in both the rural world and the city and, in the cities, his attention turned to social establishments whose "physical plants" bear interactions that, by the very rules that mediate them, challenge the standards of societal normality, especially in "our Anglo-American society"—which he also termed "our Western society" (see respectively, Goffman, 1959, p. 106, 1963a, p. 132, 1961a, p. 16). If in 1956 the psychiatric hospital was the "place" of "profane" acts, to where "modern society" brings the "transgressors of the ceremonial order" (Goffman, 1967, p. 94), in 1959 the author referenced other places: churches, ground floors of shops, factories, funeral homes, service workshops, gas stations, the rooms of the Hotel Shetland, radio and television stations, and houses (Goffman, 1959, pp. 109, 114–120, 134–135). Two years later, in addition to the psychiatric hospital (Goffman, 1961a), gambling tables, children's carousels, and operating rooms entered the scene (Goffman, 1961b). In 1963, in turn, "public places" gained prominence—that is, "regions in a community freely accessible to members of that community" (Goffman, 1963a, p. 9). The term encompasses different places apart from the "genuinely public space," with unrestricted legal access, such as streets and public squares (Lofland, 1998, p. 4, 7n).

Given the wide array of physical spaces encompassed within these varied empirical research fields, it would be possible to affirm, to paraphrase a common pun in anthropology, that in Goffman we find a sociology *in* space, rather than a sociology *of* space. The physical boundaries of social establishments would therefore circumscribe no more than the referential empirical settings for the author's analyses.

Several excerpts from Goffman's work carry, however, indications that there is more at stake. In 1961, he emphasized the relationship of certain "activities of underlife" with specific "places" or "regions" (Goffman, 1961a, p. 227). Furthermore, he emphasized, as a distinctive property of gatherings in view of social groups, an "allocation of spatial position" of individuals within interaction (Goffman, 1961b, p. 11). Such arguments suggest that the location of individuals in physical space is interpretatively relevant to a sociology of interaction.

Two years later (Goffman, 1963a, p. 17), in the framework of a longer novel conceptualization of public order, physical space assumes the interpretative status of a physical conditioning of modes of communication in face-to-face interaction. Indeed, "the physical distance over which one person can experience another with the naked senses—thereby finding that the other is 'within range'—varies according to many factors: the sense medium involved, the presence of obstructions, even the temperature of the air" (Goffman, 1963a, p. 17). This orientation allows us to find in informal conversations, for example, the difficulty represented by physical distance and the interference of "furniture arrangements" (Goffman, 1963a, p. 98) and, later (Goffman, 1971, p. 19), that it would be possible to characterize gatherings of two or more individuals on the streets as "a 'with'": after all, they would carry a type of "ecological proximity."

These arguments published in 1963 and 1971 signal towards a conception of space that echoes the ecological reflections of the Chicago School. Space is a physical medium of inherently spatial social relations. Depending on the spatial conditions, different interactions become possible. Therefore, in addition to a mere *physical setting*, space interferes with social life as a *physical conditioning* factor for interactions.[9]

Both conceptions of space, in addition to the first two regarding the abstract space of interaction and of social structure, do not allow us to infer any originality in Goffman's sociological reflection on space. The interactional and social spaces are in dialogue with Simmel and Durkheim if we consider that for each of these authors space is essentially a social construct, dependent on social interactions (Simmel, 1903/1995, 1908/1995) or on collective representations (Durkheim, 1912/1994). In turn, the conception of physical space as a setting and the conception of physical space as a physical conditioning are embedded in the ethnographic and ecological tradition of the Chicago School.

However, there is still more space at stake. In one of his early articles, Goffman conceived acts or events of individuals in social interaction as "sign-vehicles or tokens," that is, as bearers of "ceremonial messages" concerning the respective selves and communicated during co-presence (Goffman, 1967, p. 55). In addition to being of a linguistic or a gestural nature, such acts or events can be "*spatial*, as when an individual precedes another through the door, or sits on his right instead of his left" (Goffman, 1967, p. 55; added emphasis). This perspective bestows the physical space with the status of a *sign*.

Goffman further developed this conception. Its first glimpses appeared in his dramaturgical characterization of the "setting," which is the "standard part of front" that individuals exhibit to each other in physical co-presence (Goffman, 1959, p. 22). The setting comprises furniture, decoration, physical appearance, and other "background items" which, taken together, would provide the "scenery and stage props" for the plethora of actions staged therein. Indeed, this is due to the fact that the presentation of self is conveyed by the individuals' intentional and non-intentional expressivity, which, for its part, is essentially semiotic in nature (Goffman, 1959, p. 2). This semiotic substance transforms physical places into "stage devices" that distinguish the ways of life of the middle and lower classes (Goffman, 1959, p. 123). If, in subsequent moments of the assortment of texts hereby analyzed, the dramaturgical metaphor was replaced by references from the fields of communication and ethology (see respectively, Goffman, 1963a and 1971), the semiotic conception of physical space remained. In the spatial environment delimited by face-to-face interactions between two or more individuals, their bodies are not only physical, but also communicative instruments (Goffman, 1963a, p. 23). Their positions and movements within the physical space are part of what Goffman calls "body idiom" (Goffman, 1963a, p. 33). Hence, he acknowledges "spatial conventions" in informal face-to-face engagements of a conversational nature: interactions depend on physical distances of a few feet at most and, on the other hand, the difficulty of direct conversations when individuals are less than a foot and a half away (Goffman, 1963a, pp. 98–99). Physical distances between individuals communicate as much as the "individual" or "flight distance" between birds (Goffman, 1963a, p. 161). The same explanatory logic remained when, in a deeper debate with ethology (Goffman, 1971, p. 195), Goffman's interest lay in showing that the individual information conveyed in social interaction indicates more or less close social relations: the spatial distance between bodies is one of the "tie-signs" between interactions and social relations.

By drawing attention to the semiotic nature of physical space in interactions, the Goffmanian oeuvre evades, on the one hand, the Chicagoan ecological conception of space as an environment characterized by a selection, distribution, and accommodation dynamics that "influences" the human beings' relationships with space and time—or, to put it briefly: space as an ecological variable (McKenzie, 1925/1967, pp. 63–66).[10] On the other hand, Goffman's work bypasses the argument that space is a "medium" plain with "resources" for social activities (Joseph, 2000a/2005, p. 79). Within the Goffmanian approach, space neither practically enables face-to-face communication activities nor is it an instrument for its accomplishment. It communicates. And it does so because it is a sign employed by human beings, who are communicative in their essence.

But precisely because it is communicative *space*, physical space is more than *one* sign. Given that space is empirically recognizable as such due to the existence of bodies able to occupy the physical-material environment and, hence, to transform the same space and themselves into signs, space also is an environment of signs; or, more precisely, an *idiom*. This is the fourth and final conception of space that I would like to heighten here.

The insight that there would be no way to reflect upon the normative order of social interaction without problematizing its "environment" appears early on in Goffman's work. In 1956, he states that from the standpoint of the ceremonial components in the activities of the interacting individuals, "environment" is "a place where it is easy or difficult to play the ritual game of having a self" (Goffman, 1967, p. 91). Three years later, and making use of the dramaturgical metaphor, the author brings the aforementioned setting to the analysis. The setting is a "fixed sign-equipment" of a larger spatial entity: the "front region," where the self presents itself (that is, "the place where the performance is given"—Goffman, 1959, p. 107). Altogether with the "back region or backstage" (that is, "a place, relative to a given performance, where the impression fostered by the performance is knowingly contradicted"—Goffman, 1959, p. 112), and with "the outside" (that is, a region apart from the front or the back regarding "a particular performance"—Goffman, 1959, p. 135), the front region composes the "region," which is bounded by barriers to perception (Goffman, 1959, pp. 107, 112, 134–135, and 106). According to Goffman, the interactions within the regions empirically obey the logic of the "behavior setting," a concept stemming from the then recent ecological psychology of Roger Barker and Herbert Wright.[11] In fact, references to Barker surface at different moments throughout Goffman's work whenever it becomes important to reiterate that certain behaviors occur in defined physical spaces. In Goffman's first book (1959, p. 106), interactions comprise associations of meaning between expectations of conduct and "places." This equation suggests that, according to the author, physical space is more than a manageable sign. As surprising and contradictory as it may seem at first glance, the fact is that, depending precisely on the physical traits at stake in empirically given social interactions—whether the front region, the backstage, or the outside—in Goffman's work physical space becomes an environment where different impressions are managed. And the physical traits themselves are conceived as signs—without excluding the possibility that the regions sometimes hold different meanings (Goffman, 1959, p. 126).

Once conceptually devised, this dimension of physical space was deployed to account for the analytical subtleties of each moment. In order to understand how the activities of underlife of the patients at St. Elizabeths Hospital could "occur," Goffman relied on ethology (Goffman, 1961a, p. 227) to focus on the "setting," which here encompasses "places" or "regions" that he named "spaces"—more or less watched over and supervised by third parties—and the inmates' personal or group "territories" (Goffman, 1961a, pp. 227–248). When, in turn, Goffman searched for the normative structure of face-to-face interaction in public places in general and, hence, attempted to theorize socio-spatial relations, he focused on the "proper public conduct" in "situations," which he then began to define as "*spatial* environments" where newcomers become members of an either already existing gathering or of one that thereby comes into existence (Goffman, 1963a, p. 18; added emphasis). Endowed with spatial emphasis, the concept of situation becomes a gateway to others of a similar spatial nature. I think here, on the one hand, in a "social situation," which Goffman defined as an environment of possibilities for mutual monitoring (therefore, for communication) that causes any newcomer to become a participant in a gathering (Goffman, 1963a, p. 243) and, on the other hand, in a "social occasion," defined as "a wider social affair, undertaking, or event, bounded in regard to place and time and typically facilitated by fixed equipment," which "provides the structuring social context in which many situations and their gatherings are likely to form, dissolve, and re-form" amid a "'standing behavior pattern'"—again in the terms of Barker (Goffman, 1963a, p. 18).

When, in turn, and in close dialogue with ethology, the connections of public life with social relationships gained prominence in Goffman's thought (1971), the territories of the self became crucial research objects. We hence realize that individuals seek at all costs to preserve the possession, control, use, and availability of these "fields" bounded by physical places, their equipment or objects, or by objects that, belonging to individuals, generally accompany them physically (Goffman, 1971, p. 28). From the standpoint of these territories, the public order is, once again, characterized by both spatial signs and an environment of signs. Nonetheless, this same environment of signs is, in a way, physically more restricted. It represents a potential danger to the *self* given that it is delimited by the "immediate world" of the individual who interacts (Goffman, 1971, p. 250). In order to name the physical space defined by "signs for alarm" of an ethological nature, Goffman conceptualizes it as *Umwelt*, a German term stemming from the field of ethology in the 1930s (Goffman, 1971, p. 252).

Endowed with this double dimension—of being both a situational environment and an environment of the self in situations—the physical space gains, in Goffman, its most elaborate theoretical feature. In addition to being setting, physical conditioning, or sign, space is an environment of signs for social interactions. This, nonetheless, does not turn it into an "environment" of the Blumerian symbolic interactionism (Blumer, 1969, p. 11), which Goffman criticized (Gonos, 1977, p. 855, 3n). According to Herbert Blumer (1969, p. 11), the environment is exclusively defined by the objects that human beings (re)acknowledge as endowed with meaning, and one and the same "spatial location" may have different environments. The Goffmanian environment, in turn, is not restricted to objects endowed with meaning, as space does restrict itself to a symbolic human construction, and this despite it bearing traits that become signs, within the interactions.

Thus, the Goffmanian physical space ultimately leans towards a contemporary relational conception of space (Löw, 2001; Fuller & Löw, 2017). After all, in both approaches the relational ordering of things and human beings becomes conceptually relevant for the definition of space. However, regardless of this common denominator, everything else is different. The relational perspective conceptually details, above all, the phenomenal dimension of the action that constitutes space. Goffman, on the other hand, is concerned with the expressive dimension of physical space that appears in interaction.

We have before ourselves, therefore, an expressive environment. Hence, there is a more precise definition of physical space than the one of an environment of signs. Physical space is an *idiom*.

Given the possibility of such an association, a novelty emerges within the sociological debate about space. Semiotic interpretations about space have a long history, even if not specifically in sociology.[12] Goffman, for his part, offers something different. By spatializing face-to-face interactions through the notion of situation, he grants physical space an innovative role in the sociological understanding of interactions. Space becomes one of the idioms that individuals mobilize when interacting therein. This idiom goes hand in hand with the body idiom while at the same time submitted to it. After all, "bodily action" is a powerful "basis" of social interaction (Goffman, 1963a, p. 34, 1n)—and only thereby also of space generation.[13] Hence, the space as an idiom is freed from any merely instrumental connotation. It is essentially expressive, communicative.

Conclusion

The mere fact that Goffman ethnographically treaded such a wide range of physical-material environments, both in rural settings and in the city, whether with restricted and unrestricted access, would be reason enough to call attention to the role of space in his sociology. We do not commonly find theoretical contributions in the history of sociology empirically rooted in ethnographic observations of social life in such varied places.

By seeking to unveil the normative logic of face-to-face interactions, believing that it resides in these same interactions—since interactions "generate" a "realm of activity" organized by "norms of co-mingling" (Goffman, 1971, p. ix)—Goffman elaborated a sociology *in* physical space. However, since he early on found in physical space a variable that interferes with interactions and, therefore, with its own normative logic, he began to problematize it sociologically. Hence, Goffman's sociology of physical space enters the scene.

My analysis first showed that Goffman's conception of social interaction bears a strong spatial dimension. Even the simplest "presentation of self in everyday life," also the title of his first book,[14] necessarily means that individuals and those who interact with them are located interactively and socially in the restricted space-time of situations. To interact invariably means putting social places in check: the places occupied within the interaction and social structure—the latter, in fact, all the while explicitly inspired by Durkheim and Radcliffe-Brown. Such a perspective warrants for what I have named interactional and social space the status of theoretical assumptions within Goffman's sociology of space.

Furthermore, the analysis revealed that physical space is not a mere physical setting of interactions. It is moreover physical conditioning, sign, and idiom of interactions that locate individuals, through different ways, interactionally and, thus, socially.

This complex dynamic ultimately leads to six synchronous dimensions of space and, therefore, also to a *hexa-dimensional conception of space, which includes a four-dimensional physical space*. The approach bears two contributions to present-day sociology: its conceptual uniqueness and its empirical applicability. The first input is grounded on Goffman's six-fold space, which structurally differs from all the usual conceptions of space that enliven the history of sociology: space either as a social construct, an ecological variable, a dialectical product, or a relational outcome of action.

Regarding, in turn, the applicability of Goffman's approach, his four-fold conception of physical space is particularly helpful to sociologists for apprehending empirically given rules of social interaction. From the standpoint of the social situations through which daily life empirically unfolds—the realm of "moments and their men" (Goffman, 1967, p. 3)—what matters is the fact that physical space may *simultaneously* be setting, conditioning, sign, or idiom for different ways of interacting and of relating socially. Amidst this complexity, it is up to sociologists to perform an ethnography of the empirical reality in order to distinguish analytically and interpretively—and hence perhaps also conceptually—the rules of conduct that mediate these interactions. To this end, Goffman has provided a palette of notions.

Both inputs to sociology suggest that we are facing a relatively detached, conceptually flexible manner of dealing with physical space in order to better understand its role in social life. This comes as no surprise if we remember that Goffman's work is based on a rather unsystematic approach to his research issues (see Smith, 2006). It is precisely from this aspect that I finally arrive at the two contributions which Goffman's sociology of physical space offers particularly to present-day architects and urban designers.

His approach first shows that the daily interaction of architects and urban designers with clients, construction workers, practitioners, public servants, policymakers, and/or scholars involuntarily bears a crucial spatial dimension that widely transcends the physical space projected, planned, and designed by these same professionals. This socio-spatial trait of social interaction should therefore not be ignored in favor of a project, plan, and design that is as much as possible socially inclusive and just—which are two of the major challenges of the present-day "urban condition" throughout the world.

And hence I arrive at the second possible lesson of Goffman's sociology of physical space to architects and urban designers. The physical space that lies at the heart of architectural and urban-design practice is only *one* spatial element among various others that are symbolically mobilized by human beings in the situations of interaction they involve themselves in daily. Hence, the projected, planned, and designed physical space should not be essentialized by its authors as "telling its own tale." From the standpoint of Goffman's approach, this kind of physical space may simultaneously be a setting, a conditioning, a sign, and an idiom of social interaction. An awareness of this circumstance may help architects and urban designers to deliver socially better enrooted projects, plans, and designs.

This contribution suggests that, last but not least, Goffman's sociology of physical space contains a lesson that applies to sociologists, anthropologists, architects, and urban designers altogether. Even though Goffman's privileged empirical setting was "our Anglo-American society," his conceptions of space effectively allow us to infer spatial dimensions of social interactions that are not exclusive to Western society. Hence sociology meets anthropology, but also architecture and urban design. And Goffman reaffirms, whether consciously or otherwise, the existence of yet another space. It is the intellectual space that creatively congregates all of these disciplines within the dialectical unity of what is diverse—and theoretically crucial—due to the complexity of the socio-spatial processes that underpin the urban condition in the current early 2020s.

Notes

1. Apart from its preface, which has especially been conceived for the present book, this chapter is a heuristically shortened and modified version of a German journal article (Frehse, 2016) that critically reviews and updates the findings of a first Portuguese journal publication (Frehse, 2008). I am grateful to the Alexander von Humboldt Foundation for the postdoctoral scholarship which during the year 2010 allowed me start the since then ongoing intellectual interchange with German spatial sociologists of which this chapter is one outcome.
2. This bibliographic research was made possible thanks to a visiting fellowship (2020) of the Centre of Latin American Studies of the University of Cambridge, to which I hereby also express my gratitude.
3. All translations from languages other than English are my own.
4. I think here in the methodological distinction by Florestan Fernandes (1959, p. 36) between "descriptive" and "interpretive explanations" in sociology.
5. This Simmelian viewpoint found further development in the works of Leopold von Wiese (1924/1968), Pitirim Sorokin (1927), and Pierre Bourdieu (see one of Bourdieu's first references to Simmel in Bourdieu 1966/2005, p. 18).
6. The book was first published as a monograph at the University of Edinburgh in 1956.
7. In 1963 the author argues that, "[m]ore than to any family or club, more than to any class or sex, more than to any nation, the individual belongs to gatherings, and he had best show that he is a member in good standing" (Goffman, 1963a, p. 248). This perception of the theoretical importance of the order—and space—of interactions will persist throughout Goffman's life-time. In one of his last and posthumous texts he concludes that "[t]his body to body starting point, paradoxically, assumes that a very central sociological distinction may not be initially relevant: namely, the standard contrast between village life and city life, between domestic settings and public ones, between intimate, long-standing relations and fleeting impersonal ones" (Goffman, 1983b, p. 2).
8. In a 1980 interview, Goffman stated that this would be his label should he need one (Treviño, 2003, p. 7).
9. This conception, by the way, pairs with another one that, according to Isaac Joseph in an interview with Brazilian researchers, underpins the "ecological approach," according to which space is a "complete medium ['meio' in the original Portuguese formulation] where the activity of adaptation and cooperation of the individual members of groups finds resources" (Joseph, 2000a/2005, p. 79; see also Joseph, 1998/2000b, p. 57).
10. This theoretical approach also traverses the early publications by Robert Park and Ernest Burgess regarding the city of Chicago (Park & Burgess, 1925/1967).
11. Barker was the founder of the so-called ecological psychology, which was methodologically grounded on detailed observations of the relationships between human behaviors and "natural settings"—non-experimental—that he empirically found at the research station he established with colleagues in a small Kansas town in the 1950s (see, among others, Hall, 1969, pp. 1184–1186, and Carneiro & Binde, 1997, pp. 277–285).
12. I recall here, among others, Walter Benjamin's reflection on 19th-century Paris (Benjamin, 1938/1983–2006; Bolle, 1996), but I also have in mind more recent considerations regarding the relations between space and sign (Bachelard, 1957/1996; Cannevacci, 1993/2004).
13. The use of the term "generation" aims to underline that Goffman's interactionist approach differs both from the dialectical perspective on the "production" of space—that is, of space being simultaneously a product and producer, hence a mediation, of social practice (see particularly Lefebvre, 1974/2000, p. xx)—and from the relational approach to the "constitution" of space (Löw, 2001). For more details, see Frehse (2020, pp. 1–15, 18–20).
14. Differently, the first edition of the German translation, in 1969, was titled *Wir alle spielen Theater: Zur Selbstdarstellung im Alltag* (*We All Perform Theater: The Presentation of Self in the Everyday*); in Portuguese, the book was first published in 1975 with the more than inaccurate title *A Representação do Eu na Vida Cotidiana* (*The Representation of the Me in Everyday Life*).

References

Abbott, A. (1997). Of Time and Space: The Contemporary Relevance of the Chicago School. *Social Forces*, 75(4), 1149–1182.

Bachelard, G. (1996). *A Poética do Espaço* (A.P. Danesi, Trans.). São Paulo, Brazil: Martins Fontes. (Original work published 1957).
Benjamin, W. (2006). *Passagens* (I. Aron & C.P.B. Mourão, Trans.; P.F. Camargo, Techn. Rev.). Belo Horizonte, Brazil: Editora da UFMG. (Original work published 1983).
Blumer, H. (1969). *Symbolic Interactionism*. Englewood Cliffs, NJ: Prentice-Hall.
Bolle, W. (1996). As Siglas em Cores no *Trabalho das passagens*, de W. Benjamin (J. Briant & M.A. Chiarella, Trans.). *Estudos Avançados*, *1*(27), 41–77.
Bourdieu, P. (2005). Condição de Classe e Posição de Classe. In *A Economia das Trocas Simbólicas* (S. Miceli et al., Trans.; 6th ed., pp. 3–25). São Paulo, Brazil: Perspectiva. (Original work published 1966).
Cannevacci, M. (2004). *A Cidade Polifônica* (C. Prada, Trans.; 2nd ed.). São Paulo, Brazil: Studio Nobel. (Original work published 1993).
Carneiro, C., & Binde, P.J. (1997). A Psicologia Ecológica e o Estudo dos Acontecimentos da Vida Diária. *Estudos de Psicologia*, *2*(2), 277–285.
Durkheim, É. (1994). *Les Formes Élémentaires de la Vie Réligieuse* (3rd ed.). Paris, France: PUF. (Original work published 1912).
Fernandes, F. (1959). *Fundamentos Empíricos da Explicação Sociológica*. São Paulo, Brazil: Companhia Editora Nacional.
Frehse, F. (2008). Erving Goffman, Sociólogo do Espaço. *Revista Brasileira de Ciências Sociais*, *23*(68), 155–166.
Frehse, F. (2016). Erving Goffmans Soziologie des Raums. *Sozialraum.de* (Online), *8*. Retrieved from http://sozialraum.de/erving-goffmans-soziologie-des-raums.php
Frehse, F. (2020). On the Temporalities and Spatialities of the Production of Space. *SFB 1265 Working Paper Series*, *4*, 27 p. Retrieved from https://sfb1265.de/einblicke/publikationen/working-paper-nr-4-on-the-temporalities-and-spatialities-of-the-production-of-space/
Fuller, M.G., & Löw, M. (Eds.). (2017). Spatial Sociology: Relational Space after the Turn. *Current Sociology*, *65*(4), Monograph 2, 469–639.
Gerhardt, U. (2003). Of Kindred Spirit: Erving Goffman's Oeuvre and its Relationship to Georg Simmel. In A.J. Treviño (Ed.), *Goffman's Legacy* (pp. 143–165). Lanham: Rowman & Littlefield Publishers.
Goffman, E. (1951). Symbols of Class Status. *The British Journal of Sociology*, *2*, 294–304.
Goffman, E. (1959). *The Presentation of Self in Everyday Life*. New York, NY: Anchor Books.
Goffman, E. (1961a). *Asylums*. New York, NY: Anchor Books.
Goffman, E. (1961b). *Encounters*. Indianapolis, IN: Bobbs-Merrill.
Goffman, E. (1963a). *Behavior in Public Places*. New York, NY; London, UK: The Free Press/Collier-Macmillan Limited.
Goffman, E. (1963b). *Stigma*. Englewood Cliffs, NJ: Prentice-Hall.
Goffman, E. (1967). *Interaction Ritual*. Garden City, NY: Anchor Books.
Goffman, E. (1971). *Relations in Public*. New York, NY: Basic Books.
Goffman, E. (1974). *Frame Analysis*. Cambridge, MA: Harvard University Press.
Goffman, E. (1979). *Gender Advertisements*. Cambridge, MA: Harvard University Press.
Goffman, E. (1981). *Forms of Talk*. Oxford, UK: Basil Blackwell.
Goffman, E. (1983a). Microsociologie et Histoire. In P. Fritsch (Ed.), *Le Sens de l'Ordinaire* (pp. 197–202). Paris, France: Editions du CNRS. (Original work published 1982).
Goffman, E. (1983b). The Interaction Order: American Sociological Association, 1982 Presidential Address. *American Sociological Review*, *48*(1), 1–17.
Gonos, G. (1977). "Situation" versus "Frame": the "Interactionist" and the "Structuralist" Analyses of Everyday Life. *American Sociological Review*, *42*(6), 854–867.
Hall, E.T. (1969). Review: Ecological Psychology: Concepts and Methods for Studying the Environment of Human Behavior by Roger G. Barker. *American Anthropologist*, *71*(6), 1184–1186.
Jensen, O.B. (2010). Negotiation in Motion: Unpacking a Geography of Mobility. *Space and Culture*, *13*(4), 389–402.
Jensen, O.B. (2013). *Staging Mobility*. London, UK: Routledge.
Joseph, I. (2000a). *Erving Goffman e a Microsociologia* (C.S. Rizek, Trans.). Rio de Janeiro, Brazil: Editora da FGV. (Original work published 1998).
Joseph, I. (2000b). *La Ville sans Qualités*. La Tour d'Aigues, France: Éditions de l'Aube. (Original work published in 1998).

Joseph, I. (2005). Entrevista com Isaac Joseph [by Lícia do Prado Valladares & Roberto Kand de Lima]. In L.P. Valladares & R.K. Lima (Eds.), *A Escola de Chicago* (pp. 69–92). Belo Horizonte, Rio de Janeiro, Brazil: Editora UFMG/Iuperj. (Original work published 2000).

Lefebvre, H. (2000). *La Production de l'Espace*. Paris, France: Anthropos. (Original work published 1974).

Lofland, L. (1998). *The Public Realm*. New York, NY: Aldine De Gruyter.

Löw, M. (2001). *Raumsoziologie*. Frankfurt a. M., Germany: Suhrkamp.

McKenzie, R. (1967). The Ecological Approach to the Study of the Human Community. In R.E. Park & E.W. Burgess (Eds.), *The City* (pp. 63–79). Chicago, IL; London, UK: The University of Chicago Press. (Original work published 1925).

Park, R.E., & Burgess, E.W. (Eds.). (1967). *The City*. Chicago, IL; London, UK: The University of Chicago Press. (Original work published 1925).

Radcliffe-Brown, A.R. (1952). Taboo. In *Structure and Function in Primitive Society* (pp. 133–152). Glencoe, IL: Free Press. (Original work published 1939).

Schroer, M. (2006). *Räume, Orte, Grenzen*. Frankfurt a. M., Germany: Suhrkamp.

Simmel, G. (1904). Fashion. *International Quarterly, 10*, 130–155. (Original work published 1895).

Simmel, G. (1950). Discretion. In K.E. Wolff (Ed.), *The Sociology of Georg Simmel* (pp. 320–324). Glencoe, IL: Free Press. (Original work published 1908).

Simmel, G. (1995). Soziologie des Raumes. In *Aufsätze und Abhandlungen 1901–1908* (vol. 1, pp. 132–183). Frankfurt a. M., Germany: Suhrkamp. (Original work published 1903).

Simmel, G. (2006). *Questões Fundamentais da Sociologia* (P. Caldas, Trans.). Rio de Janeiro, Brazil: Jorge Zahar Editor. (Original work published 1917).

Smith, G. (2006). *Erving Goffman*. London, UK; New York, NY: Routledge.

Sorokin, P. (1927). *Social Mobility*. New York, NY: Harper and Brothers.

Treviño, A.J. (2003). Introduction: Erving Goffman and the Interaction Order. In A.J. Treviño (Ed.), *Goffman's Legacy* (pp. 1–49). Lanham: Rowman & Littlefield Publishers.

Waizbort, L. (2001). Elias e Simmel. In L. Waizbort (Ed.), *Dossiê Norbert Elias* (pp. 89–111). São Paulo, Brazil: Edusp. (Original work published 1999).

Wiese, L. (1968). *System der allgemeinen Soziologie als Lehre von den sozialen Gebilden der Menschen (Beziehungslehre)*. Berlin, Germany: Duncker & Humblot. (Original work published 1924).

Winkin, Y. (1988). Goffman à Baltasound. *Politix, 1*(3), 66–70.

5

BROKEN WINDOWS, REVISITED

Reinhold Martin

The following text was first published in 2016, as one of ten short essays collected in *The Urban Apparatus: Mediapolitics and the City*.[1] Its immediate context was the emergence of the Movement for Black Lives (or Black Lives Matter), in the aftermath of the protests against the police killing of an unarmed Black man, Michael Brown, on August 10, 2014, in Ferguson, Missouri, as one among countless acts of police violence against people of color in the United States, and in particular, against young Black men and women. Despite the protests, the killings did not stop. The barbaric police killing of George Floyd in Minneapolis, Minnesota, on May 25, 2020, the police killing of Breonna Taylor in Louisville, Kentucky, and the vigilante murder of Ahmaud Arbery in Glynn County, Georgia, along with the prior deaths of numerous others by police violence ignited an unprecedented uprising that swept across the United States and reverberated worldwide. The 1999 police killing of Amadou Diallo in New York, recounted as follows, stands here for the intersection of two intimately related processes that are among that uprising's deeper sources: the rebirth of classical liberalism's *homo oeconomicous* ("economic man") as an entrepreneur, the archetypal subject of neoliberal globalization, and the violent maintenance of urban order as an aesthetic as well as legal-political concept guiding police discourse and practice.

Architecture and urbanism have played a significant role in consolidating these tendencies. In the following chapter, I explain how the figure of the broken window came to represent the specific police practices involved, as well as how, more generally, neoliberalism's cost-benefit calculations came to account for and project aesthetic as well as social order as the basis for urban life. Early steps were taken in 1968, in the economist Gary S. Becker's landmark article, "Crime and Punishment: An Economic Approach," which reconceived the potential criminal as a rational economic actor making cost-benefit calculations. To this was added the theory of "broken windows" policing, as popularized by the eponymous article by George L. Kelling and James Q. Wilson in 1982, described later, that led to harsh prison sentences for petty crimes like breaking windows. Extrapolating from Becker and others, Kelling and Wilson argued that minor offenses were indicators of future, more serious criminal behavior that could only be offset by raising the costs. Where, as I explain, Becker's argument depended on explicitly racialized assumptions, Kelling and Wilson presented their approach as one that reconciled the interests of a predominantly white police force with those of predominantly Black neighborhoods. To these documents I add here a third. After two decades that saw the spread of "broken windows" policing and related practices throughout the United States, in 2002 the attorney and legal scholar

Neal K. Katyal published a law review article, "Architecture as Crime Control," that sought to recalibrate the ratio of environmental control to police violence, proposing to decrease the latter by increasing the former (Katyal, 2002). Although Katyal's article did not influence policy to the same extent that the Becker-Kelling-Wilson discourse did, it confirms the constitutive function of *order*, both social and aesthetic, as a dimension of neoliberal capitalism.

Katyal aims to extend the task of order maintenance from the law, the courts, and the police to the physical environment. For this he seeks the advice of what he calls "architectural theory," adapting the analyses and recommendations of reformist urbanists such as Jane Jacobs and Oscar Newman for the purpose of "crime control." Design responses that enhance "natural surveillance," establish territoriality, build community, and harden targets, Katyal argues, are better suited than law enforcement as a front-line deterrence. Violating the social norms that are secured by these spatial techniques, he suggests, raises the "perpetration costs" of breaking the law, including the perceived social costs of breaking a window in the full view of others. Katyal, who has read the warnings of Michel Foucault on the panoptic diffusion of police power, thereby conceives of the city as an instrument of social order. In this, he takes his modest place in a long line of reformers whose arguments might even strike a moderating chord among those who have taken to the streets more recently in defense of Black lives. After all, is not the soft deterrence of environmental signals—what Jacobs called an awareness of "eyes on the street" and Newman, "defensible space"—preferable to the batons, tear gas, and bullets of an increasingly militarized police?

Katyal, who has since risen to public prominence and served as Acting Solicitor General of the United States under US President Barack Obama, argues that his approach ultimately "calls into question the 'broken windows' theory of social order" (Katyal, 2002, p. 1138). But in fact, rather than challenging the central premise to the "broken windows" hypothesis, of crime as entrepreneurial calculus, Katyal merely extends the source of market signals from the permanent threat of brute force wielded by the police (the locus of the "broken windows" theory) to the softer but no less sinister threats issuing from an ambient, signifying environment designed according to the precepts of an anachronistic behavioral psychology. Scholars of architecture and urban history will not be surprised by his sources. Along with Jacobs and Newman, these include Christopher Alexander, Kevin Lynch, Donald Appleyard, Alexander Garvin, Amos Rapoport, and Edward T. Hall. The early efforts of the Congress for the New Urbanism are among his positive examples. Well aware of the risks of architectural or spatial determinism, Katyal insists that his proposals supplement traditional law enforcement rather than replace it. But with each carefully crafted, pre-emptive defense, his argument slips closer toward its inevitable destination, which is also his point of departure: that, like society at large, the city must be reconceived as a marketplace in which symbolic, social capital is produced and exchanged alongside the material goods and services, such as windows and their maintenance, around which liberal political economy was built. As we shall see herein, the human capital so prized by neoliberals—of which the racialized "criminal" is typical rather than exceptional—is liberalism's paradigmatic *homo oeconomicus*, reborn.

In response, critical theorists and historians of architecture and urbanism might ask: how do social order and aesthetic order coincide within the discursive practice of broken windows policing and its affiliates? Rather than accept analytic conventions that separate social concerns from aesthetic ones, the notes that follow on broken windows propose that cities are machines for the production and reproduction of order, and that order—including the white supremacist racial order contested in the streets—is, in turn, a way of life that depends on attributing to material things—like windows—aesthetic qualities and police powers of their own.

New York, August 2020

Broken Windows

Here is an equation: $O_j = O_j(p_j, f_j, u_j)$, where O is the number of criminal offenses a given individual, j, is likely to commit during a particular period of time, p is the probability of his or her being convicted per offense, f is the punishment per offense, and u is a "portmanteau variable" representing a cluster of other variables, "such as the income available to him in legal and other illegal activities, the frequency of nuisance arrests, and his willingness to commit an illegal act." The equation was published by the economist Gary S. Becker in "Crime and Punishment: An Economic Approach," an influential article that first appeared in 1968. When generalized, Becker's equation describes the "supply" of criminal offenses in a given population, in an approach that "follows the economists' usual analysis of choice and assumes that a person commits an offense if the expected utility to him exceeds the utility he could get by using his time and other resources at other activities" (Becker, 1974, pp. 9–10). In other words, Becker translates criminal behavior into a rational economic choice describable in logico-mathematical terms.

In the same article, Becker incorporates the overall number of criminal offenses in a given situation, O, into another equation that describes the total societal loss, L, as follows: $L = D(O) + C(p, O) + bpfO$, where D is the net cost or damage per offense, p is again the probability of conviction per offense, C is the cost of combating offenses, and b is a coefficient for determining the severity of punishment, f, per offense. This equation establishes a policy-oriented criterion, L, which enables more than the intuitive optimization of variables. Here is the Nobel-winning economist again, at length:

> If the aim simply were deterrence, the probability of conviction, p, could be raised close to 1, and punishments, f, could be made to exceed the gain: in this way the number of offenses, O, could be reduced almost at will. However, an increase in p increases the social cost of offenses through its effect on the cost of combatting offenses, C [i.e., more police, etc.], as does an increase in f if $b > 0$ through the effect on the cost of punishments, bf. At relatively modest values of p and f, these effects might outweigh the social gain from increased deterrence. Similarly, if the aim simply were to make "the punishment fit the crime," p could be set close to 1, and f could be equated to the harm imposed on the rest of society. Again, however, such a policy ignores the social cost of increases in p and f.
> (Becker, 1974, p. 14)

According to Becker, optimal settings depend in part on the behavioral tendencies of the offenders. Theoretically, "risk preferrers" and "risk avoiders" might respond differently to different values of p (probability of conviction) versus bf (severity of punishment) (Becker, 1974, p. 18). In sum, Becker offers a cost-benefit analysis of criminal behavior from the perspective of the potential criminal that also measures costs and benefits to the state. Referring to Becker's article as well as to his later work on human capital, Michel Foucault perceives this perspective as characteristic of neoliberal economics, which begins "from the point of view of the person who decides to work [or to commit a crime] rather than from the point of view of capital or of economic mechanisms." But, Foucault emphasizes, this shift takes effect only insofar as the subject is reconstituted as *homo oeconomicus*.[2]

Writing much more recently, in 2011, Becker's former student the urban economist Edward Glaeser credits Becker for pioneering an economic criminology premised on incentivizing compliance through strict enforcement and strict punitive codes. In New York City, these have included New York State's 1973 "Rockefeller drug laws," mandating a 15-year sentence for possession of four ounces of illegal drugs, and "broken windows" policing, initiated to broad acclaim in the 1990s by Mayor Rudolph Giuliani and Police Commissioner William Bratton, "which calls for strong penalties for even minor infractions, such as jumping subway turnstiles to avoid paying the fare" (Glaeser, 2011, pp. 110–111).

The underlying theory of law enforcement associated with the latter approach was first advanced by George L. Kelling and James Q. Wilson in "Broken Windows: The Police and Neighborhood Safety," a widely read nine-page article that appeared in the March 1982 issue of *The Atlantic*. Kelling, a criminologist, worked for the Metropolitan Transit Authority and consulted with the New York Police Department on the theory's implementation; Wilson was a political scientist who did his graduate work at the University of Chicago. The passage from which the article—and the policy—took its name links crime with visible disorder:

> Social psychologists and police officers tend to agree that if a window in a building is broken and is left unrepaired, all the rest of the windows will soon be broken. This is as true in nice neighborhoods as in rundown ones. Window-breaking does not necessarily occur on a large scale because some areas are inhabited by determined window-breakers whereas others are populated by window-lovers; rather, one unrepaired broken window is a signal that no one cares, and so breaking more windows costs nothing. (It has always been fun.)
>
> (Kelling & Wilson, 1982)

Most striking about this passage, and about Kelling and Wilson's argument in general, is that it moves the source of criminality into the physical environment in a manner that blends social constructivism with rational choice.[3] Put differently, it locates crime in the city's physical and institutional infrastructures by refiguring those infrastructures as a series of boundary conditions that, like a window, must be maintained. Failure to do so is, in effect, failure to raise the parameter p, the likelihood of conviction, to a sufficiently high level in Becker's equation, which the new model assimilated even as it revised the former's utilitarian premises.[4] Kelling and Wilson argue that "breaking more windows costs nothing" when environmental indications, or "signals," are that petty offenders will go unpunished (that is, that "no one cares"), creating a general impression of lawlessness that encourages escalating cycles of criminality. They do not explain, however, why breaking windows (or crime in general) is "fun" and therefore inevitable, only that it must be dissuaded by strict enforcement tactics, which in practice significantly raise incarceration rates such that order visibly reigns over disorder.

The policy was implemented in New York through a crackdown on misdemeanor offenses such as jumping subway turnstiles to avoid paying a fare and, most famously, by targeting the city's "squeegee men" who, unsolicited, washed car windshields at traffic lights in hopes of being paid for their services. The "broken windows" policy was therefore literally infrastructural, in the sense that its paradigmatic sites were subway turnstiles and street intersections. But more importantly, it was infrastructural in the sense that, as boundary conditions, windows—both real and imaginary—served as gateways that, like Maxwell's demon, separated out two states of being—one orderly, the other disorderly—and with them two subject categories.[5]

A window, here, is a threshold between environmental order and environmental disorder that takes the form of what Kelling and Wilson call a "signal." It is also, in their account, a filter between orderly and disorderly beings, "not," as they say, "violent people, nor, necessarily, criminals, but disreputable or obstreperous or unpredictable people: panhandlers, drunks, addicts, rowdy teenagers, prostitutes, loiterers, the mentally disturbed" (Kelling & Wilson, 1982). More generally, a window is a filter between "regulars," who follow the rules (and who "know their place"), and "strangers," who are viewed with suspicion (Kelling & Wilson, 1982). Regulars do not break windows; strangers might. Urbanists will recognize these categories and the forms of surveillance to which they correspond as the "eyes on the street" promoted by Jane Jacobs and the "defensible space" of Oscar Newman. To be sure, such distinctions, and such ways of ordering the world—backed up as they are by an armed police force—invite a Foucauldian reading that rightly emphasizes their social and discursive production. But equally, they invite a reading that takes the distinction between order and disorder as literally as Kelling and Wilson's would-be criminals supposedly take a broken window and, like "strangers" out to have some "fun" by smashing things up, addresses that distinction on the aesthetic plane.

For what is aesthetics here but a struggle between Apollonian order and Dionysian "intoxication," between sanitized "dreams" enforced by the police and "the tumultuous, wild chase across all the scales of the soul under the influence of narcotic stimulants or when the drives of spring are unleashed"? (Nietzsche, 1999, p. 122). That these words are Friedrich Nietzsche's reminds us that the sobriety of social science is underpinned by a will to power that rests, to some considerable degree, on aesthetic foundations. That is, the foundations of social science remain embedded in the interplay of imagistic dreams and libidinal intoxication. Breaking windows is "fun," but for whom? For "disreputable or obstreperous or unpredictable people"? Or in the imaginaries of those who wish, above all, to tame the sublime fear of such people—the fear of strangers—through the boundless agencies of art, which in this case entails nothing less than the ordering of the world?

A Foucauldian reading of "broken windows" discourse also emphasizes that the subject of the "criminal" is, to a significant degree, produced by the discourse of the police, just as the "delinquent" is an outcome—rather than an a priori category—of the carceral apparatus around which Foucault centers his account of the disciplinary society.[6] But, compelling as it is, this does not fully explain the mixture of pleasure and pain—the calculated mixture of what Kelling and Wilson call "fun" and what Becker calls "cost"—around which police discourse is organized. For this mixture is surplus to Foucauldian power-knowledge, which nevertheless remains among its constituent conditions.

In an attempt to account for what he calls the "taming of the tenements," or of the city's persistent threats, Glaeser notes the more than threefold increase in incarceration that ran parallel to the implementation of "broken windows" policies nationwide, and observes that

> [m]illions of young men have been brought into the prison system for non-violent drug crimes. Some of these men would have done worse things if they had been free, and their incarceration helped reduce crime rates. But many of them would have led perfectly productive lives. The loss of their freedom and future prospects is the terrible price of reducing crime rates by increasing incarceration rates.
>
> *(Glaeser, 2011, p. 111)*

Revising the cost-benefit schema, Glaeser suggests, in effect, optimizing for p (probability of conviction) instead of f (severity of punishment) by increasing the number of police in the streets, as New York City did during the 1990s, an investment on the part of the state that he speculates is "at least as cost-effective as longer prison stays" (Glaeser, 2011, p. 111). To this he adds relatively low-cost examples of optimizing for more efficient policing through enhanced surveillance technologies and the face-to-face approach of enlisting community members in the process, a technique known as "community policing" (Glaeser, 2011, pp. 112–113).

Glaeser makes these recommendations in a popular book titled *Triumph of the City*, in which the overall message is that the benefits of urbanization outweigh its costs. As with crime, so with everything else; cities are brimming with entrepreneurs, including would-be criminals. Adjust the equations to incentivize compliance. Minimize cost, but invest wisely in disincentives when necessary. Moreover, in Glaeser's eyes, cities are a good investment for another, related reason, for they are populated by human capital, or what Foucault called "abilities-machines" (Foucault, 2008, p. 229). In a near parody, Glaeser speaks of the "concentrated talent" of the big city and celebrates the resourceful, bootstrapping entrepreneurialism of those living in Rio de Janeiro's favelas who, as rural-to-urban migrants or descendants thereof, are following a "path to prosperity" that nevertheless brings "fortune to some and suffering to others" (Glaeser, 2011, p. 116, 75). Committed as he is to an actuarial language of pros and cons, which he names the "urban paradox" for its naturalizing of the coexistence of wealth and squalor, Glaeser repeatedly concludes that, from a societal point of view, cities, rather than villages or suburbs, represent the investment most likely to pay off, by making us "richer, smarter, greener, healthier, and happier," as his book's subtitle would have it.

In this subtitle, and in Glaeser's discourse more generally, we find telling evidence of an advance in the career of neoliberalism from that which Foucault sketched out so vividly in his lectures at the Collège de France in 1978–1979 under the title "The Birth of Biopolitics." There, Foucault speaks of "abilities-machines" when discussing Becker's work on criminality and on human capital as exemplifying the emergence of a neoliberal *homo oeconomicus*, especially in linking investment to education. Foucault asks, "What constitutes this investment that forms an abilities-machine?" He answers that it can mean hours spent by a mother with her child, or "the simple time parents spend feeding their children, or giving them affection as an investment which can form human capital" (Foucault, 2008, p. 229). Foucault, like Becker, sees this investment as primarily instrumental or utilitarian in character, wherein "abilities" are constituted functionally by being operationalized: parental affection leads, indirectly, to enhanced economic performance. Family life, education, health care, and mobility all extend economic rationality—the production of human capital—into realms previously taken as extraeconomic, if not existential, in nature. Hence, for example,

> [m]igration is an investment; the migrant is an investor. He is an entrepreneur of himself who incurs expenses by investing to obtain some kind of improvement. The mobility of a population and its ability to make choices of mobility as investment choices for improving income enable the phenomena of migration to be brought back into economic analysis, not as pure and simple effects of economic mechanisms which extend beyond individuals and which, as it were, bind them to an immense machine which they do not control, but as behavior in terms of individual enterprise, of enterprise of oneself with investments and incomes.
>
> (*Foucault, 2008, p. 230*)

The neoliberal extension of such entrepreneurialism to the level of populations and its generalization into extraeconomic spheres partially explain why Foucault titled his lectures "The Birth of Biopolitics" and yet spent most of the year on economic theory, barely touching on biopolitics as it is classically understood (a failure for which he repeatedly apologizes in the lectures). It also correlates with Glaeser's paean to rural-to-urban migration as the "path to prosperity." But Foucault's underlying productivism (we could even say functionalism) does not fully explain the qualitative rather than purely quantitative rewards promised by urbanization according to Glaeser, for whom an urban population is, yes, a "richer" one but a "smarter, greener, healthier, and happier" one as well.

In a subsequent interview, Glaeser, whose father was an architecture curator at the Museum of Modern Art in New York, deflected a question regarding neighborhood preservation with a disclaimer: "One of the beauties of being an economist, rather than an architect, is I have no standing on aesthetic issues" (Jenkins, 2015). On the contrary: standing on the side of order, he, with Becker, Kelling, Wilson, Bratton, and a host of others in the background, continues to build a politico-economico-aesthetic discourse, with associated policies, around taming the drunken delinquents and addicts of the postglobal city. In its most recent form, which Glaeser's work exemplifies, this discourse converts the calculating, Apollonian, rationally choosing *homo oeconomicus* into an intoxicated Dionysian god. Disclaimers notwithstanding, this new Dionysus is racially marked, a fact that connects the aesthetics of neoliberal urbanism—fixing broken windows—with police violence that targets young Black men and the disproportionate incarceration rates that come with it.

In 1979, in France, Foucault said of traditional racism that, when compared to the calculations of investment in human capital (he gives the example of sociotechnological genetic selection), "while something to be feared," it "does not seem to me to be the major political issue at the moment" (Foucault, 2008, pp. 228–229). But Foucault underestimated the constitutive role played by race in elaborating the concept of human capital in the first place. Becker concludes *The Economics of Discrimination*, an early, market-based study of racial discrimination first published in 1957 and revised in 1971, with a laconic summary: employers and employees have variable "tastes for discrimination" that lead them to incur various "non-pecuniary, psychic costs." A "discrimination coefficient" can be formulated from these variables. These coefficients are, in turn, "influenced by more fundamental variables," which may be inferred "[b]y relating discrimination coefficients to an economic analysis of price determination through the market mechanism" (Becker, 1971, pp. 153–154). Correlating such variables with others, such as the relative concentrations of Black and white populations in certain job markets, relative levels of education, residential segregation, and so on, Becker produces "a case study in the quantitative analysis of non-pecuniary variables" (Becker, 1971, p. 162).

Amadou Diallo was a 23-year-old Guinean immigrant, described by the *New York Times* as a "street peddler," who was actually a subject of entrepreneurial mobility and, as such, a unit of human capital preparing to study computer programming in New York (Starr, 2014). On a February night in 1999, he was struck by 19 of 41 police bullets while standing in his doorway in the Bronx, reaching for his wallet. Diallo was from the postcolony; it is therefore possible, likely even, that his reaching for his wallet was a gesture of deference to the state, an instance of interpellation that reflected the fatal misrecognition of one form of racially profiled policing— the one that checks your papers—for another, which fixes windows.

Georg Simmel wrote of the window that, unlike the door, its "teleological emotion . . . is directed almost exclusively from inside to outside: it is there for looking out, not for looking in" (Simmel, 1994, p. 8). Walter Benjamin would later reverse this teleology in glimpses through shop windows along history's "one-way street," which ended in an apocalyptic planetarium.[7] "Broken windows" policing neutralizes that teleology. As a "signal," a window, broken or unbroken, is there to be *looked at* and decoded rather than looked through. But it is also a "thing" that gathers and locates. Heidegger complained that the "nature of the thing" is all too often understated: "The consequence, in the course of Western thought, is that the thing is represented as an unknown X to which properties are attached" (Heidegger, 2001, p. 151). Neoliberal thought has anticipated this critique by assimilating the pecuniary *and* nonpecuniary variables in its equations, like the broken or unbroken window, f and p, on and off, one and zero, to an aesthetics that binds these variables to a symbolic order where the presence of order as such, and not the meaning of the symbols, is what matters. A broken window means nothing; it simply constitutes a signifying environment.[8] The same holds for a threshold or boundary condition that is in danger of being violated by strangers who belong neither inside or out; it ceases to function as a passage and becomes a screen. "Broken windows" discourse directs police attention to anyone who lingers on this screen as though on an endless bridge or in a revolving door (Siegert, 2015, pp. 201–203).

The white plain-clothes officers who emerged from a car on a darkened street and killed Diallo were members of the Street Crimes Unit (SCU) of the New York Police Department. The SCU had been enhanced by the Giuliani administration under Police Commissioner William Bratton, an admirer of Kelling's and the city's chief proponent of "broken windows" or "zero-tolerance" policing, and it was further expanded and oriented around "stop-and-frisk" policing by Bratton's successor, William Safir (Harcourt, 2001, p. 50). In the ensuing trial, the officer who had first noticed Diallo testified that the young man, who was standing in the vestibule of his building, fit the description of a known serial rapist and was behaving suspiciously, like a would-be robber. The officer acknowledged that he and his colleagues did not consider that Diallo might have lived there; nor did they consider the situation from Diallo's point of view (Fritsch, 2000). We can infer, then, that Diallo appeared to these police, who at that moment were subjects of the "broken windows" apparatus, just as he was, as a stranger marked by his race, his gender, his location in the city, and his position at the threshold between inside and outside—a "window" about to break.

Is it perverse to analyze this tragic scene from an aesthetic point of view? No, not if an aesthetic of urban order partly accounts for its outcome. Such an accounting cannot be summarized in the risk-and-reward variables laid out in equations by economists like Becker, but it lurks within them nonetheless; not simply because these equations set the stage for a neoliberal police, and the associated reordering of the urban realm, that recasts its subjects—citizens and would-be criminals alike—as *homo oeconomicus*, and therefore as subjects of capital; but also because it recasts *homo oeconomicus*, and also the "abilities-machines" of human capital in whom Foucault saw the embodiment of socially constructed economic rationality, as potentially "disreputable or obstreperous or unpredictable." Intoxicated by repeated encounters with such disorderly figures, aesthetics issues forth from the night, gun in hand, and fires.

Notes

1. Reinhold Martin, *The Urban Apparatus: Mediapolitics and the City* (Minneapolis: University of Minnesota Press, 2016). Reprinted by permission.
2. Michel Foucault, *The Birth of Biopolitics* (2008, p. 252). In contrast, David Harvey, in *A Brief History of Neoliberalism* (2007), focuses his account more consistently on neoliberal political ideology.
3. On "order maintenance" and constructivist social theory, see Bernhard E. Harcourt, *Illusion of Order* (2001, pp. 38–41).
4. On the utilitarianism of neoliberal thought in Gary S. Becker and Theodor W. Schultz, see Michel Feher, "Self-Appreciation; or, The Aspirations of Human Capital" (2009, pp. 21–41).
5. On "broken windows" policing and the formation of "orderly" and "disorderly" subjects, see Harcourt, *Illusion of Order* (2001, pp. 127–184).
6. For a compellingly detailed Foucauldian analysis along these lines, see Harcourt, *Illusion of Order* (2001, esp. pp. 150–159).
7. Walter Benjamin, "One-Way Street" (1996). On windows as thresholds, see also Georges Teyssot, *A Topology of Everyday Constellations*, esp. chap. 8, "Windows and Screens," (2013, pp. 251–284).
8. On neoliberalism and "environmental technology," see Foucault (2008, p. 259).

References

Becker, G.S. (1971). *The Economics of Discrimination* (2nd ed.). Chicago, IL: University of Chicago Press.
Becker, G.S. (1974). Crime and Punishment: An Economic Approach. In G.S. Becker & W.M. Landes (Eds.), *Essays in the Economics of Crime and Punishment* (pp. 1–54). Cambridge, MA: National Bureau of Economic Research.

Benjamin, W. (1996). One-Way Street. In *Walter Benjamin: Selected Writings* (M.W. Jennings, Ed.; E. Jephcott, Trans.; Vol. 1, pp. 444–448). Cambridge, MA: Harvard University Press.

Feher, M. (2009, Winter). Self-Appreciation; Or, The Aspirations of Human Capital. *Public Culture, 21*(1), 21–41.

Foucault, M. (2008). *The Birth of Biopolitics: Lectures at the Collège de France, 1978–1979* (G. Burchell, Trans.). New York, NY: Palgrave Macmillan.

Fritsch, J. (2000, February 26). The Diallo Verdict: The Overview; 4 Officers in Diallo Shooting Are Acquitted of All Charges. *The New York Times*. Retrieved from www.nytimes.com/2000/02/26/nyregion/diallo-verdict-overview-4-officers-diallo-shooting-are-acquitted-all-charges.html

Glaeser, E. (2011). *Triumph of the City: How Our Greatest Invention Makes Us Richer, Smarter, Greener, Healthier, and Happier*. New York, NY: Penguin Press, 2011.

Harcourt, B.E. (2001). *Illusion of Order: The False Promise of Broken Windows Policing*. Cambridge, MA: Harvard University Press.

Harvey, D. (2007). *A Brief History of Neoliberalism*. New York, NY: Oxford University Press.

Heidegger, M. (2001). Building Dwelling Thinking. In *Poetry, Language, Thought* (Albert Hofstadter, Trans.; pp. 141–159). New York, NY: HarperCollins.

Jenkins, S. (2015, May 21). Edward Glaeser, "The Trials and Triumphs of the City: Edward Glaeser in Conversation". *The Guardian*. Retrieved from www.theguardian.com/cities/2015/may/21/what-are-cities-doing-so-right-and-so-wrong-the-experts-go-head-to-head

Katyal, N.K. (2002). Architecture as Crime Control. *The Yale Law Journal*, (111), 1039–1138.

Kelling, G.L., & Wilson, J.Q. (1982, March). Broken Windows: The Police and Neighborhood Safety. *The Atlantic*. Retrieved from www.theatlantic.com/magazine/archive/1982/03/broken-windows/304465/

Martin, R. (2016). *The Urban Apparatus: Mediapolitics and the City*. Minneapolis, MN: University of Minnesota Press.

Nietzsche, F. (1999). The Dionysiac World View. In *The Birth of Tragedy and Other Writings* (R. Speirs, Trans.; pp. 117–138). New York, NY: Cambridge University Press.

Siegert, B. (2015). Door Logic; or, The Materiality of the Symbolic: From Cultural Techniques to Cybernetic Machines. In *Cultural Techniques: Grids, Filters, Doors, and Other Articulations of the Real* (G. Winthrop-Young, Trans.). New York, NY: Fordham University Press.

Simmel, G. (1994). Bridge and Door (M. Ritter, Trans.). *Theory, Culture, and Society, 11*(1), 5–10.

Starr, A. (2014, February 5). How the Legacy of Amadou Diallo Lives on in New York's Immigrant Community. *The World, Public Radio International*. Retrieved from www.pri.org/stories/2014-02-05/how-legacy-amadou-diallo-lives-new-yorks-immigrant-community.

Teyssot, G. (2013). *A Topology of Everyday Constellations*. Cambridge, MA: The MIT Press.

6
ARCHITECTURE AND THE CRITICAL PROJECT

Sven-Olov Wallenstein

No discussion of the vicissitudes of "critical theory" in modern architecture can exclude the impact of Manfredo Tafuri; read and misread, contested, rejected, declared a thing of the past, he still informs many of our current questions. Tafuri draws on a wide array of often conflicting influences: Marx and Nietzsche, Adorno and Benjamin, Heidegger, Simmel, Weber, and the classic texts of German sociology from the first decades of the 20th century, and all of these divergent traditions are brought together in a way that appears more as a violent enactment of tensions than a synthesis. Thus, it would be misleading to reduce his work to one single figure or formula; it is rather a fusion of several motifs held in a precarious balance, sometimes entering into what seems like irresolvable conflicts. This meandering quality notwithstanding, there is something like a basic intuition that recurs throughout most of Tafuri's various stories of modern architecture and his attacks on the illusions of "operative" critique and history that scan the past for solutions to present problems, and it eventually folds back on his own writing: architecture, he often argues, is structurally incapable of solving the contradictions that it addresses, which is just as much a theoretical presupposition as an empirical observation. The nature of this contradiction, however, will shift, from the fairly identifiable dialectic of city and nature, subjectivity, and "Plan," in the early work, to the multiple and shifting forces that in the later work finally make the very idea of contradiction tenuous, and instead necessitate a plurality of approaches that only with great difficulty can be brought into a dialectical matrix. The following brief remarks will attempt to shed some light on the outer ends of this development, as it were, which can be taken almost as a staging of the inner tension in the very idea of critique and critical theory.

The Crisis of the Project

The initial project that we find in Tafuri's programmatic essay from 1969, "Towards a Critique of Architectural Ideology" (1969/1998),[1] which then was reworked in systematic fashion four years later in *Progetto e utopia*, was to confront the discourse of architecture with the material contradictions of reality, to which architecture offers only imaginary solutions. Already the year before, in *Teorie e storia dell'architettura*, he had launched a critique of what he termed an "operative" critique and history, which uses historical analysis to justify the projection of a future. Operative criticism, Tafuri writes, "has as its objective the 'planning' (*progettazione*) of a precise poetical tendency, anticipated in its structures and derived from historical analyses programmatically distorted and finalized"; it is a "meeting point of history and planning" and plans (*progetta*) past history by projecting it (*proiettandola*) towards the future."[2] It would perhaps not be too far-fetched to hear as well connotations of the idea of "project" (*Entwurf, projet*) in existential ontology from Heidegger to Sartre (and even more so in the case of *Progetto e utopia*, where the first term in the English translation has unfortunately been changed to "architecture," which obscures the connection), which would imply that the project is a projection that aims for mastery and control. Tafuri's "project" thus merges several problems: apart from architectural design, we can also see traces of Heidegger's analysis of modernity and technology, Marx's theory of capital, the analysis of disenchantment in Weber, and the dialectic of Enlightenment in Adorno and Horkheimer. Tafuri can in this sense be said to ground the modern architectural project in an encompassing analysis of all the dimensions of modernity, from metaphysics and aesthetics to technology, politics, and modes of production.

Progetto e utopia is where Tafuri provides us with his most concentrated and polemically acute version of modern architecture, understood as a process unified by its inherent contradictions. The dense and schematic form of the argument is no doubt problematic, and the perception of Tafuri as a totalizing theorist, even as someone who proclaims the imminent death of architecture,[3] is largely derived from this book; conversely, it is the only text where he presents something like a sustained analysis of the logic of modern architecture as a conflicted and internally broken unity, first on the level of the relation between architecture as a single artifact and the city and then, in turn, between the city and capital.

"To dispel anxiety by understanding and internalizing its causes: this would seem to be one of the principal ethical imperatives of bourgeois art" (Tafuri, 1973/2007, p. 5, 1976, p. 1). The opening lines of the book provide a condensed view of his complex and tortuous relationship to the modernity of architecture and indicate his rather bleak view of the capacity of artistic practices under capitalism to transcend the structures that determine them. Understanding the ambivalence that marks architecture in particular, Tafuri suggests, may allow us to understand the reasons for the diremptions and anxieties that haunt the modern subject, not only as a psychological diagnosis, but above all in terms of how they condition a whole discourse of form and design that in turn produces an illusion of mastery, leading us to affirm, even desire, the most troubling aspects of our existence as if they were an expression of our own will. Architecture, we might say (even though this is never spelled out by Tafuri), takes part in the production of a particular kind of subjectivity.

The introductory definition of the task of bourgeois art, to dispel anxiety by understanding and internalizing its causes, furthermore points to the unconscious entente between capital and the intellectual avant-garde, or a kind of malevolent ruse of reason, whose entanglement of sublimation and affirmation eventually reaches its point of culmination in the heroic phase of modernism. In this process, architecture, together with other arts, plays the role of trailblazer: in anesthetizing the subject (or better: by producing a subject that derives pleasure from being desensitized, from an "aesthetic" of a particular kind), it paves the way for another compliant subjectivity; it programs a new experience through a subterfuge that lets modernism appear as a protest against alienation and fragmentation while it in fact is one of the primary instruments for accelerating and rendering it not only acceptable, but also desirable.

Tafuri presents us with a long history, which goes back to the first part of the 18th century. Here the mimetic exchange between art and nature, exemplified by Abbé Laugier, enters into a phase organized around the city, which becomes the locus of a new type of architectural discourse that is made possible by a repression of its own conditions. When architecture assumes the task of shaping social relations required by the emerging capitalist order, it becomes caught up in a negative dialectic between urban form and the solitary object that will eventually dissolve the classical tradition. Throughout the 19th century, this process is inflected through the emergence of new architectural discourses that attempt to come to terms with the urban phenomenon. Architecture, Tafuri suggests, was in fact the first art form that was compelled to accept reification, and it faces the task of integrating design into a single overarching project to organize production, distribution, and consumption within the space of the city. This it did, however, in the guise of a "Utopia of form" that made it march backwards into the future. Tafuri divides this process into three steps:

1. *The creation of an urban ideology* that overcomes the romantic critique of modernity, which still resonates in the urban utopias of the 19th century
2. *The artistic avant-gardes*, which prepare the synthetic proposals of architecture in the form of seemingly contradictory and even destructive moves, which coalesce through a kind of cunning of reason
3. *The development of the Plan as ideology*, which Tafuri reads as the final stage of architectural modernism, before the advent of the Wall Street crash and the fundamental restructuring of capitalism, a restructuring that transferred the agency of planning from architecture to government bureaucracies and international capital

The project now becomes part of the capitalist machine, and utopia is relegated to the margins of architectural experiments that have little impact on the organization of society.

Tafuri's argument in *Progetto e utopia* rests on an unmistakable determinism, which in classic Marxist fashion, and in the name of a faith—never explicitly acknowledged as such, and yet surely one of its *operative* tools—in the linear development of history, a priori rejects all "reformism" as ideology and as a refusal to acknowledge the true problem. As Hilde Heynen remarks,[4] Tafuri analyzes all the theories that could be seen as attempts to redirect the development—the garden city in all its varieties, the American Regional Planning Association, Frank Lloyd Wright's Broadacre City, Bruno Taut's *Auflösung der Stadt*—in terms of a nostalgia for Tönnies's *Gemeinschaft*, and their anti-capitalism is scorned as a "rejection of the highest level of capitalist organization, the desire to regress to the infancy of humanity" (Tafuri, 1973/2007, p. 112, 1976, p. 122).

These hard and seemingly uncompromising statements in *Progetto e utopia* are mitigated considerably in Tafuri's subsequent work on modernism (leaving aside here the formidable scholarship on the Renaissance that would follow, which obviously complicates the idea of his work as following one single trajectory),[5] notably the massive two-volume *Modern Architecture* (1976/1979, with Francesco Dal Co) and *Storia dell'architettura italiana*, which is the last book-length study he devotes to the present.[6] It is as if the unswerving negativity of *Progetto e utopia* somehow was a necessary step, a way of getting rid of modernism's utopias and linear histories, by presenting them with the grimmest possible counter-version of their own claims, in order to free a different sense of history as multiple and undecided.

The Project of Crisis

At the other end of this trajectory, in which the initial claims were ceaselessly reworked, each time rendering them more and more opaque and self-reflexive, we find the methodological preface to *La sfera e il labirinto*, "Il progetto storico" (1980), where the self-reflexivity of the very language of critique almost at every step strikes back at the methodological assurance of the 1969 essay. Seen in retrospect, Tafuri's work thus rather appears as a constant self-questioning, suffused with precisely the type of anxiety that modern art and architecture, as he interprets them, once set out to master; it is a discourse that increasingly comes to return to its conditions of possibility, not in order to rediscover a lost foundation or project a possible utopian future, but to undo the nexus between project and utopia characteristic of modernity. In this sense, the crisis is not a given situation that motivates the work, but its own aim and *telos*: the crisis is itself the project (Biraghi, 2005, pp. 9–53).

The essays in *La sfera e il labirinto* develop themes ranging from Piranesi to the present, and in many respects they trace the same historical trajectory as *Progetto e utopia*, although without the linear narrative that subtended the earlier book. The larger theoretical claims that will be in focus here are laid out in the introductory section, which presents a set of new methodological perspectives. While continuing his attempts to develop an account of architecture rooted in historical materialism, Tafuri also introduces a whole spectrum of other materialisms—of the body, the signifier, of language and discourse—that give rise to many unresolved tensions relating. They all bear on the three terms that together make up the title of the 1969 essay that I have here drawn on as contrast. First, on the very sense of *architecture* as both heteronomous and fragmented, yet endowed with a particular distance toward the world that conditions it; second, on the role of *critique* as a form of writing that continually must question its own status and tendency toward closure; and third, on the status of *ideology* as something that cannot be dispelled as mere false consciousness, but in fact permeates the whole of intellectual labor, while maintaining the ability of the analysis to somehow situate and pierce through its veils to point towards its material conditions. Confusing, sometimes even contradictory, and more like the record of an inner struggle than a systematic exposition, his reflections stage the tension between the two terms in the book's title—the pyramid that transcends the everyday and aspires to a synoptic view and the labyrinth that throws us down into the messiness of the world—often to the point that a particular paragraph seems to be canceled by the following one. History, Tafuri writes, citing Carlo Ginzburg, is akin to a jigsaw puzzle that can never be brought to a conclusion, a labor of Sisyphus that not only results from the complexity and wealth of materials to be treated, but also must take upon itself the task of questioning the nature of the object, even the very nature of reality as such. "The real problem," Tafuri states, "is how to project a criticism capable of constantly putting itself into crisis by putting into crisis the real" (Tafuri, 1990, p. 9).

The "crisis of the real," its *krisis* in the Greek sense of division and splitting, does not imply any rejection of the claim that there would be a "real" as such, or that it would be "impossible" (as in Lacan's famous dictum *le reel, c'est l'impossible*).[7] Even though Tafuri occasionally seems to enter into the vicinity of the various theories of simulation and of reality as merely an effect of discourse that were emerging at the time, he ultimately rejects them, although not without first letting them infiltrate his own writings, which is one of the reasons for their meandering and hesitant quality, attributes that go so far as to make the texts cry out to be deciphered rather than read, more so than any of his previous texts. Ultimately, Tafuri suggests, for historical writing this is a problem of language, and the language problem he earlier had diagnosed in the emptying out of the classical vocabulary and the hesitant emergence of new ones at the end of the 18th century, now invades critical discourse itself. This discourse cannot avoid speaking a multiplicity of languages, and it must draw on a vast array of vocabularies borrowed from disciplines whose reduction to a common structure remains fundamentally tenuous. "Architecture," as shorthand for many overlapping fields, cannot be reduced to a language that would be its own, but can only be grasped as dispersal.

But is it at all possible to write a history that respects this multiplicity? Does not the act of writing necessarily produce a particular reduction, and more specifically, does the Marxist framework to which Tafuri—although with increasing distance—still adheres not require a concept of totality and determination in the last instance that must always override fragmentation, as merely a surface effect in consciousness, i.e., as ideology? The writing of history, Tafuri suggests, is always a production, an analytical construction, just as much as a "deconstruction of ascertainable realities" (Tafuri, 1990, p. 3), but that writing is itself implicated in the objects that it treats means that the historical project must always be the project of crisis as a goal to be reached rather than something befalling discourse from without. Still, in order for discourse to not just turn around itself, it must also point to that which resists its appropriating force, fracturing and implicating it while yet providing it with an object that still, no matter how distantly, promises a truth—a truth that cannot, even though there is no way to simply release it from the veils that cover it, be understood as just one more move in the space of ideology. Writing is a movement that loses itself in the object, decomposes and recomposes it, guiding a truth that remains just as elusive as indispensable.

Architecture, Critique, Ideology

What gradually emerges here, I think, is a need to allow three terms—*architecture*, *critique*, *ideology*—to coexist at the same level, which renders their respective borders fuzzy in a way that here calls for an at least somewhat more detailed comment. Rather than a critique *of* architectural ideology, which sets up a top-down relation, of principles and applications, subject and object theory and practice, such a proposal would ascribe a particular kind of agency to each term and provide them with a laterality of a different kind.

Architectural form, Tafuri suggests in "The Historical Project," should rather be understood as a boundary of the object that at the same time is a limit of language, imposed as an historical crisis that prevents any fullness of form, subjective or objective, from ever being established. There will be no unique name or term for this crisis, as Nietzsche, as well as Marx, has taught us, and "words that are petrified and hard as stones"[8] must be taken apart so as not to turn into the impenetrable monuments that are particularly erected by architectural history. The stones pile up, but it is neither sufficient just to tear them down again nor to probe the interstices between the rocks where new crevices can always be found, new subterfuges invented, and new games played; what is needed, Tafuri claims, is an analysis of the battle that is constitutive of space as a contradictory layering. This battle, however, cannot as such be dated to any specific point or event in time, as if there first would have been a harmonious order that subsequently was lost, which to some extent was the underlying hypothesis of *Progetto e utopia*—a kind of negative foil that Tafuri would no doubt have rejected, but which his narrative cannot help reproducing—where the moment signaled by the name Laugier was the turning point from which the dialectic of enlightenment evolved. The historical spaces that must be uncovered are now understood as inherently complex, made up of words, stones, technologies, and practices, none of which can be given exclusive priority.

In *Progetto e utopia*, the avant-garde was positioned as a transitional phase whose various forms eventually passed "the decantation chamber" (Tafuri, 1973/2007, p. 90; 1976, p. 98) of the Bauhaus, where they were tested with a view to their efficiency and capacity to become functional within a universal design strategy. Architecture became as a temporary link in a larger chain, beyond which the Plan as a comprehensive instrument was gradually transferred from architecture to the level of State and Capital, with the 1929 crash as the decisive turning point. Now, the claim seems inverted: the unity must be fractured from the outset, and progressive and regressive tendencies, anti-urban nostalgia, communalist and anarchist elements intermingle, cross, and fuse, to the point of making many of these projects impossible to locate in terms of political claims. This complexity in turn necessitates methodological eclecticism on the part of the historian, so that finally the very term "architecture," Tafuri writes, must be used in the broadest sense: no common denominators would allow for a clear-cut classification of all its uses and ramifications.[9] But if this means to destroy the "work," Tafuri cautions us that it is not done in order to reach something like the "Word," which he here associates to Foucault's archeology as it was set out in the mid-1960s, i.e., a set of rules that would organize "things" solely through the schemata of discourse. Instead, the avant-garde hypotheses must be seen in relation to the history of urban planning as the history of assemblages that span across the whole of the social field.

This means to undo the traditional role of the architect and, seen in this light, the proposals of *Progetto e utopia* appear less a series of statements of end and closure, and more an invitation to pursue the task of linking architecture (understood in a broad sense that includes technologies, models of organization, and planning), critique (as the project of a history that would be able to decompose and recompose the elements of the trajectory of modernism in a way that cuts across disciplinary borders), and ideology (as the element of thinking and acting that includes illusions as well as partial truths, and does not allow for a thought that would simply see reality as it is, since this reality is made up of subject and object positions that include the historian's own). What this analysis can offer, Tafuri writes, is

> an intermittent journey through a maze of tangled paths, one of the many 'provisional constructions' obtainable by starting with these chosen materials. The cards can be reshuffled and to them added many that were intentionally left out: the game is destined to continue.
>
> *(Tafuri, 1990, p. 21)*

Moving beyond Tafuri's specific vocabulary, and yet, I believe, following the path he sketched out, we could say that, in order for critique to become productive, it cannot refer exclusively to buildings, bricks, and mortar, nor simply zoom out and step up to another level, to environments and large-scale urban structures, but should, more generally, explore spatial signifying practices that also include texts, images, and various modes of representation. These all revolve around that kind of material instantiation that is commonly referred to as architecture, but also extend out into intellectual culture as a whole. This fluid status, which conjoins terms like presentation and representation, reality and its image, materiality and immateriality, is one of the reasons why theory and practice cannot be opposed in terms of, for instance, the intelligible and the sensible. There is always something sensible and material in all thought, architectural or other, because it has an embodiment that may take on all kinds of guises, but which is never simply an external clothing of an inner sense. Inversely, there is never something purely material and mute: nothing is simply *there*, in space or time, without extending out into the imaginary and the sphere of concepts, as well as detaching itself, if ever so slightly, from the temporal present. Just as all theory is already a claim about our way of inhabiting the world and prefigures an embodiment, all ways of being in the world have their horizons and apertures toward the intelligible, if there is to be a world at all—a world which is not a closed set, but exists by virtue of the gaps and porosities, the leakages and lines of flight that it produces inside of itself.

If architecture must be seen in an expanded sense, the same thing applies to critique. A history, Tafuri writes, that in this way reconstructs itself as a perennial transformation must become a criticism and a doubt capable of continually turning back on themselves; it is not a series of philological proofs, or the establishing of links between different fields, but rather "probes what appears to be a void", seeks the interstices between technologies and languages without suturing them into a signifying whole, and "projects the crisis of techniques already given" (Tafuri, 1990, p. 13), by which we should no doubt also understand the techniques of historical interpretation. But—and Tafuri immediately turns the tables once more—if there is no solution to the project of history as crisis, we must just as little simply stop in the face of the multiple, "in astonishment at the edge at the enchanted forest of languages" (Tafuri, 1990, p. 13). If historical analysis is incapable of demystifying per se, it is nevertheless part of a social struggle, and must risk a temporary "inactuality," which seems to detach it both from the past as a set of given facts and documents, as well as from the present as a circumscribed contemporaneity. While its immediate relationship to practice remains blocked, it upholds a place in the battle of space, and its instruments—we might say with and against Tafuri—while lacking any definitive instrumentality, cannot avoid being made to *operate*, become *operative* in a different sense than the one rejected a decade ago, precisely because they cannot, must not, form a self-enclosed whole that could be presented in a discourse on method.

There is an obvious relationship of this term to a whole tradition running from Kant and Hegel through Marx up to Benjamin and Adorno, but I would like to understand it in a more general sense, so that it comes to include positions that not only deviate from the legacy of dialectical critique, but also seemingly stand opposed to it, of which Foucault is one obvious example. What is at stake here is the sense of critique as reflection on our historical present—a history of the present, or an "ontology of actuality,"[10] as Foucault says in some late texts, where he explicitly connects his work to the Frankfurt school—i.e., a reflection that attempts to excavate conditions, possibilities, and limitations of production, which on the one hand is inevitably inscribed in the structures of the current world, and on the other hand takes issue with it, attempts to go beyond it, or at least taps into its contradictions.

In Tafuri's earlier rejection of operative history, the idea emerges of critique that destroys illusions and ideologies, but does not provide any guidelines for practice. In the later writings this stance is not simply abandoned, but made more complex. There is surely a distinction to be made—even though it must remain porous and allow for numerous breaches—with respect to time, i.e., between theory as a way of reading and interpreting architectures that already exist, either as past works that need to be opened up or as present ones that call out for judgment, and theory as a constructing, projecting, and imagining of a critical capacity belonging to architectures that do not yet exist. The relationship between past, present, and future is not a linear one, as seems to be presupposed when critical theory is deemed useless for a practice to come. It seems more promising to understand the time of critique like a complex loop: it is present work that makes it possible to open up the monuments of the past beyond mere passive admiration and philology, just as it is such a reinterpreted past that in turn strikes back at the present, because both of them, in different ways, come toward us from the future. The activity of critique, in keeping with the Greek etymology of the term, would be a splitting that tears apart the three aspects of time in order to configure them differently; it is an unhinging of time from its axes that allows how contemporary works to burst open past ones and lets us discern in them that which did not add up, but was concealed underneath their seemingly unbroken surfaces.

Finally, how should we then understand the term "ideology," which Tafuri never defines? It can no longer be in terms of a confrontation between discourse and reality—between theories (note the plural) and history (singular), as he had suggested in 1968—but must be done in a way that breaks with the classical *camera obscura* model proposed by Marx in *The German Ideology*, in which ideology gives us an inverted picture of the world, so that ideas pertaining to the superstructure and not material processes come to be seen as the determining factors. As a general theory, this formula in many respects seems far too simplistic. First, in a curious trading on metaphors from technology and physiology (which Marx is far from the only one to use), it appears to naturalize ideology; second, it makes the dispelling of ideology's mirages into the fairly straightforward task of reversing a picture whose content would as such be correct.

Instead, Tafuri suggests, ideology functions in groups (*per fasci*; the Italian term is certainly not fortuitous here), as can be seen in the case of the poetics of the avant-garde, which displays the full political spectrum, from left to right. This polymorphous quality, and the way in which ideology is capable of performing all kinds of functions, indicates that it cannot simply be eliminated by analysis, as if it were only a mirage to be dispelled by the clarity of consciousness. The distance that this sets up in relation to the earlier work is marked out when Tafuri claims that it would be useless to "tear into the methods of 'operative criticism'" (Tafuri, 1990, p. 11), at least to the extent that this would pave the way toward a restructuring of the disciplines. Operative criticism is ideology too, but as the analysis of project and utopia gradually folds back into the idea of an historical project that, itself, although without being utopian, must question and perhaps even negate (*ou*) its own place (*topos*), the distinction between the operative and the critical turns out to be far from clear. If analysis and project at present are divided, Tafuri writes, this is no longer just in the sense that had been suggested earlier, i.e., that the first would be unable to give precepts to the latter, but also, and more fundamentally, because the very project of history finds itself challenged, and any claim to the opposite means that it would be "obliged to betray itself consciously" (Tafuri, 1990, p. 11). The final page of an historical account must be taken only as a suspension, a "pause that implies ellipsis marks" (Tafuri, 1990, p. 12).

Instead of the established "texts" of finished works, Tafuri opts for a fragmentation that signals a constant "beyond" against which analysis must measure itself, and which produces the constant ruptures in modern architecture that the "monumental constructions of the Modern Movement" (Tafuri, 1990, p. 14) and its official historiographers attempt to cover over. To trace this process of fragmentation—and here Tafuri strikes a more recognizable Marxist note—means to follow the dialectic of concrete and abstract labor, intellectual labor and modes of production, and the history of architecture must relate both to concrete projects and their implications for a general history. This amounts to an "explosion" of the work and dissemination of its unities, all of which must become the object of separate analysis, and in this sense there can be no single methodology that takes account of the totality of the work; the critical act is rather a "recomposition" or "re-montage" that breaks the magic circle of language by showing its foundations, but also indicates the mode of functioning of this language, which is not merely that of a distorted ideological reflection that analysis should correct.

Here, the alternative that permeates these methodological reflections recurs: either we may simply immerse ourselves in the free play of valences, following Barthes and the *plaisir du texte*, or we must return to external factors. Both are to some extent legitimate: the former is the operation performed by operative history, which notwithstanding its claims to historical analysis floats outside of time and space, and forms a "mass of weightless metaphors" (Tafuri, 1990, p. 15); the second, with which Tafuri no doubt aligns himself, measures language against its outside, which, he underlines, need not be taken as vulgar Marxism that erases the specificity of architecture. The model here is Benjamin's "The Author as Producer," which suggests that neither form nor content should be taken as themselves essential, since what must be analyzed is the position of the work within the relations of production.[11]

At every step, this Benjaminian idea of production calls into question the capitalist division of labor, as well as signals the need for an analysis of "structural cycles," i.e., the way in which architecture is integrated into larger historical processes. This is indicated by the historical role of ideology, and the historicizing of its concrete intervention opens up a new field of inquiry: we must, Tafuri writes, "enter into the magic castle of ideologies" in a way that prevents us from being caught up in a "hypnosis" and an "engrossing game of mirrors" (Tafuri, 1990, p. 16). This means to "unravel the intricate and labyrinthine paths traveled by Utopia" (Tafuri, 1990, p. 16), which was already the proposal of *Progetto e utopia*. Here, however, there is also a different move that just as much must be accounted for, the "knight's move," as this idea was formulated by Viktor Shklovsky (2005), which is an idea significantly missing from *Progetto e utopia*. There is a "swerve" that gives the work a particular autonomy by taking a step aside from the real, producing an estrangement.[12]

It is useless to define ideology simply as false consciousness, Tafuri writes, since no work simply reflects a pre-existing ideology, which does not mean that the swerve is not charged with ideology; there is always a margin of ambiguity, as well as compromises that must be made for the distance to the real to become effective. Rather than a set of merely distorting images, ideology operates already in the formation of subjects and objects; its structures may just as well be feeds of resistance, it is never simply an enemy without (nor within), and critical theory has to account for all of that, without assuming that it can master its own contradictions. Interpretation, we could say, is itself *a second work*, and to excavate contradictions and tensions in the object is a creation, neither superior nor inferior to the first work, and it cannot avoid embodying contradictions that it cannot master. Neither work nor interpretation is the key to the other; instead, both have multiple points in common, though without being reducible to a third underlying matrix. For Tafuri, the critique of the architectural project in the end had to turn toward the critical project itself, the crisis of project eventually becoming the project of crisis, which does not invalidate the initial claims, but provides them with an afterlife that extends into the present and beyond.

Notes

1. Pier Vittorio Aureli notes that Tafuri's conception of a "critique of architectural ideology" and his rejection of operative criticism should be seen in the context of a new understanding of intellectual work, where intellectuals have become workers in a system that incorporates the forces that used to resist. Rationally planned and reformed capitalism, scientific management, and modernization became attractive options, and were identified as the new strategy of capital by the Operaista movement. The strategic invention of a "counter-plan" (*contropiano*) implied an appropriation of the most advanced parts of capitalist culture, all of which finds its echoes, Aureli notes, in current Italian political thought on cognitive work as "immaterial labor". This required that the architect and planner were understood as intellectual workers, and not just as manipulators of formal design solutions. Seen from the perspective of the larger political context, Aureli argues, the reading of Tafuri's work as the promotion of a "death of architecture" proves to be misleading. See Aureli, "Intellectual Work and Capitalist Development: Origins and Context of Manfredo Tafuri's Critique of Architectural Ideology," (2009).
2. *Teorie e storia dell'architettura* (Tafuri, 1968/1988, p. 161); *Theories and History of Architecture* (Tafuri, 1980, p. 141). *Progettazione* has here been translated as "planning," in other passages as "design."
3. The idea that Tafuri proclaims the death of architecture (made more emphatic by the drawing of Aldo Rossi, *L'architecture assassinée*, which became the cover of the US edition), was something that he always denied, even though it is occasionally difficult to avoid. For Tafuri's shifting assessments of Rossi, from the positive claims in *Teorie e Storia* about Rossi's *L'Architettura della Città* as delineating a genuine possibility for critical invention in the city to the negative judgment of the later work on the analogous city and its retreat into subjective fantasy, see Teresa Stoppani (2010) and Marco Biraghi (2005, pp. 185–197).
4. See Heynen's discussion of "Das neue Frankfurt" in *Architecture and Modernity* (1999, pp. 44–71), and of Tafuri (Heynen, 1999, pp. 130–137); cf. also Müller (1984).
5. This has sometimes been taken to indicate that there would be two sides of his work: the highly polemical readings of modernism that tend toward overarching theoretical claims, and the subsequent interpretations of the Renaissance that immerse themselves in historical details and "micro-histories" that would seem to burst asunder any possible global synthetic framework. Today, as Marco Biraghi suggests, there is rather a tendency towards a "*maximum* integration" of its various facets (2005, p. 6).
6. For a more detailed discussion of the intermediary steps, see my *Architecture, Critique, Ideology: Writings on Architecture and Theory* (Wallenstein, 2016, chap. 1).

7. The use of the term "the real" might be taken as a reference to Lacan, and Tafuri seems to imply when he wants to take a distance from the "Lacanian left" (Tafuri, 1990, p. 2). The meaning of terms like "left" and "right" is, however, far from obvious. Tafuri's formulation might be taken in the sense that the "left" would understand the symbolic order as historical through and through, whereas the "right" would uphold a more emphatically structural view that sees historical transformations of language as mere fluctuations, ripples that can never shake the great Law of the Father and the Signifier. A bit further on, Tafuri cautions us that the "privilege attributed by Lacan to the pure materiality of the signifier" should not be identified with any "infantile attempts at reconstructing a lost fullness for disenchanted words" (Tafuri, 1990, p. 6), but he leaves the positive meaning of this materiality unexplained. K. Michael Hays has attempted to formulate a systematic theory of architecture on the basis of the Lacanian symbolic, but only with a general reference to Tafuri's negative view of the resurgence of the "language problem" in the 1960s; see Hays (2010, pp. 1–21), on Tafuri 3–4.
8. Nietzsche, *Morgenröte*, No. 47, cited in Tafuri (1990, p. 7). Today, Nietzsche writes, we must, unlike the ancients who thought that they had made a discovery when they forged a word, stumble over rock-hard, immortalized words, and rather break a leg than a word ("Jetzt muss man bei jeder Erkenntnis über steinharte verewigte Worte stolpern, und wird dabei eher ein Bein brechen, als ein Wort."). The image of stone and petrification plays a similar role in Marx, where the role of critique is to set hardened relations in movement, force them to dance, by singing back to them their own melody: "man muss diese versteinerten Verhältnisse dadurch zum Tanzen zwingen, dass man ihnen ihre eigne Melodie vorsingt!" (Marx & Engels, 1976, p. 381).
9. "It seems doubtful," Sigfried Giedion notes already in 1928, "whether the limited concept of 'architecture' will indeed endure. We can hardly answer the question: What belongs to architecture? Where does it begin, where does it end? Fields overlap: walls no longer rigidly define streets. The street has been transformed into a stream of movement. Rail lines and trains, together with the railroad station, form a single whole" (Giedion, 1928; 1995, p. 90).
10. This ontology is opposed to the "structural analysis of truth" that leads from Kant's first Critique to the first phases of analytical philosophy as well as to the epistemological claims of early phenomenology, and instead understands the question of truth as situated, historical, and finite, as a series of shifting horizons that must include the present of the questioner. It is here that Foucault once more encounters the later work of Heidegger (and to a lesser extent Hegel) and the question of what it means for truth to have a history, without being simply reducible to empirical conditions, i.e., truth as a series of problems imposed on thought. Foucault develops this concept in several essays and texts from his last years, notably the introductory lectures in Kant in *Le Gouvernement de Soi et des Autres: Cours au Collège de France, 1982–1983* (2008).
11. Here it must be noted that Tafuri shifts the perspective of Benjamin, which in "The Author as Producer" is not that of the historian, but precisely the one that Tafuri wants to avoid, i.e., that of a partisan critic supporting particular forms of contemporary work. The context of Benjamin's essay is the debate of the period on the political efficacy of literature and on whether a formalist or the content-oriented criticism is the most relevant, to which Benjamin responds by declaring the distinction invalid.
12. This theme is already broached in *Teorie e Storia*, and as Panayotis Tournikiotis has suggested, in spite of the rejection of operative critique, it seems reasonable to reconstruct a Brechtian poetics between the lines. Such a position would be a substitute for the kind of critical architecture that Tafuri deems a priori impossible, and yet, a posteriori, one must be able to glimpse somewhere—if critical thinking is not to end up in a pure despair—an architecture that in a planned estrangement dissolves myths without offering any reconciliation, places us before impossible contradictions, and yet claims certain responses to be more adequate than others. See Tournikiotis, *The Historiography of Modern Architecture* (1999, pp. 214–219).

References

Aureli, P.V. (2009). Intellectual Work and Capitalist Development: Origins and Context of Manfredo Tafuri's Critique of Architectural Ideology. *Site, 2009*(26–27), 18–23.

Biraghi, M. (2005). *Progetto di Crisi: Manfredo Tafuri e L'Architettura Contemporanea*. Milan, Italy: Christian Marinotti.

Foucault, M. (2008). *Le Gouvernement de Soi et des Autres: Cours au Collège de France, 1982–1983* (F. Gros, Ed.). Paris, France: Gallimard/Seuil.

Giedion, S. (1928). *Bauen in Frankreich: Eisen, Eienbeton*. Leipzig, Germany: Klinkhardt & Biermann Verlag.

Giedion, S. (1995). *Building in France, Building in Iron, Building in Ferroconcrete* (J.D. Berry, Trans.). Santa Monica, CA: Getty Center.

Hays, M. (2010). *Architecture's Desire: Reading the Late Avant-Garde*. Cambridge, MA: The MIT Press.

Heynen, H. (1999). *Architecture and Modernity*. Cambridge, MA: The MIT Press.

Marx, K., & Engels, F. (1976). Zur Kritik der Hegelschen Rechtsphilosophie. In *Karl Marx/Friedrich Engels Werke* (vol. 1). Berlin, Germany: Dietz.

Müller, M. (1984). *Funktionalität und Moderne: Das neue Frankfurt und seine Bauten 1925–1933*. Cologne, Germany: Rudolf Müller.

Shklovsky, V. (2005). *Knight's Move* (R. Sheldon, Trans.). Normal, IL: Dalkey Archive Press.

Stoppani, T. (2010). L'Histoire Assassinée: Manfredo Tafuri and the Present. In S. Bandyopadhyay et al. (Eds.), *The Humanities in Architectural Design: A Contemporary and Historical Perspective*. Milton Park, UK: Routledge.

Tafuri, M. (1976). *Architecture and Utopia: Design and Capitalist Development* (B.L. La Penta, Trans.). Cambridge, MA: The MIT Press.

Tafuri, M. (1980). *Theories and History of Architecture* (G. Verrecchia, Trans.). London, UK: Granada.

Tafuri, M. (1988). *Teorie e Storia dell'architettura* (4th ed.). Bari, Italy: Laterza. (Original work published 1968).

Tafuri, M. (1990). *The Sphere and the Labyrinth: Avant-Gardes and Architecture from Piranesi to the 1970s* (P. d'Acierno & R. Connolly, Trans.). Cambridge, MA: The MIT Press, 1990.

Tafuri, M. (1998). Towards a Critique of Architectural Ideology. In K.M. Hays (Ed.), *Architecture Theory Since 1968* (S. Sartarelli, Trans.; pp. 6–35). Cambridge, MA: The MIT Press. (Translated from original work "Per una critica dell'ideologia architettonica". *Contropiano, 1969*(1)).

Tafuri, M. (2007). *Progetto e Utopia: Architettura e Sviluppo Capitalístico*. Bari, Italy: Laterza. (Original work published 1973).

Tafuri, M., & Dal Co, F. (1979). *Modern Architecture* (R.E. Wolf, Trans.). New York, NY: H.N. Abrams. (Original work published in 1976).

Tournikiotis, P. (1999). *The Historiography of Modern Architecture*. Cambridge, MA: The MIT Press.

Wallenstein, S.-O. (2016). *Architecture, Critique, Ideology: Writings on Architecture and Theory*. Stockholm, Sweden: Axl Books.

7
RUINS OF THE FUTURE[1]

Otília Arantes

"I Woke Up That I Dreamt"

In May 1987, Susan Buck-Morss, then professor of Political Philosophy and Visual History at Cornell University, after handing the original manuscript of a 500-page book about Walter Benjamin's Arcades Project to her editor (Buck-Morss, 1993), embarked for Moscow as a casual tourist. She was imbued with the idea that a visit to the capital of socialism in the 20th century, 60 years after Benjamin spent two harrowing months there, could perhaps serve as a purely visual epilogue—something akin to a final inspection, albeit conducted by dint of the situations that presented themselves. This "vision" was informed by her recently completed research, in which we learn that Benjamin once explained to Martin Buber, from whom he received a commissioned article about Moscow, that his intention was to depict the city in such a way that the factual dimension of the concrete manifestations of life in Moscow became in itself a theory, following a notorious recommendation by Goethe (Buck-Morss, 1993, p. 28). Without theoretical digressions, he hoped to extract from certain images of the city, its "internal position," including therein the political sense of the term. Ambivalent images, undoubtedly.[2]

True to his method, Benjamin preferably wandered through street markets and fairs, which spread a colorful display of renounced objects across the snow-covered streets: "shoe polish and writing materials, handkerchiefs, dolls' sleighs, swings for children, ladies' underwear, stuffed birds, clothes hangers" (Benjamin quoted in Buck-Morss, 1993, p. 29). During that critical moment for the success of the revolution, he was in pursuit of far more decisive indicators than production quotas—although without the latter operating in full swing, the objective of a society beyond scarcity would be unattainable. Once this threshold was crossed, the true purpose of the revolution would come to light: social, evidently, and not merely economic. Once material needs were satisfied, the scale of the revolution should tip toward community and cultural needs, were it not unreasonable to speak of aesthetic needs, which was in fact the case.

If Buck-Morss is correct, Benjamin was already convinced at that point that the ultimate criterion, within this crucial field, was the "vibrancy of collective fantasy" (1993, p. 29), whose signs he believed he could see in those unofficial street markets. That is to say, the generative vision of the Arcades Project, as much as its corresponding materialistic pedagogy,[3] had been crystallized for some time: the bizarre idea that "commodities here as elsewhere—like religious symbols in an earlier era—store the fantasy energy for social transformation in reified form"

(Buck-Morss, 1993, p. 29). Admittedly, in the Moscow street bazaars this transfiguring fantasy was expressed, in those years of the 1920s, in a pre-industrial form, just as the city squares had not yet been desecrated and destroyed by European urban kitsch. The ultimate test would take place as the consumption level equated with Western Europe.

When the author disembarked in Perestroika-era Russia, the last stage of this test was underway. She observed it for five years during consecutive stays, in which she witnessed the fall of the Wall, the extinction of the Soviet Union, and the first devastating side effects of the subsequent economic shock treatment. But the experience of the collapse of Soviet modernization was also an extraordinary proving ground for the interpretation schemes of her previous book, duly enlarged and free from the academic corset of infinite gloss of a timeless fashion, namely the idea that "the construction of mass utopia was the dream of the twentieth century" (Buck-Morss, 2000, p. ix). Such is the first sentence in the unusual book resulting from that philosophical reunion. It was as philosophical, in fact, as Benjamin's original impulse to seriously consider the rubble of mass culture in equal standing for the disruptive course of history.[4]

It is worth remembering—now in the Buck-Morss synthesis—that since Max Weber rediscovered the fundamental intuition of the Enlightenment, it has become a sociological staple that modernity was a colossal process of demystifying and disenchanting the world. In the company of the surrealists, however, Benjamin's argument went in the exact opposite direction of this presumed evidence of our time: under the conditions of capitalism, industrialization-urbanization would be responsible for a surprising *re-enchantment* of the world. Thereby, under the surface of a growing systemic rationalization, "on an unconscious 'dream' level, the new urban-industrial world had become fully re-enchanted. In the modern city, as in the ur-forests of another era, the 'threatening and alluring face' of myth was alive and everywhere" (Buck-Morss, 1993, p. 254). Thus, taking mass culture seriously and, subsequently, the producers of the "collective" imagination, such as photographers, graphic artists, and above all architects—who, in Giedion's opinion (adopted by Benjamin), had since the 19th century led architectural forms to perform the role of the subconscious in such a way that, ultimately, all architecture had become the house of the collective unconscious dream which enveloped the new world of commodities—meant considering mass culture not "merely as the source of the phantasmagoria of false consciousness, but as the source of *collective energy* to overcome it" (Buck-Morss, 1993, p. 254, emphasis added). Therefore, this truly outlandish project approaches modernity as a dream world, in turn associated with a no less heterodox conception of the revolution as a collective awakening from this mythical sleep.[5]

Hence, *Dreamworld and Catastrophe: The Passing of Mass Utopia in East and West* (Buck-Morss, 2000). The title could not have been more Benjaminian, starting with the use, in an unprecedented context, of one of the structural concepts of the Arcades Project: "dreamworld"; even if the real historical matter, stated in the subtitle, is a comparison between two competing, albeit interconnected, versions of the same systemic process of total modernization—East and West. In other words, an entire conception of the world—the belief that a reshaping of the world by way of industrialization-urbanization would lead the masses to paradise—had collapsed on both sides, contrary to what the common sense believed, anesthetized by the overwhelming victory of the West, forgetting that the ruined Soviet Union was no less Westernized than its Fordist enemy, at least since the times of its own Taylorism. Two forms of "dreamworld" were compared at the very moment of a false awakening. Just like the kidnapped Prince Sigismund in Calderón's *Life is a Dream*, the confronting masses on both sides of the conflict "woke up that they dreamed,"[6] strictly speaking, to a nightmare, a catastrophe which, according to the author, awaited us at the other end of the 20th-century mass utopia. Thus, "the most inspiring mass-utopian projects—mass sovereignty, mass production, mass culture—left a history of disasters in their wake" (Buck-Morss, 2000, p. xi). The book reviews a vast iconography of power, the remains of technological entertainment on one side, and on the other, forms of industrial work, vanguard aesthetic and political myths, housewares, and nuclear artifacts, etc. Always a dreamworld symmetrically mirroring the other, in order to disarm, once and for all, the shared stereotypes on both ends about the intrinsic antagonism between both systems.

Now for a brief detour in this incursion into the almost post-Soviet world: even within the monster's womb, the "dialectic of awakening" remained reluctant to extinguish itself. Perhaps one of the most astonishing "dream houses" (Benjamin) of the Stalinist era was the Moscow metro, to which Buck-Morss devoted two inspired pages (Buck-Morss, 2000, pp. 208–209), and which I summarize as follows. Each station was a total environment, combining architectural design, mosaics, and sculptures, all conveniently arranged to depict a theme. Everything, ornament and luxury, allegedly palatial architecture for the working class, and in fact an immense iconography of power, national even, or above all and anyhow sumptuous interior decorations for the fantasy of the masses, with access guaranteed by some symbolic kopecks. It has commonly been said that the wonderful subterranean world of the Moscow metro was meant to mask the tragic failure going on above that underground, a mix of fairy tale and *avant la lettre* theme park.[7] That much is true. Nevertheless, in those final years of the Perestroika, when asked about their childhood memories of that extraordinary subway, the Moscow residents recalled a magical place, whose phantasmagoria, which varied during each season, seemed ingrained in their daily routine. To them, traversing through that enchanted space seemed akin to entering a cathedral, except for the presence of the human torrent that dragged them absentmindedly, sometimes in favor or against, on the way to school. Our author still wants to believe that "socialist" dreamworlds such as this, precisely because they are so deeply ingrained in a utopian childhood fantasy, end up acquiring a critical power in the adult memory.

Thus, when reviewing numerous parodic images of the unfastening Soviet world, during those years of indefinite transition, the author saw plenty of defeat, but also nostalgia for a world that was "*supposed* to be." The argument merits a full transcription, in line with Benjamin's idea

(a)

FIGURE 7.1 Interiors of Moscow's subway stations. Photos taken in 2014 and 2018.

(b)

FIGURE 7.1 (Continued)

regarding the imperative need to wake up from the world of our parents: but what to do when parents of an entire generation never dreamt?

> The gap between the utopian promise believed in by children and the dystopian actuality that they experience as adults can indeed generate a force for collective awakening. This is the moment of disenchantment, of recognizing the dream *as* dream. But a political awakening demands more. It requires the rescue of the collective desires to which the socialist dream gave expression, before they sink into the unconscious as forgotten. This rescue is the task of the dream's interpretation.
>
> *(Buck-Morss, 2000, p. 209)*

A mercy vote or otherwise, in any case inflated under the arches of a real 20th-century Arcade.

At the same time, she notes: the mass democratic myth, of an industrial modernity, had simply become, in Susan Buck-Morss' expression, "a rusty idea," discarded by the post-collapse modernizations that similarly scrapped the factories designed to make this idea into reality. With the difference, by no means negligible, that the literally devastated land on the Soviet side corresponds, at most, on the other side to a "scenario of ruins," upon which postmodernisms at their peak would stage all kinds of *aesthetic sublimations of disaster*. The gleaming scenery of skylines framing social "ruins" of all kinds, from redundant living labor to derelict neighborhoods, traversing through the ghost towns of industrial unemployment, such as the town of Flint in Michael Moore's documentary,[8] not to mention the technological and infrastructural carcasses abandoned along the way of a Development that did not exist in the periphery. Or in the so-called Second World, starting with this other version of the awakening of the socialist dream: the so-called Chinese disenchanted gradualism, which, through its reconversion to market economy, left behind mountains of junkyard, ruined factories, as well as low-value workers, as seen in Wang Bing's film about the collapse of the Tiexi industrial district in the Shenyang province.[9]

Still on the topic of Russia, Stephen Graham and Simon Marvin wrote about a downright "demodernisation" in the 1990s (Graham & Marvin, 2001, p. 26). On this basis, what would the widely propagated Russian comeback of the Putin Era mean? What new bastard dreamworlds could arise from the ashes, in the middle of the 21st century, in a so-called emerging society, and invest their soul and social energy in other environments designed to house other artifacts of manufactured mass culture? For example, the 46-story City Palace tower designed by the Scottish group RMJM in an old industrial site, or Gazprom's giant Okhta Tower, and many other major construction projects, led by the Western star system, spearheaded by Foster as the largest building in the world, with an area of 2.5 million square meters—the Crystal Island—or the largest tower in the world at more than 2000 feet tall, commissioned by the greatest South African real estate magnate, Shalva Chigirinsky, etc.[10]

The book dates back to an earlier time and halts at this threshold. It registers only the growing and stifling atmosphere of mass cynicism, wondering if a reason still exists to mourn the perishing dreamworlds, ultimately compatible with terrifying agencies of economic and political power: world war machines, mass terror technologies, and violent forms of labor exploitation. Still acknowledging, of course, that such dreamworlds are outmoded, and yet the aforementioned deadly machines of power continue to operate (Buck-Morss, 2000, p. 276).

Ruins of the Future

Although Susan Buck-Morss' subject is the Soviet awakening to catastrophe, after an entire era dreaming of the upcoming era—as Michelet would say, seconded by Benjamin—her book does not arrive at the Benjaminian chapter on ruins, even if such atmosphere brimmed in those final years. According to Masha Gessen, after Chernobyl, catastrophe had become a Russian national obsession (1997, p. 24). Perhaps for judging, in accordance with the Baudelairian arch of the Arcades, that the Soviet fantasies themselves of total production, which so faithfully mirrored the capitalist dreamworld, carried with them, together with the Stakhanovist debris, the ruins of the future.

In this regard, it would not be farfetched to remember that Walter Benjamin,[11] although consciously reviving allegorical techniques in his Arcades Project, never allowed the baroque understanding of ruin, decidedly metaphysical and centered on the inevitability of decay and disintegration, to contaminate his materialist perception that the wreckage accumulated by mass culture is not a call to resignation. If the historical disasters therein represented are a harbinger of a possible catastrophe, inscribed in the very fragility of the social order, then perhaps there was still the possibility of arriving in time to activate, as he said, the emergency brake, or to erase the trail of gunpowder already set ablaze by the chemical weapons of World War I (Benjamin quoted in Buck-Morss, 1993, p. 125). Nonetheless, he could already glimpse the tragic end of that increasingly tenuous dream: as the 1930s drew to a close, along with the rise of Nazi-fascism and communist capitulation, and the mass dream market spreading to the point of expanding and disfiguring his collective dimension to the confines of the working class, Benjamin also inflected the course of his utopian hopes in that 19th-century tangle of stupidity and sublimity, premonitions, vulgarity, and self-parody. After all, those dream houses were indeed "armed camps with guns pointing in the direction of the Faubourg Saint-Antoine," as recalled by T.J. Clark when commenting on the "Arcades" (2003, p. 44). And also, at the same time alerting that those reservations of the marvelous were in fact pathetic enclaves of dreaming in a great desert of afflictions, and Paris was increasingly frightening, empty, disenchanted even—in the author's deliberately anachronistic terms. In retrospect, the 19th-century capital seemed less and less enveloped by dream and increasingly invaded by the *spectacle* (Clark, 1999, 2003).

FIGURE 7.2 Passage in Galerie Vivienne, Paris, France (1823). Photo taken in 2011.

In fact, this "other side of dialectics," which Clark sets out to decipher in authors such as Mallarmé, Manet, Cézanne, or Seurat, is not absent from that tangle of notes that constitute Walter Benjamin's paradoxical book. After all, we cannot forget that the character par excellence of the 19th-century bourgeoisie in that capital city was none other than Baudelaire. His task was not only to decipher the enigmatic character, which the poet had politically and poetically assembled for himself, but, more specifically, what would have led Baudelaire to suggest in prose and verse, precisely when facing Paris' most modern face, that all that luminous facade, sparkling brand new, reminded him of a *city in ruins*. In contrast to his contemporaries, spellbound by the splendor of that urban *rêverie* fresh out from the Haussmannian image plant, his response merged the melancholy of those who saw everything—"*palais neufs, échafaudages, blocs*" as in the famous verses—to become allegory, and violent anger, the destructive wrath of anyone willing to invade this world and ruin its glittering buildings.[12] And we know the Benjaminian solution to the enigma: at the heart of the entirely novel experience of modernity, the discovery that the degradation of the world, which had inspired the former Baroque allegory, was now rooted at the heart of a society exclusively producing commodities. "The devaluation of the world of objects within allegory is outdone within the world of objects itself by the commodity," as we read in *Zentral Park*.

Having concluded our digression, let us return to Russia: it would be no exaggeration to state that, in the midst of "demodernisation," the convergence of wreckage and commodity produced, on the one hand, the major business of the privatization industry, and on the other, an outbreak of apocalyptic prophets, headed by Solzhenitsyn's final incarnation as a doomsday professional.[13] The ultimate manifestation of the elective affinity in the degradation between the respective kingdoms of commodity and allegory, certainly not like at the peak of Baudelaire's Parisian High Capitalism, but in a land devastated by the extreme collapse of a mass utopia, as we have seen, i.e., in Benjaminian terms as outlined by Susan Buck-Morss.

Comparatively, we once again briefly review the Chinese ruins of the future, not only in the tangible manner as we face each other, thanks to Wang Bing's film.[14] Perhaps a Baudelairian predisposition—capable of reawakening, in the face of an extraordinary scenario of demolitions and buildings, an analogous allegorical feeling of a new urban age—may yet emerge in the current Chinese scene, inspiring a diagnosis of a much more comprehensive period than the Russian outcome. (For the time being, only retrospective, the latter awaiting perhaps for another Haussmannian furor, as in the construction fever days in St. Petersburg.) And yet, everything seems to progress at an unparalleled speed towards the impending catastrophe, as in the Soviet counterpart, even if times are different. In China's major urban transformation, both the cyclopean scale as well as the historical velocity of the process are so impressive that they assume frighteningly dystopian dimensions. A path, as we have seen, also adopted by Russia and, apparently, with even greater risks of a precocious awakening.

I am not, of course, suggesting any impeding disaster, much less implying someone's tremendous anachronism, as if "flanning" the new Beijing under construction, or the future (?) Moscow, brooding like the poet, "*tout pour moi devient allégorie*." In any case, there's no harm in remembering that, in the poet's melancholy when crossing the new square of Carrousel (impossible not to call to mind Tiananmen), there still echoed a downfall worthy of a Trojan disaster—his "*mémoire fertile*" still resonates as he thinks of Andromache in the poem's first verse—the vanquished Revolution of 1848, whose procession of massacres and deportations evokes throughout the poem and its emblems: African captives, exiles, defeated of all sorts, sailors abandoned on desert islands, in short, "*quiconque a perdu ce qui ne se retrouve jamais.*"[15]

In any case, whatever the scenario, we will be chasing something akin to the survival remnants of those dreamworlds, whose birth certificate Benjamin dated from the urban daydreams of the bourgeois century par excellence. And such it ended, as soon as the aerial bombings of World War II began to factually reduce European cities to ruins. In Buck-Morss' conclusion: with the war's demonstration of the intrinsic vulnerability of the modern city,

> the significance of the modern metropolis as the ideological centerpiece of national imperialism, of capital and consumption, disappeared with these air attacks. The planet's metropolitan population has never been greater. Its cities have never appeared more similar.

FIGURE 7.3 Demolition of Butte des Moulins for Avenue de l'Opéra, Paris, 1870.

> But in the sense that Benjamin recorded in his history of the city of Paris, there can be no "Capital City" of the late twentieth century. The *Passagen-Werk* records the end of the era of urban dream worlds in a way the author never intended.
>
> (Buck-Morss, 1993, pp. 328, 330)

The prototype "Paris, capital of the 19th century" would never be replicated. Even amidst the construction of the modern mass utopia during the brief 20th century, New York and Moscow could no longer catalyze the respective politically invested collective dreams in a single synoptic space—both in the world of industrially produced artifacts and in the built environment.

Conclusive chapter? If I am not mistaken, not yet. The awakening of such a utopian dream was not immediate, far from it. Although still more intensely dominated by the overwhelming spectacle of commodity, the newly born 20th century packaged new waking dreams of collective bliss—even those which Buck-Morss tried to settle the scores, traveling to the Perestroika-era Soviet Union, months after closing such a drastic diagnosis, ending the age of capital-of-the-century metropolises. New York seems to have been an emphatic case. Barely had the lights faded in the Paris of Aragon and Breton, degraded by Hitler's macabre tour, and the feeling that the capital of the new century was beginning in Manhattan was already unanimous, beyond the stereotypes of mere propaganda. Among the many coronations, the one by architect Rem Koolhaas is not only the most inventive, but its apparent entrenched extravagance reveals only involuntary affinities with Benjaminian archeology, radical politicization notwithstanding. His version of the capital of the first half of the 20th century distinguishes itself precisely by the fantastic delusion of the urban entrepreneur, prone to the most surprising whims of the commodity form. And the most intriguing thing in this remarkable intersection is that the "delirious New York," rediscovered by the architect's tardy surrealist imagination, is rigorously contemporary with Walter Benjamin's diagnosis of Paris during the Second Empire (Koolhaas, 1994).

The American Dream

A dream—a mass dream, no doubt—rises to the skies from Manhattan, where it will, as we know, ultimately crumble. In the meantime, nonetheless, delusional fantasies, paranoid even, populate New York (it is no accident that Koolhaas turns to the *paranoïaque-critique* of Salvador Dalí and the Surrealists to interpret this eruption/congestion of endless towers). From the top of these towers, one is able to see the limits of the island, inspect its domains, no pun intended, and perform *le tour du propriétaire*. A class self-awareness, engendered by a bird's flight, thus channeled "spurts of collective energy," acknowledged and delighted as in shared "megalomaniac goals," as if the ambitions of capital enveloped ordinary daydreams. In his view, an ambitious and popular architecture (Koolhaas, 1994, pp. 25, 10)! This may be the great American novelty: fantastic cities that expand upwards, where apparently a working class, increasingly organized and demanding, seemed to believe that it could finally wake up in paradise. And yet, nothing could be more unreachable, fragile, and threatening than these mountains that populate Manhattan (Tafuri, 1980): singular, anarchic, individual events—in a permanently unstable balance between each corporation and the collective organization of capital. All of which made New York, as Koolhaas aptly observes, the "capital of the perpetual crisis" (Koolhaas, 1994, p. 11)—as well as capitalism, of course.

The novelty of the blossoming American organizational capitalism was precisely to grant Rabelaisian dimensions to something akin to a colossal accumulation pattern. It is no coincidence that from it emerged the birthplace of the skyscraper, or rather, of the height race, inherent to the emerging typology towards the infinite mirrored tower, as the sky is the limit and endless accumulation, as an end in itself, the *hybris* par excellence of capitalism. Everything happens, ultimately, as if the very concept of a building that could scratch the sky carried within it a brand to be surpassed: until now, and still for a long time, the tallest in the world. And in this "world," the evidence of an ongoing "worldwide" competition, even at the time of its invention, the first specimens of its kind only existed in the United States in the last decade of the 19th century, more precisely in Chicago and New York. A "world," in fact, which at that inaugural moment mainly referred to a very specific social universe, comprising rival firms and the respective egos of their executives and shareholders. To which we could add the bewildered audience of ordinary citizens, who were as stunned by the regressive character of this medieval tournament as the inhabitants of San Giminiano during the emulation of the towers of the families that skinned them. No wonder Adorno and Horkheimer inaugurate their classic chapter on the "culture industry" with the example of the monumental and luminous buildings of the new corporations.

Nevertheless, at the same time a population allowed itself to be deceived by such demonstration of strength and inventiveness, as if they were its true creators (which in a way they were), experiencing a continuous state of ecstasy before this mythical island—in a kind of "exacerbated collective experience" by such a dream factory (Koolhaas, 1994, pp. 9–10).[16] After all, Manhattan is almost a transposition of another dreamworld, albeit real: the neighboring Coney Island, with the first mass-scale entertainment centers in the world; Steeplechase: a popular peninsula, filled with unusual attractions, such as an elephant-shaped hotel, amusement parks with all manner of electric-powered objects—the loop-the-loop, the shoot-the-chutes, the barrels of love, the mechanical horses, the Ferris wheel, the triumphal arches, and so on; and right next door, the inaugural model of all subsequent theme parks around the world, the world-famous Luna Park, a lunar landscape populated with needle-shaped structures—the first city of towers without any function—extravagant, arranged somewhat at random, in a "free style," according to the wish of one of its entrepreneurs, Frederic Thompson, predominantly East Asian, with spirals and lookouts. It was true illusionist paraphernalia, produced by the novelty of electric lights: "In the wilderness of the sky and ocean rises the magic picture of a flaming city" and "with the advent of night a fantastic city all of fire suddenly rises from the ocean into the sky. . . . Fabulous beyond conceiving, ineffably beautiful, is this fiery scintillation" (Thompson quoted in Koolhaas, 1994, p. 41)—the circus, the giraffe, the German village, the semiarid regions of South America, a hanging garden, named Babylon Garden, or the Gates of Hell, the Great Train Robbery, etc. As Koolhaas noted, "Luna Park suffers from the self-defeating laws that govern entertainment: it can only skirt the surface of myth, only hint at the anxieties

FIGURE 7.4 Dreamland Tower, Coney Island, 1906.

accumulated in the collective unconscious" (Koolhaas, 1994, p. 42). Meanwhile, Thompson, in his lunar office, dreamed of conquering Manhattan and for that purpose takes a first step, in 1904, when he acquired a block on Sixth Avenue.

The final link in this Manhattan genetic sequence is conceived by former senator and real estate developer William H. Reynolds: "a park to end all parks," fittingly named Dreamland—a post-proletarian park, according to him, appealing to all classes. A single deck, facing the sea, like a large ocean liner in which several walkways would allow 250,000 people to enjoy the entire complex. All amusement machines reappear once again on a monumental scale. Mini-cities replicate mythical European cities. Finally, conducted by guides in Mephistopheles costumes, visitors arrive at Lilliput, the city of dwarves, where everything is theatrically allowed, in a kind of "institutionalization of misbehavior," according to Reynolds (Koolhaas, 1994, p. 49). Or watch the Fall of Pompeii, the zenith of a series of simulated catastrophes—as if exorcising the anticipated catastrophe in Manhattan itself (Koolhaas, 1994, p. 51).[17] The end of the world was staged by way of a continuous fire, in a haunting, albeit circumscribed make-believe, which comes to reality in 1911 when a short circuit in the electrical wiring, assisted by the sea wind, spreads throughout Dreamland. The catastrophe was not announced until 24 hours later, as the press believed it was yet another Reynolds trick. The park was already in decline, he said, perhaps because he was unable to reconcile elitist taste and popular imagination. After all, as Koolhaas writes, "the potentially sublime is . . . cheap and unreal" (Koolhaas, 1994, p. 67). For Reynolds, disaster came in handy: the architectural beauty was being wasted. He, too, would transfer his energies to Manhattan.

The passage from these dream-cities to business-city transpires almost without any rupture of continuity:

> To support the alibi of "business," the incipient tradition of Fantastic Technology is disguised as pragmatic technology. The paraphernalia of illusion that have just subverted Coney Island's nature into an artificial paradise—electricity, air-conditioning, tubes, telegraphs, tracks and elevators—reappear in Manhattan as paraphernalia of efficiency to convert raw space into office suites.
>
> *(Koolhaas, 1994, p. 87)*

A Frontier in the Sky

And so was defined the reinvented skyscraper in Manhattan, within a literal fantasy setting in which access was, nonetheless, charged in very real money. A historically accurate definition, furthermore, if we recall the myth of the frontier and how it walked hand in hand with the territorial expansion of American capitalism. In light of this, it is not surprising that nation and accumulation become entangled, and that the 306 skyscrapers built in New York between 1890 and 1908 not only became the paradigmatic image of American architecture and urbanism—creating, with their unique and disparate forms, apparently irrational and programmatically unstable when compared to the maximum rationality of the original reticulated city plan, an extraordinarily unusual urban ensemble—but also the most eloquent discourse regarding the new business culture fostered by American corporate capitalism, in addition to hailing the efficiency of its real estate offices—from incorporation to project—in the exponential appreciation of the built space. In this fetishistic sphere par excellence, in which narcissism coexists with all the violence of the imaginary, in fact strictly "corporal" after 1930, the Empire State Building would reign supreme.[18] A building where at its top, as one may recall, the final battle takes place in the famous *King Kong* film—another monstrous personification of the American king size, which requires no further comment.

This hyper-dimension syndrome, intensified to the brink of an implosion presaged since forever[19]—lest we forget the archetypal gorilla arrived in New York shortly after the Big Bang on Wall Street—lies at the origin, paradoxically, of the source of the tallest buildings in Manhattan, and the no less important architectural ensemble, the most monumental, broad, multi-purpose, corporate, and presumably popular, of the time, with its open spaces, hanging gardens, etc. (a truly "pragmatic Luna Park" in Koolhaas' aptly fitting description): the notorious Rockefeller Center!

A city within a city. A center for work and recreation alike. A concentrated formula and supreme image of American power amidst a crisis. The symbol par excellence of the New Deal: maximally rational, an oasis of order, calculated in minutest details to generate maximum efficiency and earnings, situated on the most profitable square meter at the time on a never-before-seen scale of real estate speculation and land appreciation. If the Rockefeller family benefited from the crisis within an environment of scarcity and poverty, it also employed 75,000 workers and won the patronage trophy, in addition to creating cultural and leisure spaces, thus playing, from an effective and symbolic viewpoint, an important role in the economic revival of that period—as Manfredo Tafuri thoroughly demonstrated in his study of American skyscrapers (Tafuri, 1980, pp. 472–481; also pp. 461–483). However, the apparent impersonality of the Rockefeller Center—with its "colossal mediocrity" in Mumford's critical definition—perhaps represented, for this very reason, a model to be replicated and, as a result, generated the "formal disenchantment of the mountain," unlike the previous series of isolated demonstrations. The Great Depression seemed to have finally awakened Americans from their dreamworld. Although an undertaking of this magnitude would still harbor, despite everything, or perhaps for that very reason, a certain ideological residue of reconciliation of trusts and collectivity on an urban scale (Tafuri, 1980, p. 484), it was as if it had magically resolved all Manhattan paradoxes—or at least that was what Koolhaas intended when referring to it as a true master stroke of architectural cannibalism:

> The Center is the apotheosis of the Vertical Schism: Rockefeller Center = Beaux-Arts + Dreamland + the electronic future + the Reconstructed Past + the European Future, "the maximum of congestion" combined with "the maximum of light and space," "as beautiful as possible consistent with the maximum income that should be developed."
> *(Koolhaas, 1994, p. 178)*[20]

Perhaps it is no accident that such an ambition for magnitude, perfectly embodied in such an undertaking, is so deeply ingrained in the history of the projection of power of the American big business elite that the last chapter, in equal measure hyperbolic and paranoid about the Chinese scarecrow (to return to the previously suggested parallel), begins by paying tribute to an atavistic veneration for *bigness*. Still on this notion (among other related ones), our architect, Rem Koolhaas (once again), edifies a set of categories from which he claims to project, for example, the famous building for the Chinese Television in the Beijing Olympics—a double tower framing an entire media and business district, whose design imperatively refers to the Rockefeller Center, the peak culmination of his delirious New York—but which, above all, will allow him to map the *terra incognita* of Chinese hyper-urbanism.

One could say that, since that inaugural moment, the whole world then aspired to have its own Manhattan and enter the race towards the skies. It is therefore not surprising that when the Petronas Towers in Kuala Lumpur were completed in 1996, the American media were the first to register the narcissistic wound: for the first time since 1891 the tallest building in the world was now non-Western and no longer situated in the United States—the shallow urban-architectural

FIGURE 7.5 Rockefeller Center and RCA Building from 515 Madison Ave, New York, 1933.

Ruins of the Future 119

FIGURE 7.6 Petronas Tower, Kuala Lampur, designed by Cesar Pelli (1998). Photo taken in 2010.

sameness was obviously beside the point. Back then—today [2009], remote, according to the velocity of capital rotation—six of the fifteen tallest buildings in the world were Chinese. And to finally announce the upcoming Asian century, the American magazine *Progressive Architecture*, taking for granted that architecture is the field where major historical changes are deciphered, congratulated itself, on behalf of the profession, on the modernity and scale in likeminded businesses, on how the Chinese and other Asian countries were feverishly committed to erecting, competing among themselves, increasingly tall towers, as ostensible proof and pledge of a who-knows-what new ultra-modernism, developed at a futuristic speed. *In any case, the most powerful reason for shock and awe.*[21]

In one word: the *bigger* the better! Everything suggests we are entering a new long wave of cosmic phantasmagoria, equally governed by a new megalomania of epic proportions, driven by the fetish of "pure numbers, of abundance, of excess, of mere spatial expansion," in the words of Walter Benjamin commenting on Haussmann's Paris, but involuntarily glossing over the Faust of the last act of his "colonization" of the universe. We should also recall that, at the imperialistic peak—after all the Great War had just ended—of the first wave of capitalist investment in urban space, the Lukács of *History and Class Consciousness* had developed the idea of "reification," and all its burden of alienation and presage of an emancipatory explosion, while also reflecting upon the decided spatial connotation of the overwhelming abstraction in which the new social relations took place. He thus concluded Simmel's inaugural approach on the intrinsic link between the metropolis and the abstraction of the monetary economy.[22]

The compulsive Asian gigantism of our time carries with it the memory of the previous two cycles, or waves: the blank slate of the Moderns and the rampant American expansion, which emerged from the Great Depression. We are undoubtedly facing a mutation by excess—certainly an expansion to "some new, yet unimaginable, perhaps ultimately impossible, dimensions" (Jameson, 1991, p. 39).[23]

Outlaw Paradises

The current [2009] scenario is undoubtedly different: nowadays, in a planet devoid of capital, in the Benjaminian sense of a single center irradiating all urban *féeries*, a new homogenizing mythology resurfaces with all its petrified procession of *son et lumière*: the myth of the Global City. Cities, three thus far,[24] recognized by the celebratory literature on the subject, encircled by a competitive system of mobile hierarchies of cities aspiring to the status of *world cities* and, therefore, poles of attraction to host significant links in the accumulation chain. For or against, as conformism and dissent oscillate, urban forms known to be dualized, polarized, segregated, etc. However, by being total introverted spaces, such fragments of *"Luxe, calme et volupté"* spread across the meshes of these networks of beatitudes, carrying with them replicas that not only rival, but sometimes supplant the extreme urban design of the original matrices. All in all, and returning to our guiding thread, one could say that such *extreme spaces* came to harbor the aforementioned final endurance of the dreamworlds. Benjamin had entrusted his revolutionary hopes in their reversal through a disenchanting awakening and, while this may no longer seem credible, it has nonetheless become the concept-password-of-entry into the phantasmagoric universe of global wealth.

Let us recapitulate a second time. As we stand on another threshold—20 years after the dystopian anticlimax portrayed by Buck-Morss—we should turn and face the class dimension of those strongholds, once dreamworlds of the 19th-century bourgeoisie. It is not that Benjamin ever doubted that the arcades and their tributaries, the other "dwellings of collective dreams" of that golden age of ancestral kitsch—winter gardens, railway stations, wax museums, casinos, etc.—were a fantasy of intimacy forged in the worst bourgeois terms. His problem was the growing bourgeois colonization of the utopian "collective dreaming," whose vibration he had sensed even in the cultural rubbish of the century that embodied the spirit of that class. At least, that is how T.J. Clark understands it in the essay quoted earlier, in which he writes:

> perhaps we have come to a moment, oddly, when the other side of the nineteenth century dialectic needs to be reasserted: not only the wishes and potentialities threaded improbably through the negative, but, even more, what the century's proudest forms (its actual achievements) of lucidity and positivity went on disclosing of terror—of true *abîme*—built into the bourgeoisie's dream of freedom.
>
> *(Clark, 2003, p. 48)*[25]

A matter of emphasis, perhaps, but above all, of historical periodization. In fact, the more the bourgeois mask of those strongholds is decanted without becoming anything other than a present of crudest domination, the more somber becomes the Benjaminian reconstruction of the history of the dominated: a history without consolations, an "appalling montage of working-class poverty, exploitation, nihilism, and suicide." There is no redeemer, as it is necessary to separate materialism from bourgeois mental habits once and for all, and finally stop narrating the history of the urban proletariat "under the sign of redemption, with the Party or the revolution or the 'socialization of the means of production' as always the Messiah who will give suffering a meaning, a destiny" (Clark, 2003, p. 44). Signs of the times, no doubt. To be more specific: the post-collapse of now, which has lasted for a turn of the century.

FIGURE 7.7 Dubai construction workers. In the background, the tallest building in the world—Burj Dubai, 2008.

(a) (b)

FIGURE 7.8 World Trade Center, New York, designed by Emery Roth & Sons and Minoru Yamasaki Associates (1976). Aerial view taken in March 2001 and during the attack on September 11, 2001.

For it is on this other threshold that the most intimate truth of the urban houses of the bourgeois dream shines brighter, as the extremes of a new era stretch in its predatory purity—if one may be brutally direct—the new arcades of the present urban age of extremes, which Mike Davis and Daniel Monk called *Evil Paradises* (2007).[26] Two brief commentaries and I shall close this prologue to the world of dreams in the 21st century.

The book brings together case studies of what could be called a political economy of extreme space manifestations of luxury, in all their most extravagant variations. A geography of fantastic places where winner takes all: not even a remnant of social contract, not to mention ordinary labor clauses, in this inside-out utopia, where "the rich can walk like gods in the nightmare gardens of their deepest and most secret desires" (Davis & Monk, 2007, p. ix). Whoever said "it is glorious to be rich" knew what they were talking about, in addition to parodying Max Weber. From the crystal archipelagos of Dubai or Moscow, to the Olympic delusions of Beijing, to the private cities of California, opportunely cloned by Johannesburg or Cairo, from the Habsburg-style condominiums of Budapest to Medellin fortified by the "good drug," one finds alternative universes for privileged forms of human life.

Our duo of authors wonders if such a spiral of desires for infinite consumption, absolute social separatism, maximum physical security, and unrestricted architectural monumentality could still be compatible with the mere moral survival of humanity. As for the genealogy of these monstrous artificial havens, the authors do not hesitate: they descend from the same impossible mythical strongholds of false Victorian consciousness and their interiors upholstered by the worst of intentions. No more, nor less than the aforementioned *Dreamworlds*. Such dream houses, reoriented in their original murderous direction, were emphasized by the aforementioned precise philological commentary of T.J. Clark as well as inspired by the current state of the world. For Mike Davis and Daniel Monk: literally *terminal*. In other words, the ghostly trickery of the towers in the United Arab Emirates or China, as well as the Olympic mega-structures in Beijing, shamelessly ground themselves on the massacring labor of a mass of immigrants, camped in indescribable quarters. All in all, such archipelagos of utopian luxury and supreme lifestyles are cocoons of armed anxiety, on a planet of slummed megacities. The price of these dreamworlds is the human catastrophe, which can be measured by the blazing speed in which they desperately try to consume, in the course of a lifetime, all the good things of a land on the verge of depletion.

Not much remains for the old Benjaminian hope for emancipation, fueled in principle by the utopian dimension of such fantasies in their earliest times. As reiterated, this river has dried up. The constellation of such extreme urban formations thus maps the "terminal, not anticipatory, stages in the history of late modernity" (Davis & Monk, 2007, p. xvi). Benjamin for a moment evoked a society that dreamed of waking up. In the technological paraphernalia of these ultimate dream homes, one readily ascertains: "They have no alarm clocks."

Acknowledgments

I am grateful for the suggestions by Paulo Arantes, and to my interlocutors, Adrián Gorelik, Laymert Garcia dos Santos, Roberto Schwarz, Pedro Arantes, Ruy S. Lopes, Luiz Recaman Barros, and Leandro Medrano.

Notes

1. This chapter serves as a prologue to a study on urbanization processes in Asia (Arantes, 2011).
2. Regarding this still innocent mention of the term *image*, from this point onwards it would be advisable to remember, especially when applied to the urban environment, the Benjaminian notion of "dialectic image." To be on the safe side, better to prevent common misunderstandings. Evidently, there is no point in reconstructing for the umpteenth time the entire debate surrounding this concept. As we may recall, Adorno, to quote just the most authoritative objection, saw in those so-called dialectical images nothing more than montages. I shall limit myself to quote Benjamin himself: according to him, extracted from their original context, these images, or fragments, would be capable, as "images that rise up" from the past, or from reality—as in Baudelaire's allegorical compositions—to undo the illusions and fetishes, such as the world of commodities, for example, fathomed in *Arcades Project* (Benjamin, 1999). In short, looking at history, the images would be nothing less than "dialectics at a standstill" [N 2a, 3]. And what he has in mind when referring to such dialectical images are not the harsh contrasts, but as he clarifies when writing about an adaptation of Faust, "the dialectical contrasts, which often seem indistinguishable from nuances. It is nonetheless from them that life is always born anew" [N 1a, 4]. Benjamin seems to want to extract this mobilizing force from the many images he collects, especially those that emerge from the past as allegories of the present: "But the rags, the refuse—these I will not inventory but allow, in the only way possible, to come into their own: by making use of them," he writes [N 1a, 8].
3. In other words, a historical evocation against the grain, not as mere memorabilia, but to allow the revolutionary class to disentangle, from the cultural residues accumulated therein, lessons for its political practice. (See previous note, see also chapter IX in Buck-Morss' quoted book "A materialistic pedagogy.")
4. Without ignoring, however, the commitment of mass culture to fascism, which leads him, therefore, to analyze it through its multiple forms and possible critical potentialities.
5. Within his approach to surrealism, however, Benjamin made a cautionary note by stating the difference between his *Arcades* and Aragon's *Paysan de Paris* (a book which he confessed fascinated him): "whereas Aragon persists within the realm of dream, here the concern is to find the constellation of awakening . . . the dissolution of 'mythology' in the space of history. That, of course, can happen only through the awakening of a not-yet-conscious knowledge of what has been" [N 1, 9].
6. In the (hip-hop) version of the classic Spanish baroque by the São Paulo theater group, Cia. *Bartolomeu de Depoimentos.*
7. It is no coincidence that Svetlana Boym, in *The Future of Nostalgia*, observed that the turn-of-the-century Moscow architecture is nothing more than a "second-wave native postmodernism," in a capitalist version of the communist revival (Boym, 2001, p. 113).
8. The film in question is *Roger and Me*. Another striking document of this world in ruins is the photo essay by Camilo José Vergara, *American Ruins* (1999).

9. In an interview, the director explained that when he saw such a premature industrial cemetery for the first time, he was initially attracted by those still-warm fossils, as if contemplating a "person's past ideals." When commenting about the filmmaker's strictly allegorical vision, Lu Xinyu noted that, unlike the Soviet films of the 1930s which celebrated refineries and steelmakers from the five-year plans, *West of the Tracks* is neither heroic nor elegiac: "Today the factories have become the ruins of an ideal. But the memory of that ideal is not extinguished in the film; it lives on in the majesty of these images, because it is rooted in the peculiarities of *this* industry and those who laboured in it" (Xinyu, 2005, p. 131).
10. Projects that currently—late 2008/2009—begin to have an uncertain future, like everything else, due to the major global crisis. Dreams of grandeur that disintegrate before they even begin.
11. As our author remains ever vigilant. See Buck-Morss (1993, p. 170).
12. For a summary of the chapter on ruins, see Buck-Morss (1993, ch. 6).
13. Regarding the latter, see the book quoted by Masha Gessen (1997). As for the fabrication of capitalism without capitalists in Eastern Europe, that is another chapter for another time.
14. Or in such films as Jia Zhang-ke's *Still Life* and *24 City*.
15. Regarding this interpretive approach to the poem *Le Cygne*, see Oehler (2004).
16. We are also indebted to Koolhaas for the descriptions of these dreamworlds, which were, in a way, "incubators of the Manhattan forms" on Coney Island.
17. See the entire chapter about the *Dreamland* (Koolhaas, 1994, pp. 43–78).
18. Fittingly, in Koolhaas' book (1994) quoted thus far, the Empire State and Chrysler buildings take on an anthropomorphic and even erotic dimension, as illustrated in an appendix by the painter Madelon Vriesendorp, presenting both buildings in bed, "*après l'amour*"—the interpretive key could be found, according to the author, within a "paranoid" fantasy (as we saw earlier, in a transposition of the method used by the surrealists, especially Salvador Dali, and at the same time theorized by Lacan, whose first essay, precisely about paranoia, was published in *Minotaure* magazine in the early 1930s). Also revealing is a masquerade ball at the time in New York, in which the elite of entrepreneurial architects are dressed in costumes alongside the Manhattan's skyscrapers.
19. Susan Sontag, in a 1965 essay dedicated to the "imagination of disaster," when writing about the "primitive gratifications" provoked by science fiction films that present "the depiction of urban disaster on a colossally magnified scale," only briefly mentions *King Kong* under the category of old monster movies, in which the Thing heads "for the great city, where he had to do a fair bit of rampaging, hurling buses off bridges, crumpling trains in his bare hands, toppling buildings, and so forth" (Sontag, 1965/2001, p. 214). After 9/11, of course, the horizon, as it were, cleared up, converging to a single blind spot. Induced by the *mise en scène* of such attacks as a catastrophe-film genre, which the American public had eagerly consumed in the 1990s (a decade of "unexplained anxiety," in Mike Davis' words), a whole repertoire of saturated images of fear and prophecy is re-represented overnight, as if confirming—as if necessary!—"a permanent forebonding about urban space as a potential Ground Zero." Among the countless presages of the Manhattan apocalypse (and we could promptly evoke Carlos Drummond's "1938 Elegy"), one of the first cited was a 1931 painting by Orozco, *Los Muertos*, "which depicts the Manhattan skyscrapers being broken apart like piñatas" (Davis, 2002, p. 3).
20. For an assessment of Koolhaas' unequivocally ambivalent point of view, or his "cynical realism" in the face of negative criticism, or the parallel between Koolhaas and Tafuri, whose texts on New York are almost contemporary, see the Preface by Adrian Gorelik to the Brazilian edition (2008).
21. In an article for *Revista da Folha Morar* (May 30, 2008, pp. 20–22), the Washington correspondent, Sérgio Dávila, refers to the fact that, from a list of the ten most renowned Western architects in activity, few will not have a project currently hired in China, whether concluded, in execution, or on paper. And that all of them, without exception, distinguish themselves for giving form to an ostentatious "delirium," whether through a conception in the project itself or the use of exorbitant materials, not to mention the barbaric scale of such *follies*. Furthermore, Dávila alludes to an article by Richard Lacayo, found in the May/June 2008 edition of *Foreign Policy*, about this extemporaneous proliferation of monuments to the newly emerging wealth, sown, not by accident (united by the same link of unrestricted power-making) by members of the global architectural star system, along a geopolitical strip that stretches from Gazprom's headquarters in St. Petersburg, and the Crystal Island in Moscow, through the Persian Gulf Emirates, to Central Asia (Azerbaijan and Kazakhstan), and from there to the Far East, not to mention the new enclaves of high-tech neo-cities in the Arabian desert. The question is not necessarily stated in this order and with such focus, but through the prism of the new division of the world, touted by the American neocons and recycled by the Bush fiasco: on the one hand, the league of liberal democracies, and on the other, the autocracy of the new semi-peripheral wealthy (cf. e.g., Kagan, 2008). The new delusions in concrete or titanium constitute what the American author calls "architecture of the autocracy," without realizing, however, that the designed imagination of each one was shaped exactly on the other bank of the river, the Western

liberal side, during the fading lights of the Modern Movement. We could thus ask ourselves, as the new world configuration ruminates, or rather, the "rise of the rest" in a decidedly post-American world, what is the formula of the new ideologues of American power (cf. e.g., Zakaria, 2008): involuntary parody of the former elective affinity of the Modern Cause with the developmentalist-authoritarian *ethos* of a certain "doomed to be modern" periphery, as one would say (cf. e.g., Arantes, 2015)? It would be grotesque if it were not false, as it would be pathetic to confuse Development with the current global migration of accumulation centers, although the literature has treasured Asian growth machines as Developmental-States, once, of course, the Age of Development had ended as a geo-culture for the legitimation of historical capitalism, as stated by Immanuel Wallerstein, for example. Notwithstanding, Sérgio Dávila titled his article "Architecture of Alienation," without further explanation. In fact, this is also what it is about, if we ultimately look at the unique dynamics of these post-urban modernizations.

22. See Simmel (1903/2010). For a commentary, see Arantes (1993, pp. 108–113).
23. The expression belongs to Fredric Jameson to characterize the postmodern "hyperspace."
24. At least in the strongest sense of the term. Cf. Sassen (1991).
25. For an idea of this new moment in history which, according to the author, would require a drastic change in the evaluation of those "dream houses," I mention his following book, published alongside Iain Boal, Joseph Matthews, and Michael Walts (Clark et al., 2005).
26. As we see, the subtitle of the book *Dreamworlds of Neoliberalism* is not a mere coincidence.

References

Arantes, O. (1993). A Ideologia do Lugar Público na Arquitetura Contemporânea. In *O lugar da arquitetura depois dos Modernos* (pp. 95–155). São Paulo, Brazil: Editora da Universidade de São Paulo.
Arantes, O. (2011). *Chai-na*. São Paulo, Brazil: Editora da Universidade de São Paulo.
Arantes, O. (2015). Mário Pedrosa Today. In G. Ferreira & P. Herkenhoff (Eds.), *Mário Pedrosa, Primary Documents* (pp. 68–72). New York, NY: The Museum of Modern Art.
Benjamin, W. (1999). *The Arcades Project* (H. Einland & K. McLaughlin, Trans.). Cambridge, MA; London, UK: The Belknap Press of Harvard University Press.
Boym, S. (2001). *The Future of Nostalgia*. New York, NY: Basic Books.
Buck-Morss, S. (1993). *The Dialectics of Seeing: Walter Benjamin and the Arcades Project*. Cambridge, MA: The MIT Press.
Buck-Morss, S. (2000). *Dreamworld and Catastrophe: The Passing of Mass Utopia in East and West*. Cambridge, MA: The MIT Press.
Clark, T.J. (1999). *The Painting of Modern Life: Paris in the Art of Manet and his Followers*. Princeton, NJ: Princeton University Press.
Clark, T.J. (2003). Should Benjamin Have Read Marx? *boundary 2*, *30*(1), 31–49.
Clark, T.J., Boal, I., Matthews, J., & Walts, M. (2005). *Afflicted Powers: Capital and Spectacle in a New Age of War*. London, UK: Verso.
Dávila, S. (2008, May 30). Arquitetura da Alienação. *Folha de São Paulo*, Morar.
Davis, M. (2002). *Dead Cities and Other Tales*. New York, NY: The New Press.
Davis, M., & Monk, D. (Eds.). (2007). *Evil Paradises*. New York, NY: The New Press.
Gessen, M. (1997). *Dead Again: The Russian Intelligentsia after Communism*. London, UK: Verso.
Gorelik, A. (2008). Arquitetura e Capitalismo: os Usos de Nova York. In R. Koolhaas, *Nova York delirante: um Manifesto Retroativo para Manhattan* (pp. 6–23). São Paulo, Brazil: CosacNaify.
Graham, S., & Marvin, S. (2001). *Splintering Urbanism*. London, UK: Routledge.
Jameson, F. (1991). *Postmodernism, or, The Cultural Logic of Late Capitalism*. Durham, NC: Duke University Press.
Kagan, R. (2008). *The Return of History and the End of Dreams*. New York, NY: Knopf.
Koolhaas, R. (1994). *Delirious New York: A Retroactive Manifesto for Manhattan*. New York, NY: The Monacelli Press.
Lacayo, R. (2008, May–June). The Architecture of Autocracy. *Foreign Policy*.
Oehler, D. (2004). *Terrenos Vulcânicos*. São Paulo, Brazil: Cosac Naify.
Sassen, S. (1991). *The Global City, New York, London, Tokyo*. Princeton, NJ: Princeton University Press.
Simmel, G. (2010). The Metropolis and Mental Life. In G. Bridge & S. Watson (Eds.), *The Blackwell City Reader* (2nd ed., pp. 103–110). Malden, MA; Oxford, UK; West Sussex, UK: Wiley-Blackwell. (Original work published 1903).

Sontag, S. (2001). The Imagination of Disaster. In *Against Interpretation and Other Essays* (pp. 209–225). New York, NY: Picador. (Original work published 1965).

Tafuri, M. (1980). The Disenchanted Mountain: The Skyscraper and the City. In G. Ciucci (Ed.), *The American City: From the Civil War to the New Deal* (pp. 389–527). London, UK: Granada Publishing.

Vergara, C.J. (1999). *American Ruins*. New York, NY: The Monacelli Press.

Xinyu, L. (2005). China's Rustbelt Epic. *New Left Review*, (31), 125–136.

Zakaria, F. (2008). *The Post-American World*. New York, NY: Norton.

PART II
Rethinking Spatial Rhythms

8
HENRI LEFEBVRE AND THE MORPHOLOGY OF A SPATIAL DIALECTIC

César Simoni Santos

Introduction

The widespread idea that the Marxist thinker's work "actualizes Marx's thought" or "resorts to the Marxian method for interpreting contemporary society" involves a trap. The hypothesis put forth here presents Henri Lefebvre as more than an excellent reader of the works of Marx, more than one of its prime promoters or, even, as more than a rigorous operator of the methods and categories of Marxian thought. We regard Lefebvre as a thinker who took up the task of redefining and developing, on a methodological level, the nexuses and structures most adjusted to the transformations he could also distinguish on a theoretical level. The idea that Lefebvre continues Marx's ideas is not wrong, but has helped to gloss over important dimensions of his work precisely where it presents its most innovative and revolutionary aspects; in other words, where it does not coincide with his precursors.

At first, with the intention of demonstrating the specificity and richness of Lefebvrian thought in the construction of a spatial dialectic, apart from the preface to the second edition of *Logique Formelle, Logique Dialectique* (1969/1983), two other moments of the philosopher's work shall be considered with the objective of highlighting the connections between the theoretical and methodological dimensions. The theoretical arrangements and connections found in *La Fin de l'Histoire* (1970) and in *Hegel, Marx, Nietzsche* (1975/2020) offer important subsidies for the support of an hypothesis presenting on the specificities of the Lefebvrian methodological perspective, resulting from a dialectical morphology or structure quite different from those found in Hegel or in Marx. Closer to the end of the argument, other works by Lefebvre, such as *The Urban Revolution* (1970/2003), *The Reproduction of Social Relations of Production* (1973/1976), *The Production of Space* (1974/1991, 1974/2000), and the essay on *Utopie Expérimentale* (1961/2001), are relied upon. Our aim is to explore the emergence of the spatial dimension in the theories and related methodologies of Lefebvre and to illustrate the power of this arrangement.

The Critique of an Exclusively Historical Dialectic Based on the Critique of Reason

The original triad uniting Hegel, Marx and Nietzsche, the fundamental authors at the base of Henri Lefebvre's considerations on history and reason, remits in a single gesture to theoretical and methodological fields. The reading according to which the modern world would be simultaneously Hegelian, Marxist and Nietzschean, present as much in *Hegel, Marx, Nietzsche* as in *La Fin de l'Histoire*, brings with it elements which reach beyond the contents of the real. This is also one of the premises of a new type of dialectical relation. If the modern world presents itself as bearing "something intolerably paradoxical" (Lefebvre, 1975/2020, p. 3), that allows us to understand and reveal the content of these three distinct doctrines, frequently taken as incompatible, then a necessity arises for reading the forms of interaction between these contents of reality and these distinct sources of thought.

It is along this path that we propose the outlining of a hypothesis, regarding the forms of articulation between terms of a Lefebvrian dialectic, foregrounding the relations that can be established between each of these sources of thought, inasmuch as they carry with them a specific form of relation between history and historicity. In this regard, apart from the potency of a thought that restitutes on another level its commitment to totality, the radical character of Lefebvre's critique of reason and history bears a dimension that serves the apprehension of some particularities of what we sometimes call *the morphology of the dialectical thought of Henri Lefebvre*.

An Arrangement According to the Position Before Hegel

While many theorists remained faithful to history and historicity as fields in which to deconstruct ideologies, alienation, and the bindings of domination, as revolutionary fields *par excellence*, Lefebvre sets out on an intellectual enterprise that makes modernity's horizon of expectations relative, and calls into question the dominion of the progress of time in the rhetorics of emancipation. It is from his radical critique of reason, history, and the state that begins the path toward the reconsideration of contents and dimensions excised by a good portion of modern thought from philosophies of emancipation or, as Lefebvre would have it, from "historian thought."[1] Thus, in Lefebvre's considerations and in the project of his radical critique, the body, passions, madness, inebriation, sex, daily life, and experience acquire particular importance. These dimensions do not comply with the rational premises or the grand project of Western rationality, which are normally overcast by bureaucratic order, by economic calculation, and by philosophy. According to this perspective, the abstraction constituting history is not developed strictly as a form of perceiving time, an illusion for organizing life and societies, a narrative: this social form of rationalized organization of time assumes a statute of reality, which Lefebvre situates in the field of "concrete abstractions."

Hegel figures in Lefebvrian thought as one of the thinkers who most aptly captures the meanings of history. Beyond the revolutionary force of reason, which moves the world, Hegel captured the meaning of history in all its magnitude and totalitarian predisposition in his *Philosophy of History*, extolling the state as its outcome, objective, and synthesis and, in this conclusive turn, reaffirming "the bourgeois, rather than democratic, aspect" (Lefebvre, 1975/2020, p. 53). The very form and materiality of reason, the state operates on the register of eternity, of bureaucratic systems and logical series, with a pretense of perfection. Therefore, marking the end of history: "with the modern state time comes to an end, and the result of time is displayed (actualized in total presence) in space" (Lefebvre, 1975/2020, pp. 8–9).

However, beyond the movements of supersession[2] and stagnation contained in the (theoretical and practical) principle of the positive realization of history (as presented by Hegel), two other critical paths open up toward the critiques of history and historicity. The first gives priority to the critical contents of historicity, to the contradictions hiding behind an image of coherence and identity, as well as to the structural crises holding together the catenations of history as predicted by Hegel. The second path foregrounds the critique of reason, recognizing the reductive contents of the rationalization of time's progress and claiming a place for dimensions and contents excised from history—a re-encounter with the thought of Marx and Nietzsche as critics of history and reason.

The examinations of the collapse of history and its critical denouement, of its justifications and promises, of its transformation into ideology and its subsequent critique all have Marx's thought as their starting point. Nietzschean thought, which calls for the return of Dionysus, the exiled god, the god of dance, of inebriation, of play and sexuality and madness, points toward the abstraction of which history is made and toward the reductive element that, through this abstraction, bear directly on life. Hence the consideration of extrarational contents and instinctive, pulsional, and affective dimensions, exiled by the hegemonic experience of time in the modern epoch. According to this point of view, the rationalization of time and of temporal organization is selective and excluding. Forms of accumulation, of progress and succession cannot incorporate antagonistic elements. That is, those elements that stand apart or are disarticulated from the chain of connections of history's great rational project. They cannot incorporate, ultimately, the irrational dimension of life.

Thus, in Lefebvre's thought, relations are established between the aforementioned authors with regards to each of their positions before history:

a) Hegel, who formulates the problem of history suggesting a positive denouement while announcing the end of history through the realization of the elementary categories that govern its movement, appears as the starting point for defining the other positions.
b) Marx, who observes the contradictions in which Hegel saw identity, points toward the ideological character of the Hegelian representation and recognizes the critical tendency that the fluxes of events carry with it under the designs of capitalism.
c) Nietzsche also turns against history in the sense it acquired with Hegel, but no longer expects anything to come of it or from its unfolding; neither the revelation of an inverted truth nor its critical self-destruction.

According to Lefebvre, "The Nietzschean critique starts from the same place as that of Marx: Hegel and Hegelianism as theory of the state. . . . The same starting point, but in diverging directions" (Lefebvre, 1975/2020, p. 142). This suggests relations which may be expressed according to Figure 8.1.

The strong element that completes the thematic orientation of critiques around the notions of history and historicity remits to the movements of thought among the authors considered by Lefebvre. In this field, however, new forms of relation and possible groupings between the authors suggest modifications in the scheme of Figure 8.1, where Marx and Nietzsche appear together, initially, on the side of critique directed simultaneously at history and Hegel, who appears isolated in the defensive field of history, in the positive interpretation of its unfolding. Among the authors mobilized by Lefebvre, crucial differences between forms of superseding history reveal very distinct positions regarding the movements of thought and the elements selected in order to compose critiques of history and historicity. From here we may propose another schematic drawing, in accordance with the morphology of dialectic revealed by Lefebvrian thought, between formal logic and dialectics itself.

On History and Its Supersession

We may gleam from Lefebvre's reading (1970, 1975/2020) that Marx, observing the dynamics of capitalist accumulation, set himself against a positive conception of history and revealed its crises and its indissociable critical nature from the inside, using history itself. In this sense

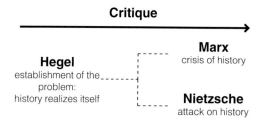

FIGURE 8.1 According to positions before history.

critique is a wager on the temporal unfolding of historical categories as the main mechanism of superseding history itself. Marx's critique of the Hegelian conception bears a dimension resting upon labor and the position of the negative.

Lefebvre frequently resorts to a theory of social classes in order to present the Marxist position in this debate. According to this approach, the wager on the proletariat as revolutionary class sustains an equally negative comprehension of history. Therefore, it is not a question of expecting from subaltern classes the realization of a project (culminating in the regime that exploits them) but its subversion, its negation, and supersession as a movement with emancipatory contents. This would bestow Marxist thought, according to Lefebvre, with historical content and a wager on the temporal and categorial unfolding typically engaged in what he calls "historian thought" (1970). "History, which according to Hegel had been completed, continues for Marx. Uncompleted time does not freeze (reify) in space. . . . This is the original form that the Hegelian dialectic acquires with Marx" (Lefebvre, 1975/2020, p. 14).

However, in *La Fin de l'Histoire*, Lefebvre had already observed that history as the register and development of the spirit, as the progress of grand emancipatory projects or even as the realization of the forms of reason, had for some time shown no meaningful advances. The same may still be stated if history is considered in its negative or revolutionary aspects. In this way Lefebvre presents the empirical and contextual constraints that bind together and justify his hypothesis, allowing him to leap forward toward a radical critique of a different nature and of newfound scope. This involved the utopian and revolutionary abandonment of history: in opposition, no longer in accordance with it. In resorting to a sort of non-historical alternative to history, or to one that was dependent on the unravelling of the historical flux itself, as Hegel had predicted, from an identitarian viewpoint, or as Marx had, according to the critical unfolding of capitalist contradictions, Lefebvre brings to his own critique elements from other matrices of thought. It is a question of searching for "another exit, another hypothesis: that of an end that does not coincide with the finalities looked upon by the creators of historian thought" (Lefebvre, 1970, p. 14). This is where Nietzsche finds his place and potency in Lefebvrian thinking:

> For Hegel, for Marx, for other thinkers of history, it is certain that there is a post-history, but that comes from history in an almost natural way. . . . Nietzsche was the first to face the hypothesis of a civilization different from ours, since it is born out of a repudiation of history, of historicity and of the historical, of the past and its knowledge taken as useless overloads, burdens of memory, increasingly sterile inventory of the realized. The birth of this civilization would imply a radical cut, a total discontinuity, a renewal in methods of knowledge, therefore a repudiation of historian thought.
>
> *(Lefebvre, 1970, pp. 14–15)*

On the level of the motions of thought, arranging the authors in groups yields a different configuration than arranging them according to their general stance before history. While the first diagram presents the separation between an affirmative and identitarian stance and a critical-negative orientation, a new drawing becomes possible according to the form that the supersession of history assumes in each of the authors of the triad. Here resides the possibility of apprehending relations with history on another level, meaning a way to capture Lefebvrian dialectical thought from another morphological configuration. In this regard, the form and movement of critique is of greater importance: while bringing forth the original Nietzschean reflexion, it groups together, on one side, Hegel and Marx and, on the other, Nietzsche. This would define a grouping scheme as presented in Figure 8.2.

Regarding positions taken before history, observations around the register of unfoldings and movements of social categories present us with, on the one hand, a strain united as a function of the expectation and consideration of events in historical time, through underscoring of its critical or positive aspects and, on the other, an attitude that denounces history itself and its order-giving reason as the origin of the falsehoods tearing life apart. This arrangement acquires meaning because Marx, his criticisms of Hegel and of the very order of time under capitalism notwithstanding, is situated on the side of what Lefebvre calls "historian thought," and so, like Hegel, situates the foundation of social activity in practical and categorical developments of time and history.

The theme of the end of history for Lefebvre is directly associated with this stance before history, taken as a medium and object of practice and understanding. On one side, the foretold, pointed out, deduced, potential ends resulting from internal (immanent) unraveling in the very course of history, one of which is positive and identity-based, as in Hegel, the other of which is critical and negative, as in Marx: both, however, are in the field of waiting for directions from the motions of history itself. On the other hand, the hypothesis of an exit: an abandonment and discarding of history as a whole, from which we may expect no plausible solution, given that this whole is not only a symptom or a version but the cause of civilizational illness. Thus, stances taken before history reverberate through three different ends, clearly captured by Lefebvre as much in *La Fin de L'Histoire* and *Hegel, Marx, Nietzsche*:

a) A Hegelian end, resulting from the motions of the spirit in time in search of its self-realization, found in the Modern State.
b) A Marxist (more than Marxian) end, resulting from critical unravelings and tensions within the accumulation process itself as well as from the lack of identification between the

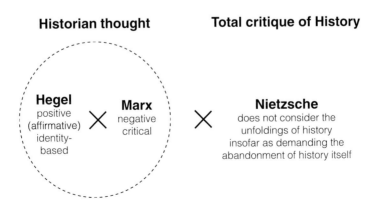

FIGURE 8.2 According to positions before historian thought.

proletariat and the state of exploitation maintained by capitalism, which finds a conclusion at the end of capitalism.
c) A Nietzschean end, which rejects history completely while singling it out as a burden of memory and register of castration, calling for the exiled dimension of the body, of passions, instincts, enjoyment, dance, use, inebriation, and madness.

On this level, particular aspects related to the motions of each author become clearly outlined. Given that these matrices are considered here as resources for unveiling the real world and the fundamental contents of modernity, the "exit from history," inasmuch as it contains its supersession, should be considered simultaneously "according to the Hegelian and Marxist sublation (*Aufheben*), but also according to Nietzschean overcoming (*Überwinden*)" (Lefebvre, 1970, p. 15).

> Here we see clearly the radical difference between Hegelian and Marxist supersession, which preserves antecedents and preconditions at a higher level by "raising" them . . . and the Nietzschean supersession, which denies, rejects, disowns, belies, refutes, casts into the abyss.
>
> *(Lefebvre, 1975/2020, p. 177)*

If we resort to the difference in translation that appears in the authors' choices of words, a discord in the very process and form of apprehending reality appears, as do each author's own articulation of a possible utopian horizon. *Aufhebung*, which preserves the profound sense of dialectical supersession as imagined and utilized by Hegel and Marx (maintaining due differences), remits to a movement that, at the same time in which it negates the superseded term, conserves it in the process of supersession and affirms it in the process of negation (determinate negation).

> Even given Marx's divergent stance regarding the results of history and historicity, Lefebvre observes the relations between him and Hegel and their respective currents of thought from a dialectical viewpoint. Proceeding in this manner, or said in this manner, Marx continues Hegelianism, he retains the substance of Hegelian historicity . . . however, Marx submits the form (system) of Hegelianism as well as its content (results of history) to his radical critique
>
> *(Lefebvre, 1970, p. 42)*

rehabilitating dialectic at the center of life and critical analyses. From this viewpoint, Lefebvre interprets the very relation between Marx and Hegel according to the terms of dialectic supersession (*Aufhebung*), in a relation of simultaneous dependence and opposition. "In Marx, Hegelian theory does not disappear but is transformed" (Lefebvre, 1970, p. 42). This is the moment of critical supersession, repositioning the negative as an element critical of the positive identity of the Hegelian system (Figure 8.3).

The notion of dialectic supersession (*Aufheben*) used to understand the relationship between Marx and Hegel, or between Marxist and Hegelian thought, also considered in their effective dimensions as contents of reality, emphasizes conservation and reaffirms the negated term in its own supersession and does not signify (whence its pertinence) the abandoning or discarding of the negated object. Thus, Lefebvre simultaneously derives from the relations each source and establishes with history and from the movement of supersession itself established between them, a path for observing the dialectic existing between Hegelian dialectic and Marxist dialectic in a motion that negates while conserving and introjecting. In this way, he states that "Marx's dialectical thought had a relationship with Hegel's dialectical thought that was itself dialectical, which means unity and conflict" (Lefebvre, 1975/2020, p. 11). In this universe of relations,

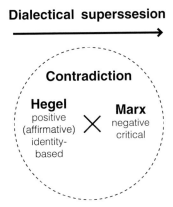

FIGURE 8.3 Dialectic between Hegel and Marx.

"Marx took from Hegel the essentials of his 'essentialist' thought . . . hence the meaning of history" (Lefebvre, 1975/2020, p. 11).

Nietzsche, in his own turn, is incorporated into the triad in the position of the radical element bearing contents of rupture, itself pertaining to a non-historical field of intelligibility, which turns against Hegelian thought and history itself. This is why the presence of Nietzsche in the triadic Lefebvrian field totalizes (takes as a whole) in one sole field both Hegelian and Marxist thought, slackening, mitigating, and blurring the opposition between Hegel and Marx. Nietzschean critique, calling for the return of the god exiled by the Apollonian rationality of western *logos*, attributes to Socrates and to Hellenism the notion of history as the end of creative impulse and separation between Eros and Logos. Thus, "Nietzsche ironically adds to the alienations described by Marx and Hegel a further *alienation by history* (an alienation of history by history itself)"[3] (Lefebvre, 1970, p. 72).

Already present in Marx, the supersession of philosophy active in Nietzsche is observed by Lefebvre in its indissociability from the supersession, abandonment, and discarding of history. For him, in the field of alienations, abstractions, and civilizational deceptions, "history, as knowledge, as fictional genesis, disguises becoming in place of revealing it. The same is true of Philosophy. Tragedy, music, these becomings have nothing in common with the becoming of knowledge and the (philosophical and historical) knowledge of becoming" (Lefebvre, 1970, p. 79): they are fruition and appropriation and invoke the exiled dimension.

Thus, observing the stance taken before history, from a perspective focused on the senses and meanings of history and on the becoming of humanity (society or civilization), as much as from a perspective closer to issues of method and the motions of thought, it is worth noting that Nietzsche's place in the Lefebvrian triad reorganizes the whole arrangement. This renewed arrangement places Marx on the side of Hegel and opens up space for considering the radical character of Nietzschean thought, defined according to another type of critique of history.

> Nietzschean overcoming (*Überwinden*) differs radically from Hegelian and Marxian *Aufheben*. It does not preserve anything, it does not carry its antecedents and preconditions to a higher level. It casts them into nothingness. Subversive rather than revolutionary, *Überwinden* overcomes by destroying, or rather by leading to its self-destruction that which it replaces. This is how Nietzsche sought to overcome both the European assertion of

> logos and its opposite obverse side, nihilism. Is it necessary to add that this heroic struggle against Judeo-Christian nihilism on behalf of and through carnal life has nothing in common with hedonism? There is a triad (three terms), but in the course of the struggle what is born casts the other terms into nothingness (sends them *zu Grunde*, as Heidegger would say), with the result that they then appear as "foundations", depths. Dialectical? Yes, but radically different from either the Hegelian or the Marxist dialectic. By the role, the import, the meaning of the *negative*. By the intensity of the tragic.
>
> *(Lefebvre, 1975/2020, p. 26)*

This is how the tragic supplants logos and nihilism in an original and originary dialectic.

> The notion of supersession persists but is profoundly modified: it is less an issue of superseding a given historical moment through history than one of superseding (overcoming) the nihilism resulting from the fact that history itself has superseded nothing. In this manner, history and historicity will be abolished. Nietzschean *Überwinden* differs from Hegelo-Marxist *Aufheben*.
>
> *(Lefebvre, 1970, pp. 73–74)*

Thus, "Nietzsche goads his contemporaries, challenges them; from that point on he is outside of their community . . . he sits outside of historical time" (Lefebvre, 1970, p. 69).

On the other hand:

> Marx posited a meaning of becoming, of history, without demonstrating it; he accepted Hegelian (Western) logos without subjecting it to a fundamental critique. Hegel's still-theological hypothesis passed through the sieve (the "break") in Marx's thought. No more than Hegel did Marx question the origin of Western rationality, its genesis or genealogy: Judeo-Christianity, Greco-Latin thought, industry and technology. Marx was content with an attenuation of Hegelian theology (theodicy) and the epic of the Idea.
>
> *(Lefebvre, 1975/2020, p. 34)*

In this way, the combination suggests a scheme that can be represented from a grouping of authors included in the field of so-called historian thought on one hand, despite its internal contradictions, and totalized by a contradiction on another level, defined here by the position occupied by Nietzsche (Figure 8.4).

On the plane of the utopian horizon and of history's role at the center of theoretical conceptions, the arrangement can be reorganized according to a summarized positioning of each of the authors in the triad.

> Hegel thus foresaw a state that generated its conditions of formation and equilibrium, a self-generating and self-reproducible system. Marx, on the contrary, foresaw in the name of the proletarian revolution a leap forward of becoming, a new "generation," without repetition but without loss of the past. Nietzsche . . . made the demand for a complete break that transcended the past".
>
> *(Lefebvre, 1975/2020, p. 177)*

Nietzsche requires nothing from reality; he flouts it while projecting new destinations which come into being after the abandoning of the historical past.

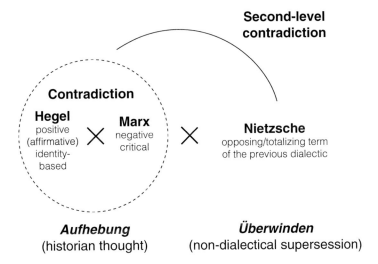

FIGURE 8.4 Lefebvrian dialectic according to the triad of authors.

If he had little to say about capitalism and the bourgeoisie, this was because he despised them and also because he condemned them en bloc, not deeming to see there an "object" worthy of interest, and also because he included them in Judeo-Christianity.

(Lefebvre, 1975/2020, p. 134)

This schematic representation bears, in general terms, many structural aspects for the comprehension of the morphology of Lefebvrian dialectical thought itself, as the following section shall address. Thus, apart from the contents associated with the critique of history and historicity and that denounce its crisis, we suggest the establishment of a dialectical thought arranged in order to observe the contradictions of space.

On the Relation Between Formal Logic and Dialectic at the Base of a Spatial Dialectic

In a way, some elements of the structure glimpsed through the articulation of the terms of the triad were already present in Lefebvre's claims regarding the rights of dialectic in the contemporary world. There would also be, on this plane of the author's considerations, a dialectic operating on a second level articulating social contents, themselves already dialectical, inheriting their contradictions from history, to the realm of forms. The relation between dialectically defined social content and formal logic, itself of a dialectical nature, is at the center of this consideration. Thus, from this viewpoint, a dimension of the Lefebvrian theoretical-methodological project is defined. One that, faced with the faltering and crisis of history and historicity, seeks an opening for understanding the contradictions of space: the same theoretical effort that highlights and transports the spatial dimension to the field of critical social theory, restituting the potential that space effectively acquired as much in relation to the formulation of concrete social problems in actuality and, consequently, its theoretical elucidation as to practical actions.

Such a project is inscribed simultaneously in two main lines of commitments to theory. In the first place, if it fell upon Marx to "rescue" dialectics from the arbitrary confines of history and of the movement (or, precisely, the stagnation) that threatened it in the Hegelian system, Lefebvre took it upon himself to rescue it from Stalinism, to whom the state doctrine implanted in the USSR had begun to reflect, in the name of Marxist supersession of Hegel's legacy, the same or very similar totalitarian aspirations already identified in the teleological orientation of Hegelian philosophy.[4]

In the preface to the second edition of *Logique Formelle, Logique Dialectique*, Lefebvre defends himself from accusations of assimilation into Hegelianism coming from different influential Stalinist currents in France, inverting the playing field and taking aim at the Hegelian system and the totalitarian vocation of Stalinism in one stroke, while opening up a new path in his project of radical critique of the state, toward what he would later call "the state mode of production," the title given to volume 3 of *De L'État*. On the plane of dealings with dialectic, combined and attached to this critique, a strong stance against the systemic conception that constrains horizons and blocks the universe of the possible begins to take form. The crisis of historicity cannot, in this manner, remain attached to the horizons and destinations of dialectic as put forth in the Hegelian system. The end of history could not be the practico-sensory equivalent to the end of dialectic: from this point on, the second strain of commitments in the theoretical-methodological project outlined in the preface to *Logique Formelle, Logique Dialectique* is drawn out.

With the intent of rescuing dialectic from the exclusive movements of history and historicity, projected beyond the uncoupling operated by Marx upon the Hegelian system, Lefebvre opened up a new path toward renewing and amplifying the scope and claims of dialectic in critical social interpretation. In observing the faltering of historical socio-temporal order and in dedicating attention to the vibrant social dimensions not contemplated in the project of rationalizing "the great spirit of the world," it was not enough to subvert the playing field or invert the signs of social analysis. History proved incapable of realizing its promises, while some of its ends became compatible with a universe of coercions, with the State and the empire of value functioning as epitomes of the formalisms responsible for social order (bureaucracy, the law, justice, commodities, money, exchange value). Its very ruins, furthermore, served to illustrate the dimensions neglected by speculative dialectics, reinforcing the demand for a comprehension which might access the contradictions of space. This path was followed in Lefebvre's theoretical-methodological project with the reconsideration of the place of formal logic in the face of dialectic thought.[5]

The starting point of this project, therefore, is a refusal in seeing formal logic as a mere deviation, or as the foundation of the mystifying illusions of social analysis, the source of an equivocal or ill-informed reflection, something to be expelled from critical speculation. This is because of two reasons that here determine each other mutually.

First because, in the movement of thought, the empty form, or the logical form which attaches itself to contents and reduces them to their formal expressions, for not containing the complexity, movement, and simultaneously positive and negative determination that are particular to its internal dialectic, constitutes a necessary moment. That is, an unavoidable starting point, related to the universe of contents, however, in manners not always harmonious or linear.

> There is no other path for knowledge besides the one that starts from a nothing of knowledge . . . there is no path beyond that which starts from such a *reduced* thought, that is, from a virtuality of thought, with the objective of restituting and reintegrating—in situating—that which was momentarily removed. Thus, a *project* (recapturing content) and a *trajectory* (prescribable in the meaning of content) are determined, a trajectory that will remain the same according to the "pure" form.[6]
>
> (Lefebvre, 1969/1983, p. 51)

This same project is completed with the proposition of *dialectical logic*, simultaneously elucidating 1) that formal logic takes part in thoughtful considerations of the reality of its contents, and (2) that the enunciate proposing dialectical logic does not come out of a "mistake" in Lefebvre's reading of the classical texts of dialectical thought, but from an effort directed at developing a project aimed at producing a critical knowledge relatively independent of history and historicity. In this project, the relation between formal logic and the dialectic of social contents takes on a dialectic nature itself. It is in this regard that a dialectic appears operating on "a second level," placing dialectic and dialectical thought, taken as one of its terms in relation to formal logic, admitted as an inalienable moment of knowledge. This also includes dialectical thought, even if it was discredited by speculative dialectics.[7]

It must be considered that dialectic, dialectical thought, and the movements of content only become one of the terms of this relation when placed, in conflict or in contradiction, before formal logic. Through it we may apprehend, by opposition, the *pole of content* as an active term in the consideration of dialectical logic: a dialectic, therefore, apprehended on another level. However, other contradictory terms underlie this dialectic. Taken as one of the terms in a relation, the movement of contents is contradictory, and this contradiction carries with it a "double determination." "There exist, therefore, contradictions between form and content and contradictions within the contents themselves (between them and in each of them)" (Lefebvre, 1969/1983, p. 60).

Thus, in attempting to elucidate the specificities of a morphology of Lefebvrian dialectical thought, considering the transfiguration of dialectic into one of the terms of the (also dialectic) relation with formal logic, the presented relation can be developed in a very simplified manner in the following schematic drawing (Figure 8.5).

When mobilizing *dialectical logic* in order to capture the (second-level) contradictions between formal logic (and ensuing formalisms) and the realm and activity of contents, the third term does not occupy the position of an outcome, of the supersession, synthesis, or solution of a contradiction, as seems to be the case defined by the form of articulation between the terms of Hegelian dialectic.

The schematic triangle of Hegelian dialectic establishes a hierarchy between its positioned terms in placing at its vertex the one that stands for the supersession, or synthesis, of contradictions arising from the others. Lefebvre observes in this form the limitations of speculative

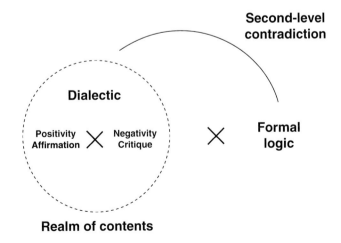

FIGURE 8.5 Developed scheme of the dialectic between formal logic and dialectic.

dialectics, the victory and vengeance of logic over dialectic itself, restricted to an ultimate synthesis in the State, the very image and symbol of reason and transparency. This form, simultaneously committed to history and its end, is very different from the one proposed by Lefebvre in his attempt to rescue dialectics. Here, the third term re-elaborates the relation, suggests a contradiction on another level, points toward the complexification of relations, not toward their resolution or supersession: thus, taking root in its own morphology, the Lefebvrian proposition of the "dialectical method" is freed from the exclusive restrictions to historian thought. "*Supersession* only bears meaning in one case, that of historicity . . . the third term can degenerate, be born and soon disappear, without there having to be 'history'" (Lefebvre, 1969/1983, p. 58). In the Hegelian dialectic, the position of the synthetic element, of the resolution and outcome of the preceding contradiction assumed by the third term, is an expression of the commitment and formal complacency of this dialectic to the movement of history itself. "The dialectic today no longer clings to historicity and historical time, or to a temporal mechanism such as 'thesis-antithesis-synthesis' or 'affirmation-negation-negation of the negation'" (Lefebvre, 1973/1976, p. 14). In this sense, the identification of the Lefebvrian dialectic with the Hegelian, by virtue of the mere occurrence of a third term, presupposes the emptying out of its meanings and significations and incurs in a grave interpretative error.

Secondly, given that we are dealing with a project that is developed not only with the pedagogical objective of an education of the gaze and of consciousness, of methodological and interpretative correctness, but with a construction concerned with *praxis* and with issues pertaining to the material world, it is worth highlighting that, in Lefebvrian thought, formal logic exists not only as an action, a moment, or instrument of intellection and intuition of the real. It is admitted in its effective presence in reality, in the determination of life, of social practices, and contents, taken in their relations in space. This is a movement into *metaphilosophy*, "included in a *general theory of forms*, searching for the connection between abstract and concrete forms, between the mental and the social" (Lefebvre, 1969/1983, p. 81). In these terms, critique must conceive of logic as not only a moment of thought, but also as a foundation for the social strategies that obscure and disguise the contradictions of the real, seeking to impose itself in its place, installing through suppression the rationality of transparency and coherence, in a movement that affronts and violates social contents: logic, separate, fetishized and hypostatic, begins to serve not only as ideology but also as a foundation acting upon the real, attempting to shape it. Thus, this spatial dialectic refers not only to the contradictions occurring in space but, more specifically, to the contradictions of space, those that are particular to it and are engendered specifically in its dimension of social life.

Method in Operation: The Concrete Dimension of the Relation Between Logic and Dialectic

According to the point of view outlined here, it is understood that the contradictions of space are elaborated in the field of dialectic, resulting from the conflict between the formal dimension, harboring political and economic strategies, and the field of complexities and contradictions specific to the contents of social space. Thus, not only dialectic, conflicts, contradictions, and differences express a concrete, sensible dimension but also formal logic itself assumes effective material expression and is confronted in practice with the contents of social life. On one side, therefore, we have socio-spatial practice, the realm of life and of the differences or effects, causes, or reasons of the reproduction of relations of production, as the domain of history-based dialectic. On the other side we have flattening, planning, norms and normalization, classification, the sieve of exchange value, the empire of form, of measurements, of the numerical, and of quantification as the foundation of a science of space. As components of an (abstract) mental space that enters into conflicts with the concrete dimensions of social space and its contents, making efforts to reduce them. Concrete dimensions of logic and dialectic both appear here as moments of a spatial dialectic.

Nevertheless, it is at the moment in which the relations between logic and dialectic, form and content, emerge as the foundation for understanding social space, and consequently concrete space, that the theoretical-methodological project reaches its highest expression. Here it presents its power of apprehending reality according to a dialectic not enclosed within the unveiling of the contradictions of and in history. To observe and consider the formal dimension as one of the poles of dialectic established before different and contradictory contents constitutes a necessary stage in the development of this project. In other words, to observe and consider the ways through which formal logic, abstract and mental in principle, acquires materiality when imposing itself over social space (through sketches on a drawing board or through laws written in books) emerges as one of the foundations for the development of a concrete spatial dialectic. Observing and considering this movement, which attributes concrete dimensions to formalisms and formal logic as part of a strategy that selects, filters and separates the social contents of space, engaging in open conflict with them, supplies the necessary character of this renewed spatial dialectic.

Thus,

> Logic stakes a larger claim than it did for Hegel or Marx. . . . It is a question of formal logic and its application to a determinate content. Strategies (which are presented as logics of this or that: of society, of the thing, of the commodity, of growth, etc.) are a result of using logical form in this way.
>
> *(Lefebvre, 1973/1976, p. 16)*

In these terms, in the passage from the mental to the social, or when logic is superimposed as an abstract form over concrete space, "the relation between logic and dialectic raises problems" (Lefebvre, 1973/1976, p. 16).

> It is impossible today to eliminate logic as such, and equally impossible to vacate the dialectic. They are no more separable than theory and practice, or knowledge and ideology. Let us take the example of social space. Social space is where the reproduction of the *relations* of production (superimposed on the reproduction of the means of production) is located; at the same time, it is the occasion for and the instrument of a form of planning (land development), i.e., of a logic of growth. . . . *This, then, is what is new and paradoxical: the dialectic is no longer attached to temporality.* . . . To recognise space, to recognise what "takes place" there and what it is used for, is to resume the dialectic; analysis will reveal the contradictions of space. The abstract space of the mathematicians and epistemologists is answerable to logic. The route from this mental space to social space is already, implicitly, a dialectical movement.
>
> *(Lefebvre, 1973/1976, pp. 16–17)*

Thus, the second-level contradiction and the role of formal logic as negative polarity are at the base of Lefebvre's critical thought and guide his critique of the state, of urban planning and urbanism, among other fields that appear in the same position. One of these fields, neither more nor less important than the others and deeply connected to them, is the one which signals toward the relations between the universe of practices of *inhabiting* and their functional and reductive confinement in *habitat*.

Seeking to critically capture the origins and means of exercising the violence intrinsic to the reductive rationalism implicit in the instruments of control and management of life and the uses of space, pertaining also to the market's range of strategies, Lefebvre puts into focus the contradictions between *inhabiting* [*habiter*] (as the realm of daily practices, containing contradictions arising out of history and of conflicts between different terms, a clash of rhythms, representations, practices, and expectations) and *habitat* (the reduced experience of space that gives priority to abstract space over lived space). Resulting from a rationality specific to industrial society, the simplified function of *habitat* reduces life to the elementary acts of eating, sleeping, and reproducing.

> During the reign of habitat, habiting [*habiter*] disappeared from thought and deteriorated strongly in practice. It required the metaphilosophical meditations of Nietzsche and Heidegger to restore the meaning of the term. Habitat, ideology and practice, had even repressed the elementary characteristics of urban life, as noted by a very shortsighted ecology. . . . Habitat was imposed from above as the application of a homogeneous global and quantitative space, a requirement that "lived experience" allow itself to be enclosed in boxes, cages, or "dwelling machines."
>
> *(Lefebvre, 1970/2003, p. 81)*

The projects of architects and engineers that seek an economic solution for life, who seek to standardize and functionalize the forms of using space, be it in the home or in the city, reduce to a minimum any gestures or daily experience. This is particularly clear in a city that strictly followed, or intended to follow, the teachings of a functionalist Corbusian framework, such as Brasília. It also becomes clear in the "ultra-economical" and functional projects that guide the production of social housing and that equally advance as a concept through all social strata. Therefore,

> Concrete space is the space of habiting: gestures and paths, bodies and memory, symbols and meanings, the difficult maturation of the immature-premature (of the "human being"), contradictions and conflicts between desires and needs, and so forth. This concrete content, time inscribed in space, an unconscious poiesis that misunderstands its own conditions, is also misunderstood by thought. Instead, it takes off into the abstract space of vision, of geometry. The architect who draws and the urbanist who composes a block plan look down on their "objects," buildings and neighborhoods, from above and afar. These designers and draftsmen move within a space of paper and ink. Only after this nearly complete reduction of the everyday do they return to the scale of lived experience. They are convinced they have captured it even though they carry out their plans and projects within a second-order abstraction. They've shifted from lived experience to the abstract, projecting this abstraction back onto lived experience. This twofold substitution and negation creates an illusory sense of affirmation: the return to "real" life.
>
> *(Lefebvre, 1970/2003, pp. 182–183)*

The principles allowing for and giving direction to this critique reveals the dimension of violence not quite captured by perspectives that remained tied to a dialectic of historical time. The passage from the mental to the social makes the violence implied in abstraction effective.

> A logic of reduction/extrapolation is applied to the blackboard as to the drawing-board, to the blank sheet of paper as to schemata of all kinds, to writing as to contentless abstraction.

> This modus operandi has even graver consequences ... [than the] space of the mathematicians. ... Violence is immanent to instrumental space, which seems rational, evident ... the mental space of castration [is thus formed].
>
> *(Lefebvre, 1974/1991, pp. 298, 306, 309)*

This apprehension of the phenomenon can be extended into other fields of observation. The original critical considerations that attack the state and bureaucracy as large-scale expressions of abstract rationality and of abstraction actualized as violence, while operating the leap from the mental to the social, when it attempts to impose itself in place of life, replacing it in the process. These considerations recognize the sources of this violent reduction of the meaning of life in urbanism and in territorial planning as well. Understanding that spatial planning, as it was experienced in its time in France, proposed "nothing less than carving, rationally modeling the space" (Lefebvre, 1974/2000, p. xviii), Lefebvre begins looking for the connecting elements that would allow him to approach this hypertrophy of the recourse to logic and abstraction, as the source of exercises of state power as well as of the violence conveyed through implementing functionalist and rationalizing urban plans.

> Lastly, we find that abstract space so understood is hard to distinguish from the space postulated by the philosophers, from Descartes to Hegel, in their fusion of the intelligible (res extensa) with the political—their fusion, that is to say, of knowledge with power. The outcome has been an authoritarian and brutal spatial practice, whether Haussmann's or the later codified versions of the Bauhaus or Le Corbusier; what is involved in all cases is the effective application of the analytic spirit in and through dispersion, division and segregation.
>
> *(Lefebvre, 1974/1991, p. 308)*

Planning, and urban planning specifically, are frequently founded on programmatic thinking, they "operate over possible (virtual) objects and confront them with experience inasmuch as one wishes the imagined object to enter into practice, to be actualized, in a word. This thought also seeks to invent forms, but concrete forms" (Lefebvre, 1961/2001, p. 130). Normally established on an "*a priori* construction" and on "abstract utopia," "[planning] deals with the ideal city (*cité*) with no relation to determinate situations" (Lefebvre, 1961/2001, p. 130). Moreover, "it proposed to human beings a program of daily life. It seeks to offer multiple rationally ordered means of reaching the budding individuals and partial groups in a community. It proposes a harmony" and thus "assumes its moral responsibility ... programmatic thought, thus defined, involves an ideology" (Lefebvre, 1961/2001, pp. 132–133).

Therefore, in simultaneously realizing that 1) the plane of logic and, more specifically, formal logic, is not indifferent to its contents (even if they are not immediately identified with it) while suggesting a dialectical relation between the terms; and 2) that this dialectical relation is not built solely on an epistemological level but participates in daily life, Lefebvre arrives at a dialectic suited to observing the contradictions of space, which is the movement and concrete meaning of these contradictions. "For this reason, what is called for is a repeated, and repeatedly refined, analysis of the relations between form and content" (Lefebvre, 1970/2003, p. 171).

> The study of the logic of space leads to the study of its contradictions (and those of space-time). Without that analysis, the solutions to the problem are merely dissimulated strategies, hidden beneath an apparent scientificity. On the theoretical level, one of the severest critiques of urbanism as a body of doctrine (not altogether successful) is that it

> harbours a socio-logic and strategy, while it evacuates dialectical thought in general and the dialectical movements specific to urbanism in particular—in other words, internal contradictions, both old and new (one aggravating and masking the other).
>
> *(Lefebvre, 1970/2003, p. 171)*

This is how,

> The dialectic is back on the agenda. But it is no longer Marx's dialectic, just as Marx's was no longer Hegel's. Besides, it does not much matter what Hegel and Marx wrote about this or that in particular, and especially about the dialectic. What matters is to grasp movement and non-movement in the *present*, to grasp what it is that shifts and collides with that which does not shift.
>
> *(Lefebvre, 1973/1976, p. 14)*

Besides carrying out critique, this dialectic emerges as an arena of possibilities in a renewed utopian project. This is equal to saying that dialectic does not succumb, no-contest, to formalisms or to the rationalities seeking to dominate everyday life. In the Lefebvrian project, there is a place for that which does not fit, for that which does not subject or adjust itself immediately to the reductive plane of forms and formalisms, like the "residue," the "resistance," or the new projecting themselves into the virtual: a dimension excised from the realm of contents that does not dissolve before the impetus of abstraction. Thus, "beside deduction and induction, the dialectically-enhanced methodology should present new operations, such as *transduction*, an operation of thought of/for a virtual object, for constructing and actualizing it. This would be a logic of the possible/impossible object" (Lefebvre, 1969/1983, p. 49).

Formal logic, positive and well-adjusted, rejects or does not comprehend the right to difference and negates the very movement of negation in the dialectical contents of social space and its contradictions. A negation, then, of the very contents to which these remit. Such a logic cannot, for these reasons, fully embrace these contents, leaving out residual elements that return as resistances and, frequently, social conflict. Thus, the very relation between a *science of space* and a theory of the *production of space* "correspond to the articulation between logic and dialectic."[8]

After All, a Re-Encounter With Marx

> This project of space . . . implies a superseding (Überwinden) on the scale of the world, casting the dead results of historical time into abolition. It contains a concrete test, bound up with practice and the totality of the possible, according to Marx's most radical thought, bound up too with the entire restitution of the palpable and the body, according to Nietzsche's poetry.
>
> This project rejects into the nothingness of dead results the Hegelian space, the work of the state, where this establishes and displays itself. As the work and product of the human species, space emerges from the shadow, like a planet emerging from an eclipse.
>
> *(Lefebvre, 1975/2020, p. 203)*

The expectation of outlining a few specificities of Lefebvre's theoretical-methodological project has been suggested since the beginning of the present discussion. It proceeded and advanced while developing arguments in two fields that are particularly important for a thought committed to unravelling the contradictions of space, namely: the radical critique of history and historicity, situated on a more theoretical field, and the design of a dialectical logic operating in-between the field of formal logical and that of contents, which are already dialectical in and of themselves.

Regarding critical considerations of history, emphasis on elements of continuity between Hegel and Marx might, however, lead us to understand that Lefebvre had failed to attribute appropriate importance to one of the most recognized and important accomplishments in the history of modern philosophy: the radical character and force that critique acquires thanks to the activity of the negative in Marx, including, specifically, his relationship with Hegelian theory. However, this is not the case. At a certain point, it became necessary to operate a double distancing, which means simultaneously having to criticize the official doctrine and state philosophy that Marxism was on its way to becoming and not succumbing to the seductions of the new logical science that encroached upon Marxism's doctrinal body, both suspended in an immobility resulting from logic's triumph over dialectic. It is at this point that Lefebvre re-encounters the early writings of Marx and that his demands for a corporeal element, for the full force of social practice, find support in the reflections of Nietzsche. Thus, in skirting both a philosophy of the state and the trappings of a certain type of marxology, reclaiming the rights and place of the complexity of everyday life and space in critical theory, which had long since been expelled from philosophical debates, Lefebvre reinstates the revolutionary nucleus of Marxism. This is noticeable not only in the critical-analytical instruments created but also in the possibilities inaugurated by the renewed critical nature of this theoretical-methodological project.

Notes

1. For Lefebvre, "historian thought" (*pensée historienne*) is different from what is habitually called "historical thought" (*pensée historique*). With it Lefebvre wishes to differentiate between a dated or history-based thought (historical thought) from a thought that operates exclusively within history's field of intelligibility or that establishes its commitments with its reproduction (historian thought).
2. Translator's note: the Portuguese word "superação" has been translated as "supersession" when it has a general sense. Clear exceptions were made where "overcoming" appears, remitting to the Nietzschean *überwinden*. The verb "to sublate" is employed in order to characterize the Marxist and Hegelian *aufheben*.
3. "The Greece of creative impulse discovered tragedy and the tragic, music and feasts, the soothing of anguish in joy, before separating Eros and Logos.... Socratic Greece, that of logic and *logos*, of the City-State, of "pure" knowledge and historical narrative, marks the end of ancient Greece and of its creative force ... the end of Greece, this conclusion that historians seek to explain, contains a double lesson: it was the end of *a* history and an end *through* history" (Lefebvre, 1970, p. 76).
4. The dialectical materialism synthesized by Stalin appeared as "a synthesis between a 'real nucleus', materialism, and a 'rational nucleus', dialectic. An abstract and definitive synthesis, operated and proclaimed on a philosophical plane" (Lefebvre, 1969/1983, p. 31). "It was an attempt at totalization, a *philosophical-political system*, that is, a new Hegelianism, a philosophy of and by the State, supposed result of the end of the philosophy of history and of the history of philosophy ... reduced history to the genesis of that State" (Lefebvre, 1969/1983, p. 31). "Dialectical thought became its opposite; essentially critical, it ultimately emptied out into a dogmatism, presenting abusive systematization: official, institutional 'dia-mat'. In this systematization, the word 'dialectic', that is, dialectical thought, reduced to a single word, became the vehicle of an ideology that, precisely, actively liquidates 'negativity', critical reflexion. On the other hand, the systematization carried out in the name of dialectic (tending toward the closing-off of the system under the pretense of a movement demanding opening) absorbed logic into dialectics. What was the result? Lacking in logical support and reference, in rules for employing concepts, without this becoming an impediment to congealing in dogmatic discourse, dialectic thought was no longer distinguished from sophistry, from eristics" (Lefebvre, 1969/1983, p. 38).
5. It is worth pointing out that, in its occurrences in the preface in question, the possible proximity between the expressions *dialectical thought*, *dialectic*, and *speculative dialectics*, remitting to Hegelian philosophy's theoretical universe and its unravellings, is not present with regards to the notion of *dialectic logic*, constitutive of the Lefebvrian project as such.
6. In his critique of the Hegelian system, marked by the closure that confines history and movement, Lefebvre also singles out the contempt that speculative dialectic showed in relation to formal logic as one of

its problems. "Logic should appear as a *moment* in the process: formally elaborated and, notwithstanding, still open, unclosed (open upon and to whatever comes afterwards). In other words: as a well-determined *moment*—that of determination—in a *movement* that cannot be restrained without dissolving" (Lefebvre, 1969/1983, p. 33).

7. The schematic presentation proposed by Lefebvre in order to illustrate the role, position, and form of articulation of the elements of his theoretical-methodological project prioritizes the mediating condition of *dialectical logic*. A drawing of this schematic representation was presented by Lefebvre with the following structure: formal logic—dialectical logic—Dialectic or Dialectical thought (Lefebvre, 1969/1983, p. 86). It is not this formula, then, that should be used as an exercise in expostulating the morphological dimensions of Lefebvre's dialectical thinking. The priority given to the place of dialectical logic does not make sufficiently clear the accentuated difference in nature between the mediating role attributed to it and the condition of the involved terms, namely formal logic and dialectic.

8. "The science of space (mathematics, physics) has affinities with logic, with the theory of ensembles, systems and coherences. But knowledge of the productive process, which introduces this most general of products—space—into social existence, has affinities with dialectical thought, which grasps the contradictions of space. Here again, it is the juncture between logic and dialectic that is the problem" (Lefebvre, 1973/1976, p. 18).

References

Lefebvre, H. (1970). *La Fin de l'Histoire*. Paris, France: Éditions de Minuit.
Lefebvre, H. (1976). *The Survival of Capitalism: Reproduction of the Relations of Production*. New York, NY: St. Martin's Press. (Original work published 1973).
Lefebvre, H. (1983). *Logique Formelle, Logique Dialectique* (3rd ed.). Paris, France: Anthropos. (Original work published 1969).
Lefebvre, H. (1991). *The Production of Space*. Oxford, UK: Blackwell. (Original work published 1974).
Lefebvre, H. (2000). *La Production de l'Espace* (4th ed.). Paris, France: Anthropos. (Original work published 1974).
Lefebvre, H. (2001). Utopie Expérimentale: Pour un Nouvel Urbanisme. In *Du Rural à l'Urbain* (pp. 129–140). Paris, France: Anthropos. (Original work published 1961).
Lefebvre, H. (2003). *The Urban Revolution*. Minneapolis, MN: University of Minnesota Press. (Original work published 1970).
Lefebvre, H. (2020). *Hegel, Marx, Nietzsche or, the Realm of Shadows*. London, UK: Verso Books. (Original work published 1975).

9
ANTHROPOPHAGIC PHENOMENOLOGY[1]

Encounters at Lina Bo's SESC Pompeia Cultural and Leisure Center

Natalia Escobar Castrillón

Anthropophagy, or the concept of devouring the other, has had different connotations and rhetorical functions throughout modern Brazilian history. The earliest available written accounts building a history and myth of corporeal metaphors in the country dates back to the 16th century, when European colonizers, such as the German Hans Staden (c. 1525–c. 1576), allegedly reported the first-hand observation of an indigenous tribe's cannibalistic rituals (Staden, 2008, p. 17).[2] In contrast, scholars such as William Arens (1941–2019) questioned the veracity of cannibalistic accounts around the world, arguing that they were rather a cultural device for building hierarchies; his opinions fueled a contested debate.[3] Contemporary scholars have argued that, although some forms of cannibalistic practices may have existed in Brazil, many available accounts were distorted depictions from a colonial gaze that aimed to construct a narrative of cultural superiority to justify imperial projects (Martel, 2006); however, cannibalistic practices were not specific to Brazil, since they have been reported or imagined in tribes around the world, including on the European continent (Avramescu, 2009). At the same time, some archeologists and anthropologists have argued that there are evidences of cannibalistic practices in Brazil, but that these rituals were not mere acts of violence, and rather, were more complex cultural practices that ranged from simulated gestures to scare the colonizers to the honoring of the deceased population through the consumption of their bodies (Mora, 2008; Islam, 2011), a hypothesis that resonates with religious metaphors such as the Christian Eucharist. This controversial debate has inspired multiple cultural and artistic practices interested in rethinking the concept of otherness and of cultural domination, being particularly relevant for modern avant-garde cultural practices and contemporary post-colonial theories. *I will argue that following avant-gardes reinterpretations of this debate, the Italo-Brazilian architect Lina Bo's[4] (1914–1997) project for the Social Service of Commerce (SESC) in Pompeia triggers the experience of otherness and emancipation through architecture, what I have called "anthropophagic phenomenology."*

At the beginning of the 20th century, Brazilian artist Tarsila de Aguiar do Amaral (1886–1973) produced allegorical paintings that, along with the modernist artistic scene at the time, inspired the anthropophagic movement (Amaral, 2009, p. 32)[5] and poet José Oswald de Souza Andrade's (1890–1954) influential 1928 *Manifesto Antropófago* (*Cannibalist Manifesto*) (Andrade, 1928). This work exemplified a kind of modern cannibalism as an avant-garde practice in which Brazilians appropriated, devoured, and subverted the meaning of the European cultural legacy, producing an artistic mutation of the works. In the first half of the 20th century, this Brazilian epistemology became an international artistic reference, establishing horizontal cultural exchanges with European intellectuals.[6] In the late 1950s and early 1960s,[7] the anthropophagic movement was no more a reaction against the European colonial culture, but rather, against the uncritical absorption of the North American consumer culture that was popular at the time. Brazilian artists searched for references in local and precolonial cultural manifestations, such as indigenous practices and symbolisms, that included non-linguistic signs and embodied practices in the process of meaning-making, resulting in original phenomenological explorations. Continuing the anthropophagic explorations, the group of artists around the *Neoconcreto Manifesto*[8] introduced and rethought the foundational phenomenological theories of French philosopher Maurice Merleau-Ponty (1908–1961) in the Brazilian artistic production;[9] however, in this context these theories took on a particular socio-political meaning that they did not have in Europe at the time. Seeking to define an identity distinct from other countries in the international panorama, Brazilian artists pursued the subversion of meanings, not only through abstract operations, but also through embodied encounters with the artwork, following Merleau-Ponty's rejection of the Cartesian division between body and mind.[10] The later works of Bo seem to translate these subversive encounters into the specific medium of architecture, putting the body and the local culture of the Brazilian northeast at the center of her architectural and socio-political explorations and aspirations.

Lina Bo emigrated from Italy to Brazil in 1947, after her office was bombed during World War II, and then moved from São Paulo to Salvador de Bahia in 1958, during a prolific artistic period in the country that was abruptly disrupted in 1964 by a military coup and dictatorship that lasted until 1985. However, subversive artistic practices continued to emerge. Bo was engaged and shaped the artistic developments at the time through her professional experiences as an architect and curator in São Paulo and as professor and curator in the *Universidade Federal de Bahia* and the *Museu de Arte Moderna*.[11] She curated exhibitions and represented avant-garde productions with theater director Eros Martim Gonçalves (1919–1973), such as Bertolt Brecht's 1928 *The Threepenny Opera*,[12] influencing musician Caetano Veloso (1942–) and film director Glauber Rocha (1939–1981), among other students at the time (Aguilar, 2005, p. 121). Bo and Gonçalves also curated the 1959 exhibition *Bahia no Ibirapuera*, bringing to the southern metropolis of São Paulo the neglected cultural manifestation of northeastern Brazilian "popular culture"—which included the influence of African descendants and Amerindian cultures, and reflected the scarce material lifestyle in the *sertão* (dry inner land). From this period and Bahian cultural influence emerged the influential Brazilian artistic movements of *Cinema Novo* and *Tropicália*, among many other cultural manifestations that used art to resist the repressive dictatorship.[13] In Rio de Janeiro, environmental artist Hélio Oiticica (1937–1980), who directly influenced the *Tropicália* name and movement, developed an artistic work that he called "super-sensory objects." These objects were immersive artistic installations that aimed to expand the audience's sensorial experience in order to trigger their "expressive spontaneity, restricted by the daily routine" (Oiticica, 1986, pp. 102–105). Similarly, Bo affirmed that she felt a "visceral horror of any attempt to rationalize expression, gesture, and behavior."[14] Both artists believed in the agency of design to shape social behavior and had an interest in cultural manifestations of historically oppressed populations, such as racialized social groups.[15] Scholars have pointed at the similarities between Oiticica and Bo's explorations,[16] but there is no record of them having a personal relationship. Yet, in the notes of the architect, she writes, "Hélio: The simplification of cultural processes in the architectural field, for example, would lead to a higher valorization of spaces in relation to the body."[17] These notes demonstrate that Bo knew and reflected on the work of Oiticica and of the body in architecture.

Within the context of the dictatorship in Brazil, phenomenological explorations acquired a destabilizing quality and socio-political meaning. In contrast to the early European phenomenological theories of Martin Heidegger (1889–1976) and Merleau-Ponty, in which the body is the source of coherence and continuity in our experience of the world,[18] contemporary Austrian philosopher Dylan Trigg theorizes the concept of "abnormal embodiment" as a sort of displacement or up-rootedness experienced in places associated with traumatic past events (Trigg, 2012, p. 258). He describes the deep sense of disbelief and instability that seeing these places again after time have elapsed and physical transformations may have taken place. Trigg distinguishes between "absolute hereness," in which the body's temporality is the source of continuity and reliability in the experience of place, and "ambiguous hereness," as a sense of radical estrangement or pathology in which the body, time, and place are misaligned (Trigg, 2012, p. 260). His subject's conflicting memories produce the experience of otherness within itself as if two split subjectivities coexisted in one body. Although the works of Trigg and Bo are from different historic times, places, and disciplines, they could be connected by their reflection on otherness using their particular disciplinary means. I argue that Bo's project for the SESC Pompeia places and displaces the human body, intentionally un-grounding it and generating an ambiguous perception of spatial and temporal relationships. The architect introduces multiple and contrasting sensorial and symbolic references to the culture of historically excluded populations in Brazil, triggering the embodied architectural experience of otherness and the subversion of history, a practice that can be defined as anthropophagic phenomenology.

Anthropophagic Phenomenology at the SESC Pompeia

The SESC Pompeia complex located to the west of São Paulo (Figure 9.1) involved the transformation of a drum-packaging industrial plant built in 1938 by the German firm Mauser & Cia. Ltda., later occupied by the Brazilian packaging industry IBESA and the fridge fabricant Gelomatic.[19] Deactivated in 1970, the SESC bought the property in order to build a cultural and sportive center for its workers and the inhabitants of the developing neighborhood of Lapa. The complex consisted of a main axis that gave access to a diaphanous horizontal space under a continuous industrial shed. The space was enclosed by red brick walls inspired by British industrial structures and supported by a raw-concrete Hennebique structural system that was a technical innovation at the time. Bo got the commission in 1976 and developed a project with her trainees André Vainer and Marcelo Carvalho Ferraz (1955–). Their project preserves the existing structure but subverts it by designing embodied experiences that radically transformed their meaning.

The spaces at SESC Pompeia produce forms of abnormal embodiment as a design strategy for including multiple cultural references and for liberating the body from strict social norms and conventions, a bodily freedom that Bo identifies in the Brazilian populace in an idealized discourse:

> The wielder of civilization, of this total freedom of the body, of this *deinstitutionalization*, is the populous, the Brazilian people's very way of being, whereas highly developed western countries and the *middle class* (including here certain type of intellectual) anxiously seek a way out of the hypocrite and limiting freedoms that they destroyed centuries ago.[20]

In an interview with Bo's collaborator Carvalho Ferraz, he explains:

> I am almost sure that Lina tried to make phenomenology a driving principle for her architectural designs. She seems to suggest that architecture is to be inhabited and felt not just spoken. It has to have an experiential effect. What she meant is that the space imposes a behavior.[21]

FIGURE 9.1 Aerial view of Lina Bo's SESC Pompeia's Cultural and Leisure Center, São Paulo, Brazil.

The political theorist Antonio Gramsci, of whom Bo was an avid reader, affirmed that the social production of space is commanded by a hegemonic class as a tool to reproduce its dominance.[22] Bo's design strategies show an awareness of the strong relationship between power and space-making and the possibilities for subversion by using the abstract and concrete tools of architecture. The SESC Pompeia presents this awareness both literally and symptomatically. Bo alters old spatial relationships and introduces specific elements in the industrial complex, which allows for simultaneous and sometimes contradictory bodily experiences that avoid the normative experiences of space. These experiences resonate with Trigg's notion of abnormal embodiment, but in Bo's architectural work, they acquire a particular socio-political goal: the liberation of the body-mind through an ambiguous experience and the "*deinstitutionalization*"[23] of perception that will be presented through different examples throughout the complex. In an interview about the SESC Pompeia, she explains: "we followed contemporary principles, where a word such as recuperation has no place . . . this space has been created for new manifestations."[24]

Anthropophagic Phenomenology **151**

The notion of abnormal embodiment can be an imposed condition due to historical contingencies, such as human or natural catastrophes and traumatic experiences and/or rigid political regimes. However, we could also think of an architecture that intentionally triggers abnormal embodiment as a political statement for social inclusion by allowing for the coexistence of multiple subjectivities in place. The acceptance of otherness within oneself can result in more tolerance to differences outside ourselves. These reflections potentially intersect with studies on post-colonialism, race, and gender theory.[25] This approach builds on the theory of Merleau-Ponty while also introducing an element of purposeful disembodiment, as defined by Trigg. The late works of the architect Lina Bo in Brazil are coetaneous with the phenomenological explorations in the arts, and her work exemplifies some of these theoretical explorations through architecture.

Bo's preliminary drawings depict a series of sensorial landscapes (Figure 9.2) that include a fire-pit, a pond, river pebbles, bright and plastic colors, rough textures and finishes, temperature contrasts, a fountain, noises, scents, light reflections, as well as material intrusions providing specific and disruptive unhomely and haptic experiences within the existing sober industrial complex. She compares the newly designed inner water pond with the Northern San Francisco River; the new raw-concrete sports towers with the anonymous architecture of Brazilian fortresses lost in the seashore; the public spaces with the "*terreiros*"[26] or sacred sites for the Afro-Brazilian religion of Candomblé as well as the exterior fountain or collective shower when she wrote, "the waterfall in the square is an image from the Northeast, it's a waterfall bath, the Waterfall at Mata Grande where Father Xangô lives;"[27] the new wood deck with a "*solarium Indio*";[28] and the entire complex with a *cidadella* or traditional walled European city, supporting

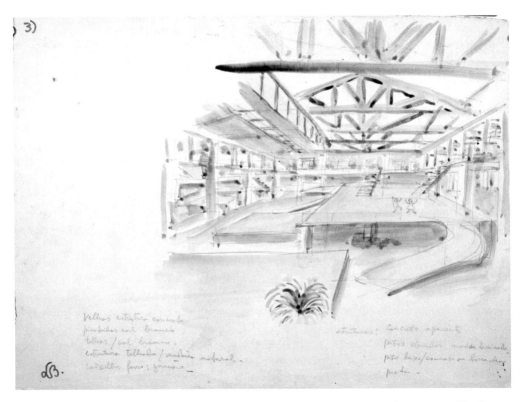

FIGURE 9.2 Lina Bo's sketch of the SESC Pompeia's collective space conceived as a sensorial landscape.

the coexistence of different readings of the building, mixing and "cannibalizing" previous cultural associations within the Brazilian reality.[29] In addition, on another drawing reflecting about the landscaping for the complex, Bo develops an inventory of plants that have symbolic meanings for Brazilian culture because of their healing or ritualistic associations (Oliveira, 2006). These experiences are not mere sensorial stimuli disconnected from intellectual and socio-political realities; rather, they are intentional references to the culture of historically oppressed social groups in Brazil, such as the numerous populations of Indigenous and African descendants that inhabited the northern regions of the country.

Under the pre-existing industrial shed, Bo qualified spaces by introducing elements that produce atmospheres and experiential intensities and contrasts rather than using conventional architectural divisions. In her description of the project, Bo affirms: "The architectural design of the SESC Pompeia Factory Leisure Center came from the desire to build another reality. We included just a few things: some water, a fireplace."[30] In an early furniture plan of SESC, what seems to be a circular-shaped reception desk is transformed in later drawings into a hearth that Bo initially designed for an outdoor space besides the complex entrance, but later placed within the shed's diaphanous space, acting as a marker. Therefore, the building receives visitors by inviting them to join a bodily experience by sitting around a fire-pit as a collective social ritual. The hearth appears as a sign for warmth but also as its primordial experience. The stone base absorbs and releases the heat, the fire lights the dark space, and the reflecting metal tube of the chimney hangs from the ceiling, collecting the smoke but also marking a space of gathering from the distance. In contrast, Bo places a pond in a dialectical spatial and experiential relationship with the fire-pit, producing a sense of incompatible sensorial stimuli. The pond is primordially the experience of freshness and humidity that touches the skin, but also cools the stone floor and triggers the movement of hot air to the ceiling's openings. The pond includes a small fountain of vertical pouring water that distorts light reflections and adds noises and dynamism to the experience. This pond is a dynamic mirror, a generator of activity, and a technical solution that transforms and contributes to an always-changing experience of the space. Whereas the fire-pit invites visitors to gather and stay around it, the sinuous shape of the pond invites visitors to pursue a peripheral movement around the nave, gaining a perspective of the whole.

These sharp contrasts create a sense of instability that is enhanced by additional ungrounding spatial qualities. The hearth, traditionally a centering element, acquires in Bo's project a decentering role that resonates with Trigg's concept of ambiguous hereness. The tooth-saw shed and its supports virtually divide space into equal modules. The fire-pit appears to be placed in a random position that does not seem to respond to classical relationships of symmetry, centrality, or monumentality. Far from the main entrance, off the axis of symmetry of the structural module, and misaligned with the closer door, the hearth becomes a decentering experience rather than being a grounding element (Figure 9.3). Although the shed could have suggested to the architect a disconnection between content and envelope that would justify these misalignments, at other instances the architect recognized the spatial features that the fire-pit's position denies. Within this spatial module, a simple stone bridge marks the axis of symmetry, although forcing a perpendicular direction. The possibility to stand still at the center of the modular nave perceiving its symmetry is at odds with all the elements pertaining to Bo's intervention. In addition, the hearth is visually aligned with the SESC complex's entrance. Therefore, it provides a center for its immediate surroundings, a misalignment within the modular space, and a marker that orients visitors from the beginning of their building's experience. These decisions show the architect's awareness of existent spatial qualities and her conscious challenge of them through the design of diverging experiences.

FIGURE 9.3 The decentering chimney and pond at the SESC Pompeia's collective space.

Bo's work cannot be inscribed in a single movement or school at the time, but rather she worked closely with artists who blurred disciplinary limits. However, there are some resonances between her work at the SESC Pompeia and other architectural and artistic explorations at the time. The organic shape of the pond and her original sketches showing large-scale plants under the shed resonate with the work of Brazilian landscape architect Roberto Burle Marx (1909–1994) that includes the design of tropical and water gardens using autochthonous species. Bo met him in 1947 in Rio de Janeiro and visited his residence in 1952. Burle Marx imagined the embodied and dynamic perception of gardens as visitors walk through, and he designed accordingly (Birksted, 2004, p. 92). He also considered the effects of lighting and reflection in relation to water in his designs. These qualities seem to be crucial in Bo's designs for the collective space under the shed, but also for the landscape of the complex. The decentering and destabilizing quality of Bo's arrangements also reminds observers of Hélio Oiticica's immersive objects that aim to free the body from habitual behavior. In addition, as part of Bo's personal library, we can find a copy of Claudia Andujar's 1978 photograph book *Yanomami*. Andujar (1931–) develops a system of representation adequate to the dynamism of the Amazonian Yanomami tribe's rituals that resulted in blurred images, where the mystical event was not literally or realistically represented. Rather, Andujar captured the atmosphere with shimmering lights, smoke, confusion, movement, tilted angles, doubled elements that are juxtaposed, as well as mixed faces, figures, artifacts, and nature, in which foreground and background intermingle. Andujar's photographs encapsulate the complexity of a single moment in a *felt-seen* image characterized by richness and ambiguity rather than an objectified culture. Similarly, Bo designed heterogeneous and dynamic landscapes and experiences.

Between 1982 and 1986, Bo designed three new towers for the expansion of the complex in which she pursued typological, spatial, and material subversions, generating unexpected experiences. Two of the towers contain sports facilities that are stacked vertically instead of spreading horizontally on the ground floor, which was an innovation at the time. The architect generated a sculptural volume by connecting the towers with a series of expressive bridges of an almost anthropomorphic quality. She also designed a third independent tower that recalls an old chimney that was demolished before the SESC acquired the land. However, the new tower is instead a water tank, radically transforming the previous association of this typology with air pollution and industrial production. The water tank becomes the symbol of the new spirit of work and leisure, by projecting flowers instead of smoke through the iconography that the architect also designed for the complex.

Different from the operations within the shed, the new towers produce an experience of abnormal embodiment not because of their spatial features, but because of their ambiguous aesthetic temporal references to the far past and future. The towers can be connected to historic architecture characterized by its roughness and massiveness, such as a fortress or bunker. Bo wrote: "Reduced to two pieces of land, I thought of the marvelous architecture of Brazilian military fortress lost in the sea, or hidden throughout the country, in cities, forests, in the isolation of desserts and interior lands."[31] The towers can also be read as arcane objects from prehistoric times, such as caves, stone hedges, obelisks, or totems. Their primitivism is inflicted by the use of raw concrete as almost the only external material but with rough finishes and an irregular facade's openings only covered with vernacular wood lattices. Bo describes these openings as "the prehistoric holes of caves with no glazing, nothing,"[32] which contributes to readings these contemporary buildings as a kind of architectural archaism and contemporary ruin.

However, at the same time, this architecture points to the future. On a sketch, Bo designs an urban landscape of towers around the SESC complex following the exact same design of her towers but multiplying its scale, and she writes, "view for a possible future of SESC" (Figure 9.4). The structural use of raw concrete reminds viewers of modern silos and progressive industrial constructions related to labor, such as the image of the Atlantic City's pier tower that Bo kept for reference in her personal archive. In the interior, a concrete waffle slab allows for huge spans without supports. This constructive system, along with the flying bridges joining two of the towers, displays the modern structural capacity of reinforced concrete and the possibilities of technological innovation. This reference to industrial aesthetics reminds readers of Le Corbusier's (1887–1965) project for modern architecture (Le Corbusier, 1923). However, in the case of Bo, she was not seeking to distill this industrial architecture, but rather to show non-aestheticized materials and construction process in a display of the presence of human labor. She left irregularities and the traces of the construction process on the water tank's surface, where a series of circular wood scaffoldings generated a succession of concrete rings. She uses fabric from sandbags' leftovers inside the wood scaffolding that intensified the irregular concrete joints between sections. In the design of the workshops' walls under the shed, she used cement and concrete brick walls, and allowed for the cement to pour beyond the surface without eliminating or flattening what was commonly considered material residues. For the cement floors, she designed the intrusion of small tile fragments (Figure 9.5). These operations insist on the use of modern materials but rendering the presence of the human hand, rather than presenting a fully industrialized construction that she associated with a bourgeois aesthetics. In 1982, when the construction of the towers began, Bo curated an art exhibition at SESC that was preceded by a description titled *The Beautiful and the Right to the Ugly*. The architect wrote:

> The expression kitsch emerged in Germany at the end of the 19th century when the Industrial Revolution took power definitively. This is the stigma of the high educated bourgeoisie and less fortunate actors of this same class, that through industrialization

FIGURE 9.4 Lina Bo, "View of a Possible Future," sketch of the SESC Pompeia's sport towers.

FIGURE 9.5 Material and aesthetic explorations at the SESC Pompeia's workshops and exhibitions space.

began to have access to the Arts' Treasures and to the "beautiful." This small exhibition is not an integration of Kitsch, it is a humble example of the RIGHT TO THE UGLY, which is the fundamental base of many civilizations, from Africa to the Far Orient, who never knew the "concept" of Beauty, which is the concentration camp of Western Civilization. From all this process, even less fortunate people were excluded: The Populace. And the Populace is never Kitsch, but this is another story.[33]

The intrusions and irregularities insist on human labor and the impurity of materials and seek for an unfamiliar aesthetic language that prevents the passive consumption of architecture. Bo writes in her personal notes:

The "Beautiful" is easy, what is difficult is the ugly, the truly ugly. I wish that the Sportive Complex of the SESC Pompeia Factory were ugly, even uglier than the "Museum of Art of São Paulo." It is a silo, bunker, container.[34]

The towers represent an ancient past previous to the standardization of vertical construction and the use of concrete, while on the other hand, a desire for a future different from the European cultural colonization, the abstractness of the modern architectural movement and the engineering developments of the Paulista school. What manifests itself is the freedom of a past time, a repressed desire for a self-explanatory construction and materiality, the right to make irregular and imperfect surfaces, the handmade, and in sum, the desire for alternative and liberating aesthetic discourses.

Bo's approach sheds light on how we could address the socio-political challenges that 21th-century architecture is facing in the demand for social inclusion and diversity. Rather than producing autonomous objects disconnected from social realities, her practice is a kind of architectural activism that aims to include and make visible oppressed cultural manifestations and worldviews in space. However, the architect does not turn to literal references or folkloric interpretations of these cultures. The example of the fire-pit and the pond illustrates architectonically how contrasting cultural references and embodied experiences can coexist, creating an inclusive spatial experience. In addition, the example of the towers challenges the exclusionist bourgeois aesthetic imported from Europe throughout the 20th century, which represented a single version of modernity and development. Rather, Bo's underlying socio-political agenda addresses "the people from the Northeast, working leather and empty tins, the village-dwellers, the blacks and the Indians, the masses who invent and contribute to the creation of something that is tough, dry, hard to digest" (Bo, 2013). Her anthropophagic architectural experience at SESC Pompeia suggests the embodied experience of the repressed of history and the shuttering of prevailing and exclusionist notions of modernity and its associated definitions of beauty, culture, behavior, subjectivity, and space.

Notes

1. Self-coined term to designate an embodied alterity that disrupts the traditional corporeal synthesis of the phenomenological experience. I borrowed the term *anthropophagy* from the influential Brazilian avant-garde artistic movement of the first half of the 20th century.
2. This was the earliest European account of the Tupi Indians written in the 16th century by German mercenary Hans Staden, who alleged that he was captured and escaped that tribe. His account haunted the European imagination and nurtured the constructed distinction between a civilized Europe and a primitive Brazil in which colonial projects are grounded.
3. "In other words, the question of whether or not people eat each other is taken as interesting but moot. But if the idea that they do is commonly accepted without adequate documentation, then the reason for this state of affairs is an even more intriguing problem" (Arens, 1979, p. 9).
4. Lina Bo adopted the surname "Bardi" from her husband as it was and still is a tradition in many countries around the world. By this practice, women bear a mark of their husbands that is not reciprocal and that in many cases entirely replaces their names. This practice is one of the many manifestations of the structural machismo that prevails in our society against which this article takes a stance. We are responsible for revising and challenging traditions that perpetuate gender-based discrimination in the name of objectivity and neutrality. The architect was born Achillina Bo, using only her father's surname, because the use of maternal surnames is still forbidden in Italy by the Constitutional Court Decision No. 286, at Gazetta Uufficiale No. 52 (Dec. 28, 2016).
5. Tarsila de Amaral and Oswald de Andrade were part of the *Grupo dos Cinco* (Group of Five) that also includes Anita Malfatti, Menotti Del Picchia, and Mario de Andrade (D'Alessandro & Oramas, 2017, p. 39, p. 171).
6. International artists, such as French poet Max Jacob (issue 6 of *Revista de Antropofagia*) or Indian philosopher Jiddu Krishnamurti (issue 8), among many other international artists and intellectuals, responded with sympathy to the Manifesto Antropófago. According to do Amaral, "the movement excited, scandalized, irritated, enthused, infuriated and grew in members from Northern to Southern Brazil, in addition to attracting the sympathy of intellectuals from our neighboring countries. It also had reverberations in Paris, with indignant protests aroused by my painting *Antropofagia*" (Amaral, 2009, p. 33).
7. Between 1956 and 1964, the populist governments of Juscelino Kubitschek (1956–1961), Jânio Quadros (1961), and João Goulart (1961–1964) pursued structural social improvements. This period was characterized by political stability, decentralization, and economic growth, cultural and artistic production, international exchanges, and trans-disciplinary dialogues that were characterized by a search for local identity.
8. The Neoconcreto Manifesto was signed by Amílcar de Castro, Ferreira Gullar, Franz Weissmann, Lygia Clark, Lygia Pape, Reynaldo Jardim, and Theon Spanudis, and Mario Pedrosa.
9. In the *Neoconcreto Manifesto* we can find the following direct reference to Merleau-Pontry's theory: "We do not conceive a work of art as a "machine" nor as an "object," but as a *quasi-corpus* [quasi-body], this is, as something that is not exhausted in the external relationship of its elements; something that, decomposed in parts for analysis, can only be fully grasped phenomenologically. . . . [It] supersedes and transcend mechanistic relationships (of an objective Gestalt) and creates for itself a tacit signification *(M. Ponty)* that emerges for the first time" (Gullar, 1977, p. 82).

10. Maurice Merleau-Ponty's approach was a response to the Cartesian division between body and mind that relies on the former as the only source for truth. See Merleau-Ponty, 1962.
11. A detailed account of Bo's involvement with avant-garde artists in Salvador de Bahia in the 1960s can be found in Risério (1995); see also Lina Bo, (undated), *Cinco anos entre os brancos* (*Five years among the white men*), São Paulo, Brazil: Acervo do Instituto Lina Bo e Pietro Maria Bardi.
12. The work offers a critique of the capitalist world. It opened on August 31, 1928 at Berlin's *Theater am Schiffbauerdamm*.
13. For a better understanding of the artistic movements at the time, see Basualdo (2005, pp. 22–93).
14. Lina Bo, lecture notes, my translation, Acervo do Instituto Lina Bo e Pietro Maria Bardi, São Paulo.
15. In the case of Lina Bo, there is an over-time evolution of her understanding of the culture of African and indigenous descendants in Brazil that switches from a neocolonial characterization of their art as primitive (Bo, 1951) to a profound expression of freedom and political agency (Bo, 2013).
16. To read more about the parallelisms between Bo's and Oiticica's spatial explorations, see Wisnik (2012).
17. Lina Bo, lecture notes, my translation, Acervo do Instituto Lina Bo e Pietro Maria Bardi, São Paulo.
18. Merleau-Ponty's notion of experience is based on the synoptic presence of human existence where no conceptual abstraction and neither pure experience can replace the intertwined and co-constituent relationship between the body-subject and the world (Merleau-Ponty, 1962).
19. Jose Roberto Ferreira Cintra, "IV A constituição da área atual: centro cultural e desportivo Pompeia," in Levantamento Historico CCD Pompeia, undated, Acervo do Instituto Lina Bo e Pietro Maria Bardi.
20. Lina Bo, "SESC Pompeia—Sport," 1977, my translation, Acervo do Instituto Lina Bo e Pietro Maria Bardi, São Paulo. The excerpt presents Bo's original highlighted words.
21. Marcelo Ferraz, interview with author, July 17, 2017, São Paulo.
22. Lina Bo had a collection of Antonio Gramsci books in her personal library that was heavily highlighted and annotated, showing her deep engagement with his theories. In particular this piece is from the book Gramsci, Antonio. *Opere di Antonio Gramsci: Lettere dal carcere*, Torino: Giulio Einaudi Editore, 1947. Bo's personal library at Acervo do Instituto Lina Bo e Pietro Maria Bardi, São Paulo.
23. Lina Bo, "SESC Pompeia-Sport," 1977, my translation, Acervo do Instituto Lina Bo e Pietro Maria Bardi, São Paulo. The excerpt presents Bo's original highlighted words.
24. Lina Bo, "Ajustar o novo ao antigo, a preocupação," April 11, 1982, *Folha de São Paulo*. Acervo do Instituto Lina Bo e Pietro Maria Bardi, folder no. 1.0046 (my translation).
25. See the works on identity politics by Sara Ahmed or Maria Lugones.
26. "terreiro hall" in Lina Bo, "Teatro," SESC Pompeia, April 22, 1980, Acervo do Instituto Lina Bo e Pietro Maria Bardi, São Paulo.
27. Lina Bo, "The Pompeia Factory," 1986, my translation, Acervo do Instituto Lina Bo e Pietro Maria Bardi, São Paulo. And Oliveira, 2006.
28. Lina Bo, "The Pompeia Factory," 1986, Acervo do Instituto Lina Bo e Pietro Maria Bardi, São Paulo.
29. These comparisons can also be found in Lina Bo, Notes, "Sesc Pompeia," 1977, my translation, Acervo do Instituto Lina Bo e Pietro Maria Bardi, São Paulo; and "A Bowl of Soup for People," in Lima (2013).
30. Lina Bo, "The Pompeia Factory," 1986, my translation, Acervo do Instituto Lina Bo e Pietro Maria Bardi, São Paulo.
31. Lina Bo, "SESC Pompeia," 1977, my translation, Acervo do Instituto Lina Bo e Pietro Maria Bardi, São Paulo.
32. Lina Bo, notes for interview with *Casa Vogue*, no. 6, São Paulo, Nov.–Dec. 1986, 134, Acervo do Instituto Lina Bo e Pietro Maria Bardi, São Paulo.
33. Lina Bo Bardi e Equipe do SESC, "Primeira Exposição de Artes dos Funcionarios do INAMPS," at SESC Fabrica da Pompeia, São Paulo, 1982, my translation, Acervo do Instituto Lina Bo e Pietro Maria Bardi, São Paulo. Original emphasis.
34. Lina Bo, notes, my translation, Acervo do Instituto Lina Bo e Pietro Maria Bardi, São Paulo.

References

Aguilar, G.M. (2005). *Poesia Concreta Brasileira: As Vanguardas na Encruzilhada Modernista*. São Paulo, Brazil: Edusp.

Amaral, T.A. (2009). *Tarsila do Amaral*. Madrid, Spain: Fundación Juan March.

Andrade, O. (1928). Manifesto Antropófago. In A.A. Machado & R. Bopp (Eds.), *Revista de Antropofagia* 1(1). Cannibalist Manifesto (L. Bary, Trans.). *Latin American Literary Review* 19(38), Pittsburgh, Dept. of Modern Languages, Carnegie-Mellon University, 38–47.

Arens, W. (1979). *The Man-Eating Myth: Anthropology and Anthropophagy*. New York, NY: Oxford University Press.

Avramescu, C. (2009). *An Intellectual History of Cannibalism* (A.I. Blyth, Trans.). New Jersey, NJ: Princeton University Press.
Basualdo, C. (2005). *Tropicália: A Revolution in Brazilian Culture*. São Paulo: CosacNaify, Museum of Contemporary Art Chicago.
Birksted, J. (Ed.). (2004). *Relating Architecture to Landscape*. London, UK: Taylor & Francis.
Bo, L. (1951). (Unnamed). *Habitat*, (1), 72.
Bo, L. (2013). Planning the Environment: "Design" at an Impasse," (1976). In S. Rubino (Ed.), *Architecture Words 12: Stone Against Diamonds*. London, UK: Architectural Association.
D'Alessandro, S., & Oramas, L.P. (Eds.). (2017). *Tarsila do Amaral: Inventing Modern Art in Brazil*. Chicago, IL: Art Institute of Chicago, New York Museum of Modern Art.
Gullar, F. (1977). Manifesto Neoconcreto. In A. Amaral (Ed.), *Projeto Construtivo Brasileiro na Arte (1950–1962)* (pp. 80–84). Rio de Janeiro, Brazil: Funarte. (Reprinted from *Jornal do Brasil*, March 22, 1959).
Islam, G. (2011). Can the Subaltern Eat? Anthropophagic Culture as a Brazilian Lens on Post-Colonial Theory. *Organization*, 19(2), 159–180. https://doi.org/10.1177/1350508411429396
Le Corbusier (Charles-Édouard Jeanneret). (1923). *Vers une Architecture*. Paris, France: Éditions Crès.
Lima, Z.R.M. (2013). *Lina Bo Bardi*. New Haven, CT: Yale University Press.
Martel, H.E. (2006). Hans Staden's Captive Soul: Identity, Imperialism, and Rumors of Cannibalism in Sixteenth-Century Brazil. *Journal of World History*, 17(1), 51–69. https://doi.org/10.1353/jwh.2006.0031
Merleau-Ponty, M. (1962). *Phenomenology of Perception* (C. Smith, Trans.). New Jersey, NJ: Humanities Press.
Mora, V.V. (2008). Cuerpos, Cadáveres y Comida: Canibalismo, Comensabilidad y Organización Social en la Amazonia. *Antípoda, Revista de Antropología y Arqueología*, (6), 271–291. Retrieved from www.redalyc.org/articulo.oa?id=814/81400614
Oiticica, H. (1986). *Aspiro ao Grande Labirinto*. Rio de Janeiro, Brazil: Rocco.
Oliveira, O. (2006). *Subtle Substances: The Architecture of Lina Bo Bardi*. Barcelona, Spain: Editorial Gustavo Gili.
Risério, A. (1995). *Avant-garde na Bahia*. São Paulo, Brazil: Instituto Lina Bo e Pietro Maria Bardi.
Staden, H. (2008). *Hans Staden's True History: An Account of Cannibal Captivity in Brazil*. Durham, NC: Duke University Press.
Trigg, D. (2012). *The Memory of Place: A Phenomenology of the Uncanny*. Athens, OH: Ohio University Press.
Wisnik, G. (2012). Public Space on the Run: Brazilian Art and Architecture at the End of the 1960s. *Third*, 26(1), 117–129. https://doi.org/10.1080/09528822.2012.647660

10

INCREMENTAL HOUSING

A Short History of an Idea

Nelson Mota

Introduction

Over the last decades, sustainable development became a catch-phrase to frame narratives related with the built environment. The apex of this debate was the Habitat III Conference convened by the United Nations in 2016 in Quito, Ecuador. The New Urban Agenda (NUA), based on 17 Sustainable Development Goals, is arguably the most prominent outcome of Habitat III. While the NUA (Habitat III Secretariat, 2017) addresses aspects that touch upon the field of operations of a wide range of disciplines, urban and architectural design are also called to take the responsibility to contribute to achieve some of its goals and targets.

Access to adequate housing is one of the critical challenges arising from the rapid urbanization that will take place in the coming decades. The shared vision for the NUA highlights the importance of establishing "cities and human settlements that fulfil their social function, . . . with a view to progressively achieving the full realization of the right to adequate housing as a component of the right to an adequate standard of living, without discrimination" (Habitat III Secretariat, 2017, p. 5). Furthermore, the NUA stresses the importance of cities and human settlements that are "participatory, promote civic engagement, engender a sense of belonging and ownership among all their inhabitants" (Habitat III Secretariat, 2017, p. 5).

In the context of the debate on strategies to accomplish the sustainable development goals, incremental housing has been proposed by housing scholars as a contribution to the development of adequate housing that can enable citizens' participation and enhance a sense of belonging and ownership (Wakely & Riley, 2011; Lindert, Smets, & Bredenoord, 2014). Slowly but steadily, incremental housing has also penetrated the jargon of architects and urban designers since the 1970s.[1] However, there is not yet a clear definition of what incremental housing is, what it does, and who does it. In this context, this chapter aims to shed some light on this concept and discuss how it can implicate the role of the architect, architecture, and the city in the 21st century.

Before moving further, it is important to settle an answer to the first question: what is incremental housing? According to the Merriam-Webster dictionary, the adjective "incremental" means "of, relating to, being, or occurring in especially small increments." For example: "*incremental* additions" or "*incremental* change." Accordingly, I would define incremental housing as a conceptual approach to the design of houses that can gradually accommodate vertical and/or horizontal changes and expansions, evolving from the initial configuration in a series of increments over time. House types with these characteristics can thus be assembled under the notion of incremental housing.

While its popularity is growing in housing scholarship and architectural narratives, incremental housing approaches seem to remain at odds with the hegemonic structures of power that influence global and local housing policies. Since the neoliberal turn of the 1980s, housing programs all over the world have been mostly rooted in a form of economic rationality geared to satisfy the needs of, and to partner with, the market. From that moment on, a major paradigm shift in housing policies started taking shape. The paradigm of the state as provider of housing that prevailed throughout the decades of welfarism was suddenly replaced by the paradigm of the state as enabler of private initiatives. Despite some remaining cases of welfarism still being operational in countries like the Netherlands, or the Nordic countries, over the last four decades the use value of housing has been quickly replaced by its exchange value. Rather than promoting housing as a social good, states all over the world shifted their policies to stimulate home ownership, indeed promoting housing as a commodified asset (Fishman, 2018).

Housing programs rolled out over the last two decades in such diverse geopolitical realities as India, South Africa, or Brazil testify to this change (Bredenoord, Lindert, & Smets, 2014). Their focus on short-term efficiency—a typical feature of neoliberalism—created detrimental consequences to the livelihoods of millions of citizens. In this context, incremental housing has been looked upon as a possibility to create a more inclusive, resilient, and sustainable approach to the production of affordable housing (Bredenoord & van Lindert, 2010; Wakely & Riley, 2011). It is not clear, however, what mechanisms need to be put in place to make incremental housing a possible solution to solve the affordable housing crisis that is threatening the way we live today. It is even less clear how it could influence the way we will live in the cities of the 21st century, shaped by a relentless process of planetary urbanization (Brenner & Schmid, 2012).

Many housing scholars stress the importance of de-commodifying the development of affordable housing to tackle the rising social and spatial inequality triggered by the neoliberal system (Marcuse & Madden, 2016; Martin, Moore, & Schindler, 2015). Others highlight the importance of challenging the enabling strategy that gained momentum in housing policies disseminated after the neoliberal turn (Yap, 2016).

Paraphrasing John Turner's famous axiom, there is a growing consensus that housing as a product should again be replaced by housing as a process. It is in this context that a critical review of incremental housing approaches is necessary. As this text will show, incremental housing approaches deconstruct the binary polarity of housing-as-a-*process*/housing-as-a-*product*. As such, this text will examine the extent to which the ambiguous political agency and accountability of incremental housing practices can be instrumental to rethink the current models of housing production.

A great deal of the scholarship produced on this topic has been primarily focused on aspects related to governance and policy. It has been far less discussed, however, what does *housing as a process* mean today for the architecture discipline and to meet the targets of the New Urban Agenda. To what extent can housing design contribute to promoting a more inclusive society? And, more specifically, how can design and governance be interwoven to promote the right to housing and the right to the city using incremental housing approaches?

To try and provide some possible answers to these questions, in this text I will examine the historical evolution of incremental housing approaches developed since the interwar period (1920s–1930s) until the turn of the 2020s. In this chapter I will use "incremental housing" as an umbrella term to describe different housing approaches and house types designed to accommodate growth and change through time. There are indeed a few other terms used to designate this housing approach or these types of house: "growing," "expandable," or "evolutionary" houses; "aided self-help housing" and "sites-and-services."

While all of these terms can be placed under the umbrella of "incremental housing," they are not interchangeable. In effect, they mean different things, in different historical moments. They all have in common, however, the fact that their popularity is inversely proportional to economic stability. In other words, incremental housing approaches usually coincide with times of scarcity of resources, fiscal austerity, or economic recession. Sometimes, all of these combined.

The Growing House

One of the first publicized experiments on incremental housing design came about in the early 1930s, a period characterized by a world crisis that depleted the financial resources of families and governments worldwide. But it was also a period when social inequality was on the rise and the livelihoods of the poor were being seriously threatened. It was in this context that the German landscape architect Leberecht Migge published in 1932 *Die wachsende Siedlung nach biologischen Gesetzen* (*The growing settlement according to biological laws*). In this book, Migge developed a project for a farming community that included a design for a "growing" house. Migge's idea of a productive landscape followed up on Adolf Loos' projects for self-sufficient communities, designed for the outskirts of Vienna in the 1920s (Hochhäusl, 2014). In Migge's growing settlement, the architectural definition of the house was not overlooked. Rather, he designed the house as an organism that could evolve through time, from just a shed, to a small 25-m^2 core-house, to a 100-m^2 two-bedroom house with indoor areas for food production (Haney, 2010). The project was designed to be feasible using a limited palette of materials and easily accessible craftsmanship and construction tools.

Also in 1932, Migge, together with other leading exponents of German *Neues Bauen*, participated in the exhibition *Das Wachsende Haus* (The Growing House), curated by Berlin's chief city planner Martin Wagner (Fezer, Hager, & Hiller, 2016). Both Migge's book and Wagner's exhibition were attempts to answer the acute housing crisis experienced at the turn of the 1930s, as well as a critique to the prevailing paradigm of housing production in Germany. Wagner's growing house condemns the detrimental lifestyles of the metropolis, as well as the social inequalities reproduced by existing urban-planning and architectural measures. Wagner's critique of the status quo highlighted the interdependence between typological solutions and the political economy of housing. As Tatjana Schneider (2016, pp. 193–194) asserts, "the rigid standardization of worker's housing and the commodification of living space, . . . came to assume not only a use value, but also a speculative value." For Wagner and most of the *Neues Bauen* architects, the growing house was promoted as a design and technological experiment, but also as a way of empowering and emancipating working-class families, providing conditions to improve their sanitary conditions, and acquiring some level of self-sufficiency.

Aided Self-Help

While the growing house approach was being discussed in Central Europe, another approach to the development of self-sufficient communities, "aided self-help," was being developed in parallel as a policy to cope with resource scarcity. "Aided self-help" approaches started at the beginning of the 20th century, included in the housing policies of some Nordic countries. According to Richard Harris (1999, p. 283), Sweden's national "Own Homes" Loan Fund of

FIGURE 10.1 Illustration of the "Growing Siedlung," as published in Leberecht Migge's *Die wachsende Siedlung nach biologischen Gesetzen* (1932).

1904 was the first program to include aided self-help housing. However, aided self-help did not gain traction as a full-fledged housing approach until the end of World War I. From the 1920s on, this would change dramatically. In a context of post-war recovery, it was used in European cities such as Stockholm and Vienna, but also in the young Soviet Union, "as a pragmatic, untheorised, response to severe housing shortages and political unrest after the First World War" (Harris, 1999, p. 282).

Afterwards, through the hand of people such as the American engineer and urban planner Jacob L. Crane, self-help housing policies would also be developed in North America. Then, from the 1950s on, it would be widely used in development aid, chiefly as an alternative for ill-defined public housing policies. In his canonical book *Man's Struggle for Shelter in an Urbanizing World*, published in 1964, Charles Abrams dedicated an entire chapter to "Self-help, Core housing, and instalment construction" (Abrams, 1964, pp. 164–181). From the 1960s through the 1980s, "assisted" or "aided" self-help housing approaches became popular as a methodology used in development aid by global players such as the United Nations, the Ford Foundation, USAID, and the World Bank.

The British architect John Turner would become an influential voice spreading the word on the virtues of self-help communities (J. Turner, 1968). His work would set the background against which the International Design Competition for the Urban Environment of Developing Countries was created. Organized by the staff of *Architectural Record* in 1973, this competition was thought of as a contribution to the United Nations Habitat Conference, which would be held in Vancouver in 1976. Its goal was to establish a privileged *forum* to discuss experiments in the architecture of self-help communities. The site selected for the competition was Dagat-Dagatan, an area of reclaimed fishponds located in Manila's Tondo Foreshore. In the brief of the competition, the part dedicated to the guidelines for the housing design instructed the competitors to clearly specify what was supposed to be provided as a *bare minimum*. The feasibility of the proposals, considering the limited financial resources available, was highlighted as a key criterion for the evaluation of the entries. However, the brief explained, "additional improvements, expansion possibilities and additions to the floor space and finishes should also be indicated whenever applicable" (Seelig, 1978, p. 30).

With 476 projects submitted, the competition was a huge success. The project submitted by Sau Lai Chan, a young Malaysian graduate of North-East London Polytechnic, provides a good illustration of how the idea of "self-help community" influenced architectural thinking and projects in the mid-1970s.

Chan's project, which won third prize in the competition, was done to obtain his master's degree thesis from Manchester University in 1975. It showed an approach to the architecture of self-help communities based on a cluster of core-house units. Each cluster was meant for a community of 10 to 30 households. The cluster was organized around a communal courtyard, with a water tap, laundry areas, and a windmill for generating electricity. At the scale of the dwelling unit, Chan proposed a core-house with a small footprint (9x5 m for up to 7 persons and 11x5 m for up to 10 persons). Each house was delivered to the residents by the government with a few built elements only: concrete footings, timber load-bearing structure, and roof. Each individual family would "complete the construction of its own home at its own pace as determined by its skills and resources" (Seelig, 1978, p. 59).

Sau Lai Chan's project shows how the concept of self-help influenced the 1970s' approach to housing design. At all the different scales of the project, the architect deliberately avoided fixing the spatial configuration of the settlement and the social and spatial practices that it could accommodate. Instead, the architectural project focused mainly on the definition of the infrastructure of public spaces and patterns of association to promote meaningful social spaces and accommodate vernacular domestic practices.

Sites-and-Services

Following up on the "self-help" tradition, the "sites-and-services" approach was strongly focused on the interwoven relationship between top-down design of the infrastructure (services) and

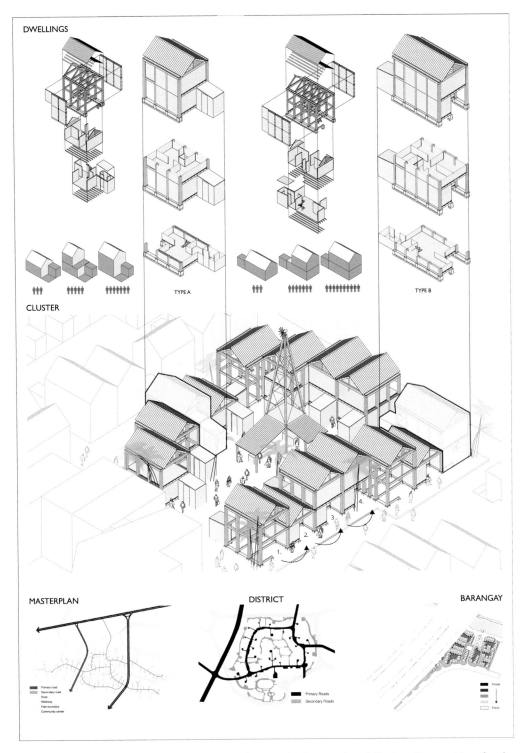

FIGURE 10.2 Project submitted by Sau Lai Chan to the International Design Competition for the Urban Environment of Developing Countries (1976).

bottom-up incremental improvement of the houses built on the plots (sites). According to Jan van der Linden, the sites-and-services approach had an historical precedent in the allotment garden movement that developed from the middle of the 19th century onwards in Europe (Van der Linden, 1986, pp. 40–46). The driving motives for the ideologues of the allotment garden movement were contradictory, though. For conservative organizations such as the Dutch "Anti-Social-Democratic Union of Railway Employees 'Right and Duty'," it was a way of promoting God, Family and Property (the slogan in the organization's banner), fighting the spread of socialism. For the labor movement, however, allotment gardens were seen as "an antidote against the alienating effects of factory work and city dwelling" (Van der Linden, 1986, pp. 41–42). In any case, the allotment gardens were initiated with a top-down approach but designed to give the laborers freedom to decide on the micro-management of their plot. Eventually, in countries like England, Wales, and the Netherlands, allotment gardens were instrumental to promote a shift from charity to self-help, advancing the emancipation of the laborers (Van der Linden, 1986, p. 43).

Developed mainly in the 1970s and 1980s, the sites-and-services approach shares with the allotment garden movement its ideological ambiguity. On the one hand, it was based on high-level decision-making and policies, usually at governmental level, with the support of international aid organizations or financial institutions. On the other hand, it was intended to give room for the progressive emancipation and empowerment of the low-income groups living in cities of the developing world.

There were three fundamental premises in the sites-and-services approach: resilient urban infrastructure, security of tenure, and self-help housing practices. These premises also have aspects in common with the aided self-help approach described previously. The main differences are in the scale and agency of the program. While aided self-help was mostly focused on the scale of the dwelling and the resources and tools of the household and local community, sites-and-services schemes were designed from scratch by national and international organizations to create new townships or urban districts, supported by an infrastructural network procured and developed by public governmental institutions.

In their *Urbanization Primer*, Horacio Caminos and Reinhard Goethert (1978) made the case for the sites-and-services approach as an alternative for mass housing. For these authors, the solution was either providing "complete dwellings to a few beneficiaries, or to provide only basic utilities and services to a much larger sector of the population" (Caminos & Goethert, 1978, p. 6). The latter would become the framework for most of the housing initiatives sponsored by development aid agencies. Eventually, the "sites-and-services" approach, mostly due to the sponsorship of the World Bank, would be responsible for the development of several millions of incremental dwellings built in the 1970s and 1980s (Williams, 1984).

In *Urbanization Primer*, Caminos and Goethert compiled a comprehensive set of project assessment, site analysis, and design criteria to optimize the development of efficient sites-and-services schemes. Their research on the optimum layout for the sites-and-services developments would set the standard for worldwide dissemination of this approach. However, the popularity of the sites-and-services approach in the 1980s would also propel some critical reviews from leading architects operating in the developing world. For example, two of the most well-known Indian architects, B.V. Doshi and Charles Correa, have explicitly rejected the mechanist, technocratic, and rigid design guidelines associated with the sites-and-services approach (Correa, 1989, pp. 14–30). In the mid-1980s both developed housing projects that showed an alternative approach to the sites-and-services schemes, in particular, and to incremental housing, in general. B.V. Doshi's project for the Aranya township and Correa's Belapur neighborhood advanced design strategies to mitigate the rigidity of the guidelines proposed by Caminos and Goethert.

In both cases, there was a strong emphasis on the clustering strategy and in the sequence of spaces that mediate the transition between the city and the dwelling unit. In their projects, Doshi and Correa also went beyond Caminos and Goethert's technocratic approach, introducing guidelines regarding architectural image and materiality that were instrumental to establish a connection with the vernacular patterns of inhabitation.

While these two notable designers introduced a high level of sophistication in their designs for residential communities, the bread and butter of departmental bureaucrats in international agencies and in local planning offices was characterized by a higher level of pragmatism. However, the results were not necessarily compromised. The Bombay Urban Development Project, sponsored by the World Bank and developed in Mumbai during the 1980s, is a case in point. This project had the ambitious goal of improving the living conditions of 100,000 households (500,000 inhabitants) living in slum hutments and squatter areas of Mumbai, creating "legal, environmentally-acceptable neighborhoods under the project through the provision of infrastructure improvements, long-term, leasehold tenure, and loans for home improvement" (The World Bank—South Asia Projects Department, 1985, p. 17).

The main component of this project was the Land Infrastructure Serving Program (LISP), dedicated to develop 85,000 serviced residential, commercial, and small industrial plots, using the sites-and-services approach in 12 different locations spread over Mumbai's metropolitan region. The project for one of these locations, Charkop, provides a compelling illustration of the fundamental tenets of the sites-and-services approach.

Charkop was a vast area of reclaimed marshland located on the northwest of Mumbai's peninsula. Under the auspices of the World Bank project, 15,420 plots were created in an area of approximately 180 hectares. The Charkop sites-and-services project was coordinated by Vidyadhar Phatak, an urbanist working for Bombay Metropolitan Region Development Authority (BMRDA), with the technical assistance of Alain Bertoud (World Bank). The key features of the project are the design of the typical residential cluster and a clear hierarchical street grid and open space network (Padora, 2016, pp. 179–196).

Each typical cluster included 35 plots varying from 25 m² (3.5x7m) to 40 m² (3.5x11.5m). Despite the relatively small size of the plot, over time each household could expand the house vertically, growing the habitable area incrementally with self-initiated expansions. Over the last 30 years, the projected incremental growth happened as planned. The social, economic, and environmental qualities of the neighborhood were not undermined by this incremental growth, though. In fact, the opposite is true. Charkop became a sought-after area showing, according to a recent study (Owens, Gulyani, & Rizvi, 2018, p. 268), a high level of liveability.

Not all the sites-and-services schemes developed in the 1970s and 1980s show such good results as Charkop. The success stories usually demonstrate an alignment of three key conditions: locations close to possibilities of income generation, reliable infrastructure, and affordable housing finance. Regarding design, there was one fundamental aspect: adequate plot size and configuration, clustered in meaningful communities.

Evolutionary Houses

The "sites-and-services" projects were mainly implemented in the developing world and were generally characterized by a high level of control, both in terms of urban design and governance. The architectural definition of the house was seldom included in these programs. Conversely, in the post-war period, "evolutionary houses" gained momentum as a new concept to define house types that could accommodate growth and change through time. They became an important field of research for post-war architects.

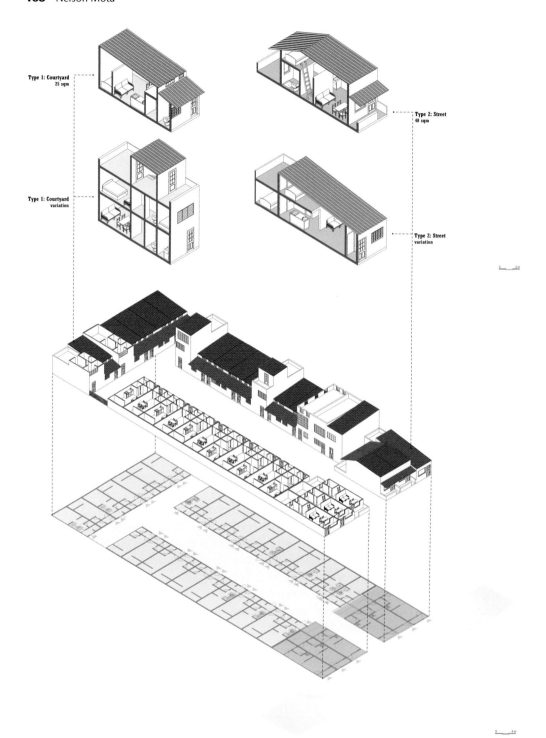

FIGURE 10.3 Axonometric perspective of the typical cluster for low-income families in the Charkop sites-and-services scheme (Kandivali, Mumbai).

Some of the most active groups participating in the post-war CIAM (*Congrès Internationaux d'Architecture Moderne*) congresses showed already an interest in growth and change at the ninth CIAM congress, held in Aix-en-Provence in 1953. It became a central topic during the discussion on the habitat for the greater number. This theme was famously discussed by Michel Ecochard, where he and his fellow members of the CIAM group ATBAT-Afrique showed projects to accommodate large groups of rural migrants in the French protectorate of Morocco (Avermaete, 2012).

The notion of *habitat évolutif* (French for "evolutionary housing") would stem from the discussions at CIAM IX and be developed further by architects such as Ionel Schein, Claude Parent, and Georges Candilis. In his notes while attending the 1953 CIAM congress, the Romanian-born French architect Ionel Schein wrote: "Function Living: It varies according to the evolution of society. What men builds to dwell should be able to perpetually change" (quoted in Berselli, 2015, p. 6). Schein's interest in the dynamic nature of dwelling practices comes back again, in 1953, in an essay dedicated to evolutionary housing that he wrote together with Claude Parent in *L'Architecture d'Aujourd'hui* (Parent & Schein, 1953).

Some years later, in the 1956 CIAM congress held at Dubrovnik, the interwoven relation between housing for the great number and *habitat evolutif* would evolve into a specific focus on the "problem of growth and change," with a commission fully dedicated to reflect this theme (Mota, 2014, pp. 423–425). In the preparation for the 10th CIAM congress, the topic of "growth and change" would be highlighted as a key factor for the creation of a Charter of the Habitat. In the draft framework prepared in 1954 by the CIAM X commission, the importance of acknowledging the dynamic nature of social and spatial practices was stressed, and how they should be accommodated in each particular house for each particular type of community. "Architecture and planning," the framework document stated, "must lose something of their finite character. Habitat should be planned and constructed so as not to resist their own spontaneous development (the development of those they serve)" (CIAM 10 Commission, 1954).

For the new generation of architects coming of age during the 1950s, the concept of *habitat evolutif* or evolutionary housing would remain a topic of intellectual investigation and experimentation in the following decades. In 1959, Candilis, Josic, and Woods published in the magazine *Techniques et Architecture* their proposal for evolutionary housing (Candilis, Josic, & Woods, 1959). As Tom Avermaete explains, in their project, the dwelling unit was put forth as an evolutionary habitat, "a living environment that has to be relentlessly appropriated, annihilated and re-appropriated" (2005, p. 174).

The engagement of architects with the idea of evolutionary housing would increase during the 1960s. Some of the most ground-breaking architectural experimentation of the time, such as Oskar Hansen's (1961) Open Form theory, was dedicated to projects that explored evolutionary housing. In the Netherlands, evolutionary housing was part of John Habraken's theory of supports (Habraken, 1999) and Constant's "New Babylon" project. In France, it was a key feature in Yona Friedman's "Spatial City" (*Ville Spatiale*), and in England, Cedric Price played with evolutionary housing in his "Fun Palace" (Anderson, 2019). The work of Constant, Friedman, and Price would remain influential mainly in theoretical debates, as arbiters of an insurrectional architecture, as Michel Ragon (1977, pp. 13–19) put it. However, Habraken's structuralist theory of supports would be taken further with the creation of the Foundation for Architects Research (*Stichting Architecten Research*, SAR) and a worldwide dissemination of its method for the design of mass housing (Bosma, Hoogstraten, & Vos, 2000).

Next to these novel architectural narratives, the notoriety of evolutionary housing approaches would be boosted by one event, the PREVI-Lima competition. PREVI-Lima would become one of the most famous experiments, exploring the potential of evolutionary houses as the basis for a new approach to the production of affordable housing. This experience was triggered in 1965 by the joint initiative of the United Nations and the Peruvian government, whose president was Fernando Belaúnde, an architect, to invite Peter Land, a British architect and urban planner. According to Peter Land, incremental housing was one of the fundamental principles that framed the experiment. The urban design should be based on the possibility of future expansion, and the concept of a growing house should be used to accommodate the growth of households over time (Land, 2008, p. 12). The brief of the competition, published in the April 1970 issue of *Architectural Design*, was clear about this feature: "The dwelling was not to be conceived as a fixed unit but as a structure with a cycle of evolution" ("Previ/Lima. Low Cost Housing Project," 1970, p. 188).

PREVI would become a housing experiment, gathering projects from some of the most outspoken supporters of the notion of "open architecture," as well as other notable international and Peruvian architects. In total there were project submissions from 26 architects/architectural offices, including acclaimed international names such as Oskar Hansen, Fumihiko Maki, Candilis, Josic & Woods, Aldo van Eyck, James Stirling, and Christopher Alexander (Land, 2015).

The project presented by Aldo van Eyck offers an innovative approach to incremental housing. The most striking feature in Van Eyck's project is the hexagonal shape of the plots, where the initial basic houses would be built with a rectangular footprint. The odd shape of the remaining triangular areas, Van Eyck argued, would "discourage further building by the inhabitants in any direction which would result in the loss of external space or internal light—a frequent development in self-build *barriada* housing," as well as loss of "a genuinely urban character" ("Previ/Lima. Low Cost Housing Project," 1970, p. 205). The layout of the basic houses and their expected incremental growth took into consideration climate considerations, allowing cross-ventilation through the core of the house. Climate considerations were also instrumental for the clustering strategy, shaping the pedestrian paths to take advantage of the cooling breezes in the summer and protection from winter winds.

Interestingly, the devices of control defined by Aldo van Eyck and most of the other PREVI-Lima architects proved to be powerless in shaping the residents' self-initiated transformations. A study conducted on the actual conditions of the houses 30 years after completion shows that in most cases the inhabitants went much further than the architect's wildest imagination (García-Huidobro, Torriti, & Tugas, 2008). In any case, this study also shows the importance of the spatial configuration of the plot and the strategy for clustering the dwelling units. While each house may grow and change through time, the structure of public and social spaces remain and sustain resilient urban communities.

Expandable Houses

The concept of "expandable houses" is closely related with that of "evolutionary housing." There are occurrences for the term "expandable houses" in the early 1950s that overlap chronologically with the emergence of *habitat évolutif*. I would argue, however, that there is one subtle difference in the use of these two terms. While "evolutionary housing" was the preferred term used by those exploring growth and change from a more theoretical—or even academic—framework (e.g., Parent, Candilis), "expandable houses" was favored more by agents related with the production of housing. For example, an unsigned article published in February 1952 in the American magazine of building *House & Home* was entitled "Does the Expandable House Make Sense?". The epigraph of the article summarized the relevance of the question: "with higher down payments shrinking the house market, the cry of 'half a house is better than none' is heard over and over again." The author thus concluded: "It's a good time to take a

Incremental Housing **171**

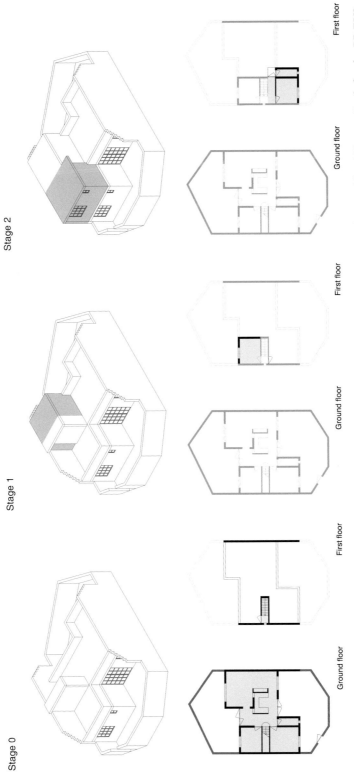

FIGURE 10.4 Axonometric perspective of the expected stages of growth and change of the dwelling units designed by Aldo van Eyck for the PREVI-Lima competition.

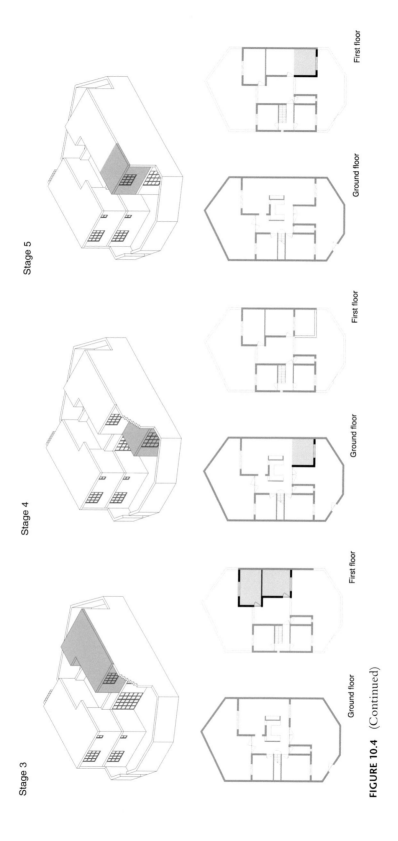

FIGURE 10.4 (Continued)

closer look at the expandable house" (*House and Home*, 1952, p. 114). The article moves on to offer pragmatic advice on how to "make expansion work," showing a collection of examples of expandable houses, conceived by builders, engineers, and architects, with clear influences of the American vernacular tradition.

Distilling vernacular examples of "expandable houses" as an inspiration for new designs gained currency. In 1959, the magazine *Ekistics* published extracts from a booklet produced by Bandung's Regional Housing Centre (Indonesia), illustrating "four house types designed to be expandable in accordance with the growth of family needs and family incomes" (Indonesia, 1959). The project draws inspiration from the Indonesian dwelling tradition, expressed in the options regarding building materials and techniques as well as climate design.

The use of expandable houses would also be encouraged in processes based on self-help initiatives. The *Manual for Self-help Housing*, published by the United Nations in 1964, testifies to this: "Certain desirable design features are especially useful in self-help housing, and should be considered and employed by any architect" the manual recommends. And it goes further stating that "the most important and valid aim is to make the house expandable; and this should be true whether maximum or minimum self- help houses or complete, shell, nuclei, or core houses are to be designed" (United Nations, 1964, p. 384).

As discussed earlier, through the 1970s, approaches to the design of mass housing based on the *habitat évolutif* approach were seen as a vehicle for the democratization of architecture. This was the period when flexibility and adaptability became fetish concepts for architects engaged with proving housing that could adapt to the changing needs of users. The time was also ripe to explore expandable systems for housing.

Skjetten Town, a new settlement projected for almost 2,000 households to be located in the vicinity of Strommen, approximately 20 km east of Oslo, Norway, is an exemplary experiment with expandable houses. Nils-Ole Lund was the coordinator of the team that won the competition for a new low-rise high-density housing district, launched in 1965 by the municipality (Hultberg, 1971). While there were some multi-story blocs included in the plan, the majority of the households were accommodated in the expandable two-story, 6.4m-wide row-houses. The project for the row-houses was based on a modular system, with a fixed core and multiple possibilities for expansion. These expansions, however, should be framed within the structural grid, using industrialized, factory-produced components to be assembled on site. To stress further the openness of the project, the designers created a house manual, meant to support the residents' self-initiated expansions, demonstrating the possibilities of the system as well as the technical and economic implications.

The motto of Lund's team's winning proposal was "Variation—Order—Community—Privacy." This motto demonstrates the team's attempt to negotiate contrasting values, combining order with possibilities for individual expression, and securing the privacy of each household while promoting a sense of community. The focus on the spatial agency of the residents was central to the project. Writing in 1973, Nils-Ole Lund (2012, p. 25) stated that "at Skjetten, one did not try to find a general housing type, but sought rather a system that could make each house as distinct as possible." And he further asserted that "in the same way that each family is different from every other family, so is their need different when it comes to dwelling."

The Skjetten project illustrates the potential of incremental housing to be used as a design approach for a more humanistic approach to mass housing. As Mari Hvattum (2012, p. 9) puts it, "instead of the paternalistic model of post-war planning, the multi-disciplinary 'Skjetten team' sought a less patronizing way of making architecture, one that considered the residents as individuals rather than as average abstractions."

174 Nelson Mota

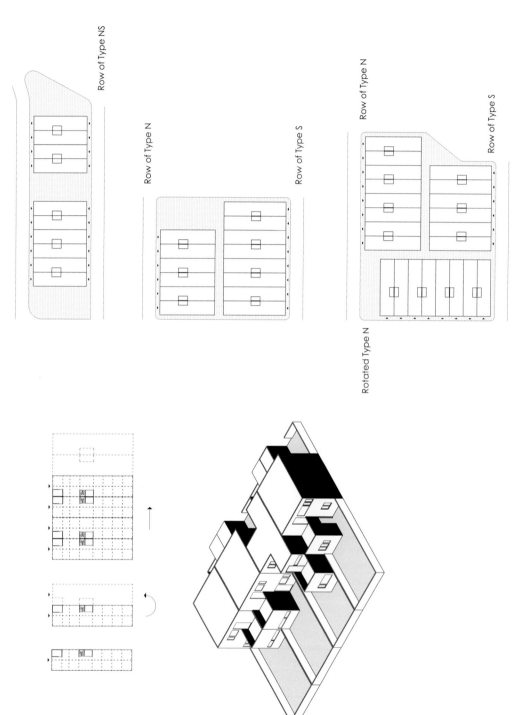

FIGURE 10.5 Clustering strategy for typical dwelling plots in Skjetten.

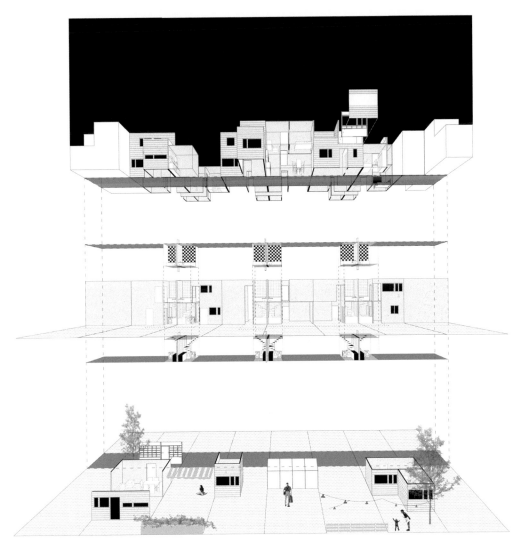

FIGURE 10.6 Illustration of the basic design principles of Skjetten Town.

Incremental Housing

The terms discussed in the previous sections are still used to describe contemporary projects. The project "Rumah Tambah" and the "Modular expandable housing concept for Peru" developed by a multi-disciplinary team of Peruvian architects and engineers testifies to this ("Modular Housing by Arana & Suasnabar Architects Lets You Add Rooms," 2019; "Rumah Tambah | Urban-Rural Systems," n.d.). However, since the turn of the 21st century, "incremental housing" progressively became the preferred term to describe approaches to the design and development of houses able to accommodate growth and change through time. The first occurrences of "incremental housing" in scholarly articles started in the early 1970s, a time when most of the terms discussed earlier were still widely used.

In 1973, the Indian civil engineer and urban planner Shirish B. Patel wrote a piece in the journal *Economic & Political Weekly* in which he suggested a research program for urban housing, with a set of investigations necessary to solve the Indian perennial crisis in the provision of housing for the lower-income sections. For Patel an in-depth investigation into the possibilities of using "incremental housing" was urgent. However, Patel warned:

> the real difficulty is to start with the cheapest form of construction and incrementally upgrade it to the next better level, without destroying entirely the initial construction and starting over again, and without damaging seriously the livability [sic] of the house while construction is in hand.
>
> *(Patel, 1973, p. 673)*

For Patel, the incremental housing approach should be combined with, and associated to, a selection of local materials and labor to implement those incremental improvements, securing the tenure of the householder, and a selection of convenient site locations, affordable but connected to transportation systems and opportunities for income generation.

In the last decades of the 20th century, precious few cases followed Patel's criteria for a successful implementation of incremental housing approaches. The Charkop sites-and-services project, mentioned prior, is one of those exceptions. The list, however, is not extensive. Recently, the popularity of incremental housing approaches has risen conspicuously. This upsurge was underpinned by the visibility of the "Quinta Monroy" project, developed between 2003 and 2006 by the Chilean architectural office Elemental for Iquique, a coastal city in the north of Chile (Aravena & Iacobelli, 2013).

This project was Elemental's answer to the progressive withdrawal of the Chilean government in the provision of housing for the lower-income groups and the relentless reduction of housing subsidies provided by the state. One of the direct consequences of this process was the reduction of the size of the dwelling units for the poor, as well as their displacement to underserved peripheries far from the urban centers and main areas of work and income generation. To tackle these challenges, Elemental's proposal was based on four principles. First, they encouraged the establishment of families in a consolidated urban area. Second, they sustained that incremental construction should be done without neighborhood deterioration. Their third principle was that all future expansions should be safe and affordable. Finally, they advocated design with community participation (Aravena & Iacobelli, 2013, p. 98). Quinta Monroy was used as a test case for this strategy, and it proved successful, at least in terms of media visibility and international prestige for Elemental.

Disseminated worldwide, this project would be responsible for launching Elemental as the world reference for social housing projects based on the incremental development approach. The social concern of the Elemental design approach would also be instrumental to promote one of the office founders, Alejandro Aravena, to the architectural star system and eventually win the coveted Pritzker Prize, in 2016. As the Brazilian architect Pedro Arantes writes in his *The Rent of Form*, "the [Pritzker] award to Chilean Alejandro Aravena in 2016 seems to show that the 'social' dimension has finally been acknowledged by the system of values and higher decorations of the privileged architectural circle" (Arantes, 2019, p. 206). For Arantes, however, this acknowledgment does not suggest any departure from the status quo engaged in pursuing ways to monetize architectural innovation. Rather, he adds, Aravena "is a hero of the poor, invented by the rich, and therefore a hero under control. He does not attack the system, but recycles it" (Arantes, 2019, p. 230).

Despite its controversial contribution to enhance social equity, Elemental's experiments with housing undoubtedly revived the interest in design strategies for incremental housing that had been somewhat dormant in the mainstream architectural media during the last decade of the 20th century. Furthermore, I would argue, this revived interest in incremental housing triggered a reconceptualization of the role of the architect, inducing a renegotiation of the boundaries between design decision-making and governance.

Negotiating Design and Governance

As the previous sections demonstrate, the different approaches to the design and development of incremental housing are historically determined. Over the last century, incremental housing approaches navigated always in two different disciplinary fields: design and governance. These two fields were not always balanced, though. In some cases, design decisions were at the core of the approach, whereas in other cases, the focus was primarily placed on managerial strategies.

In the growing house approach, for example, there was a strong focus on design as the medium to explore the most advanced technological possibilities available at that time in the industrialized world. The optimization of the layout of the floor plan and the solutions to integrate pre-fabricated elements in the construction of the dwelling units were front and center in the designers' research. The stakes for the designers were high. They were invested with the responsibility to regenerate society. In a time of scarcity, the growing house approach embodied the hope for a new way of life, which should be able to overcome the detrimental consequences of life in the metropolis. It was simultaneously an attempt to improve the living standards of the society but also meant to be a technologically advanced product, rather than a DIY approach (Urbanik, 2020, p. 247).

In the post-war period, the redemptory reliance on technology to improve the living standards of the citizens would fade away from the main narratives of architects and urban designers. The focus on the efficient production of mass housing, using standardization and closed forms was heavily contested, though. Starting with the post-war CIAM congresses and moving into the Team 10 meetings, the theme of "growth and change" influenced a whole generation of architects and urban designers active in the period the French call *les trente glorieuses* (1945–1975). Over this period, rather than an obsession with control and permanence, the discourse moved to flexibility, openness, and democracy. The role of the architect was readjusted to give agency to other stakeholders in design decision-making processes. First and foremost, citizens' participation gained currency in housing design as a required feature to enable an architecture of democracy (Jones, Petrescu, & Till, 2005).

With this paradigm shift, form and design were not alone anymore at the center of the operations. The importance of managerial aspects surfaced as a key component of incremental housing approaches. The aided self-help movements that developed in the interwar period and were further disseminated in the aftermath of World War II put a strong emphasis on governance. Defining the different systems of home ownership, selecting appropriate locations for the development of new housing settlements, and providing access to adequate financial instruments were key components of the "aided self-help" and "sites-and-services" approaches. The development of Charkop (1984–1990) in India, with the sponsorship of the World Bank, illustrates the importance of managerial decisions for incremental housing approaches.

Incremental housing requires an interwoven relationship between design and managerial decisions. More so, I would argue, than other approaches to the production of affordable housing. The particular nature of incremental housing challenges hegemonic power relations and reveals agonistically the conflicting interests of the stakeholders involved in mass housing production. Developers, designers, builders, and residents have to re-adjust their role in the process and navigate constantly between top-down decisions and bottom-up initiatives.

This complex network of relations, as well as the ambiguity inherent to the agency of the different stakeholders, makes incremental housing approaches simultaneously fragile and appealing.

Its fragility is associated with the fact that promoting self-help initiatives to foster the agency of the citizens in shaping their own living environment is politically weak. This weakness stems mainly from two factors. On the one hand, the lack of organized social constituency in self-help initiatives antagonizes the building industry, trades—including some architects and urban designers—and policy makers (Harris, 1999, p. 301). On the other hand, its political philosophy navigates in ambiguous territories. For example, some approaches are influenced directly or indirectly by such distinct ideas as those advanced by the social planning of Patrick Geddes or by the critique of the capitalist system by anarchists like Kropotkin. While the first was an inspiration for the work of advocates of self-help housing such as Jacob L. Crane (Harris, 1998) and Charles Abrams (Henderson, 2000), the latter featured front and center in John Turner's manifesto towards people's autonomy in building environments (Turner, 1972; Gyger, 2019). The political weakness of incremental housing approaches is also evident in its vulnerability to be appropriated by ideologies that diverge from its constitutional aims. For example, the "sites-and-services" approach has been recuperated by neoliberal ideas, like those of the Peruvian economist Hernando de Soto (2001), based on strategies to stimulate low-income households to become homeowners and enhance the role of the markets in the provision of affordable housing.

The way the "freedom to build" is enacted depends a great deal on the housing type proposed. For its particular characteristics, an incremental housing approach relies heavily on what it does for the household, the smallest social structure of a community. As the overview of the different approaches to incremental housing discussed herein shows, the spatial configuration of the housing settlements is predominantly based on the single-family house type. This did not happen without a clear social and political agenda.

From Leberecht Migge's "growing houses" to Charkop's "core-houses" the use of schemes based on single-family housing communities was ideologically motivated. Offering conditions for the self-reliance of each family was instrumental to mitigate social tensions and reduce people's dependency on governmental support. It was also a vehicle to promote the commodification of housing. Promoting the single-family house as the basic element for incremental housing schemes was instrumental to enhance the security of tenure and eventually homeownership. Consequently, with an initial input of governmental bodies, the house could develop its status as an asset (most of the time, the main asset) of a family. This precious commodity would then create communities of homeowners with access to bank loans and other financial instruments secured by real estate, the most trusted collateral. Additionally, security of tenure would also increase the government's catchment basin to collect property tax. At first sight, this looks like a win-win-win proposition.

Some voices, however, have been unveiling the "dark side" of this operation. Architecture and urban design scholars Camillo Boano and Francisco Vergara Perucich are a case in point. In their piercing critique of Elemental's approach to incremental housing, they considered the "good half-house" strategy as a neoliberal method to produce social architecture (Boano & Vergara Perucich, 2016, p. 62). Rather than a counter-hegemonic approach to the design of good architecture to the poor, Boano and Vergara Perucich (2016, p. 70) contend that Quinta Monroy illustrates "a utilitarian approach to social architecture for neoliberal goals." Elemental's project, they advance, is more a good economic strategy than a good mode of spatial production. Ultimately, it's a win for financial institutions, but not necessarily a win for the people or a win for the city.

Boano's and Vergara Perucich's critique of Elemental's neoliberal method to produce social architecture highlights the disciplinary and political ambiguity of incremental housing approaches. Rather than conforming to the binary polarity of "housing as a product/housing as a process," incremental housing approaches entail the combination of diverse spatial agencies in managerial and design *processes* to enable the progressive development of a *product*.

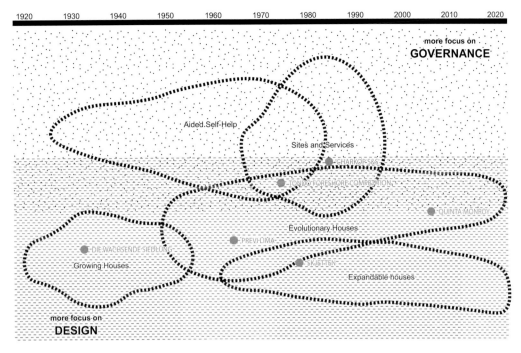

FIGURE 10.7 Balance between design and governance in different incremental housing approaches.

Conclusion: Give Time a Chance

Since the Industrial Revolution (if not since forever), we live in a permanent housing crisis. In the 21st century, or at least in the foreseeable future, this everlasting housing crisis will only get worse. Over the last century, incremental housing approaches have been implemented to try and tackle the shortage of affordable housing. It was used by capitalist and socialist regimes. It was embedded in housing policies integral to planned economies but also to neoliberal programs. And now, what will be its role to face the housing challenges in the post-neoliberal world?

The different approaches to incremental housing discussed in this text suggest that architects and urban designers can play an important role in contributing to developing better livelihoods. Recent reviews of incremental housing settlements, which were frowned upon at the time they were built, are now praised for having created resilient urban communities (McGuirk, 2015, pp. 67–80; Owens, Gulyani, & Rizvi, 2018; Rouissi, 2019). This suggests that *time*, which is a basic ingredient of any incremental housing approach, is a key factor to take into account in the development of sustainable housing approaches. The articulation of design and managerial decisions is yet another key feature of incremental housing approaches. On the one hand, design decisions such as clustering strategies, plot configuration, dwelling layout, and selection of building materials and construction techniques determine decisively the social and environmental quality of urban communities. In incremental housing approaches, these design decisions can result from collaborative practices, rather than be enacted by hegemonic processes designed to reproduce the power relations that exclude the urban poor. On the other hand, managerial decisions such as the definition of homeownership models, adequate locations, and access to housing finance play a key role in the economic sustainability of each household, in particular, and urban communities in general. In incremental housing approaches, these managerial decisions can be instrumental to provide security of tenure, easy access to income-generating activities, and affordable rents, loans, and mortgages.

The intrinsic political ambiguity of incremental housing approaches may not be a detrimental factor for the architecture and city of the 21st century. Conversely, it may be a precious tool to activate the role of architects and urban designers as key players in shaping the spatial production for a world undergoing a process of planetary urbanization. As this historical review shows, incremental housing approaches have a strong impact on social and spatial practices, labor, and fluxes of people and materials. Using their inherent capacity to negotiate and mediate different types of expertise and disciplines, architects and urban designers can revive incremental housing approaches to influence the urban metabolism of cities in the 21st century and create a better social life for the city to come.

Note

1. A search for the keywords "incremental housing" performed on three of the most comprehensive databases of scholarly articles and publications in the field of architecture and urban design produced the following results: Avery Index of Architecture Journals: 33 results. The oldest record is dated from October 1978; Science Direct: 91 results. The oldest record is dated from 1983; Jstor: 112 results. The oldest record is from April 1973. Search performed on May 26, 2020.

References

Abrams, C. (1964). *Man's Struggle for Shelter in an Urbanizing World*. Cambridge, MA: The MIT Press.
Anderson, C. (2019). Good Life Now: Leisure and Labour in Cedric Price's Housing Research, 1966–1973. *Footprint, 13*(1), 11–30. https://doi.org/10.7480/footprint.13.1.2139
Arantes, P.F. (2019). *The Rent of Form: Architecture and Labor in the Digital Age* (A. Kauffmann, Trans.). Minneapolis, MN: University of Minnesota Press.
Aravena, A., & Iacobelli, A. (2013). *Elemental: Incremental Housing and Participatory Design Manual*. Ostfildern, Germany: Hatje Cantz.
Avermaete, T. (2005). *Another Modern: The Post-War Architecture and Urbanism of Candilis-Josic-Woods*. Rotterdam, Netherlands: NAi Publishers.
Avermaete, T. (2012). Accommodating the Afropolis: Michel Ecochard's Alternative Approach to the Modern City. In M. Angelil, & R. Hehl (Eds.), *Informalize! Essays On The Political Economy of Urban Form* (pp. 18–52). Berlin, Germany: Ruby Press.
Berselli, S. (2015). Une Correspondance Architecturale: Ionel Schein "Enfant" de Le Corbusier. In *LC 2015—Le Corbusier, 50 Years Later*. Valencia, Spain: Universitat Politecnica de Valencia. http://doi.org/10.4995/LC2015.2015.1042
Boano, C., & Perucich, F.V. (2016). Half-Happy Architecture. *Viceversa, 4*, 58–81.
Bosma, K., van Hoogstraten, D., & Vos, M. (2000). *Housing for the Millions: John Habraken and the SAR (1960–2000)*. Rotterdam, Netherlands: NAi Publishers.
Bredenoord, J., & van Lindert, P. (2010). Pro-Poor Housing Policies: Rethinking the Potential of Assisted Self-Help Housing. *Habitat International, 34*(3), 278–287.
Bredenoord, J., van Lindert, P., & Smets, P. (Eds.). (2014). *Affordable Housing in the Urban Global South: Seeking Sustainable Solutions*. Abingdon, Oxon: Routledge.
Brenner, N., & Schmid, C. (2012). Planetary Urbanisation. In Gandy, M. (Ed.), *Urban Constellations* (pp. 10–13). Berlin, Germany: Jovis.
Caminos, H., & Goethert, R. (1978). *Urbanization Primer*. Cambridge, MA: The MIT Press.
Candilis, G., Josic, A., & Woods, S. (1959). Proposition Pour Un Habitat Evolutif. *Techniques et Architecture, 19*(2), 82–85.
CIAM 10 Commission. (1954). *Draft Framework for CIAM X Congress with Dutch Supplement*. BAKEg34. Het Nieuwe Instituut, Bakema Archive.
Correa, C. (1989). *The New Landscape: Urbanisation in the Third World*. Butterworth Architecture.
De Soto, H. (2001). *The Mystery of Capital*. London, UK: Black Swan.
Fezer, J., Hager, M., & Hiller, C. (Eds.). (2016). *Martin Wagner: The Growing House: Das Wachsende Haus*. Leipzig, Germany: Spector Books.

Fishman, R. (2018). The Global Crisis of Affordable Housing: Architecture Versus Neoliberalism. *Architectural Design*, *88*(4), 22–29. https://doi.org/10.1002/ad.2317.

García-Huidobro, F., Torriti, D.T., & Tugas, N. (2008). *Time Builds!* Barcelona, Spain: Editorial Gustavo Gili.

Gyger, H. (2019). *Improvised Cities: Architecture, Urbanization, and Innovation in Peru*. Pittsburg, PA: University of Pittsburgh Press.

Habitat III Secretariat. (2017). *New Urban Agenda*. Quito, Ecuador: United Nations.

Habraken, N.J. (1999). *Supports: An Alternative to Mass Housing* (B. Valkenburg, Trans.). Urban International Press.

Haney, D.H. (2010). *When Modern Was Green: Life and Work of Landscape Architect Leberecht Migge*. New York, NY; London, UK: Routledge.

Hansen, O. (1961). La Forme Ouverte Dans l'Architecture—l'Art Du Grand Nombre. *Le Carrè Bleu*, *1*, 4–7.

Harris, R. (1998). The Silence of the Experts: "Aided Self-Help Housing", 1939–1954. *Habitat International*, *22*(2), 165–189.

Harris, R. (1999). Slipping through the Cracks: The Origins of Aided Self-Help Housing, 1918–53. *Housing Studies*, *14*(3), 281–309.

Henderson, A.S. (2000). *Housing and the Democratic Ideal: The Life and Thought of Charles Abrams*. New York, NY: Columbia University Press.

Hochhäusl, S. (2014). Grass Roots Modernism: Architecture and Organization in Austrian Settlements and Allotment Gardens, 1921–1925. In N. Elleh (Ed.), *Reading the Architecture of the Underprivileged Classes* (pp. 119–136). Farnham, UK: Ashgate Publishing, Ltd.

House and Home. (1952). Does the Expandable House Make Sense?, February 1952.

Hultberg, E. (1971). An Adaptable and Expandable System for Row Houses. *Ekistics*, *31*(183), 176–178.

Hvattum, M. (2012, Spring). Nordic Nomumentality. *Nordic Journal of Architecture*, *2*(1), 8–10.

Indonesia, Regional Housing Centre. (1959). Expandable Houses. *Ekistics*, *8*(46), 134–136.

Jones, P.B., Petrescu, D., & Till, J. (Eds.). (2005). *Architecture and Participation*. London, UK; New York, NY: Taylor and Francis.

Land, P. (2008). The Experimental Housing Project (PREVI), Lima: Antecedents and Ideas. In F. García-Huidobro, D.T. Torriti, & N. Tugas (Eds.), *Time Builds!* (pp. 10–25). Barcelona, Spain: Editorial Gustavo Gili.

Land, P. (2015). *The Experimental Housing Project (PREVI), Lima—Design and Technology in a New Neighborhood*. Bogotá, Colombia: University of Los Andes in Bogota.

Lindert, P., Smets, P., & Bredenoord, J. (2014). Pro-Poor Housing Policies Revisited. Where Do We Go from Here? In P. Lindert, P. Smets, & J. Bredenoord (Eds.), *Affordable Housing in the Urban Global South: Seeking Sustainable Solutions* (pp. 397–403). Abingdon, Oxon: Routledge.

Lund, N.-O. (2012, Spring). Skjetten Town, Norway. *Nordic Journal of Architecture*, *2*(1), 22–29.

Marcuse, P., & Madden, D. (2016). *In Defense of Housing: The Politics of Crisis*. London, UK; New York, NY: Verso.

Martin, R., Moore, J., & Schindler, S. (Eds.). (2015). *The Art of Inequality: Architecture, Housing, and Real Estate—A Provisional Report*. New York, NY: The Temple Hoyne Buell Center for the Study of American Architecture.

McGuirk, J. (2015). *Radical Cities: Across Latin America in Search of a New Architecture*. London, UK: Verso.

Modular Housing by Arana & Suasnabar Architects Lets You Add Rooms. (2019). *Dezeen*. Retrieved on February 20, 2019 from www.dezeen.com/2019/02/20/mini-living-modular-housing-peru-arana-suasnabar-architects-video/.

Mota, N. (2014). *An Archaeology of the Ordinary: Rethinking the Architecture of Dwelling from CIAM to Siza*. PhD Dissertation. Delft, Netherlands: TU Delft.

Owens, K.E., Gulyani, S., & Rizvi, A. (2018). Success When We Deemed It Failure? Revisiting Sites and Services Projects in Mumbai and Chennai 20 Years Later. *World Development*, *106*(June), 260–272. https://doi.org/10.1016/j.worlddev.2018.01.021.

Padora, S. (2016). *In the Name of Housing, A Study of 11 Projects in Mumbai*. Mumbai, India: Urban Design Research Institute.

Parent, C., & Schein, I. (1953). Essai Pour Un Habitat Individuel Évolutif. *L'Architecture d'Aujourd'hui*, *49*(October), 4–5.

Patel, S.B. (1973). A Research Programme for Urban Housing. *Economic and Political Weekly*, *8*(14), 671–676.

Previ/Lima. Low Cost Housing Project. (1970). *Architectural Design*, *4*, 187–205.

Ragon, M. (1977). *L'Architecte, le Prince et la Démocratie: Vers une Démocratisation de l'Architecture*. Paris, France: Albin Michel.

Rouissi, K. (2019). Housing for the Greatest Number: Casablanca's under-Appreciated Public Housing Developments. *The Journal of North African Studies*, 1–26. https://doi.org/10.1080/13629387.2019.1692411.

'Rumah Tambah | Urban-Rural Systems'. (n.d.). Retrieved on June 1, 2020 from https://urs.sec.sg/category/rumah-tambah/.

Schneider, T. (2016). The Growing House of the Shaping of Time. In J. Fezer, M. Hager, & C. Hiller (Eds.), *Martin Wagner: The Growing House: Das Wachsende Haus* (pp. 193–196). Leipzig, Germany: Spector Books.

Seelig, M.Y. (1978). *The Architecture of Self-Help Communities*. New York, NY: Architectural Record Books.

Turner, J. (1968). The Squatter Settlement: An Architecture that Works. *Architectural Design*, *38*(August), 355–360.

Turner, J. (1972). 'Housing as a Verb'. In J. Turner & R. Fichter (Eds.), *Freedom to Build: Dweller Control of the Housing Process* (pp. 148–175). New York, NY: Collier Macmillan.

United Nations, Dept. of Economic and Social Affairs. (1964). Manual on Self-Help Housing. *Ekistics*, *17*(103), 375–384.

Urbanik, J. (2020). "The Growing House"—The Way to Solve the Housing Problem in Interwar Germany. In J. Charytonowicz, & C. Falcão (Eds.), *Advances in Human Factors in Architecture, Sustainable Urban Planning and Infrastructure* (pp. 243–255). Advances in Intelligent Systems and Computing 966. Cham: Springer Nature Switzerland. https://doi.org/10.1007/978-3-030-20151-7_23.

Van der Linden, J. (1986). *The Sites and Services Approach Renewed: Solution or Stopgap to the Third World Housing Shortage?* Aldershot, UK: Gower.

Wakely, P., & Riley, E. (2011). The Case for Incremental Housing. *Working Paper 1. Cities Alliance Policy Research and Working Papers Series*. Washington, DC: Cities Alliance.

Williams, D.G. (1984). The Role of International Agencies: The World Bank. In G.K. Payne (Ed.), *Low-Income Housing in the Developing World: The Role of Sites and Services and Settlement Upgrading* (pp. 173–185). Chichester, UK: John Wiley & Sons.

The World Bank—South Asia Projects Department. (1985). *Staff Appraisal Report. Bombay Urban Development Project*. Staff appraisal report 4794-IN. The World Bank.

Yap, K.S. (2016). The Enabling Strategy and Its Discontent: Low-Income Housing Policies and Practices in Asia. *Habitat International, Housing the Planet: Evolution of Global Housing Policies*, *54*(May), 166–172. https://doi.org/10.1016/j.habitatint.2015.11.026.

11

THE BUBBLE, THE ARROW, AND THE AREA

Urban Design and Diagrammatic Concepts
of Human Action

Daniel Koch

In 1964, the American planning giant Gruen Associates, a consultancy founded by Austrian emigré Victor Gruen[1] in 1951, developed a plan to regenerate the city center of Fresno, California, making national headlines by closing its main street to car traffic and opening the Fulton Mall—a pedestrianized remake of the old four-lane Fulton Street. The plan focused on creating a pleasant social urban environment including vegetation, sidewalk cafés and restaurants, a range of seating opportunities, stores and art galleries, and local small public/collective transport aids. This is a further development of ideas presented in Fort Worth, Texas, in 1956 to create a pedestrianized oasis in the city center free of noise, pollution, and traffic, which would allow a pleasant yet vibrant social urban public place. While relying heavily on investment in car infrastructure, the point of these investments was always the "bonus" potential created by the elimination of the *surface movement* of mechanized transport:

> In some cases, large plazas and squares could be provided where space, until then utilized for automotive accessory facilities, became available. In other cases, streets were narrowed either by adding new structures on both sides or by introducing structures on one or both sides or by introducing structures within the area formerly used for vehicular purposes. It was proposed that some streets be roofed over so that they might form protected, air-conditioned business and shopping environments; for others, colonnades and arcades were proposed, to furnish protection from sun and rain. Thus a pattern of great variety and interest was created, providing a continuous change of pace and atmosphere to those who would work in the core or visit there.
>
> *(Gruen, 1964, pp. 219–220)*

Gruen's work pioneered developments in the United States, and regardless of whether developments that claimed to build on his work also shared his intentions or operated as superficial copies, they had significant influence on downtown developments. The intent in Fort Worth, Fulton (Figure 11.1), and subsequent sites worked on by Gruen Associates was to reinvigorate or create anew "traditional" inner cities to combat the growing prevalence of the mall. Yet much of the configurative and systemic-structural principles at work in these examples draw on similar modernist planning principles: for instance, the Swedish SCAFT model (Statens Planverk, 1968) that was the foundation of the Swedish "Million Program" suburb and the "ABC City."[2]

184 Daniel Koch

FIGURE 11.1 Gruen Associates' illustration of the future Fulton Mall.

As much of the discourse on these developments recognizes, Gruen's plans, much like the more recognizably modernistic suburban planning, required large investments in the planning and execution of car traffic infrastructures, which may suggest that they were all to some extent made for the car. However, when turning to the illustrations of the type of life and local atmosphere that was envisaged in the plans, there is a distinct itch of contemporaneity. Despite shifts in graphics and representation, the milieus presented look remarkably like, for instance, White's illustrations of the development of Söderstaden in Stockholm, from 2017 (Figure 11.2); Gehl's illustrations of "the living city" in their work for Trelleborg in 2017; Gensler's work for Baltimore's Southwest Partnership in 2015; Carmona and Wunderlich's (2012) visualizations of the goal for a good urban design; or Strategisk Arkitektur's proposal for Stenungsund in 2019, as a few example of a ubiquitous phenomenon. In all of these examples, *good* stands for socially, economically, and ecologically sustainable illustrated by means of vibrant pedestrianized public spaces claimed to foster inclusion, cohesion, and community generation in a leisurely sociable environment. These plans all tend to share another tendency: while creating more pedestrianized public space, they include massive investments in placing car roads (and on occasion rail commuter traffic) underground, creating parking possibilities (or "mobility hubs") at the edges or under these spaces, ensuring efficient access to these oases of public life from the outside as well as their swift circumvention underground. But these systems are to facilitate the pedestrian city, as Jane Jacobs notes on Gruen's plans for Fort Worth:

FIGURE 11.2 White Arkitekter AB's winning proposal for Söderstaden-Hovet in Stockholm in 2017.

> The plan by Victor Gruen Associates for Fort Worth is an outstanding example. It has been publicized chiefly for its arrangements to provide enormous perimeter parking garages and convert the downtown into a pedestrian island, but its main purpose is to enliven the streets with variety and detail. This is a point being overlooked by most of the eighty-odd cities that, at last count, were seriously considering emulation of the Gruen plan's traffic principles.
>
> *(Jacobs, 1958, pp. 162–163)*[3]

This observation can be made with reference to an even earlier period—as Gruen does, pointing to an illustration in *Harper's Weekly* in 1881 that critically compares a street scene in Paris with a street scene in New York (Gruen, 1964, p. 30). This very image is reproduced in *The Harvard Design School Guide to Shopping* alongside images from the arcades of Paris, other European city streets, and many other illustrations of an ideal urban life from the late 19th century on (Chung et al., 2001). Similar conceptualizations of urban design as primarily concerned with producing pleasant spaces for socialization and experience can be identified again and again in planning literature and architectural and planning practice.[4] The notion that a good public space is a populated public space, where "populated" equals a certain mode of populating (or: populating as in surface socializing and leisure) is implied not only in such images but also in a range of conceptual and theoretical contexts. One can find a similar disposition in many of Le Corbusier's illustrations as well: in the oft-reproduced illustration of *Ville radieuse*, the environment in the foreground is most reminiscent of, if anything, the outdoor seating at a local French café, and even in the distance one can see how traffic has been put underground in order to free the pedestrian surface from its contamination.[5] This is not an isolated phenomenon, nor is it a very selective reading of history. In reviewing the way living environments are illustrated in journals and magazines, one finds that although building morphology, plan shapes, traffic structures, and other factors may vary markedly, the portrayal of living environments maintains a noticeable consistency.

Many, if not most, of the proposals mentioned here echo or prefigure a well-known narrative engrained in the UN Sustainability Goals (United Nations, 2015): to create dense and lively ("vibrant") urban settlements. Let us, for now, set aside the internal conflicts between the UN Goals as such and look at how a focus on the type of environment described can be seen to respond to many or even all of them. Such environments, after all, lack any signs of many important societal functions; their place in the urban fabric; the life of the labor force that is employed to perform them, to maintain their infrastructures, to produce their goods and staff their facilities; as well as with respect to the technologies and other products required to support the leisurely experience and socialization they demand (Koch, 2018; Lefebvre, 1991). The illustrations are nearly invariably free from hospitals, police stations, delivery trucks, garbage collectors, recycling stations, street cleaners, factory fronts, or other necessary components of a wider contemporary society.[6] Of course, one can argue that this depends on selective use and interpretation of the UN Goals, just as Gruen notes how his own work was appropriated, or McMorrough (2001) argues is the case with the works of Jacobs. It also conforms to tendencies to make an antidote to select problems into universal resolutions: in this case, a specific urban environment that is universalized. Such a move is supported by a view that planning is problem solving—a means to care for the ills of urban settings (Rittel & Webber, 1973). From this point of view, if overcrowding, pollution, sanitation, and low material standards were the "ills" that modern planning was to solve—and to a remarkable degree did—then residential segregation, lack of local public spaces that serve to form bonds between people, and an abundance of car use appear to be the "ills" that are to be thwarted today. Yet solutions look remarkably similar.

If we turn to the way that *intentions* were formulated in modernist planning practice, a similar tendency to focus on pleasant urban environments with a social atmosphere inspired by "traditional cities" is also present. For instance, we can look to the comments of Dergalin and Stäck, two Swedish architects (the former later became Professor in Urban Design at KTH) on the development of the area of Rinkeby in Stockholm—an area that is today used to exemplify how "modernist planning" is antithetical to urbanity, by those for whom urbanity is understood as in the vibrant public space of the traditional city, and intimately connected to the Car Society. Writing in 1964, the architects note:

> The goals for the work with the masterplan have included, amongst other things, to create the possibilities for an intense, concentrated, and richly composed environment in the new living area. This is a living area that combines some of the traditional city's intensity, concentration, and order with the periphery's greenness, spaciousness, and freedom from disturbances, to create an urban environment with safe, pleasant and comfortable pedestrian streets and enclosed park environments.
>
> *(Dergalin & Stäck, 1964, p. 119, translated by the author)*

We can illustrate these continuities further by comparing the Swedish post-war legacy within suburb planning to urban planning arguments that are made today. For instance, in how Erik and Tore Ahlsén (1944) argue for their work in Årsta Centrum in that social relations need to build from active interaction rather than passive co-presence, requiring spaces of socialization and activity to be *integrated into the paths and places of everyday life*. Or how Albert Aronsson reflects on his work with Vällingby Centrum:[7]

> Already from the beginning it was clear that if we within the given volume, which was small in comparison to the "big city," could not create some of the pulse, the buzz, the

light, and the rhythm that signifies a "well developed" urban life, Vällingby Centrum would come off as a fraud.

(Aronsson, 1956, p. 78, translated by the author)

So: solutions to social, economic, and ecologic sustainability tends to lie in plans that in many ways appear rather as variants on that which they vehemently claim to oppose. Visions of the sustainable planning paradigm to, for instance, build communities of around 10,000 inhabitants and provide them with convenient and efficient mobility solutions and pleasant, vibrant public spaces to ensure the formation of social communities are strikingly familiar. They also often share similar selectively chosen references with historical examples of preindustrial settlements as support.[8] This is despite the fact that, as for instance Chapin and Hightower show in 1965 and is further problematized by Hanson and Hillier in their critique of correspondence thinking, such a direct relation between community and the location of housing is demonstrably problematic (Chapin & Hightower, 1965; Hanson & Hillier, 1987). Despite this critique, creation of "communities" continues to be allocated a central role in urban development on the basis of a vaguely defined link between "physical neighborhoods" and (a, singular) "social community" (Blokland, 2017).

How could these ideals persist for such a long time, without challenge? Even though many arguments made by contemporary urbanists often claim to correct the wrongs of the modernists—and particularly to correct *what the modernists aimed to achieve?*

I do not pretend that battlegrounds between different ideals cannot be identified within the history of urban design—there is no doubt that there exist vastly different models of cities, and the claim is not that there is an interchangeability between urban planning ideals. But as Elizabeth Wilson (1991) notes, struggles with socio-economic transformations in society tend to be buried in debates about style and the visual appearances of buildings. Hence, while I acknowledge that differences between positions are important, my aim is to point to certain continuities that tend to be buried in a discourse of opposition. I am here interested in how these models relate to certain aspects of human, non-human, and social action and culture; I seek to argue that, despite vast changes in aesthetic, social, and cultural ideals, the ideals of urbanity and subjectivity upon which such models are constructed appear remarkably resilient and highly dependent on the modern subject and modern subjectivity.[9] I will argue that throughout these changes the notion of the *intentional subject* dominates, whether rational or not, which arguably is part of how we are conditioned to become subjects to begin with (Butler, 2005; Ferguson, 2009). As Butler notes, a common query that both generates subjectivity and also places expectations on the subject is the question "Why?" As subjects, we are expected to be able to provide answers to this particular question for almost any action we undertake or any location we are at—and as Anthony Giddens (1984) notes, we are remarkably good at providing answers whether they are true or not. This insistence on the intentional subject, which sometimes is constructively and critically used to challenge the rational modern subject, remains a variant of the Freudian ego and allows cities to be simultaneously "unprogrammable" and definitely "programmable"—*if we just find out what people want to do*. To cut to the chase: a *psychological* or *psychosocial* model pervades our reasoning and practice in relation to the city, and this model feeds into planning and design by supplying these disciplines with an idealized, active, and intentional subject who makes use of space (urbanity, architecture, etc.) in order to achieve pre-existing aims, and who is actively and deliberately engaged in experiencing the environment as such. But what are the *structuring acts* that such a conceptualization demands from its practitioners and subjects?

By a somewhat opportunistic drawing of parallels, I will attempt to throw a curveball into the discourse by exposing the fact that the Car Society and the Car-less Society look, in fact, rather alike. This involves also exposing a series of epistemological, and even ontological, problems within contemporary urban discourse, particularly with respect to how urban design and planning practice have treated matters of subjectivity and action. My analysis concerns conceptual structures and is based on a close reading of the use of diagrams. Diagrams have a long history but emerge as common methodological tools more distinctly in the modern movement and serve to highlight aspects of modes of thinking in ways that remain crucial to contemporary discourses and practices. Diagrams can both be conceptual or mental ways to organize thought, and act as a direct approach employed in practical planning and design contexts (Foucault, 2002; Frichot, 2014, 2019; Stengers, 2011). Here, I engage diagrams as structuring devices of thinking; as "material objects that are not 'ready-made' but rather unfolding elements of situational practices" (Svetlova, 2015, p. 70) or as concepts that are thought *with* (Hillier, 1996); and as conceptualizations that relate to subjectivity, individuals, "the social," people's desires and actions, the built environment, and "the mental, social, and environmental ecologies" (Guattari, 2000) that are embedded in planning practices, where a central issue concerns correspondence thinking—i.e., whether a diagram is considered to correspond to the "real world" (i.e., the built structure or the human behavior) that it models. In this, I agree with Paul Emmons' description of "the current dominance of the functional network diagram" as evidencing "that the diagrammatic orders we choose to employ not only shape and reflect our ways of thinking but also our ways of imagining" (Emmons, 2006, p. 453). The diagrammatical devices I will work with are: the bubble, the arrow, and the area.

The Bubble

As noted by Emmons (2006), some of the particularities of modern architecture were in fact the result of ways of conceptualizing the world that have today become normalized organizational techniques. These include the invention of the bubble diagram. Originating in the works of Carl von Linnaeus, amongst others, the bubble diagram organizes the world into a set of (usually discrete) categories and defines their interrelations. While Linnaeus used bubble proximity to describe relations, the most common version of the bubble diagram today makes use of the electric circuit model, drawing connections with lines. This use of lines to describe relations, which can also be found in early diagrams such as that proposed by physician and naturalist Vitaliano Donati, allow for more complex connections between categories. We can see how the relational dependency of proximity in Linnaeus' more geographical map is released, and bubbles can drift relatively freely. As Emmons notes: "Bubble diagrams are topologic as they indicate spatial relationships rather than metrical floor plans. So long as the diagrammatic lines connecting spaces are not severed, they can be stretched, bent, or twisted as the architect imagines various plan organisations" (Emmons, 2006, p. 452).

This frees up a range of potentials: since it allows a multi-faceted set of relations to be mapped in a two-dimensional diagram, complex relations can be represented even when proximity relations become impossible to determine. But in this freedom the capacity of the diagram to operate with the material conditions brought by the complex programs of architectural design is also limited. The strength of the bubble-line diagram—namely, its ability to separate out and to link together—also becomes one of its problems.

The conceptual operation of *the bubble* becomes clear in the work of the Japanese architect Kiyoyuki Nishihara (1968), who attempted to describe the difference between "Western" and "Japanese" home architecture through relations between program and space (Figure 11.3). Nishihara describes the difference of the Japanese and the Western home as that:

> The West operates on the idea that each function has its own space. Eating requires suitable space, as does sleeping. The very names bedroom, dining room, bathroom, clearly

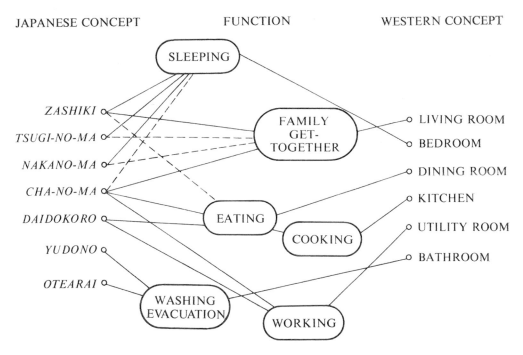

FIGURE 11.3 Kiyoyuki Nishihara's comparisons between the functional approach to spaces in the West and in Japan.

show the attitude that one function should have one designated room shut off from the other spaces by four walls. The Japanese house, however, names its rooms by their location—*okuzashiki*, the inner sitting room or *nakanoma*, the middle room—without direct reference to function.

(Nishihara, 1968, p. 108)

Even though this is not discussed by Nishihara, this diagram builds on a particular programmatic description of "family life," a description that is the basis of the modern movement's functionalism and which—one might note—still circulates in much architectural thought, sometimes, remarkably, as an antidote to functionalism. But why is family life understood as being organized in this way? And why would it be sensible to aim for a one-to-one correspondence between spatial and this particular understanding of social organization?

It may make initial sense to provide cooking with a specific location, depending on food and food preparation culture (Foucault, 1982; Madge, 2007). It is less self-evident, though, why "family get-together" is separated from eating (together), or why different modes of eating should be co-located. What is the *raison d'être* behind pushing all socializing into one bubble (unless it involves the preparation or intake of food)? While the diagram may not pretend to describe *all* family life, it nevertheless clusters a fleetingly differentiated set of practices and activities into a manageable set of entities that can be translated to architectural solutions at the expense of omitting power relations and the socio-cultural spatial effects of complex family structures, etc. As Foucault (2002) demonstrates, the structures and actions that generate such orders are embedded with values, priorities, and perceptions that, while not easily readable in the final "sensible" categories, operate to structure our understanding of that which is organized as well as what sort of operations constitute sensible organizing principles.[10]

We can see here, how the bubble diagram does three things: 1) it separates the continuity of family life into distinct bubbles of activity; 2) it frees the bubbles from one another, making it possible to re-arrange them as long as links are ensured appropriately; and 3) it suggests that a *social/use bubble* corresponds to a *spatial bubble*, which can then be designed on both a system and "bubble" level. The logic also suggests that this is, in fact, a sensible description and generates false pretenses of conformity between conceptual realms: while one can categorize *eating* as an important part of living in a home, this does not mean it is the most spatially relevant categorization of use—or that the conceptualization matched subsequent, actual use (Peponis, 1989).

These kinds of bubbles maintain intimate ties to neighborhood planning. Drawing on the works of Clarence Perry (1929), and studies like those of Christaller (1966) and von Thünen (1966) for notions of distributions, sizes, and hierarchies, many forms of neighborhood center planning distinctly demonstrate the conceptual shortcomings of the "bubble" in their overly simple classifications of (public) space. In all of its simple abstractness, the Swedish planner Bertel Granfelt (1968) makes an illustrative point in his diagrams addressing the relation between contextual-situational dependency of activities and the inability of a system of centers of discrete scales (no matter what scales are chosen) to provide for the complex range of activities that they are supposed to hold (Figure 11.4).

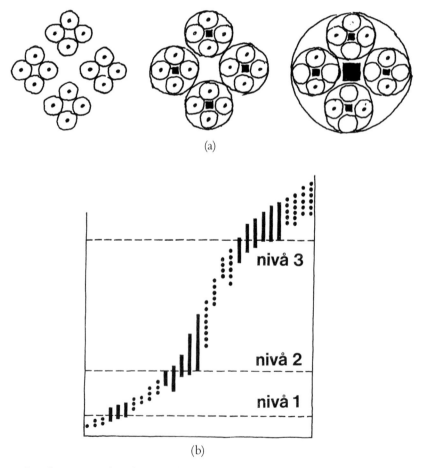

FIGURE 11.4 Local, communal, and regional centers in the draft regional plan of Stockholm in 1966 (top) and Granfelt's critical diagram (bottom).

If one can criticize the bundling of diverse social activities in homes as evidencing an insufficient understanding of the plurality of daily social engagements, then *public space*, as understood through what Victor Gruen tried to achieve in his malls, is treated with the same kind of reductive thinking; as bubbles for *vibrant and pleasant urban socializing*. Gruen's intention was to recreate the kind of public space that was found in European cities in US suburban landscapes (McMorrough, 2001; Wall, 2005). Within the then-existing US landscape, consisting largely of spread-out domestic subdivisions and labyrinthine road structures, the solution was to literally create a bubble—the multi-purpose mall—which would combine three aspects of the European city center: shopping, (public) service, and public space. Like conceptual bubbles, these centers distinctly separate inside from outside and have a plastic relation to their surroundings.[11]

Here, the bubble's *detached* relation on both physical and conceptual levels enables it to operate autonomously, to maintain relations with other bubbles in particular ways, and to be artificially created in a decontextualized manner. While malls can be considered literal bubbles, the key aspect is the *conceptual* bubbles that underlie these structures. Gruen's approach illustrates how "public space" is being separated from other space in discourse and practice, and this separation of public space into its own plastic entity is what is at stake. Once "public space" as a design question is separated out from other types of space, the logics of the bubble can be applied to the concept, and the ideal (the leisurely, lively, and vibrant central square) can infect the entirety of public space, allowing every location to be expected to provide that ideal and to be considered a failure if it does not.

This line of thinking can be found in historical urban design discourse. For instance, Jane Jacobs (1954) praises Gruen's work with the Northland Mall,[12] suggesting that it holds potential as a model for how to work with the redevelopment of downtown areas—something Gruen did in the aforementioned Fort Worth plans (Gruen, 1964). What needs to be recognized is that the concept of public space that is deployed in Fort Worth is largely the same as in the Northland Mall—while the project is more sensitive to its surroundings, the existing architecture, and the opinions and wants of locals. That is, the bubble is still there and operates in the same way—it is just less discernable as it has been transformed through its formal plasticity to appear as streets and squares. The model for inner-city public space was, literally, the mall, with its artificial density of presence that can only be maintained by the exterior contribution of incoming visitors. This logic still seems to be valid in the majority of pedestrianized city centers, as well as in plans for new pedestrian cities, although car parking may be replaced by "transit stations" or "mobility hubs."

The Arrow

While often interlinked with bubble diagrams, *the arrow* is another technique deployed in making flow charts and mapping flows in conceptual diagrams—and thus in structuring and arranging plans through understanding topologies of relation and the structures of (specific) flows. As Macarthur and Moulis (2005) note, while lines representing movement in an architectural diagram might seem obvious, this was an invention of modernism in the specific sense of representing movement flow patterns. While the movement axis was central to, for instance, the Beaux Arts model of teaching design, the role of lines and arrows in the bubble diagram brings with it another type of relation to the line: where the axes of the Beaux Arts were geometric abstractions of architectural sequence and order that ran *through* spaces and thereby structured geometry, the line in the bubble diagram operates by "a-geometrically" linking bubbles that concretely represent abstracted connections. In this, the axis and the arrow operate in opposite manners, conceptually: one *defines and restricts* spatial organization in relation to geometry, and the other *frees up and liberates* the same by detaching topology from geometry.

Here, we can see how such diagrammatic practices are comparable to other developments that to an extent precede them, which increasingly separated spaces of flows and spaces of being. While this development grows gradually forth from negotiations between power structures, rights of privacy and control, and the needs and desires for movement and access (Evans, 1978; Hanson, 1998), this differentiation of space grows exponentially as *the bubble* of activity can be freely and efficiently interlinked via the *arrow* and thereby manipulated as pure topology.[13] However, the arrow as mediator of efficiency also poses challenges for how we understand flows and the capacity of flows to populate places, since the figure for flows, as Emmons notes, is *the figure which is meant to minimize time in movement* (Emmons, 2014, p. 548). He notes further the way in which the American efficiency engineer Charles Day sorted out efficiency diagrams for industries in the beginning of the 20th century by making use of flow lines and flow charts: once the solution was finished, a building merely needed to be designed around it. But one of the first examples of using arrows to illustrate flows and to address the notion of efficiency outside of industry and technology is that of Christine Frederick (1913), presenting her well-known diagram of the flow of preparing an omelet in a bad and a good kitchen arrangement (Figure 11.5). While it should be noted that "flow lines reflect an imagined possible future ambulation rather than determining how a person will actually move" (Emmons, 2014, p. 549), uses of flow charts often tend to conflate one into the other. In this, they reflect the ways that bubble diagrams of organizations and relations sometimes are conflated with geometrical solutions of plans.

The capacity of the arrow to sort out movement and its tendency to structure thinking around efficiency and convenience can also be found in the works of Victor Gruen. He uses a similar argument and graphic language as Frederick in his description of the "suburban labyrinth" (Figure 11.6) and his plea for introducing a multi-purpose center in order to gather services in one place (Gruen, 1973). Gruen argues this will reduce the time taken by people driving around, instead allowing them to be where they want to be: at home, enjoying public life, or making use of the mall services. Here, we can note how the traditional vibrant city he seeks to emulate in many respects would be better represented by the figure of the "Suburban

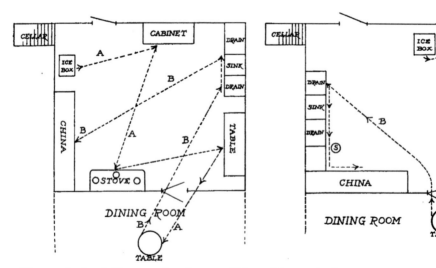

FIGURE 11.5 Christine Frederick's illustration of "bad" and "good" kitchen arrangements.

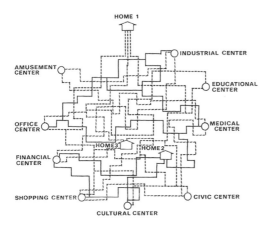 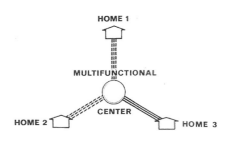

FIGURE 11.6 The "Suburban labyrinth" and its cure.

labyrinth," although with significant differences in scales and how distances are embedded in or created by the structures of the street systems. Or perhaps more clearly: if the goal of a plan is a lively square, then a solution that mimics a "good" kitchen (i.e., rationalizing and making efficient flows and accessibilities) is contradictory to the sought-after character.

The clustering of services and homes, linked through efficient transportation infrastructure, remains a pertinent model in contemporary mobility discourse. Traffic planning that favors travel decisions of a particular character further builds this logic into systems in ways that affect the (mobile) subject deeply. This is because when *the arrow* is made to stand for an intention, and used to link two or more bubbles, it connects notions of subjectivity and action. Its role in such circumstances is to facilitate as much as possible with as little effort as possible (Chapin & Hightower, 1965). Here is where we can begin to address more critically not "the arrow" as such but how it relates to notions of subjectivity and psychology embedded in notions of mobility and transport on deep and sometimes hidden levels. We can begin by studying the way that traffic analysis operates, partially because many of the foundational ideas of contemporary transport planning emerged in the 1950s to 1970s, with the *Detroit Metropolitan Area Traffic Study* (Michigan State Highway Department, 1955) and *The Chicago Area Transportation Study* (1959–62) (Chicago Area Transport Study, 1959) considered as important origins (Figure 11.7).

Embedded in this model, we can find a specific understanding of behavior, which is made especially clear by the pedagogical diagram of the four-step model that grew out of this study made by Meyer and Miller in 1984: trips are generated *first* by individuals wishing to perform specific actions; these desires subsequently *unfold* into trips (Figure 11.8).[14]

Once the challenge of mobility is understood as a problem of getting person i to where they wish to be j, via distance d, efficiency of travel can override other concerns. What the arrow (in the form of motorized transport) allows is the translation of d from space to time and effort; and a psychological model allows this conceptualization to be valid: if transportation is understood as a question of how to make the journey between i and j as efficient as possible, this requires that i "already knows" and desires j; that is, that i is a deliberate subject with internal needs and desires regardless of context. While contemporary traffic analysis operates with much more complex and nuanced models, some of which challenge this tendency, methods are still based on this principle in practice, albeit with complex networks of feedback loops (Batty, 1976; Ortúzar S. & Willumsen, 2011). The same behavioral concept is found again in the well-known "dumbbell" shopping mall layout, a model that postulates that a mall should be constructed with two

194 Daniel Koch

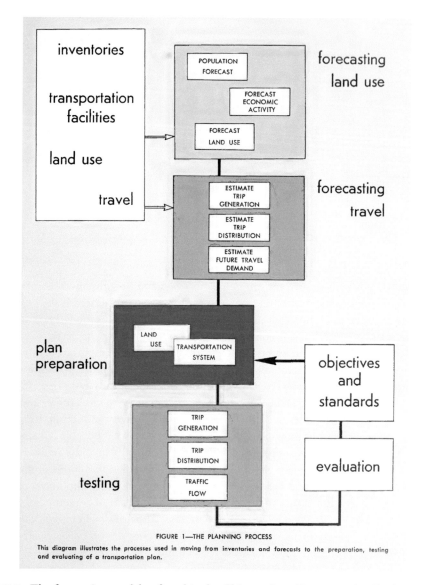

FIGURE 11.7 The forecasting model as found in the Chicago Area Transportation Study.

large "anchors"—one at each end—which will generate flows in-between where other stores can profit from drop-in customers (Beddington, 1982). This demonstrates both the power of this understanding of movement and subjectivity, and how it integrates its opposite into itself: that is, how the notion of the modern rational ego manages to also contain that of the irrational, seducible subject as its opposite in the same figure of action.

Thus, the notion of movement as an activity that takes *individuals with pre-existing desires from where they are to where they already want to be* is expressed in rational notions of flow charts and diagrams, whereby the arrow is that which enables the travel in-between. This invokes an understanding of subjectivity that is highly problematic and allocates individuals a certain kind of agency and responsibility.[15] When the Freudian ego, with its desires that both emerge from the interior of the subject and push that subject to seek out and enact them in an exterior

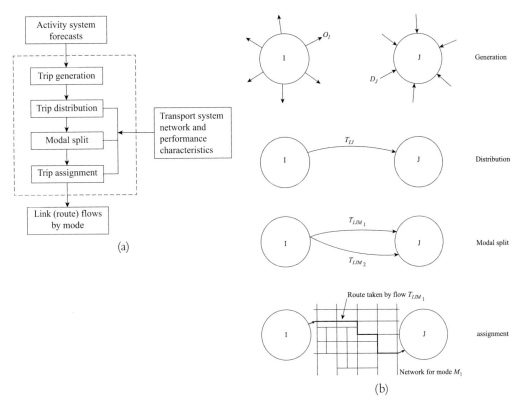

FIGURE 11.8 A diagram of the Urban Transport Modeling System and a pedagogical diagram of what the steps entail.

world (Ferguson, 1992), is combined with the release of travel from geometry, these ideas push in the same direction: the clustering of *desire fulfillment* (by way of creating few and large bubbles) and the facilitation of mobility (making it possible to get to those places). That is, there is the potential of dialectical interplay between diagram and concept, that is self-reinforcing, whereby the diagram that is to sort out movement flows becomes the diagram of how movement works, and consequently, how movement is to be generated. Movement (and urban life) is generated by *destinations*. The detachment of the transportation link d from geometry engenders efficiency in a contradictory manner: as time and distance are differentiated, solutions can take on new forms. With only small differences in speeds, a longer route quickly becomes more time-efficient than a shorter route. The Car Society, it seems, rather than favoring straight lines, favors avoidance—the circling of contexts would reduce speed rather than distance efficiency.[16]

This subject-logic is embedded in traffic planning, place-making, and shopping centers in different ways. Such a conceptualization of flows depends on the discretization of what they are to lead between—a logic that also advances clustering of origins and destinations, thereby combining the two efficiency gains of quick trips and a reduced number of trips. The arrow suggests (and depends on) the bubble in the way that it leads from the before to the after. Just because the bubble is a "vibrant pedestrianized mixed-use area," it operates no less as a bubble and poses the same requirements in terms of access, because just like the shopping mall, it is dependent on considerable influx from its context to fulfill its intentional role as lively and vibrant.

The Area

The notion of an "area" presents challenges related to the images in the beginning of this chapter and how they relate to conceptualizations of community. Communities are messy, tangled, differentiated, overlapping, and distributed things. Not only can one person's community be radically different from another person's community even when both are part of one another's community, but community is a vague concept that spans from describing a single, cohesive social unit to referring to a range of related forms of practices, relations, shared codes of conducts, or values (Blokland, 2017). Some operate more on the basis of everyday meetings, and some operate on other types of recognition. There are communities or relations that build on, in short, proximity; others that depend on (inter)personal histories (e.g., family ties); and yet others that are built around memberships such as interest groups, subcultures, or other a-spatial commonalities (Castells, 1997; Williams, 2011).[17] Furthermore, everyone is arguably part of several communities, where community belonging is at the very least an interplay between *belonging to* a group and *not being part of* another group (Bourdieu, 1984; Rose, 2002). In the face of this vast array of diverse positions on community, it is odd that both theory and practice regularly suggest that generating *a* community in *an* area is a cornerstone of sustainable development.

Unfortunately, this practice and discourse sometimes confuse *co-presence* for community on the one hand, and the potentials generated by co-presence for a deterministic result of co-presence on the other: the existence of a visible collective tends to be confused with the existence of community (Bishop, 2004). These slippages cause problems in understanding trans-spatial relations, the complexities of community formations, and what would generate deeper social relations.[18] They are also instrumentalized in a politically highly problematic act of trying to force community upon people based on a combination of spatial proximity and largely arbitrarily drawn boundaries.[19] While, as Ann Legeby (2013) argues, encountering difference in public space is important for building social cohesion, challenging segregation, and generating understanding of difference in cities, it is important to question and nuance why "community formation" must be the grounds for positive outcomes as compared to, for example, a broadened understanding of diversity of population and living conditions (further Young, 1996; Zukin, 1995). In addition, it takes only a cursory observation to note that while shares and magnitudes may differ, only portions of any urban settlement are lively at any given time. Given these concerns, how can a repetition of a particular image of sociability serve as a model for "all" public space and as a vision of social sustainability?

These challenges relate to a reading of area that understands it to operate as an abstracted concept of a *community-neighborhood bundle*, which can be summarized by recourse to two different forms of synecdoche: imposing the whole on the part and reading the part for the whole, both of which make the error of assigning homogeneity to heterogeneity.[20] To start in a perhaps unexpected end, one can turn to the *Modifiable Areal Unit Problem* (MAUP), a well-known problem in quantitative geography (Openshaw, 1983): in short, any statistical averaging or aggregation of data is sensitive to the area definition in which it is averaged or into which it is aggregated (Figure 11.9). Growing from early research demonstrating how statistical correlations of census tracts grew as the units of the census tract areas increased in size (Gehlke & Biehl, 1934), defining just what area definition is relevant for geographical statistics remains a challenge. It can concern more obvious things such as how density figures can grow or shrink whether one includes a park or not (Rådberg, 1998). If working to compare neighborhoods within a city, the choices of how to subdivide into neighborhoods will affect not only figures for each neighborhood but also the relative figures of neighborhoods compared to one another. And, as Openshaw notes, "the areal units (zonal objects) used in many geographical studies are arbitrary, modifiable, and subject to the whims and fancies of whoever is doing, or did, the aggregating" (Openshaw, 1983, p. 3)—which is demonstrated in Figure 11.9 in how Swedish

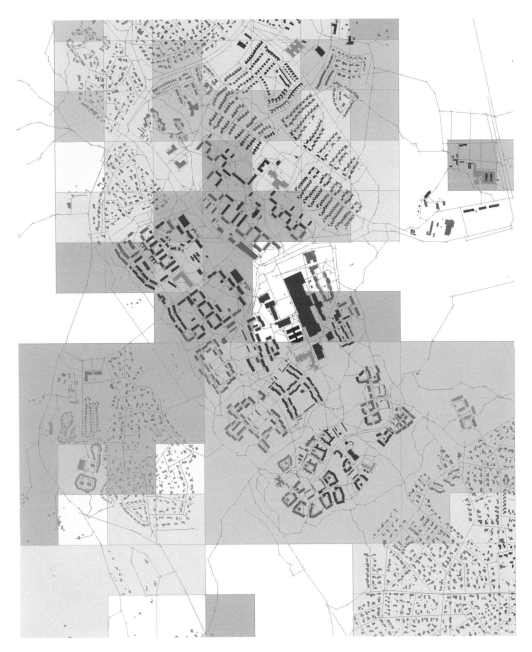

FIGURE 11.9 The geographical distribution of income statistics in Gottsunda outside of Uppsala, Sweden. Darker areas for higher income, darker building footprints closer to schools.

income statistics are geographically aggregated (Legeby, Koch, & Miranda, 2019). When these kinds of statistics are then used to understand local situations, we effectively confront a whole-for-the-part synecdoche.

This is not limited to quantitative analysis. For instance, Stockholm's earlier municipal policy "Stockholms Byggnadsordning" (Kallstenius & Fredlund, 2001) presents 12 urban types, which constitute the different areas of Stockholm distributed in discrete bubbles (Figure 11.10), while in reality Stockholm is not neatly divided into distinctly separate areas of as few as 12

198 Daniel Koch

FIGURE 11.10 Part of the typomorphological map of Stockholm and the 12 types of Stockholm's "Byggnadsordning."

The Bubble, the Arrow, and the Area **199**

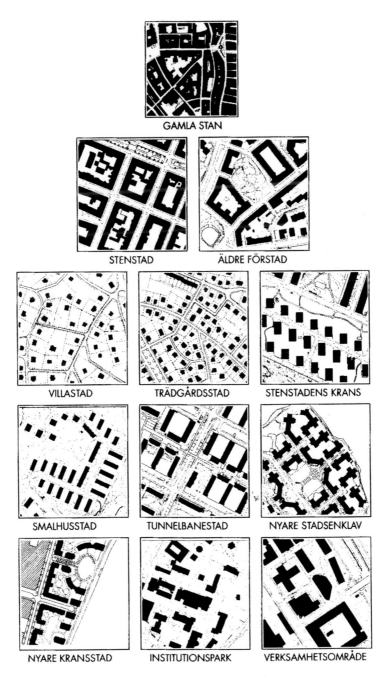

FIGURE 11.10 (Continued)

homogenous typologies. Averaging of areas here operates on areas in plural—collective averages are mapped out onto areas that are diverse, both within and between one another, as descriptors of their individual characters. Under certain circumstances, this commits violent acts of transformation of the perception of areas folding them into generic categories from which they might be quite different when looking closer. As an official document, however, it influenced development in constituting a "reality" to relate to when assessing proposals parallel to the on-the-ground reality.

For a concrete example of the part for the whole synecdoche, one can turn to the example of Gottsunda outside of Uppsala from Figure 11.9, and the Swedish Police's designation of the area as a "particularly vulnerable area" (Nationella Operativa Avdelningen, 2017).[21] Without attempting to trivialize challenges, although there are serious problems with organized crime in the area and the risk and threats this causes to others are important to recognize, these problems tend to take place in a very limited part of the area, involving a limited number of people.[22] Furthermore, while *parts* of Gottsunda can be characterized as having high unemployment rates and low education levels, other parts have remarkably high levels of education and near full employment of its population. All the same, in media and in discourse, these challenges have come to characterize and define Gottsunda, while a significant portion of the population feel both safe and proud of their area. Such stigmatization is not uncommon and often the case when whole areas are designated as problematic or dangerous, which while rooted in *parts* thereof, end up having effects on the whole through how such perceptions affect actions on many levels, from individual choices to political decisions, reaching far outside of the area itself as well (Wacquant, 2008). Conversely, whole areas can gain reputations and images that hold positive qualities based on similarly particular or local characteristics—as is the case, arguably, for most larger-scale areas characterized as "lively." Such thought figures tend to become increasingly influential the less one knows of an area, often operating in an indirect but pervasive manner (Koch, 2017).

The two forms of synecdoche thus often work interconnectedly, such as when the liveliest streets of Manhattan come to stand for Manhattan, but where then this concept of Manhattan as a whole-from-the-part grows to the expectation and understanding of everywhere on Manhattan. This does not mean that there is not an awareness of variety on Manhattan, but rather that the synecdoche operates on a conceptual level that engenders notions like "Manhattan life" to act as if it *was* indeed a plausible possibility to make the whole into what is in the part. Similarly, it risks leading planning proposals to address safety and security issues in Gottsunda *as if* the whole of Gottsunda was unsafe, as a result of *the area* being designated as such due to events in limited parts thereof.

Here we confront one of the challenges with "mixed-use" planning in relation to the diagrammatic figure of "the area." While sensitive approaches to the concept can clearly be relevant, there is a risk that zoning of mixed-use areas engenders thinking with several or all of the challenges of the area. The synecdoche-based tendency for the livelier parts of particular areas to stand for their whole becomes—in the transfer of the characteristics from the real area as inspiration to the ideal that is to be implemented, or in the transference from an existing situation to an intended new situation—conducive to an error in thought that assumes that the whole new area *can* or *will* be like the part of the original. But it is also the process that allows deviant parts—such as less-used squares or side streets with little activity along them—to be considered problems or failures while quite possibly they are necessary for intense places to work, and where the experience of them as lively or not is subject to the relativity of rhythms as such (Lefebvre, 1996).

These problems relate to what Gilles Châtelet (2000) calls problems of the cut-out, which in his terms is a violent and transformative act transforming both the cut-out and its previous surroundings. In removing the cut-out (the area) from its context and studying it "in itself," there is a range of conceptual effects in how one understands its characteristics and challenges. Planning of *areas* conditions solutions; when applied as a boundary of challenge, problem, and solution alike, this limits the problem space to what is feasible or plausible to handle within the given boundary, attempts to force all solutions to fit within the scales and bounds of the given area, and leaves the effects of solutions on other areas outside of the field of consideration. The neighborhood unit is such a conceptual cut-out of society, which not only makes it appear as possible to treat independently, but also disassociates it from societal challenges as well as a nuanced understanding of urbanity. This is embedded in most, if not all, governance practices of urban areas. The boundary line of the area—as arbitrary as it might be—serves as a structuring force of the governance project, delimiting not only who is or is not concerned, but also the game board upon which discussions and decisions are to be played out and realized.[23]

The area thus allows planning to strive for 1) a vibrant, lively center of its own, 2) a "mixed-use" ideal with "active ground floors" that will enliven it, 3) the insistence that any particular location within that area that does not fulfill the ideal of the center is a failure, and finally 4) the notion that ensuring that these goals are reached locally demands that visitors be drawn from other areas with the risk of moving the problems, as well as the successes, around rather than finding overall improvements. Conversely, the area extends itself over a surface and has two tendencies: it expects from a planner to solve its internal needs within itself, and it expresses a unity of that which is within its borders. The cut-out, as it were, merges the bubble with the area, and this merger helps us to see additionally how the transition of mall urbanity to inner-city concepts operates. It is in this interrelation that the bubble of the mall can become the ideal for public space spreading over entire areas, where the cut-out enables its conceptual execution as pedestrianized areas with (cut-away) parking houses, underground roads, and mobility centers to feed it.

Fragmented Life and Discretized Urbanity

The bubble, the arrow, and the area are graphical entities that demonstrate modes of thinking, or *modi operandi*, at work in many different approaches to urban design and planning. Rather than direct models or deliberately applied concepts, it is the way that they operate to reposition us and our understanding of the world that needs to be scrutinized.[24] The bubble diagram here both represents and enables a certain way of thinking about solutions through architectural plans, but it does not deterministically cause it. The arrow suggests a way to relate to flows, but it does not require this.

This conceptually further relates to two types of intentional subject—one rational and one irrational—that both operate in the guise of a Freudian desiring ego that enacts alterity, rationality, desire, intent, or wishes in and on the world; that takes shape in similar forms of focused (although differently differentiated and conceptualized) intents and actions. Activities become rituals in the most limiting sense, as it is by becoming rituals they can be formulated as programs, and therefore responded to by formal adaption as de-contextualized bubbles. Alternative spaces are also given a detached bubble character of alterity, infused by the same psychological construct, allowed for—and generated by—a bubble diagram of space *and* action. It is in this context that "public space" and "community" alike can be *qualitatively assessed through the quantity of people present*, where more is better, and a somewhat empty public space can be assessed as bad, inefficient, underused, underutilized, unsafe, as sites of segregation and crime, and *failed*. This, of course, forgets both the relativity of rhythms and the very easily observable situation that most public spaces are mostly rather empty of people for most of the time.

A way to further see how this relates to conceptualized structures of space and activity is through Julie Zook's work comparing the narrative structure of the films *The Naked City* (1948), *The Long Goodbye* (1970), *Goodfellas* (1990), and *Pulp Fiction* (1994), noting how the examples from New York demonstrate a certain continuity where thresholds—and the passing from scene to scene—is directly present and even emphasized, whereas those from Los Angeles rather form sets of compartmentalized scenes with jumps in-between (Zook, 2016). The latter is interchangeable with the bubble diagram but also integrates into itself the arrow and the area, as one jumps between detached bubbles, which can be extended as long as they follow the episodic scene structure. She notes further how this can be traced in the respective city's morphology.

This kind of fragmentation comes out of this discussion: the growing conceptualization of the city as a collection of discrete places for discrete (sometimes co-located) and independent activities, broken up by repetitions of in-between which, no matter their length, are there to facilitate the discrete pieces (Koch & Sand, 2009; Lefebvre, 1996). This fragmentation allows for the notion that a space "for everyone" can be a space for both a dominant and counter-cultures because both sides have been discretized and individualized and therefore are able to co-inhabit the same space (at the same time) and to consider the same space theirs. This discretization is dependent on a conceptualization of subjectivity and action embedded in much planning and design practice, which enables car-centric and anti-car conceptualizations to meet in the leisurely pedestrianized center.

No-Car, Non-Car, Not-Car

When urbanity is broken into distinct pieces of space and activity, which in their detached form correspond to one another, and when urbanity comes as a "cut-out," then contradictory conceptualizations of mobility, vibrancy, and pedestrian environments are enabled. This contradiction contributes to the emptying out of elsewheres in order to activate the here and now. Under such a model, only a few gradients of space are left, and "public" has come to mean "highly populated"; pedestrianized leisurely environments can coexist with copious roads, tunnels, and other infrastructures. Just like the arrow, the car emerges merely as an operator in this account, where what is important is the before and after. It simply facilitated efficient movement between that which actually mattered: the bubbles. If life and society is a collection of bubbles, and travel in-between is to be facilitated as efficiently as possible, then the traffic apparatus of highways, tunnels, roundabouts, and everything else does not romanticize or favor the car per se, but counterintuitively is rather all about *not* being in the car and *not* being on the road. It is simply more efficient to separate traffic and lead it the long way around if it reduces the total amount of time spent driving from *a* to *b*. This is not the same as saying that modernism did not plan for cars, but is rather to stress that it enabled the car to facilitate spending time in the bubbles, and extrapolated this capacity towards its logical end.

Modernist planning, in this sense, planned for the [not] car.

In the field of tension between building cities and environments that are bubbles where you *are not driving or being in your car* and making the connection between bubbles that have been artificially separated connected by the car, the resulting traffic apparatus by necessity spreads out and becomes dominant *between the bubbles*. In a similar manner, we now see a planning that advocates "car-less" societies, but which have not dealt with ideals of mobility nor engaged with breaking apart conceptual bubbles or the intentional subject, who enacts pre-existing desires. Such planning is, essentially, rather more of the same: it plans for bubbles of car-free zones or pedestrianized areas interconnected by (driverless, electrical) cars, where movement between these bubbles needs to be efficient and therefore is best facilitated by being provided in a separate system. Once again, this is not because of an ideology intentionally advocating cars or the Car Society, but is a result of modes of thinking and how they come to be realized in systems of implementation.

The not-car is thus distinct from but remarkably interchangeable with the no-car to the point of confusion. The *not-car* is a conceptualization that is concerned with *everything that is not driving in the car*, that is, being at home, at work, experiencing culture, sporting, socializing, etc., where planning and design aim to maximize time in these situations. The car is an enabler, a mobility concept-thing, that allows the not-car to be "at its best." Gruen's notion of the mall, very distinctively and explicitly, is *not* about the car but about maximizing time in the home and the new public space, *enabled* by brief stints inside cars. As long as no-car arguments and solutions operate with similar conceptualizations of subjectivity, activity, and mobility, one can see a drive towards confusingly similar solutions—only this time with cars underground. Logically, such ideas could reduce car use, if systems were not propagating and self-reinforcing. Ideals of mobility thereby wander on perilous ground between not-car and no-car: when the ambition is to create car-free spaces with mobility in-between, they more often than not become the same thing. Challenging the Car Society, beyond what is visible in urban environments, must deal with the logics of behavior and subjectivity.

This permeates both concepts of human action and of design and planning. In the simplest sense, it concerns planning of "meeting places," "culture hubs," "mobility centers," and so on. It concerns how observing people being at a square leads to assumption that the reason for them being there is that they want to be there specifically, which subsequently is the guiding principle for interpreting any individual or collective behavior. Activities become insular and discrete, and thereby separable, and possible to independently locate in space—and thereby also to build specific spaces for. This thinking permeates smart city solutions and developments, which argue for making it easier to find what one is looking for or providing you with information about where you might find that which you already desire, as a spatially decontextualized ego. It also permeates notions of resistance identities and alternative spaces, and finds its way into both consumer culture and anti-consumption culture, as well as discourses on architecture and architectural experience in a wide sense. This operation is further supported by readings where the activity-environment link is particular and local and thereby mobile.

All of these points invite us to rethink the role of representations and models towards a better understanding of nuances in ecologies of spaces, activities, and social relations. Rather than dismissing representations as such, it asks for a critical engagement with the mental, social, and environmental ecologies embedded in model-making, notions that participate in structuring subjectivity, action, and social structures. The subjectivity that is embedded in concrete and abstract diagrammatic operations and design thinking is what is currently at stake.

Notes

1. Victor Gruen has been given the nickname "the father of the Mall"—an epithet he notably opposes by this time (Gruen, 1964; Wall, 2005).
2. ABC stands for: *(A)rbete* (work), *(B)ostad* (housing), *(C)entrum* (center), conceptualized as covering all needs of inhabitants in their daily urban life (Stadsplanekontoret, 1952).
3. The mythical status accorded to Jane Jacobs makes it difficult to relate to her legacy, as there are risks of confusing practices emerging from her writings for Jacobs' own intentions (see e.g., McMorrough, 2001). In this chapter I engage with how *particular readings* of Jacobs' work have influenced design and planning discourse.
4. For example, Beddington (1982), Burns (1959), and Mongs (1979), or more recently the proposals of White and Gallardi+Hellsten for new Kiruna, okidoki's proposal for Vallastaden in Linköping (Sveriges Arkitekter, 2015), or Wester + Elsner's suggestion for the Globen area (Engström, 2017). These examples are not chosen in order to point fingers at specific architects or firms but act as concrete examples of a ubiquitous phenomenon, as I believe that specificity is important to demonstrate the argument.
5. Thordis Arrhenius notes that while arguably obsessed with cars, Le Corbusier seems rather to be phobic of them, as almost all solutions insist on placing them underground or otherwise excluding them from public space (Arrhenius, 2003).
6. In this sense, these illustrations form *utopias*, relegating that which enable their existence such as car traffic and parking to elsewheres and elsewhens (Foucault, 1986).

7. Both of international relevance at their time, referenced by, e.g., Wilfred Burns (1959), as examples of new ways in which pedestrianized areas and centers can contribute to a more humane future society.
8. The *Report of the United Nations Symposium on the Planning and Development of New Towns* from 1966 here mentions that while the size varies, between 6,000 and 12,000 inhabitants seem to be the most common norm (United Nations, 1966). Figures often range between 8,000 and 10,000, at times in groups of up to 30,000 (Mumford, 1954; Perry, 1929; Statens Planverk, 1968). The *Dudley Report* in Great Britain postulates 10,000 inhabitants per unit (Central Housing Advisory Committee, 1944).
9. The persistence of ideas of modern subjectivity have certainly been debated, as has levels of rationality or intentionality, in relation to cities—see, for instance, the critique set out in *The Sphinx and the City* (Wilson, 1991).
10. This means the diagram commits violent acts of separation (Châtelet, 2000), in that it requires for any part of an architectural program to either form its own bubble or subscribe itself into another bubble. While a convenient shorthand for organizing plans, it generates and enhances the idea of the functions as self-contained units with a spatial integrity of their own.
11. This can be further linked to the development of "interior urbanism" and atrium architecture as discussed by Charles Rice (2016), with its continuous evolution reiterating and reformulating the character of this interior-exterior relation (Frykholm, 2020).
12. While the review in *Architectural Forum* is signed as an editorial, Alex Wall (2005) attributes it to Jane Jacobs, as does Peter L. Laurence (2011), noting how she worked as *Architectural Forum*'s specialist on shopping centers from 1952. From there, it seems that while they did not always agree, Gruen's and Jacobs' work develops in parallel (Hardwick, 2004), and while Jacobs later disowned the idea of inner cities learning from suburbs, her respect for Gruen's work remained (Laurence, 2011).
13. This development is of course not uniform and linked to culture and class, where cultural norms have a drastic impact, often overruling "rational" limitations of size (Giuliani, 1987; Hanson & Hillier, 1982).
14. How psychological concepts are embedded in the *Chicago Area Transport Study* has been discussed by Throgmorton and Eckstein (2000), even though they focus on how specific methods and procedures are rationalized.
15. As Baudrillard (1998) points out, it places any "blame" for consumerism on a generalized "you" (meaning personalized individuals), as it is from within you that desire emerges and because of this desire you consume, which, he notes, is to confuse everything.
16. See Boeing's study of American street structures showing how car circuity—the added distance of a connection as compared to a straight axis—significantly exceeds that of pedestrian circuity also over remarkably long distances (Boeing, 2019).
17. Hanson and Hillier (1987) introduce the terms "spatial" and "transpatial" social relations to describe relations generated and upheld by proximity or regular face-to-face meetings, and relations which can grow or remain despite a lack of physical meetings. See further, Durkheim's (1933) discussions on mechanical and organic solidarity.
18. See, for instance, Claire Bishop's (2004) critique of relational art and Blokland's (2008) on discussion of trans-group understanding versus upholding of prejudices. Also Zygmunt Bauman's (2001) critical discussion on the role of community.
19. Of course, various degrees of separation into neighborhoods or areas exist in many kinds of settlements, including apparently continuous cities (Peponis, Ross, & Rashid, 1997), but boundaries are often gradual or fuzzy (Yang & Hillier, 2007).
20. For extensive research on how actions can be understood through rhetoric figures, see the work of Jean-Francois Augoyard (2007).
21. The police have identified vulnerable areas as "a geographically delimited area characterized by low socio-economic status where criminals have an impact on local society" (Nationella Operativa Avdelningen, 2017, p. 4; author's translation).
22. As discussed with the municipality and the police on several occasions; see further (Koch, Legeby, & Miranda, 2019).
23. It is important to maintain that the challenge is not the visual representation but what structures thought and action, where the existence of a masterplan or not may be inconsequential. On the contrary, refusal to make visible governing notions of ranges of decisions that are related to geography may instead bury such decisions in the rhetoric of working with processes, agreements, and stakeholder needs and desires.
24. Following Willard McCarty's argument, it builds on models holding "a ternary relationship in which it mediates epistemologically, between modeler and modeled, researcher and data or theory and the world" (McCarty, 2008, p. 55), where this ternary relationship means models also position the *modeler*, or, the one doing the work (Stengers, 2015).

References

Ahlsén, E., & Ahlsén, T. (1944). Årsta Centrum. *Arkitektur, 1944*(23), 430–433.
Aronsson, A. (1956). Vällingby centrum—från idé till verklighet. *Arkitektur, 1956*(4), 77–79.
Arrhenius, T. (2003). *The Fragile Monument: On Conservation and Modernity*. Stockholm, Sweden: KTH.
Augoyard, J.-F. (2007). *Step by Step: Everyday Walks in a French Urban Housing Project* (D.A. Curtis, Trans.). Minneapolis, MN: University of Minnesota Press.
Batty, M. (1976). *Urban Modelling: Algorithms, Calibrations, Predictions*. Cambridge, MA: Cambridge University Press.
Baudrillard, J. (1998). *The Consumer Society: Myths and Structures* (C. Turner, Trans.). London, UK: Sage.
Bauman, Z. (2001). *Community: Seeking Safety in an Insecure World*. Cambridge, MA: Polity Press.
Beddington, N. (1982). *Design for Shopping Centres*. London, UK: Butterworth.
Bishop, C. (2004). Antagonism and Relational Aesthetics. *October, 110*(Fall), 51–79.
Blokland, T. (2008). Gardening with a Little Help from Your (Middle Class) Friends: Bridging Social Capital Across Race and Class in a Mixed Neighbourhood. In T. Blokland & M. Savage (Eds.), *Networked Urbanism: Social Capital and the City* (pp. 147–170). Farnham, UK: Ashgate.
Blokland, T. (2017). *Community as Urban Practice*. Cambridge, MA: Polity Press.
Boeing, G. (2019). The Morphology and Circuity of Walkable and Drivable Street Networks. In L. D'Acci (Ed.), *The Mathematics of Urban Morphology* (pp. 271–287). Basel, Switzerland: Birkhäuser.
Bourdieu, P. (1984). *Distinction: A Social Critique of the Judgement of Taste* (R. Nice, Trans.). Cambridge, MA: Harvard University Press.
Burns, W. (1959). *British Shopping Centres: New Trends in Layout and Distribution*. London, UK: Leonard Hill.
Butler, J. (2005). *Giving an Account of Oneself*. New York, NY: Fordham University Press.
Carmona, M., & Wunderlich, F. (2012). *Capital Spaces: The Multiple Complex Public Spaces of a Global City*. London, UK: Routledge.
Castells, M. (1997). *The Information Age. Volume 2: The Power of Identity*. Malden, MA: Blackwell.
Central Housing Advisory Committee, G.B. (1944). *Design of Dwellings: Report of the Design of Dwellings Subcommittee of the Central Housing Advisory Committee Appointed by the Minister of Health and Report of a Study Group of the Ministry of Town and Country Planning on Site Planning and Layout in Relation to Housing; The Dudley Report*. London, UK: H.M.S.O.
Chapin, F.S.J., & Hightower, H.C. (1965). Household Activity Patterns and Land Use. *Journal of American Institute of Planners, 31*(3), 222–231.
Châtelet, G. (2000). *Figuring Space: Philosophy, Mathematics and Physics* (R. Shore & M. Zagha, Trans.). Dordrecht, Netherlands: Kluwer Academic Publishers.
Chicago Area Transport Study. (1959). *The Chicago Area Transportation Study. Volume I: Study Findings*. Chicago, IL: Harrison Lithographing.
Christaller, W. (1966). *Central Places in Southern Germany*. Englewood Cliffs, NJ: Prentice-Hall.
Chung, C.J., Inaba, J., Koolhaas, R., & Leong, S.T. (Eds.). (2001). *The Harvard Design School Guide to Shopping*. Köln, Germany: Taschen.
Dergalin, I., & Stäck, J.M. (1964). Generalplan för Rinkeby, Spånga Kyrka och Tensta. *Arkitektur, 1964*(5), 119–124.
Durkheim, É. (1933). *The Division of Labor in Society* (G. Simpson, Trans.). Glencoe, IL: The Free Press of Glencoe.
Emmons, P. (2006). Embodying Networks: Bubble Diagrams and the Image of Modern Organicism. *The Journal of Architecture, 11*(4), 441–461.
Emmons, P. (2014). Demiurgic Lines: Line-making and the Architectural Imagination. *The Journal of Architecture, 19*(4), 536–559.
Engström, F. (2017, November 25). Klövern och Citycon i JV för att dubbla Globen Shopping. *Fastighetsvärlden*. Retrieved from https://www.fastighetsvarlden.se/notiser/klovern-och-citycon-jv-att-dubbla-globen-shopping/
Evans, R. (1978). Figures, Doors and Passages. *Architectural Design, 48*, 267–278.
Ferguson, H. (1992). Watching the World Go Round: Atrium Culture and the Psychology of Shopping. In R. Shields (Ed.), *Lifestyle Shopping: The Subject of Consumption* (pp. 21–39). London, UK: Routledge.
Ferguson, H. (2009). *Self-Identity and Everyday Life*. New York, NY: Routledge.

Foucault, M. (1982). Space, Knowledge, Power; Interview with Paul Rabinow. *Skyline*, *1982*(March), 16–24.

Foucault, M. (1986). Of Other Spaces: Utopias and Heterotopias. *Lotus*, *48*(9), 9–17.

Foucault, M. (2002). *The Order of Things: An Archaeology of the Human Sciences*. London, UK: Routledge.

Frederick, C. (1913). *The New Housekeeping: Efficiency Studies in Home Management*. Garden City, NY: Double Day.

Frichot, H. (2014). On the Becoming-Indiscernible of the Diagram in Societies of Control. *Journal of Space Syntax*, *5*(1), 1–14.

Frichot, H. (2019). *Creative Ecologies: Theorizing the Practice of Architecture*. London, UK: Bloomsbury.

Frykholm, H. (2020). *Building the City from the Inside: Architecture and Urban Transformation in Los Angeles, Porto, and Las Vegas*. Stockholm, Sweden: KTH.

Gehlke, C.E., & Biehl, K. (1934). Certain Effects of Grouping upon the Size of the Correlation Coefficient in Census Tract Material. *Journal of the American Statistical Association*, *29*(185A), 169–170.

Giddens, A. (1984). *The Constitution of Society: Outline of the Theory of Structuration*. Berkeley, CA: University of California Press.

Giuliani, M.V. (1987). Naming the Rooms: Implications of a Change in the Home Model. *Environment and Behavior*, *19*(2), 180–203.

Granfelt, B. (1968). Service och centra som planeringsproblem. *Arkitektur*, *1968*(11), 4–13.

Gruen, V. (1964). *The Heart of Our Cities: The Urban Crisis: Diagnosis and Cure*. New York, NY: Simon and Schuster.

Gruen, V. (1973). *Centers for the Urban Environment: Survival of the Cities*. New York, NY: Van Norstrand Reinhold Co.

Guattari, F. (2000). *The Three Ecologies* (I. Pindar & P. Sutton, Trans.). London, UK: Athlone Press.

Hanson, J. (1998). *Decoding Homes and Houses*. Cambridge, UK: Cambridge University Press.

Hanson, J., & Hillier, B. (1982). Domestic Space Organisation: Two Contemporary Space-codes Compared. *Architecture and Behaviour*, *2*(1), 5–25.

Hanson, J., & Hillier, B. (1987). The Architecture of Community: Some New Proposals on the Social Consequences of Architectural Planning Decisions. *Architecture and Behavior*, *3*(3), 251–273.

Hardwick, J.M. (2004). *Mall Maker: Victor Gruen, Architect of an American Dream*. Philadelphia, PA: University of Pennsylvania Press.

Hillier, B. (1996). *Space is the Machine: A Configurational Theory of Architecture*. Cambridge, UK: Cambridge University Press.

Jacobs, J. (1954). Northland: A New Yardstick for Shopping Center Planning. *Architectural Forum*, *100*(6), 103–104.

Jacobs, J. (1958). Downtown is for People. In The Editors of Fortune (Ed.), *The Exploding Metropolis* (pp. 157–184). New York, NY: Doubleday & Company.

Kallstenius, P., & Fredlund, A. (Eds.). (2001). *Stockholms byggnadsordning: ett förhållningssätt till stadens karaktärsdrag*. Stockholm, Sweden: Stadsbyggnadskontoret.

Koch, D. (2017). Memory, Projection, and Imagination: On Challenges for Observation and Statistics Based Research. *Contour 2: Agents/Agency of Urbanity*, *2*(1), 1–15.

Koch, D. (2018). On Architectural Space and Modes of Subjectivity: Producing the Material Conditions for Creative-Productive Activity. *Urban Planning*, *3*(3), 70–82.

Koch, D., Legeby, A., & Miranda, P. (2019). Suburbs and Power: Configuration, Direct and Symbolic Presence, Absence, and Power in The Swedish Suburb Gottsunda. In *Proceedings of the 12th International Space Syntax Symposium* (pp. 264-2:1–21). Beijing, China: Beijing Jiaotong University.

Koch, D., & Sand, M. (2009). Rhythmanalysis—Rhythm as Mode, Methods and Theory for Analysing Urban Complexity. In A. Wesener & M. Aboutarabi (Eds.), *Urban Design Research: Method and Application—Proceedings of the International Conference held at Birmingham City University 3–4 December 2009* (pp. 61–72). Birmingham: Birmingham City University.

Laurence, P.L. (2011). The Unknown Jane Jacobs: Geographer, Propagandist, City Planning Idealist. In M. Page & T. Mennel (Eds.), *Reconsidering Jane Jacobs* (pp. 15–36). New York, NY: Routledge.

Lefebvre, H. (1991). *The Production of Space* (D. Nicholson-Smith, Trans.). Oxford, UK: Blackwell Publishing.

Lefebvre, H. (1996). *Writings on Cities* (E. Lebas & E. Kofman, Trans.). Oxford, UK: Blackwell.

Legeby, A. (2013). *Patterns of Co-Presence: Spatial Configuration and Social Segregation*. Stockholm, Sweden: KTH.

Legeby, A., Koch, D., & Miranda, P. (2019). Schools at 'Front Row': Public Buildings in Relation to Societal Presence and Social Exclusion. In *Proceedings of the 12th International Space Syntax Symposium* (pp. 287–2:1–219). Beijing, China: Beijing Jiaotong University.

Macarthur, J., & Moulis, A. (2005). Movement and Figurality: The Circulation Diagram and the History of the Architectural Plan. In A. Leach & G. Matthewson (Eds.), *Celebration: Proceedings of the 22nd Annual Conference of the Society of Architectural Historians, Australia and New Zealand* (pp. 231–235). Napier: Society of Architectural Historians, Australia and New Zealand.

Madge, J. (2007). Type at the Origin of Architectural Form. *The Journal of Architecture*, *12*(1), 1–34.

McCarty, W. (2008). Modeling: A Study in Words and Meanings. In S. Shreibman, R. Siemens, & J. Unsworth (Eds.), *A Companion to Digital Humanities* (pp. 254–270). Oxford, UK: Blackwell.

McMorrough, J. (2001). Good Intentions. In C.J. Chung, J. Inaba, R. Koolhaas, & S.T. Leong (Eds.), *Harvard Design School Guide to Shopping* (pp. 371–379). Köln, Germany: Taschen.

Meyer, M.D., & Miller, E.J. (1984). *Urban Transportation Planning: A Decision Oriented Approach*. New York, NY: McGraw-Hill.

Michigan State Highway Department. (1955). *Detroit Metropolitan Area Traffic Study Part 1: Data Summary and Interpretation*. Lansing, MI: Speaker-Hines and Thomas.

Mongs, L. (1979). Planer på ett centrum. *Arkitektur*, *1979*(8), 17–24.

Mumford, L. (1954). The Neighborhood and the Neighborhood Unit. *The Town Planning Review*, *24*(4), 256–270.

Nationella Operativa Avdelningen. (2017). *Utsatta områden: Social ordning, kriminell struktur och utmaningar för polisen*. Polismyndigheten.

Nishihara, K. (1968). *Japanese Houses: Patterns for Living* (R.L. Gage, Trans.). Tokyo, Japan: Japan Publications.

Openshaw, S. (1983). *The Modifiable Areal Unit Problem*. Norwick, VA: Geo Books.

Ortúzar S., J.d.D., & Willumsen, L.G. (2011). *Modelling Transport* (4th ed.). Oxford, UK: Wiley-Blackwell.

Peponis, J. (1989). Space, Culture and Urban Design in Late Modernism and After. *Ekistics*, *56*(334/335), 93–108.

Peponis, J., Ross, C., & Rashid, M. (1997). The Structure of Urban Space, Movement and Co-presence: The Case of Atlanta. *Geoforum*, *3–4*, 341–358.

Perry, C.A. (1929). The Neighbourhood Unit: A Scheme of Arrangement for the Family-life Community. In *Regional Survey of New York and its Environs, Volume VII: Neighborhood and Community Planning*. New York, NY: New York.

Rådberg, J. (1998). *Doktrin och täthet i svenskt stadsbyggande 1875–1975*. Stockholm, Sweden: Statens råd för byggnadsforskning.

Rice, C. (2016). *Interior Urbanism: Architecture, John Portman and Downtown America*. London, UK: Bloomsbury Academic.

Rittel, H.W.J., & Webber, M.M. (1973). Dilemmas in a General Theory of Planning. *Policy Sciences*, *4*, 155–169.

Rose, M. (2002). The Seductions of Resistance: Power, Politics, and a Performative Style of Systems. *Environment and Planning D*, *20*, 383–400.

Stadsplanekontoret, S.S. (1952). *Generalplan för Stockholm 1952*. Stockholm, Sweden: Stockholms Stadsplanekontor.

Statens Planverk. (1968). *SCAFT 1968: Riktlinjer för stadsplanering med hänsyn till trafiksäkerhet*. Stockholm, Sweden: Statens Planverk & Statens Vägverk.

Stengers, I. (2011). *Thinking with Whitehead: A Free and Wild Creation of Concepts*. Cambridge, MA: Harvard University Press.

Stengers, I. (2015). In *Catastrophic Times: Resisting the Coming Barbarism* (A. Goffey, Trans.). Lüneburg, Germany: Open Humanities Press/Meson Press.

Sveriges Arkitekter. (2015). *Agenda Livsmiljö: Nationell innovationsagenda för hållbara livsmiljöer med människan i fokus*. Stockholm, Sweden: Sveriges Arkitekter.

Svetlova, E. (2015). Modeling as a Case for the Empirical Philosophy of Science: The Benefits and Challenges of Qualitative Methods. In S. Wagenknecht, N.J. Nersessian, & H. Andersen (Eds.), *Empirical Philosophy of Science: Introducing Qualitative Methods into Philosophy of Science* (pp. 65–82). Cham, Switzerland: Springer International.

Throgmorton, J.A., & Eckstein, B. (2000). *Desire Lines: The Chicago Area Transportation Study and the Paradox of Self in Post-War America*. Paper presented at the Project web site of the 3 Cities Project of the Universities of Nottingham and Birmingham, United Kingdom. Retrieved from www.nottingham.ac.uk/3cities/throgeck.htm

United Nations. (1966). *Report of the United Nations Symposium on the Planning and Development of New Towns, Moscow, Union of Soviet Socialist Republics, 24 August—7 September 1964*. New York, NY: United Nations.

United Nations. (2015). *Transforming our World: The 2030 Agenda for Sustainable Development*. United Nations.

von Thünen, J.H. (1966). *Von Thünen's Isolated State* (C.M. Wartenberg, Trans.; P. Hall, Ed.). Oxford, UK: Pergamon Press.

Wacquant, L. (2008). *Urban Outcasts: Towards a Sociology of Advanced Marginality*. New York, NY: Blackwell.

Wall, A. (2005). *Victor Gruen: From Urban Shop to New City*. Barcelona, Spain: Actar.

Williams, J.P. (2011). *Subcultural Theory: Traditions and Concepts*. Cambridge, MA: Polity Press.

Wilson, E. (1991). *The Sphinx and the City: Urban Life, the Control of Disorder, and Women*. Los Angeles, CA: University of California Press.

Yang, T., & Hillier, B. (2007). The Fuzzy Boundary: The Spatial Definition of Urban Areas. In A.S. Kubat, Ö. Ertekin, Y.İ. Güney, & E. Eyüboğlou (Eds.), *Proceedings of the Sixth International Space Syntax Symposium* (pp. 091.001–022). Istanbul, Turkey: ITU Faculty of Architecture.

Young, I.M. (1996). *Justice and the Politics of Difference*. Oxford, UK: Blackwell.

Zook, J. (2016). *The Flow of City Life: An Analysis of Cinematography and Urban Form in New York and Los Angeles*. Atlanta, GA: GeorgiaTech.

Zukin, S. (1995). *The Cultures of Cities*. Oxford, UK: Blackwell.

PART III
Contemporary Spatial Forms of the City

12

THE SUBALTERN CITY

Revisiting the Materialist Critique of Urban Form

Marta Caldeira

Architectural Topographies of Urban Inequality

On Thursday, March 14, 2019, New York City's administrative, real estate, and architectural communities celebrated the preview unveiling of the latest architectural icon of socio-economic inequality in the city. The whole complex of Hudson Yards, with its sky-high towers and staggering tax incentives to privatize the largest parcel of undeveloped land in Manhattan, could certainly be seen as a colossal monument to the triumph of uneven development.[1] But the icon in question is much more modest and yet more strident, even if it is meant to be perceptible only to the subsidized residents of 15 Hudson Yards every time they will be denied access through the main door of the very building in which they reside. This architectural icon is, in short, a "poor door"—the contemporary epitome of the city's complete surrender of the housing question to the private sector. Enlisted by the New York City administration of Mayor Bill De Blasio as the sole division in its quest for affordable housing, private developers devised the two-door strategy, allowing them to fully segregate the required affordable units within buildings while taking advantage of hefty public incentives. If Mayor De Blasio's vision of affordability was built upon ideals of urban inclusion and community building, as well as trust on public-private ventures, the "poor door" thus appears as the icon of a resounding failure.

To be sure, not all voices rise univocally against the two-door strategy. In his review of the new complex, *New York Times*' critic Michael Kimmelman cautiously mentioned the "separate entrances for the wealthy condo owners and the subsidized renters" in Diller Scofidio + Renfro's residential tower at 15 Hudson Yards (Kimmelman, 2019); whereas across the Atlantic, British Prime Minister Boris Johnson, then London mayor and pro-Brexit instigator, unsurprisingly defended the segregating technique in 2015 as a matter of "dual access," thus flattening any difference and neutralizing the "poor door" power as an icon of inequality with a single brush of rhetoric (Osborne, 2014). By assenting to "separate entrances" or "dual access," city leaders were in fact condoning the inscription of a dual society into the building code. At the height of the polemic in 2015, the iconic strength of the "poor door" had moved public consternation and protests that lead De Blasio to ban the segregating technique, which was very much celebrated by local and international media (Moyer, 2015). At the time, Manhattan Borough President Gale Brewer stated, "Buildings that segregate entrances for lower-income and middle class tenants are an affront to our values." But it seems that the affront is no more. The "poor door" made its comeback and with a vengeance, now integrating the newest museum of "star-chitecture" that developer Stephen M. Ross envisioned for Hudson Yards.[2]

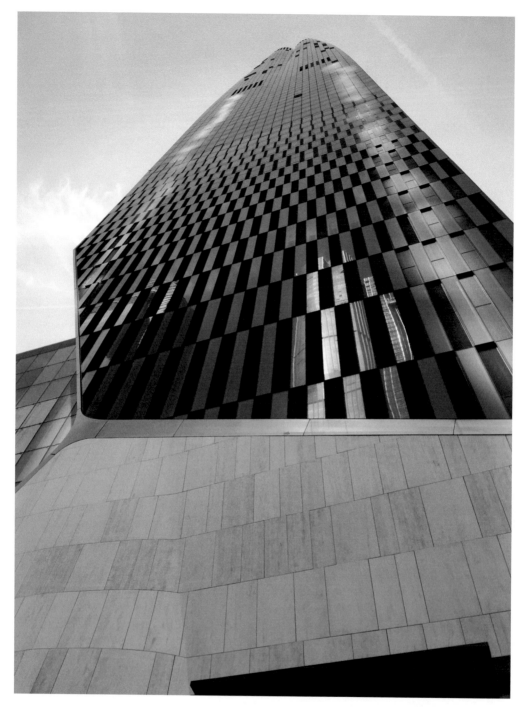

FIGURE 12.1 15 Hudson Yards residential tower in New York, by Diller Scofidio + Renfro (2019).

As an architectural icon of contemporary urban inequality, the "poor door" is, then, not a new phenomenon. Architectural critics and historians have scrutinized its role as a practice of real estate governance rooted in inequality as well as the regulating social codes through which it is enacted (Martin, 2015). And it is also not isolated, as it joins a series of other coordinates

The Subaltern City **213**

FIGURE 12.2 The two separate entrances for condo owners and subsidized renters at 15 Hudson Yards. Although giving access to the same tower, the separate entrance for subsidized units tucked under the High Line has a different legal address, 553 West 30th Street.

that shaped in recent years the architectural topography of contemporary urban inequality. The "poor door" "scandals" and "financial apartheid" loudly contested in London and New York (Eaton, 2014; Licea, 2016) could indeed be considered alongside the demise of a city program for "young people" housing in Lisbon (Henriques, 2012), the disputed federal housing vouchers in the United States and federal housing programs in Brazil,[3] or the most recent "courtyards for the homeless" in Los Angeles (Medina, 2018), among many others. This transcontinental constellation of architectural markers flags discrete instances and mechanisms through which architecture and urban policy, for better and for worse, participate in a broader effort to rebalance through housing the flaring socio-economic gap among today's urban populations. In this variegated constellation one finds different, at times overlapping, jurisdictions and scales of action—between federal and local governance—which converge in the ambition to secure a place for living for the urban underclass, be they low-income individuals or families, the urban poor, or simply the urban young. As material signifiers of inequality, affordability and attempted but failed urban inclusion, these architectural markers reveal the multi-faceted, and at times conflictive, ways in which architecture is imbricated in this perennially skewed balancing act. On one side, architecture appears as a technique of inequality and segregation—most visible in "super-tall" towers, gated communities, and "poor doors"—and, on the other side, as a technique of regulation—in the provision of public or affordable housing. Yet more than a technique, the 2015 "poor door" polemic leading to NYC's provisional ban shows how architecture can also become a powerful image for public mobilization and contestation. At stake, then, in this crossroads of urban development and inequality, architecture, and regulation, is the state of contemporary architecture in its ability to visualize, qualify, and ultimately offer an alternative image to act upon a problem that is at once socio-economic, political, and cultural.

While this constellation of markers strongly evokes an architectural topography of urban inequality, their descriptions in reality fall short. Whether decried or analyzed as symptoms of failing housing systems, these markers too often remain isolated from the highly nuanced topographies of which they constitute their most visible, and most strident, coordinates. From the early stages of modern urbanization, critical cornerstones in modern urban theory have continuously addressed questions of inequality and of sustainable ways of life across all layers of urban society. Since Friedrich Engels first posed *The Housing Question* in 1872, radically broadening the historical materialist analysis of industrial workers' housing to include both the capitalist bourgeois class and the exploited country peasants upon whom the city depended, many modernist utopias and planning models followed suit with visions of an all-inclusive (and perfectly zoned) urban future.[4] Urban ideologies, imagined settings, social structures, and aesthetics certainly varied widely between the critiques and visionary proposals. Yet all addressed instances of urban inequality by insisting, in different ways, on the need for a totalizing perspective on the city reflecting an all-encompassing view of society, of its social strata, and their spatialization in the urban fabric. In short, if the problem of inequality was to be fully comprehended, then the city needed to be understood as a single entity, as a whole urban and economic structure and socially integrated system—as a totality.

The City as a Totality

Starting in the 1960s, the idea of the city as a total entity, combined with a renewed materialist critique of inequality, signaled a decisive turn in the architectural discourses on the city. This materialist analysis of urban form would have lasting and extended ramifications in architectural and urban studies in the final decades of the 20th century. At stake was a new critical understanding of the multi-scalar ways that architecture related to urban development, both as a register of socio-economic forces to be decoded and as a means for intervention in the social, economic, and physical reality of the city. By combining a materialist theoretical framework, largely stemming from the Marxist legacy of critical theory, with a newly developed methodology based on typological and morphological analyses, the studies of cities such as those developed at the Istituto Universitario di Architettura di Venezia (IUAV)[5] that Manfredo Tafuri termed "typological criticism" and qualified as "an essentially urban criticism" had as its primary objective a class critique of architecture and the city (Tafuri, 1980). Through the study of repetitive residential types, distinct or homogeneous morphologies (especially of popular or workers' areas), and their spatial organization in the city, architects and urban theorists sought to visualize the ways through which architecture intersected with the economic and social processes of urban growth. Ultimately, the intention was to identify, in the contradictions of urban form, potential sites and strategies for intervention that, whether through services, housing, or land rent regulation, could foster more equitable forms of living in the city.

Fifty years later, recent theories in urban studies positing increasingly large territorial, global, and planetary scales of urbanization have permanently challenged the idea of city as totality at the core of the "typological criticism" of urban form. By rejecting the idea of city as a valid descriptor of contemporary urban form, these theories have tacitly denied the idea of a total—social, political, and economic—entity upon which the materialist analysis based its class critique. Moreover, many of the techniques of segregation, regulation, and urban inclusion mentioned earlier—"poor doors" and housing vouchers in particular—also seem to defy a typological approach to urban critique by severing any direct correspondence between social and urban form. While current theories of urbanization seek to chart the new scales and global processes of urban phenomena, the problem of urban inequality is, at best, only acknowledged quite briefly and in the broadest terms.[6] Their focus on the ever-increasing connectivity that bounds world populations through totalizing images of a planetary "urban society,"[7] or the equally universal idea of urbanism as "a way of life" (Soja & Kanai, 2007), such conceptions of the urban thus tend to lose sight of the widening socio-economic gaps and mechanisms that divide rather than connect. The architectural topographies of urban inequality are in this process not only flattened, but also paradoxically subsumed as yet another urban reality that connects cities across the globe.

In the face of increasing scales of the urban and its optimistic global connections, architectural concerns with the city and urban inequality have arguably receded since the 1990s. Many urban-minded architects gradually traded the proactive interdisciplinary world of critical urban studies for a seemingly safer refuge in the developers' world of iconic objects. From Bilbao's Guggenheim to the newest Hudson Yards, urban architecture was thus relegated to sell images that could propel urban redevelopment and to accentuate the topography of inequality. It seems important, then, not only to ask how architecture may reengage with issues of contemporary urbanization and urban studies, but also to inquire how it may contribute to rethinking the modes of urban description that allow both understanding current forms and imagining alternative futures. It is here that the materialist critique of urban form may offer critical grounds for reflection. Revisiting the materialist critique of urban form today does not mean opposing current theories of the urban, and much less rescuing a theoretical framework and methodology from the past. Rather, it means to examine its critical principles and methods, only now in light of contemporary urban issues and taking into account the criticism that it has faced since then. More than seeking answers, the aim of revisiting the materialist critique of urban form in the face of new critical conceptions of urbanization in urban studies is to raise questions: questions that may clarify architecture's current problem to describe the architectural topographies of urban inequality, and questions that may help us reimagine the theoretical and methodological bridges between architecture, urban form, and the regulatory techniques of affordability and inequality.

The Materialist Critique of Urban Form

Central to the criticism aimed at the discourses on architecture and the city that, in the 1970s, allowed architects to rethink their profession in social and political terms, was the urban ideal of the city that many of the texts and projects entailed. For critics such as urban geographers Edward Soja or David Harvey, for instance, the materialist studies of urban form emerging in this period—in particular those based on studies of morphologies, typologies, and formal analyses of urban structures—reflected a problematic attachment to the idea of the industrial city. They identified this attachment in three main discursive elements: an idea of the city with clearly contained limits, a town-country dialectic between the urban and the non-urban, and the concentric logic of urban growth set forth by the Chicago School.[8] And yet, one could counter this criticism with two different conceptions of the urban that were inherent to the discourses on architecture and the city already in the 1960s.

First, the 1960s discourse on urban form signaled rather a shift in the understanding of urban development, motivated precisely by structural transformations of the modern city largely deriving from the second post-war economic boom and subsequent territorial expansions. Indeed, new concepts such as "the new urban dimension" of "city-region" or "city-territory" informed the discourse. These reflect precisely a shift away from the idea of the modern industrial city, understood as a total entity centered on industrial production, and a shift toward a conception of the urban on a different scale, that is boundless, and in most cases decentralized.[9] In sum, these concepts reflect the attempts of architects to grapple with the city in its new form—that is, a late capitalist and post-industrial form—and to examine the role that architecture was to play in it. And if architects mapped the city of the past—that is, in its form of the industrial city—they did so in order to understand the processes through which it arrived in the present. Second, the insistence of authors such as Harvey or Soja on the primacy of the industrial city also reflects back on an urban tradition, predominantly Anglo-Saxon, that posits industrialization as the origin of the modern city. But this is, in fact, a contested history, especially among countries across Southern Europe with a Latin tradition of urban settlements. The studies of Spanish and Latin American cities led by the Laboratori d'Urbanisme of Barcelona become here a case in point. With 19th-century figures such as Baron Haussmann or Ildefons Cerdà, urban theorists studying territories outside the British-American-Germanic axis have argued that modern speculative urbanization often preceded and, in turn, funded industrial development, not the other way around (Solà-Morales, 1978).

Born out of the transmuting industrial city after the second post-war, materialist studies of architecture and urban form first developed in and concentrated precisely on urban centers that had undergone several phases of development, preceding even the industrial. From the very beginning, critical lenses from outside the fields of architecture and urbanism proved instrumental in the development of new analytical methods for the study of urban form. Most influential among these studies were the morphological studies developed at the famous Venice School, or the Istituto Universitario di Venezia (IUAV), which were soon adopted across Europe and beyond. With Saverio Muratori and his studies for what he termed an "operative urban history" in the 1950s, urban analysis first followed the logic of structuralism from the budding social sciences.[10] The goal was to read the relationships between architectural forms and urban fabric—between building types and morphologies—as an expression of the intersecting forces that in different periods constructed the city, forces that were economic, social, and political in nature.

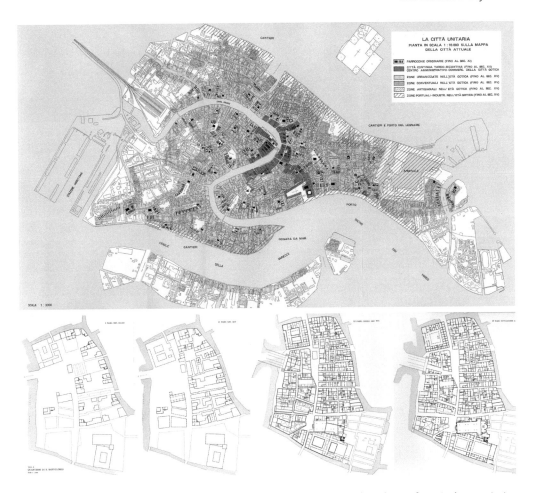

FIGURE 12.3 Saverio Muratori, morphological study and typological analysis of Venice's quartieri.

With the mounting political pressures that came to characterize the 1960s, especially in Italy, the following generation of researchers at the IUAV, led by Carlo Aymonino, continued the materialist critique of the city initiated by Muratori, only now focusing on the modern city through the lens of political economy.[11] This was, then, a critique that saw urban form as the physical manifestation of the capitalist logic of the modern city, as the place of the contradictions of society. And a critique that sought above all to analyze the structures and forms inherited from the modern city, understood as center of production and consumption, in order to make apparent the possibility of "a new urban structure, born from within the history of the industrial city," but that would be now "projected as a 'need for power' of the exploited classes" (Aymonino, 1965/1993, p. 115).

The historical imperative behind the materialist critique thus stood in sharp contrast to the more utopian modernist and post-war projections of urban futures, and equally rejected a technocratic approach to planning based on the modern system of zoning. The material analysis of urban form and structure initiated by the Venice School and soon extended to other research centers in Italy and beyond intended to reveal the structural dialectics and internal contradictions of the city.[12] This not only implied studying the development of the city as an historical product, but also that in every historical moment the city needed to be considered as a totality.

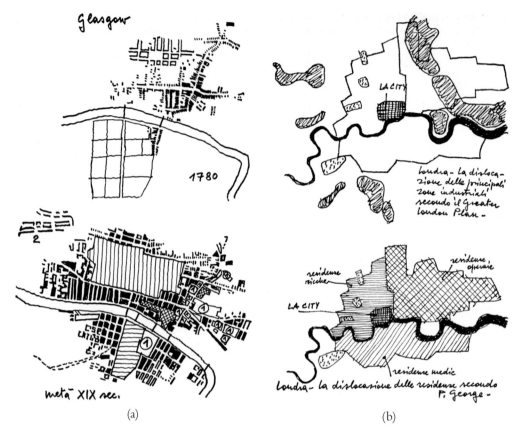

FIGURE 12.4 Carlo Aymonino, comparative morphological analyses of residential and working sectors in the urban development of London and Glasgow.

Echoing Friedrich Engels' critique of *The Housing Question*, urban morphologists thus argued that only by studying urban form as a whole—and where the physical construction and formal organization corresponded to the social and economic organization of the city—could an alternative idea of city emerge, one more equitable or at least more conscious of its classes. This was, then, the idea of city as totality encapsulated in the concept of "urban structure" at the core of the materialist critique of urban form: an idea of structure that was at once social, economic, and formal.

Making the Subaltern City Visible

This materialist approach to the city does not fit comfortably with the recent criticism of "methodological cityism" (Angelo & Wachsmuth, 2014) or with criticism that opposes "the city as a thing" to "urbanization as a process" (Harvey, 2014), because architectural or urban forms were understood to be indelibly associated with the socio-economic processes of urban development. Theorists such as Carlo Aymonino and Manuel de Solà-Morales adopted terms such as "urban phenomena" (Aymonino, 1977) or "forms of urban growth" (Solà-Morales, 1997) precisely to encapsulate both form and process in a single concept. They maintained that if urban form was both the result and support of structural processes, then interventions with urban form could be a means of manipulating the urban structure, even if only partly. Hence, the question at stake in the materialist discourses of urban form was to what extent architecture and urban form could also be conducive to urban transformation, not only in a formal aesthetic sense, but also at a structural level.

Here, it should be underlined, the role of history in the materialist approach to the city should not be confused with the historicism in the typological conservation of historical blocks under the aegis of urban renewal, or New Urbanism's nostalgic planning of pseudo-traditional downtowns based on the formal properties of historical building types and iconic morphologies. Limiting the typo-morphological apparatus to such formal and iconographic interpretations is to ignore the materialist critique that motivated the historical analyses of urban form from the start. The emphasis was not on the conservation or repetition of formal types, but rather on the identification of gaps and contradictions in urban form, inconsistencies that signaled contradictions in the urban structure and therefore flagged potential points for intervention. As material testimonies of a previous era, the many typological charts, morphological analysis, and urban taxonomies offer a singular visual record of architects' attempts to reclaim political and social agency for the urban underclasses in the face of a new age of post-industrial speculation that looked upon urban redevelopment as a fruitful source of revenue.

Carlo Aymonino encapsulated this ideological core of the materialist critique in his concept of the "subaltern city": the city of local communities and low-income workers whose subsistence was increasingly at risk and depended on the subaltern city's dialectic counterpart, the "speculative city" (Aymonino, 1965). By drawing on Antonio Gramsci's concept of the "subaltern," Aymonino qualified urban form through a social lens and humanized popular building types and poorer urban areas. In this process, he made visible population groups and urban areas that were until then neglected by planning authorities. The "subaltern city" was, however, not simply Aymonino's conceptual key to establishing a critical correspondence between urban subjects and urban form. It also became the means through which he revised the antithesis that Marx and Engels established between town and country. Aware of the significance of the town-country antithesis in the early stages of the industrial city and determined to extend the analysis to different urban areas, Aymonino translated the antithesis between town and country into the economic and hierarchic relationship between the "speculative" and the "subaltern" city. He maintained that the mutations of this relationship could be traced through the different phases of modern urban development. With the appropriation of rural territory by the bourgeois city, Aymonino argued, the antithesis between town and country was now transformed and internalized by the new urban structure into a "typological differentiation" (in buildings) and "positional differentiation" (between zones) that "corresponded to the accentuated division of labor within the urban settlement" (Aymonino, 1965, p. 31). Preceding Neil Smith's theory of uneven development by nearly two decades, the typo-morphological analysis by Aymonino already identified the forms through which urban differentiation becomes manifest in the city. In doing so, he translated the notion of ground rent from an abstract concept into the tangible realm of ground positions and building types.[13] For Aymonino, the contradictions of capitalist production originally spatialized in the antithesis between town and country were equally manifested in the relationship between center and periphery, between residential, commercial, and tertiary areas, and even among different residential areas.

By updating the dialectics of town and country, the materialist critique of urban form did not only aim to make the "subaltern city" visible but also to render it as an intrinsic and indispensable part of the contemporary city. In its translation of the Gramscian concept of the subaltern, the early logic of town and country was not reproduced, but was now actualized and reinterpreted

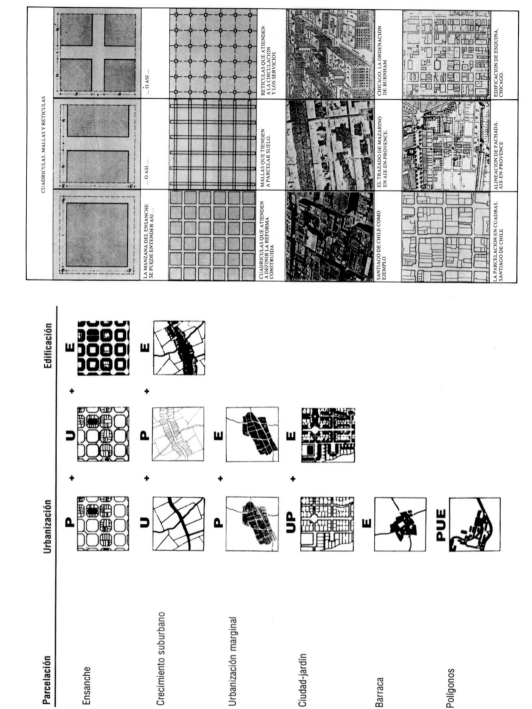

FIGURE 12.5 Manuel de Solà-Morales, taxonomy of structural typologies of urban growth (left); comparative chart Cuadriculas, Mallas y Reticulas (right).

in new, more complex spatial organizations. Through the subaltern, the contradictions and inequalities of urban capitalism were no longer located between an inside and an outside, but were now studied within the city. In the same vein, the subaltern city was no longer seen as a limited concentric formation, but as a set of socio-economic processes with a formal structure that could be extended indefinitely. Ultimately, the hope of Aymonino was that the materialist critique of urban form would make apparent the possibility of an alternative and more equitable city, born from its history but now designed to serve the needs of its underrepresented classes.

This critical framework motivated countless morphological surveys, generated typological charts, and supported urban strategies such as the preservation plan for the historical center of Bologna led by Pier Luigi Cervellati in the early 1970s.[14] For Cervellati, typological preservation was synonymous with social preservation. Based on an historical and morphological analysis of the urban fabric, the identification of what he termed the "typological structures" of low-cost popular housing became a central concern of the new plan. Cervellati maintained that the evaluation of all other urban functions were to be adjusted to these typological structures, including the municipal plans of expropriation which were vital to this operation. In the relationships that housing types established between themselves and as a whole, Cervellati saw a reflection of the social and economic structure of urban society. The ambitious urban plan for Bologna did not detach architecture from the structural totality of the city, but rather aimed to affect the course of urban development by an "integral restoration" of the center as a concerted policy for the whole city and territory. In short, by understanding preservation policy within the frame of structural development of the city, Cervellati aspired to change the course of urban development.

A similar reasoning can be found, for instance, in the 1974 analysis of urban form by Álvaro Siza and his team that resulted in the expropriation of land for a workers' neighborhood within the housing program Serviço Ambulatório de Apoio Local (SAAL) in post-revolutionary Portugal.[15] Through a sequence of morphological analyses, Siza's team reconstructed the modern history of urban development in the area of the São Victor "proletarian island," a neighborhood embedded in Porto's urban fabric and the site of the shanty community for whom the team was to design new residences. The analysis illustrated that the island was as much a part of this urban fabric as the industrial buildings and residences, just as the workers were as much a part of the urban history as the industrialists or the landowners were. For Siza and his team, this history granted the residents' right to the city and justified the rightful expropriation of the land.

The planning strategies of "centri direzionali" in Italy or service districts across Europe offer a territorial counterpoint to the previous examples. Based on morphological analyses of the city and its surrounding territories, these service centers have through decades supported the decentralization of services in response to new forms of metropolitan and territorial urbanization. And, at an even larger scale, the different forms of planning based on ideas of "urban acupuncture" become also references that drew from the legacy of materialist critique of urban form. From Barcelona since the 1990s to Medellin in the last decade, these urban plans drawn at the scale of the city strategically inserted a program intended to balance the distribution of services, urban equipment, and cultural facilities in the city.[16]

In their varying scales of approach to urban intervention, these examples clearly show how the discourse on urban form had no intention of reproducing new urban totalities. Rather, the objective was to affect the city by identifying points of contradiction and intervening locally. This sense of appropriate measure was latent in the materialist critique of urban form in the 1960s and 1970s. It became apparent in concepts such as "homogeneous zones,"[17] or "city per parts,"[18] which sought to break the analytical frame down to an intermediate scale while maintaining an idea of the whole, as well as in the typo-morphological method that connected the

222 Marta Caldeira

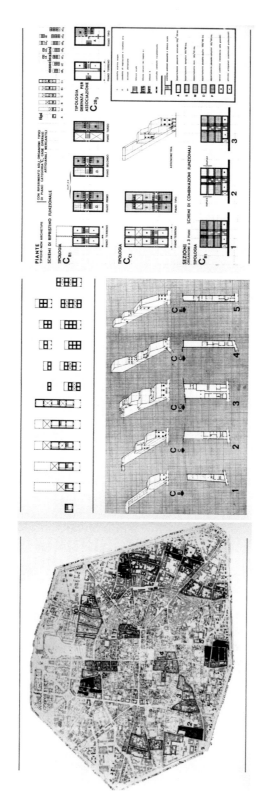

FIGURE 12.6. Pier Luigi Cervellati, morphological analysis of Bologna's urban fabric and "typological structures" of popular housing.

The Subaltern City 223

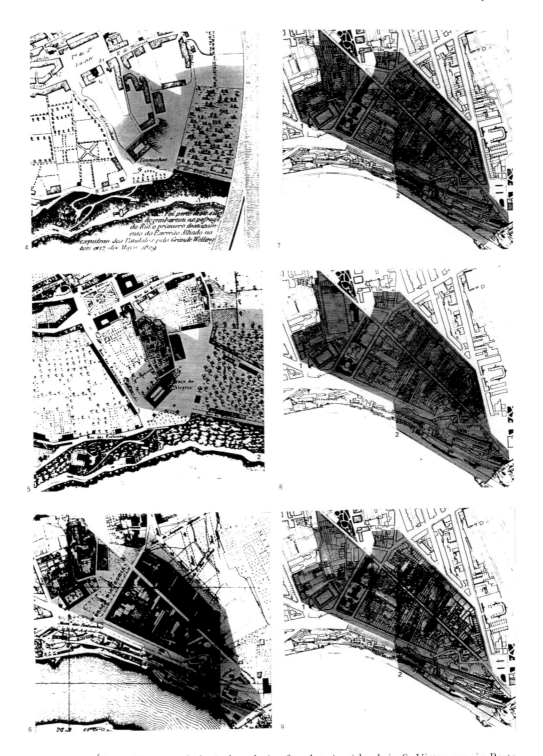

FIGURE 12.7. Álvaro Siza, morphological analysis of proletarian islands in S. Victor area in Porto, Portugal (1976).

224 Marta Caldeira

FIGURE 12.8 Joan Busquets, Plan of Areas of New Centrality, Barcelona (1986).

architectural object to the urban structure. It was also reflected in the many attempts by architects and planners to induce change locally and from within, through a reformist approach to the city and the techniques of regulation available—from housing and planning, to preservation policy, as illustrated in the examples of Bologna and Barcelona.

This vision of local interventions as having a gradual and lasting impact on total systems became once again a much-hailed basis for urban development at the turn of the millennium. Recent approaches to planning are premised on new assumed relationships between urban projects, local governance, and new scales of economy. Consider the example of what is now called "strategic urban planning," which refuses to make reference to modern planning instruments such as zoning or masterplans. Such an approach is predicated upon ideas of spatial organization, projects based on long-term guidelines, and an equal participation of public administration, the private sector, and civil society in urban governance. While seemingly local, these strategic interventions are in fact totalizing in essence: each project still implies understanding the morphology of inequality of the whole. Only now it is stretched forward in time and folds in all stakeholders, in the hopes that every single intervention in a disadvantaged area will help reduce inequality disparities and gradually impact the whole urban system.

Throughout this long trajectory of the materialist critique of urban form, the architect-urbanist stood continuously in an in-between position, mediating between the existing and the potential, and between description and projection. The power of this critique lay in the ability to capture the economic and the social in a representation of urban form: by studying what was represented, architects and planners could criticize the existing city, but could also imagine what should be represented instead. This ability stemmed from the correspondence found between the historical forms inherited from the modern city and the socio-economic processes that generated them. The architects' power of description resided, in short, in an almost direct correspondence between the topography of socio-economic inequality in the city and the architectural topography of urban form. Returning now to the "poor door" in the beginning of this text, it clearly illustrated how this correspondence can no longer be found within the contemporary condition of urban inequality. As new conceptions of the urban necessarily take on ever-expanding views of the processes behind contemporary urbanization, they not only drive the field of architecture further away from this analysis, but also from the critical questions of housing affordability, social preservation, and urban rights that guided the materialist critique of urban form in the first place. This does not mean, however, that the social and economic pressures on urban society are not there, that they are not manifested in architectural or urban form, or further still, that they do not demand a comprehensive image of the architectural topography of inequality. Quite the contrary, architecture remains critical for rendering visible the far-reaching impact of inequality and eventually imagining forms—social, economic, regulatory, and yes, also physical—to mitigate it. As Neil Smith posited, uneven development and socio-economic inequality continue to be intrinsic to the movements of capitalism. We might not have an answer to the question of "just how much inequality is acceptable?" (Martin, 2015, p. 93), but we do know when it becomes unacceptable, and thus we may well start drawing red lines. The "poor door" image of 15 Hudson Yards is only the latest reminder. The question remains as to what modes of description architects may deploy to respond to this contemporary challenge. Until then, we are left with "poor doors."

Notes

1. In his seminal thesis on uneven development, Neil Smith already in 1984 posited the redevelopment of urban land as a key process that relies on and promotes uneven development, generates capital profit from urban land rent, and is indelibly associated with socio-economic inequality. The core of Smith's uneven development remains valid, if not accelerated and intensified, in processes of urban development today (Smith, 1984).
2. "We are creating a museum of architecture and a whole new way of life," Stephen M. Ross quoted by Michael Kimmelman from his interview with the Hudson Yards developer (Kimmelman, 2019).
3. The obvious reference here is the vast housing program sponsored across the country by Brazil's federal government titled "Minha Casa Minha Vida" ("My Home My Life").
4. Among numerous examples from this period, the most obvious and iconic urban models include Ebenezer Howard's *Garden Cities of Tomorrow* (1898), Tony Garnier's *Cité Industrielle* (1904), *Ville Radieuse* by Le Corbusier (1924), or Ludwig Hilberseimer's *Grossstadt* (1927).
5. On the collective studies of cities conducted at the IUAV in the 1960s, see the school's yearbooks *Aspetti e Problemi della Tipologia Edilizia* (Aymonino et al., 1964) and *La Formazione del Concetto di Tipologia Edilizia* (Aymonino, 1965), and also the monograph *La Città di Padova* (Aymonino, 1970).
6. In their lengthy theoretical manifesto "Towards a New Epistemology of the Urban?", Neil Brenner and Christian Schmid set forth seven highly elaborate theses as a meta-theoretical groundwork for developing new forms of understanding contemporary urban phenomena. Questions of urban struggle, politics, and urban inequality appear only on the very last page of this remarkable study (Brenner & Schmid, 2015).
7. In his introduction to the volume *Implosions/Explosions*, Neil Brenner revisits Henri Lefebvre's theory in *The Urban Revolution*, with its central hypothesis that "society has been completely urbanized," as a prompt for this collection of essays examining the planetary as the new scale of urbanization.
8. The most recent critiques that David Harvey and Edward Soja directed at morphological studies of the city and a perceived contemporary crisis of representation can be found, respectively, in "Cities or Urbanization?" (Harvey, 2014) and "Regional Urbanization and the End of the Metropolis Era" (Soja, 2014).
9. The notions of city-territory or city-region emerge as urban concepts from Italian debates on the problem known as "The New Dimension." In opposition to urban planning based on zoning, the city-territory

or city-region presented a model for urban growth that relied on the strategic planning of large-scale development, potentially as a means to anticipate and program the future urban conurbation at a regional or territorial scale. In Italy, several institutions sponsored the debates on the New Dimension, including the INU (Istituto Nazionale de Urbanistica, directed in the 1950s and 1960s by figures such as Adrianno Olivetti, Ludovico Quaroni, Luigi Piccinato and Bruno Zevi) and ILSES (Istituto Lombardo per gli Studi Economici e Sociali). In 1962 Giancarlo de Carlo, director of urbanism at ILSES and defender of territorial planning, famously convened the seminar *La Nuova Dimensione della Città: La Città-Regione* (*The New Dimension of the City: the City-Region*); the same year Carlo Aymonino led the experimental design studio based on the Città-territorio at the University of Rome. Seminars on the "New Dimension" continued to take place in the following years, gathering architects, urbanists, and planners. The models and instruments proposed for a new understanding of the contemporary urban scale generated contention among the participants. Among many, see *Relazioni del Seminario. La Nuova Dimensione della Città: La Città-Regione* (Carlo, 1962); "La città-territorio. Verso una nuova dimensione" (Piccinato, Quilici, & Tafuri, 1962); *La città Territorio* (Aymonino, 1964); *Il Territorio dell'Architettura* (Gregotti, 1966).

10. Saverio Muratori led the class on *Caratteri Distributtivi di Ediffici* (*Distributive Elements of Buildings*) at IUAV between 1950 and 1959. During his Venetian tenure, Muratori developed the method for the analysis of urban form based on building typologies and urban morphology and, with his students, surveyed the historical city of Venice. Combining historical views and plans of the city with cadaster registers and site surveys, Muratori and his students produced ground-level plans for each of the Venetian neighborhoods according to four different phases: the archipelago city, the continuous city, the unified city, and "the contemporary crisis," that is, Venice in the modern period. Street photographs also illustrated the plans, allowing Muratori to complement the typological and structural analysis of the plans with an iconographic characterization of the neighborhood. The result of this research carried out in the 1950s—the visual documentation, the written critical analysis, and the methodological description—were compiled in the famous volume *Studi per una Operante Storia Urbana di Venezia* (*Studies for an Operative Urban History of Venice*) (Muratori, 1959).
11. An emblematic example is Carlo Aymonino's seminal writings on the origins and development of the modern city, first published in the volume *Origini e Sviluppo della Città Moderna* (1965). Aymonino's extensive use of critical writings from political economy and critical theory include authors such as Karl Marx and Friedrich Engels, Lenin, Stalin, Mao Zedong, Charles Bettelheim, or Ernst Bloch, among others.
12. On the impact of IUAV's approach to urban studies in France, see Jean-Louis Cohen (2015); for Barcelona, see Marta Caldeira (2016).
13. On the concept of "seesaw movement" of capitalism, see Neil Smith (1984, ch. 4).
14. For a detailed description of the Bologna plan, see P.L. Cervellati and R. Scannavini (1973).
15. On Álvaro Siza's SAAL project for São Victor, see Álvaro Siza Vieira (1976).
16. On the plan of urban development for Barcelona, see Joan Busquets (1987).
17. On the notion of homogeneous zones, see, for instance, *Aspetti e Problemi della Tipologia Edilizia* (Aymonino et al., 1964), *La Formazione del Concetto di Tipologia Edilizia* (Aymonino, 1965), and *La Città di Padova* (Aymonino, 1970).
18. On the concept of "city per parts," or "città per parti," see Aldo Rossi (1966).

References

Angelo, H., & Wachsmuth, D. (2014). Urbanizing Urban Political Ecology: A Critique of Methodological Cityism. In N. Brenner (Ed.), *Implosions/Explosions: Towards a Study of Planetary Urbanization* (pp. 372–385). Berlin, Germany: Jovis Verlag GmbH.
Aymonino, C. (Ed.). (1964). *La Città Territorio: Un Esperimento Didattico Sul Centro Direzionale di Centocelle in Roma*, series *Problemi della Nuova Dimensione*. Bari, Italy: Leonardo da Vinci Editrice.
Aymonino, C. (Ed.). (1965). *La Formazione del Concetto di Tipologia Edilizia*. Venice, Italy: CLUVA.
Aymonino, C. (1970). *La Città di Padova*. Rome, Italy: Officina Edizioni.
Aymonino, C. (1977). *Lo studio dei fenomeni urbani*. Rome, Italy: Officina Edizioni.
Aymonino, C. (1993). *Origini e sviluppo della città moderna*. Venice, Italy: Marsilio. (Original work published in 1965).
Aymonino, C., Cristofoli, C., Dardi, G., Fabbri, Gaffarini, P.M., & Rossi, A. (Eds.). (1964). *Aspetti e Problemi della Tipologia Edilizia*. Venice, Italy: CLUVA.
Brenner, N., & Schmid, C. (2015). Towards a New Epistemology of the Urban? *City*, *19*(2–3), 151–182.
Busquets, J. (1987). *Arees de Nova Centralitat*. Barcelona, Spain: Ajuntament de Barcelona.
Caldeira, M. (2016). The Education of an "Architect-Urbanist": Manuel Solà-Morales and Urban Pedagogy at the ETSAB. *FAmagazine 38*, pp. 35–47.

Carlo, G. de. (1962). *Relazioni del Seminario. La Nuova Simensione della Città: La Città-regione*. Milan, Italy: ILSES.

Cervellati, P.L., & Scannavini, R. (1973). *Bologna: Politica e Metodologia del Restauro nei Centri Storici*. Bologna, Italy: Il Mulino.

Cohen, J.-L. (2015). *La Coupure entre Architectes et Intellectuels, ou les Enseignements de l'Italophilie*. Brussels, Belgium: Éditions Mardaga.

Eaton, E. (2014, September 27). London's "Poor Door" Scandal. *KCW Today*.

Gregotti, V. (1966). *Il Territorio dell'Architettura*. Milan, Italy: Feltrinelli.

Harvey, D. (2014). Cities or Urbanization? In N. Brenner (Ed.), *Implosions/Explosions: Towards a Study of Planetary Urbanization* (pp. 52–66). Berlin, Germany: Jovis Verlag.

Henriques, A. (2012, February 1). Câmara de Lisboa extingue programa que vendia casas novas e baratas. *Público*.

Kimmelman, M. (2019, March 14). Hudson Yards Is Manhattan's Biggest, Newest, Slickest Gated Community. Is This the Neighborhood New York Deserves? *The New York Times*.

Licea, M. (2016, January 17). 'Poor Door' Tenants of Luxury Tower Reveal the Financial Apartheid Within. *Metro*.

Martin, R. (2015). Real Estate Agency. In R. Martin, J. Moore, & S. Schindler (Eds.), *The Art of Inequality: Architecture, Housing, and Real Estate: A Provisional Report* (pp. 92–131). New York, NY: The Temple Hoyne Buell Center for the Study of American Architecture.

Medina, J. (2018, October 29). A Novel Solution for the Homeless: House Them in Backyards. *The New York Times*.

Moyer, J. Wm. (2015, June 30). NYC Bans "Poor Doors"—Separate Entrances for Low-Income Tenants. *The Washington Post*.

Muratori, S. (Ed.). (1959). *Studi per una Operante Storia Urbana di Venezia*. Rome, Italy: Instituto poligrafico dello Stato, Libreria dello Stato.

Osborne, H. (2014, July 28). Boris Johnson Rules Out 'Poor Door' Ban on London Housing Developments. *The Guardian*.

Piccinato, G., Quilici, V., & Tafuri, M. (1962). La Città-territorio. Verso una Nuova Dimensione. *Casabella Continuità*, *270*(December), 16–25.

Rossi, A. (1966). *L'Architettura della Città*. Padua, Italy: Marsilio.

Smith, N. (1984). *Uneven Development: Nature, Capital, and the Production of Space*. Athens, GA: University of Georgia Press.

Soja, E. (2014). Regional Urbanization and the End of the Metropolis Era. In N. Brenner (Ed.), *Implosions/Explosions: Towards a Study of Planetary Urbanization* (pp. 276–287). Berlin, Germany: Jovis Verlag.

Soja, E., & Kanai, M. (2007). The Urbanization of the World. In R. Burdett & D. Sudjic (Eds.), *The Endless City* (pp. 54–68). London, UK; New York, NY: Phaidon Press.

Solà-Morales, M. (1978). Toward a Definition: Analysis of Urban Growth in the Nineteenth Century. *Lotus International*, *19*, 28–36.

Solà-Morales, M. (1997). *Las Formas de Crecimiento Urbano*. Barcelona, Spain: Edicions UPC.

Tafuri, M. (1980). Operative Criticism. In *Theories and History of Architecture* (pp. 142–170). New York, NY: Harper and Row.

Vieira, A.S. (1976). The Proletarian "Island" as a Basic Element of the Urban Tissue. *Lotus International*, *13*, 80–93.

13

THE CHRONICLES OF NEO

Janina Gosseye

Neo is a 27-hectare urban development project in Brussels, Belgium. Commissioned by the City of Brussels and the Brussels Capital Region and situated on the Heysel Plateau, which is a legacy site in the northwest of the Brussels Capital Region where in 1958 the World Expo took place, the project is scheduled for completion in 2023. Among its key components are a regional (70,000 m^2) shopping center, the "Mall of Europe," a concert hall, a multi-purpose convention center for international events, and a hotel.[1] On the website www.neobrussels.com, those behind the project write:

> NEO is the construction of a new district on a historical site near the Atomium. NEO is an ambitious and visionary re-urbanization based on the sustainable development of a multitude of different urban facilities and functions. NEO is a center of human, economic, commercial, touristic, cultural, leisure and home development, creating 5,000 new jobs in the long-term. NEO is a development opportunity for the whole country. . . . NEO Brussels is a "capital" project in the heart of Europe that will attract 15 million visitors a year.
>
> *("The Project," n/d)*

This introductory statement is accompanied by a two-minute video, which draws on several of the clichéd tropes that have by now become ubiquitous signifiers of this type of large, commercially driven urban development. Building on the "brand" of Brussels as the capital of Europe to market the project, the video starts with images of Big Ben, the Brandenburg Gate, and the Eiffel Tower, to then show the Atomium (Belgium's contribution to the 1958 World Expo) in Brussels, which is where the project is located. The spirited tune accompanying the video reaches a climax as it glosses over the site. After several bird's-eye views, close-ups are shown of the different areas of the new development through a sequence of panning zooms, which emphasize fluid motion over stasis, or flow over friction. White, glazed, and mostly non-descript blocks of architecture are shown bathing in a sea of green. The video then goes on to highlight some of the many recreational attractions that will be incorporated in the new development, such as the Spirouland indoor theme park and the *Cité des Enfants* or "children's city." Destined to include 21 new film theatres, the word "cinema" is also prominently present. Then, a series of clips from existing shopping centers around the world appear which confirm that global brands, such as Apple, Nespresso, Forever 21, and Sephora will find a place in the new Mall of Europe as well. Filled with people laughing, chatting, and dancing, these clips depict the mall as a place for human interaction rather than a site for individualist consumption. Finally, a sequence of hero-shots slides across the screen just before the video concludes with text touting the development as a new landscape district and a residential area for everyone, which has attracted over 800 million euros in private investment. The "Mall of Europe," viewers are told, will open in 2021, and is proudly financed by Unibail-Rodamco, CFE, and Besix.

Watching this video, it is easy to pinpoint Neo as a poster-child of neoliberal development. The project's promotional footage underlines the growing importance of big business, commerce, and global brands on our built environment. Another element that confirms its allegiance to neoliberal development is the fact that Neo is not solely supported by private funds, but relies on a substantial contribution from the public purse. Apart from Unibail-Rodamco, CFE, and Besix, the City of Brussels and the Brussels Capital Region are also investing heavily in Neo. They are injecting 335 million euros into the project, which will be used towards the development of its public spaces, green areas, mobility, sports park, swimming pool, and convention center, while the private investors are responsible for the shopping center, the housing, and leisure areas ("About," n/d). Furthermore, the land on which Neo is located is publicly owned. It was originally purchased by the City of Brussels in 1926 in preparation of the centenary of Belgium's independence ("History," n/d). Neo is thus a public-private partnership, or PPP.

Public-private partnerships were popularized at the end of the Cold War, when two concurrent trends emerged. On the one hand, there was growing support for government enablement of markets and, on the other hand, there were calls for greater government enablement of communities. At the same time, a third trend popularized, which supported the marriage of these two opposing camps on the grounds that partnerships between communities and the private sector, mediated by the public sector (i.e., the government) would achieve a synergy able to overcome certain shortcomings of each of the other two trends—rampant capitalism on the one hand, or insufficient economic stimulation on the other (Miraftab, 2004, p. 89). This third way thus both favored growth, entrepreneurship, enterprise, and wealth creation as well as greater social justice, and allocated a major role to the public sector in bringing this about. As a result, in this period following the end of the Cold War, PPPs became a preferred tool for urban development. However, in recent years, scholars of the built environment have suggested that PPPs might be the Trojan horse of neoliberal urban development (Miraftab, 2004). They claim that while in theory PPPs support power-sharing, once the process is in motion, the interests of the community are often overwhelmed by those of the most powerful member of the partnership: the private sector. As such, PPPs are said to enunciate rather than mitigate the sharp edges of neoliberal capitalism. Chronicling the pre-history of Neo, by narrating the development of earlier, comparable urban development projects in Belgium that (like Neo) relied on PPPs and had large shopping centers at their core, this chapter aims to do three things: 1) to explore the ideological foundations of PPPs; 2) to untangle why the reputation of PPPs has been tarnished, and 3) to put forward a speculative prognosis for the outcome of Neo.

Neo's Ancestors

Even though PPPs were popularized from the end of the Cold War, they have existed much longer. In Belgium, they were regularly used from the 1960s as a tool for the realization of ambitious urban development and redevelopment projects, often involving the construction of a large shopping center. A first notable example can be found in Genk, which is a city in the northeast of the country that, at the turn of the 20th century, after the discovery of charcoal in the region, started urbanizing rapidly. At that time, three mining sites opened in the Genk: Waterschei in 1909, Winterslag in 1912, and Zwartberg in 1913. Over the following decades, the city's population increased dramatically from approximately 3,500 inhabitants in 1910 up to 47,500 in 1960—mainly due to the influx of foreign laborers from Poland, Italy, Ukraine, and Turkey. With the three mining sites functioning as nuclei of growth, Genk's urban fabric became increasingly dispersed and fragmented (Rijck, Kesteloot, & Jansen-Verbeke, 1998). By the 1960s, it became clear that Genk's natural resources were finite. At that time, the mine of Zwartberg was forced to close, quite dramatically. Accordingly, Genk set out to reinvent itself, both economically and spatially. The city adopted a plan to construct a large new urban development scheme adjacent to its historic downtown, which would include a large shopping center, and which was intended to create a core that could mend Genk's metastasizing urban growth. The strategic placement of this project was a direct result of the lead role that the city adopted in its development: Genk's city council selected the site, it expropriated the land, and it also commissioned an architect of its choice to develop a design.

In 1964 architect Plumier presented his first plans: an ambitious urban complex of detached, rectilinear buildings with different heights, sizes, and functions, all located in a car-free, open-air, all-pedestrian area surrounded by parking lots. The project incorporated a large housing block, offices, an administrative center, a hotel, a café, a restaurant, a range of communal facilities such as a day-care center and a swimming pool, and also a significant proportion of shops. The buildings were all connected through an intricate system of "streets in the sky," which separated vehicular traffic from pedestrians while providing a place where people could linger, chat, and observe activities in the lower-lying areas.

By 1965, after a first review, Plumier's design had evolved from this initial multi-level, multi-functional, open-air complex to an elongated single-story open-air street, which traversed the plot from East to West. The main function of this revised scheme was commerce, although it did still include a limited set of auxiliary functions. At its most western point, it gathered two large supermarkets and a few smaller commercial units around a spacious square, while in the east it included a health clinic, a restaurant, and a hotel around a square with a generous pond. Based on this design, the municipality opened a tendering procedure and soon reached an agreement with Constructions et Entreprises Industrielles, a construction company from Brussels. Genk would sell the land that it had expropriated to this company, which in exchange would build the project following the design of architect Plumier. The company committed to completing the shopping center within five years, while the municipality pledged to execute all the necessary roadworks to ensure its optimal accessibility. In the contract that Constructions et Entreprises Industrielles (CEI) sent to the municipality in May 1965, the company suggested that the established price, 25 million Belgian Francs, was still negotiable. They wrote:

> Should Genk refrain from obliging [CEI] to construct certain of the non-profitable components . . . then the conditions of the sale could still be revised, taking into account the additional available land and the surplus value that could be attributed to it.[2]

Genk budged. Throughout 1966 and 1967, Plumier revised the plans for Genk's new urban core repeatedly, and the nature of the project changed dramatically. Generous concessions were made to the private partner, CEI, and when the envisaged grand urban development project finally opened its doors in August 1968, it no longer remotely resembled the initial plans. What was built instead was Belgium's first fully enclosed, climate-controlled shopping center that contributed little to the city's urban fabric, but was nonetheless proudly named "Shopping 1," as it (allegedly) was the first shopping center to open in the country (Gosseye, 2018).

A similar story unfolded in the Brussels periphery, where two ambitious urban development projects were launched in the late 1960s and early 1970s; one to the east of the city center of Brussels, the other to the west.[3] Around the time that these projects were initiated, many people working in the capital sought a nice home on the outskirts from where they could easily commute. The dilapidated state of the capital city, in combination with the rising popularity of cars and the expanding road network around Brussels, led to an urban exodus, and the fabric of Brussels started spreading like a blot of ink. So, when in 1963 Devimo, a real estate company, took the initiative to construct a "luxury shopping center" in Woluwe, which is one of the 19 municipalities that are part of the Brussels Capital Region, the local municipal council quickly capitalized on this opportunity to create a larger urbanization plan, which would make Woluwe a major sub-centrality in the eastern suburbs of the city. A masterplan was prepared, which proposed to combine the shopping center with cultural and leisure facilities as well as several multi-story residential units in an urban complex located along the Boulevard de la Woluwe, on either side of the Avenue Hymans. Open-air pedestrian walkways, such as the so-called *promenoir central* (central walkway), which traversed the shopping center and doubled as its "mall," were to connect the various areas of the development—both commercial and non-commercial. However, the proposed masterplan was never formally adopted by the municipality and therefore never completely realized. The pedestrian walkways, which were to embed the shopping center in its surroundings, disappeared in subsequent versions of the design and, as a result, the envisaged open-air *promenoir central* evolved into a more common enclosed, air-conditioned mall. This evolution of the design coincided with the arrival of Sears, Roebuck & Co. as Devimo's financial investors for the project. As a result, when Woluwe shopping center opened in September 1968, only a few weeks after "Shopping 1" had opened in Genk, none of the other amenities that were to surround it had been built, and this would remain so for several decades to come.

If the story of Woluwe is an example of a municipality reacting *a posteriori* to an initiative by private actors, the history of Westland in Anderlecht, which is a municipality in the western suburbs of Brussels, is like that of Genk, the paradigm of a public authority adopting a proactive approach to urban development. Convinced that Anderlecht had the potential to become the sub-capital of Brussels' western suburbs, the municipality's socialist mayor, René Bracops, entered into a partnership with Devimo, the same real estate company that had initiated the development of the shopping center in Woluwe, to construct an ambitious urban development project, which included a large shopping center. A masterplan was developed that wove together different residential neighborhoods, as well as several civic facilities in a large, park-like setting through a system of pedestrian walkways. An important component of this masterplan was a large shopping center at the western end, which Devimo pledged to build. Once this masterplan was approved, in 1971, construction of the shopping center commenced almost immediately and progressed quickly. As a result, "Westland" shopping center festively opened in 1972, before any of the other components of the scheme had even commenced construction. Then, a few months later, in 1973, with only the shopping center constructed on site, the economic crisis hit and left little resources available to continue the project, which remained manifestly incomplete.

A Trojan Horse?

These three brief examples of PPP-driven urban development projects that were realized in Belgium in the latter half of the 20th century offer some insights into the trials and triumphs of public-private partnerships. First, they give some hints as to why PPPs have accrued a somewhat bad reputation. In all three cases, little more than a shopping center was realized of the ambitious mixed-use urban schemes that were initially proposed. However, these examples also show that the reasons for this breakdown varied. In the case of Genk, the public actor yielded to the economic interests of the private actor, who (quite unsurprisingly) sought to get a better deal. Likewise, in Woluwe, most of the blame could actually be attributed the public partner, the municipal administration, who failed to formally approve the proposed urban masterplan. Finally, in the case of Anderlecht, where Westland shopping center was built, external circumstances—the economic crisis—interfered with the municipality's urban development ambitions.

These three examples *also* show that the history of PPPs dates back further than the end of the Cold War. In Belgium, as elsewhere in Europe, PPPs underwriting large urban development and reconstruction schemes were already popularized in the mid-20th century, which is perhaps not all that surprising. After the atrocities of World War II, European governments had become quite suspicious of the threat that all too extreme and nationalist expressions of citizenship posed. As a result, the question emerged how a new, modern post-war society could be shaped which shared common pursuits, but which was simultaneously devoid of totalitarian overtones. In response, the ideal of the "consumer-citizen" emerged, who was believed to be both independent and community-minded. Many planners and architects believed that a new community of consumer-citizens could be shaped through mixed-use urban developments that blended commercial functions with civic, administrative, and leisurely pursuits. The evolving thinking regarding the concept of the consumer-citizen from the mid- to the late 20th century also (to a certain extent) clarifies evolving approaches to liberalism and the evolution (or devolution?) from a welfare state to a neoliberal regime. Over the course of the second half of the twentieth century, claims by leftist writers and thinkers suggesting that consumption was a tool of "mass deception" wielded by capitalists consolidating their reigns were increasingly challenged by those on the right who suggested that markets could regulate themselves and that consumers actually enjoyed greater freedom than "oppressed" citizens. When in the early 1970s the so-called Club of Rome published their influential book *The Limits to Growth* (Meadows et al., 1972) and the economic crisis hit, the foundations of the European welfare state regime, which had been instrumental in harnessing capitalism's consumption-juggernaut, started to shake and crumbled when figures such as Reagan and Thatcher advocated that the market offered greater freedom and that consumers were better able to know and define their own needs and to pursue these rationally (Gosseye & Avermaete, 2017).

What does all this mean for Neo? The first phase that is currently being built of this ambitious project is called "Europea" ("Europea," n/d). Apart from approximately 600 housing units, this first phase—like the first phases that were constructed of the schemes that were proposed for Genk, Woluwe, and Anderlecht—consists by and large of commerce. It comprises the "Mall of Europe" that will offer about 70,000 square meters of shops, as well as 9,000 square meters of restaurants and associated hospitality functions ("Facts and Figures," n/d).

When you compare what is being constructed in this first phase with the public and communal amenities that already existed on the site—these were erected following the City of Brussels' purchase of the land[4]—it soon becomes apparent that in this first phase, very few of the project's advertised "public spaces" are realized. At the moment, the developers are basically reaping what the welfare state sowed. Furthermore, when you have a closer look at what "public spaces" *are* proposed for Neo, it appears that these are by and large subservient to the commercial ambitions of the scheme. They, for instance, facilitate the vehicular connection from the A12 motorway to the site; they provide a "green link" for pedestrians from the car park to the shops; they "reshape" the avenues to make the shops and recreational attractions more accessible and to make shopping more pleasant still, etc. However, perhaps none of this even matters as all the illustrations that are featured on Neo's website, including the lush and lively depictions of the project's "public spaces," are, as is explicitly stated at the bottom of each page, nothing more than "an artist's interpretation" which "are not legally binding" ("Public spaces," n/d). So, perhaps the Trojan horse of neoliberal urban development is not so much the public-private partnership itself, as the public partner in this partnership, who rather than defending the interests of the people all too gladly sells the prerogative to shape contemporary citizenship to the highest bidder.

Epilogue

The question could be posed what the alternative might be to this Trojan horse of neoliberal development. A return to a strong regulatory state seems unlikely. So, it is up to architects and urban designers to take up the mantle and develop strong designs that resist the commodification of the 21st-century city. When in 2006, J.G. Ballard wrote *Kingdom Come*, which was largely set in a shopping center, it was described as a "novel about a dystopian future." With every new urban development PPP that is launched these days, this dystopian future is rapidly becoming our new reality. To conclude with the words of Ballard:

> The churches are empty, and the monarchy shipwrecked itself on its own vanity. Politics is a racket, and democracy is just another utility, like gas and electricity. Almost no one has any civic feeling. Consumerism is the one thing that gives us our sense of values. Consumerism is honest, and teaches us that everything good has a barcode. The great dream of the Enlightenment, that reason and rational self-interest would one day triumph, led directly to today's consumerism.
>
> *(Ballard, 2014, p. 102)*

Notes

1. The masterplan for Neo has been prepared by Kees Christiaanse of KCAP Architects & Planners. The design of the international convention center and hotel, which constitute phase 2 of the project—also called "Neo II"—has been entrusted to Atelier Jean Nouvel.
2. Original quote: "Voor het geval, dat de Stad Genk er vanaf zou zien de ondergetekende [C.E.I.] te verplichten om bepaalde geen voordeel opbrengende onderdelen te bouwen zoals de parkeerplaatsen met verdiepingen, het dispensarium, het hotel, de brug, dan zouden de koopvoorwaarden . . . herzien worden, hierbij rekening houdend met de nieuwe ter beschikking komende oppervlakten en, de meerwaarde die hieraan mogelijker wijze zou toegekend worden." See Ontwerpcontract van immobilia aan gemeente Genk, dated May 20, 1965, 5, Bouwaanvragen 1966: Shopping Center 1 (874.1), City Archive, Genk.
3. A detailed history of the development of these two shopping centers in Brussels can be found in: Yannick Vanhaelen and Géry Leloutre (2017).
4. These public facilities, for instance, include the Centenary Stadium (today known as the King Baudouin stadium), as well as several palaces that were realized for the 1935 Universal Exhibition.

References

About. (n.d). *Neo*. Retrieved on April 25, 2020 from www.neobrussels.com/en/about/.
Atelier Jean Nouvel. (n.d). Heysel International Convention Center & Hotel—Néo II. *Atelier Jean Nouvel*. Retrieved on May 1, 2020 from www.jeannouvel.com/en/projects/centre-international-de-convention-du-heyssel-neo-ii/
Ballard, J.G. (2014). *Kingdom Come* (First published 2006). London, UK: Fourth Estate.
Europea. (n.d). *Neo*. Retrieved on May 2, 2020 from www.neobrussels.com/en/europea/.
Facts and Figures. (n.d). *Neo*. Retrieved on May 1, 2020 from www.neobrussels.com/en/the-heysel/facts-figures/.

Gosseye, J. (2018). The Janus-faced Shopping Centre: The Low Countries in Search of a Fitting Shopping Paradigm. *Journal of Urban History, 44*(5), 862–886.

Gosseye, J., & Avermaete, T. (2017). Shopping Towns Europe 1945–1975. In J. Gosseye & T. Avermaete (Eds.), *Shopping Towns Europe 1945–1975: Commercial Collectivity and the Architecture of the Shopping Centre* (pp. 1–21). London, UK: Bloomsbury Academic.

History. (n.d). *Neo*. Retrieved on May 2, 2020 from www.neobrussels.com/en/the-heysel/history/

KCAP Architects & Planners. (n.d). Neo. *KCAP Architects & Planners*. Retrieved on May 1, 2020 from www.kcap.eu/en/projects/v/neo/

Meadows, D.H., Meadows, D.L., Randers, J., & Behrens III, W.W. (1972). *The Limits to Growth: A Report for the Club of Rome's Project on the Predicament of Mankind*. New York, NY: Universe Books.

Miraftab, F. (2004). Public-Private Partnerships: The Trojan Horse of Neoliberal Development? *Journal of Planning Education and Research, 24*, 89–101.

The Project. (n.d). *Neo*. Retrieved on April 25, 2020 from www.neobrussels.com.

Public Spaces: 335 million euros of public investment for a high-quality project. (n.d). *Neo*. Retrieved on May 1, 2020 from www.neobrussels.com/en/public-spaces/.

Rijck, T., Kesteloot, C., & Jansen-Verbeke, M. (1998). *Sporen van een Mijnverleden: Sociaal Geografische Studies in de Limburgse Mijnstreek* [Traces of a Mining Past: Social-Geographical Studies into the Limburg Mining Region]. Heverlee, Belgium: Instituut voor Sociale en Economische Geografie.

Vanhaelen, Y., & Leloutre, G. (2017). Shopping Centres as Catalysts for New Multifunctional Urban Centralities: The Case of Two Shopping Centres around Brussels. In J. Gosseye & T. Avermaete (Eds.), *Shopping Towns Europe: Commercial Collectivity and the Architecture of the Shopping Centre 1945–1975* (pp. 51–64). London, UK: Bloomsbury Academic.

14

THE LEGITIMIZED REPRODUCTION OF A CORPORATE TYPOLOGY

Dispositions of Architectural Form in the LEED® Rating System

Raphael Grazziano

In his recent essay "The Aesthetics of Singularity" (2015), Fredric Jameson examines the validity of his notion of "postmodernity," developed in the mid-1980s, for the 21st century. The notion had originally been conceived of to explain a determinate historical period, from the 1970s onward, and would apply to the totality of social phenomena, "from economics to politics, from the arts to technology, from daily life to international relations" (Jameson, 2015, p. 104). Thirty years later, phenomena are surely quite different from those initially analyzed, but Jameson still considers adequate his initial judgement, of a new historic experience implied, on the one hand, in the socialist debacle and, on the other, in the leap of the means of production toward information. Adequate, Jameson writes, except for one term: his initial formulation was missing "globalization," which would only appear in theoretical debates some years later (e.g., Harvey, 1989; Sassen, 1991).

If we accept the premise of globalization's centrality in the cultural field over past decades, we shall see the full territorial extent to which certain spatial practices became widespread throughout this period. So-called spatial products were formed—the expression belongs to Keller Easterling (2007)—replicating themselves on the trail of fluxes of capital and masses of consumers. Such products became hegemonic in the global urban experience. Easterling enumerates different typologies such as logistical warehouses, resorts, and technological campuses, but what interests us here is an example that is not directly mentioned, even if alluded to in a cursory manner: corporate buildings. Such buildings were on the rise at least since the end of the 1980s, when production management activities began to acquire strength and reconfigure cities transitioning from industrial to service economies. An example of this process is the proliferation of financial centers, or Central Business Districts (CBDs), throughout different global metropolitan spaces.

Large project and consulting firms took charge of financial centers in locations ever further from their headquarters—and ever more peripheral in relation to the productive system's center. Some project imperatives arise from globalization. This is because the tenants of corporate buildings are branches of multinationals, and their headquarters stipulate quality standards to be followed for guaranteeing equivalent management conditions in disparate geographical contexts. Furthermore, office buildings—which are rented and not actually bought by these companies in order to remain liquid and guarantee the swift repatriation of dividends in the case of adversities—are real estate investments. As such, they were conceived of in order to reward their proprietors, generally funds whose investors have never visited the development. These towers, attractive to multinational corporations and real estate funds, are called "Triple A" on the market. With the intention of guaranteeing the necessities of the former as much as the expectations of the latter, these projects keep to a list of characteristics, such as ceiling height, slab size, proximity to airports, and even norms of the New York Fire Department. In order to be certified Triple A, developments must consider a series of different norms, standards, protocols, and international certifications in order to streamline contracts and financial transactions. These norms and protocols, which gradually spread through different programs and project scales, are clouds of exigencies that are not made publicly available but are taken into consideration by each developer and real estate services consultant when operating in the market.

Against this background, we propose in this text to analyze the emergence of the international office tower from the perspective of the rating system Leadership in Energy and Environmental Design (LEED®). To be more precise, we hold that a certification system such as LEED® encompasses a set of "dispositions" that strongly affects the material and typological occurrence of the office tower. Being a technical standard, LEED® establishes levels of performance to be observed, requests documentation as evidence of compliance to its guidelines, and is voluntary. Among its various credits, few are those that necessarily need to be fulfilled for the certification process to begin. According to Easterling's studies (2014) of the International Organization for Standardization (ISO), these emphases on documentation and performance processes would lead to *dispositions* of architectural form. In her understanding, a disposition is "the character or propensity of an organization that results from all its activity" (Easterling, 2014, p. 21); it is "a potential agency," "immanent, not in the moving parts, but in the relationships between the components" (Easterling, 2014, p. 72). Disposition is not the object form, that of the concrete realization of building projects, but the active form present in the norms. In the analysis of active form, an infrastructure of contemporary space is revealed, not only in the material sense commonly used, as electrical networks, sanitation, and transportation, but as management protocols and guidelines. According to Easterling, it does not matter exactly what the active form does, but especially what it does *not* do, or even what it obstructs. In short: the active form works with dispositions and not with objects, with propensities and not with things, with the medium and not with the message.

In her first formulations of the notion of active form (2012), Easterling suggests it could have an impact on the object form, a consequence ultimately suppressed from the final draft of her book *Extrastatecraft* (2014). But if LEED® establishes levels of accomplishment and evaluates architectural performance according to them, what is its disposition? Would it tend toward determinate project standards or even carry typological tendencies? Answering these questions may clarify how corporate spaces were conceived of in the last decades, especially considering how important office areas became in reshaping cities since the 1990s. It may also show how LEED®, among a wide range of norms and best practices protocols, is a concealed tool of contemporary architecture and urbanism design, underpinned by its own rationalities.

LEED® New Construction and Core and Shell Systems

Let us begin with the structure of LEED® itself. LEED® is a sustainability rating system managed since 1998 by a non-profit, the United States Green Building Council (USGBC). In the 20 years elapsed since its creation until 2018, LEED® certified almost 72,000 developments of varied uses and programs and more than 200 million square meters. In evaluating developments according to energy, water, and material consumption, aside from its implantation and the well-being of its occupiers, LEED® became a tool allowing for comparison between performances in architectural projects. It also became a tool through which branches may demonstrate concretely to their headquarters that they follow the scripts of sustainable management, or an index of development quality with which funds may prove the low risk of an investment to their shareholders.

In its first 1998 version, there was only one system, LEED® New Construction (NC), but others were gradually created: the fourth and most recent version shows upwards of 20 specific systems. According to Jerry Yudelson, a long-time USGBC collaborator, the pilot version of LEED® NC already had corporate buildings as its prime objective (2016, p. 122)—but it is only with LEED® Core and Shell (CS) that architecture for speculative buildings is addressed.

There are few differences between the NC and CS systems, and they are mainly regarding the fact that in CS there is no specific client to be considered for the project at hand, as it is mainly used by speculative projects. In the United States, the system with the most certifications became, over time, Homes, dedicated to residential developments, from single-family homes to apartment buildings. Internationally, however, the system with the most certifications is NC. If we decide to take area into consideration, instead of the sheer quantity of developments, LEED® CS becomes the main system outside of the US, with more than 80 million certified square meters. In Brazil, LEED® CS is the most widely used system, found in 43% of certified developments, of which 85% are version 3.[1]

The LEED® NC and CS systems are organized through five main categories: *Sustainable Sites* (SS), *Water Efficiency* (WE), *Energy and Atmosphere* (EA), *Materials and Resources* (MR), and *Indoor Environmental Quality* (EQ). From version 4 onwards, part of the SS category is relocated to the newly established *Location and Transport* (LT), but the evaluated categories and their values remain constant. Each fundamental category has a set of credits that are prerequisites for certification. Apart from the fundamental categories are two other extra ones: *Innovation in Design* (ID) and, onwards from version 3, *Regional Priorities* (RP). The quantity of available points varies in different versions of LEED®, but, for the purposes of this chapter, score proportions are kept relatively constant. In order to be certified, the development must submit documentation requesting specific credits in the system. This documentation is related to simulations or calculations made according to the design and construction records. According to performance assessed through the submitted documentation, the development can be simply certified or acquire the Silver, Gold, or Platinum distinctions.

The five main categories assess different aspects of a project. In LEED® NC and CS, the SS category possesses around one-fourth of the fundamental points and relates to choice of terrain and development implementation. Its credits can be grouped, on the one hand, by those relating to pre-existing natural or urban conditions, privileging natural preservation and urban infill. On the other hand, in greater number, are those credits pertaining to minimizing impact on surroundings, incentives to access public and non-motorized transport, expansion of green areas, and control of rainwater, heat islands, and light pollution.

The WE category, dedicated to hydric resources, has 10% of the fundamental points. Credits can be divided according to those concerning potable water consumption and those concerning sewage treatment inside the development, avoiding its ejectment into the city's sanitation system.

The category bearing the most possible points is EA (35 points), which is therefore of central importance in fulfilling the LEED® system requirements. Its procedures, related to energy consumption in building operation, are divided into energy consumption reduction, verification of projected mechanical and electrical systems, *in loco* production of electrical power from clean sources, and proscriptions of chemical elements harmful to the ozone layer. This category contains the *Optimize Energy Performance* credit, the most important out of the NC and CS systems, being the one with the most possible points. This credit alone is responsible for 20% of the fundamental points.

The MR category focuses on the construction materials used and involves at least three assessment fronts. The first is reduction in material consumption, be it the preservation of pre-existing constructive elements through an intervention, or be it through reuse of residue from the construction site itself. The second front is development operation and residue management. The third front, in turn, deals with issues related to the production and provenance of materials, incentives for recycled contents, proximity to the products' extraction site, and renewable materials.

Finally, the EQ category deals with environmental quality for building occupants. On the one hand, it assesses strategies for better internal air quality, through increases in ventilation and reduction of airborne chemical compounds. On the other hand, it deals with the users' comfort in issues such as illumination, temperature, and sense of confinement.

Apart from the fundamentals, the ID category gives out prizes to exceptional performances or projects that are considered innovative. The RP category includes extra points selected by the USGBC or by a local council in international situations, according to the development's specific geographic context. These points are added to pre-existing credits in the system.

Though LEED® seems to be a rather objective and equivalent system of criteria, the architects working with it do not operate with them equally. Patterns of assessment can be noted in what we have briefly presented concerning the system. These patterns of assessment can be incorporated "automatically" by designers, as expressed by one of the architects interviewed for this research: the projects' workflow would integrate solutions from the outset, predicting fulfillment of certain credits in later stages. In this sense, in lieu of starting from the multiplicity of possible points taken up by an incorporator, who will always choose those points that are easiest to be reached, or which present larger economic gains in a stipulated timeline, our methodological premise is instead the complete fulfillment of the certification. Let us also take as a premise for research the use of LEED® from the early stages of the project onward. That is, given that LEED® guidelines are followed as specified in the certificate, and not according to eventual distortions from empirical use, can we find a general spatial sense in the rating system?

Mechanization of the Environment

The first design characteristic that stands out from the LEED® certification is the improvement of a building's systems, be they hydraulic, electrical, or mechanical. The building fulfills sustainability objectives through the improved efficiency of these systems. LEED® does not demand strategies that are unusual in the corporate real estate market but rather better performances from habitual building systems. Better complementary projects are necessary, as well as, at least ideally, their inclusion in more initial stages of the architectural design. Thus, building design would establish a dialog from early stages in its development, such as in preliminary studies, with necessities of complementary projects.

Specification of these systems is so much more important given that, in speculative buildings, building systems are central to the architectural project, together with the circulation and service core and the building shell. In the spatial interval between core and shell, only these service systems are foreseen in the architectural project, the rest being decided by future tenants. It should be noted that at first this would only be characteristic of rental buildings, objects of the LEED® CS system. However, the LEED® NC system, dedicated to new construction in general and to substantial interventions in existing buildings, has an equal emphasis on building systems, which indicates how the design logic of the speculative building reverberates in the various programs evaluated by LEED®.

Though the argument that LEED® "provides the green building benchmarks, but doesn't tell applicants how to get the points" (Gottfried, 2014, p. 128) is common, what can be gleaned from the system, on the contrary, is that the assessment points guarantee larger benefits for cutting-edge architecture than for those relying on traditional techniques.

This emphasis on building systems is applied through "a suite of technological innovations, including cutting-edge insulation or windows, low-energy lighting, 'smart' thermostats with state-of-the-art heating, ventilation, and air-conditioning (HVAC) systems, or rooftop photovoltaic solar panels" (Boschmann & Gabriel, 2013, p. 223). The project is related, therefore, more to high-tech equipment than to vernacular or contextual approaches, which are not rewarded in LEED® with specific scores. These are the so-called active strategies, through which these buildings employ a technological, energy-consuming apparatus to operate and fulfill intended indexes. Those procedures that function without intervention, according to the very way the project is conceived of and constructed, are called "passive." Thus, passive procedures use natural ventilation instead of air-conditioning; opacity and thermal inertia instead of up-to-date glasses; solar light and its optimal distribution through the environment instead of artificial lights; and historically tested solutions instead of more recent technological advances.

If it is through the mechanical control of environments, and not through typological solutions, that the sustainability of corporate LEED®-certified spaces is guaranteed, then projects present less an issue of spatial configuration than one of technological regulation. The main design procedure in LEED® is not about blueprints and sections adapted to air flow and light penetration, as in common diagrams in environmental architectures, but first and foremost about mechanization of the environment. This procedure, rather marginal in the history of architecture, was developed by Reyner Banham in his *The Architecture of the Well-Tempered Environment* (1969). Banham in a sense foresaw the expansion of climatized spaces in the following decades, as much in office buildings as in shopping centers. For him, these spatial typologies of modernity had only become possible through the commercial availability of mechanical systems. Otherwise, it would be impossible to use those deep spaces, far from windows, without natural light or air flow, nonetheless conceived of to be highly occupied by people, activities, and equipment (Banham, 1969, pp. 71, 86). His argument is of interest given two aspects: 1) making spaces viable through artificial climatization, since their geometry would not allow its occupation otherwise; and 2) the fact that the commercialization of mechanical systems, more than their isolated invention, allows the generalization of typologies like those of office buildings.

If LEED® systems play a role in the history of architecture, as read by Banham, it is that of promoting and making commercially viable those mechanical systems that are increasingly efficient in their functioning and responsive in their operation, such as low-consumption air-conditioning or lighting equipment that is automatically adaptable to temperature or lighting of specific spots in the floor plan. LEED®'s role works then in two directions. On the one hand, it establishes performance criteria that guides materials and systems specifications toward common sustainability parameters. On the other hand, it enables these materials and systems commercially, as it generates a network of corporations—as producers of materials and real estate services organizations—that fund the national Green Building Councils and have representatives in the internal committees that discuss those sustainability parameters (Grazziano, 2019, chs.1, 2).

Certainly LEED® is not the only organization responsible for increasingly mechanized buildings. Banham's historiography already showed how this was a regular process throughout the 20th century. LEED®, however, reinforces the mechanization of architecture in the ecological field, an uncommon phenomenon before the 1990s, by concentrating assessment criteria on HVAC systems.

Credits such as *Fundamental Commissioning of Building Energy Systems* and *Enhanced commissioning*, found in LEED® NC and CS, are directly related to the verification of building systems, and at least 58 of the 110 points in LEED® version 3 treat the theme at least partially. Even if the credits are never specifically reduced to building systems, foreseeing solutions in ventilation and natural lighting, there is a tendency in LEED® to deal with these systems rather than passive strategies. Indeed, the absence of mechanization can obstruct the attainment of a large portion of the indexes demanded by LEED® systems, most of all in areas outside of temperate climates. This is because these indexes are ill-adapted to tropical climates, as noted by Jerry Yudelson, with regard to North-American developments:

> [T]he reality is that a new construction project that aims at LEED certification will find it pretty easy to get certified, *if* it meets all prerequisites and remembers to document specific criteria at the appropriate time. However, unusual project types may find that getting an energy model accepted could be the biggest obstacle, since meeting the minimum energy performance prerequisite depends on using a specific ASHRAE modeling protocol. In some instances, even low-energy-using projects may have a hard time meeting the energy prerequisite. An example is projects in regions that don't use any air-conditioning, such as the Caribbean or Hawaii.
>
> *(Yudelson, 2016, pp. 115–116)*

"Unusual project types" are, therefore, all those that sit outside the geographic context in which LEED® was initially conceived. Difficulty in designing buildings for operating without mechanical climatization, coupled with corporate clients' resistance to natural ventilation lead to the generalization and affirmation of active strategies in LEED® systems.

The "specific modelling protocol" mentioned by Yudelson is the *ASHRAE Standard 90.1*, developed in a collaboration between North American technical organizations.[2] The different versions of LEED® accompany the different versions of the standard. It is a requisite of two credits in the LEED® NC and CS systems in the energy category: one is a prerequisite and the other a credit concentrating the largest possible amount of points in both systems, *Optimize Energy Performance*.

As Rodrigo Cavalcante explains, the ASHRAE standard is divided into different sections and appendixes, with G being referenced by LEED® in the aforementioned two credits. This appendix, called *Performance Rating*, deals with assessing projects that perform better than the standard norm. According to this methodology, two models must be measured in a digital simulation: on the one hand, we have the actual proposed project and, on the other, a baseline building. Both modeled buildings should be the same, except for 1) the envelope properties and the size of the openings, where "the baseline building must be modeled with a thermally isolated roof, steel-framed outer walls, steel-joist flooring and WWR [Window-to-Wall Ratio] of 40% or equal to the project specification, whichever is smaller" (Cavalcante, 2010, p. 44); 2) any type of sunshade must be removed from the baseline building; 3) the project's orientation, where the baseline building must have a thermal load estimated from the average between the orientation of the proposed building and the performances in three other orientations, obtained by rotating the project by 90°, 180°, and 270°; 4) the load from artificial lighting, which must follow the prescription of the standard in the case of the baseline building; and 5) HVAC systems, which must also follow the standard prescription for the baseline. In summary, the differences between the two simulated models are the orientation, the specifications of the building systems, and the characteristics of the envelope (Cavalcante, 2010).

In order to accomplish one of the LEED® energy prerequisites, the candidate must demonstrate that the project's energy performance is better than the baseline building, being awarded more points if they perform better in a range that goes from a 10% to 48% increment.

Cavalcante made energy simulations in the Energy Plus software, with anonymous case studies and fictional projects, comparing them to what is established in ASHRAE 90.1. Through this procedure, he shows that geometries with better energy performance do not translate necessarily into a better assessment according to the standard. After all, even if a certain geometry is more efficient from a thermal standpoint, it has no impact in the mathematical calculation, being a constant (Cavalcante, 2010). As exposed earlier, the calculation variables are the envelope, building systems, and orientation, the latter to a lesser degree. Geometry is inscrutable to ASHRAE and LEED®: a first aspect of the disposition.

Envelope Architecture

If until now we have been looking at the mechanization of the environment, the second aspect is the emphasis on the envelope design. Both characteristics operate together, since the better the envelope performs, the less energy air-conditioning consumes. For this reason, the envelope tends to be sealed in order to reduce heat exchanges through ventilation. For LEED®, the envelope also needs a good thermal performance, at first obtained by reducing glass area. Glass has lower levels of thermal performance than opaque materials, so the simplest design solution is to reduce the window-to-wall ratio (WWR), which is one of the elements taken into account in the ASHRAE 90.1 simulation. Although not mandatory, the proportion of a maximum of 40% glass area is relevant in the calculations and imperative in the project, regardless of its geographical location and its urban surroundings. For this reason, architects of corporate buildings complain about the loss of autonomy in design decisions, as Alberto Botti, from Brazilian office Botti & Rubin, does in an interview with researcher Isadora Guerreiro:

> And now we have this issue with the "green" LEED people, who come up and tell you: "scale down the windows or we won't award you points." . . . Between the rules . . . by these commercialization offices, most of all by American offices, and LEED regulations and so on, architecture is becoming incredibly inflexible. Do you know what proportion LEED proposes? This building [Edifício Plantar, IG] doesn't fit. There must be a 50% span [actually 40%, RG] to 50% of the wall [actually 60%, RG]. . . . Each case is different! If this room is six meters, this window is dimensioned in a way. If it was eight meters long, and it didn't have that wall, for example, this window had to be bigger to give more illumination. So this is absurd!
>
> (Guerreiro, 2010, p. 185)

Ideally, the sealed envelope, with a 60% opaque surface, also needs to have a pure and concise form in order to comply with LEED® performance standards. An increase in the building perimeter through folds in the facade is a possible resource for acquiring points in the *Daylight and Views—Views* credit, which establishes parameters for natural light in the occupied space. However, this same measure can represent an increase in the building's thermal load, compromising scoring in the main credit of the LEED® NC and CS systems, *Optimize Energy Performance*, hence the greatest relevance to the scoring, in principle, of a smaller-perimeter project.

The limitation of the perimeter to reduce the thermal load and the low WWR can lead to less incidence of natural light inside the occupied spaces. To solve this problem in a multi-story building, skylights for illuminating deep spaces are not possible. Lighting pits in the center of the building, in turn, in addition to being formal solutions without privileges in ASHRAE 90.1, can also lead to an increase in the perimeter of the building and consequently of its thermal load. There are several strategies for diffusing natural light through environments, but the possibility of only limiting the depth of the building is of interest here. This simple solution can help to obtain points not only in *Daylight and Views—Daylight*, but also potentially in *Daylight and Views—Views* credit, in which a direct line of sight to the outside in 75% of the occupied space must be guaranteed.

Implantation and Open Space

Evidently, more sophisticated solutions can be employed in order to guarantee natural lighting, such as light shelves, sunshades in order to diminish glares, or photosensitive controls. The reduction of the building's depth, however, does not represent an increase in cost and has effects on some of the other credits, beginning with *Site Development—Maximize Open Space*, in which a reduction of the building's occupied area, so as to increase in 25% the open areas on the ground floor, is required. This reduction, in turn, leads to a greater quantity of permeable areas required in *Stormwater Design*. It also opens space for shade-producing vegetation, as required in *Heat Island Effect—Nonroof*, and for flora restoration, as in *Site Redevelopment—Protect or Restore Habitat*. This last credit suggests "clearly-marked construction boundaries" (USGBC, 2011, p. 13), a concentration of the program and a reinforcement of the distinction between building and environs, which would guarantee the preservation of part of the site's vegetation. Thus, the combination of reduced building depth, its isolation, and landscaping has a potential impact of 8 points in the LEED® NC and CS systems, if calculated according to version 3.

Taking as a reference only the motives put forth in the systems themselves, the increase in open space and vegetation resulting from these measures would lead to environmental benefits such as greater biodiversity and water infiltration, as well as to lesser thermal impact upon fauna and building occupants. However, the providing of open spaces does not necessarily entail their actual use by the population, since the NC and CS systems do not forbid fencing around the development. These open spaces can remain privately accessed, depending upon the proprietor's stipulations.

The increase in open space foreseen in the NC and CS systems does not necessarily represent an increase in activities and services for the population. Even though the systems suggest implantation in an area with abundant offers of services, therefore in a place of urban centrality, the credits make use of their surroundings without offering returns. Thus, the *Development Density and Community Connectivity* credit, according to version 3 guidelines, offers five points for the project located: 1) in an already occupied area, 2) up to 800 meters from a neighborhood with at least 10 units per acre (1 unit per 400 m^2), 3) within 800 meters of 10 basic services, and 4) in an area with a possible pedestrian route. Among these 10 basic services counted for points—restaurants, churches, parks, pharmacies, schools etc.—only one can be located within the certified project. This ensures that the project can have a single use—the one presenting higher financial advantages for the developer—instead of promoting mixed-use developments.

Accordingly, LEED® implementation requirements have double effects: on the one hand, we have buildings isolated inside of green areas, which may be fenced off without impacting the overall score; on the other hand, we have benefits provided by the myriad activities in surrounding areas, while the development is not required to present their neighbors with new options.

Large Scale

The choice of active thermal regulation strategies and high-performance materials in the envelope has an impact on the increase in the construction and operation costs of these buildings, when compared with passive alternatives. The cost rises given not only the most sophisticated equipment, including sensors and adaptable performance, but also because of the hired teams of consultants and specialists.

The main reports point to between 1% and 20% of cost increase in the certified development (Dwaikat & Ali, 2015). The lower and upper limits have several causes, such as the intended degree of certification and the developers', designers', and builders' experience in certification. In addition, there are fees paid to Green Business Certification Inc. (GBCI) for the certification process.

Larger buildings have proportionately smaller costs, not only because of the gains in scale given equipment and glass but also because of the dilution of fixed prices for certification and through area tiers with smaller costs of revision by GBCI. Analysis of the areas disclosed by the USGBC is not conclusive, as there are several projects with no area or with the wrong area. Also because, since the purpose of the area is charging fees, the figures in the disclosed data eliminate parking areas. Finally, large developments can be subdivided in the certification process, such as groups of towers, misrepresenting their scales.

For the certification of developments, then, larger areas are an advantage. As Jerry Yudelson argues:

> Fixed costs to meet prerequisites for LEED certification, energy modeling (required only for new buildings), building commissioning (required for both new buildings and existing buildings), specific design measures, operational changes, documentation and certification costs, are *prohibitive* for these smaller buildings.
>
> (Yudelson, 2016, p. 99)

Aside from the larger relative costs of small buildings, return rates are further complicated outside of urban centers, where sustainable building is hardly a relative advantage in a less competitive real estate market.

As a solution, Yudelson proposes an immediate passage into a digital environment, with the creation of an app to substitute the certification process and to standardize solutions for development cost reductions. To a certain extent, this is already the direction taken by the USGBC, albeit at a slower pace than that introduced by Yudelson, in proposing the Arc® platform, in which new certified developments are centralized online and in real time. Through it, the USGBC can constantly verify that a building is up to specifications—and, in doing so, parry one of the main criticisms directed at LEED®: the fact that certifications are given to project simulations and not to the building's actual performance. In a way, the platform could reduce the various LEED® systems—new projects, interiors, or interventions in pre-existing buildings—to only one, pertaining to the development's better standards of performance. This does not seem to be the USGBC's objective, who maintain the different LEED® systems and provide no transparency with regard to the platform's data. What seems to be in course, on the contrary, is the creation of a platform concentrating large global volumes of corporate building operation data. The plan may place the USGBC in the field of *big tech*, controlling enormous masses of data on the performance of globally localized buildings, but does not overcome the obstacle of costs coming from the technological equipping inherent to the requisites in the LEED® NC and CS systems.

A Tacit Architectural Model

We now have the four main aspects laid out by LEED® for an architecture design: 1) the mechanization of the environment to the detriment of passive solutions; 2) the prismatic, rigid envelope; 3) implantation with a highlighting of figure-ground schemes, greater soil permeability, and potentially private and mono-functional; and 4) large scale.

These characteristics are not always found in a uniform manner in LEED®-certified developments, mainly given the system's flexible and voluntary scoring. Their spatial propensity, however, can frequently be noted. This is because LEED® assessment parameters do not only follow technical principles but also respond to the spatial models of architectural sustainability being debated during the creation of the certificate. One of the most influential models was Fox & Fowle's Four Times Square building (1995–1999) (Fernández-Galiano, 2005; Glenn, 2003). Analyzing the project, Suzanne Stephens already foreshadowed the forms privileged by LEED® in the following years: "Fox & Fowle's Four Times Square is not avant-garde. The 49-story tower at 42nd Street and Broadway does not radically redefine the skyscraper as an urban building type, and its much praised energy-saving features are more symbolic than actual" (2000, p. 91).

Four Times Square has several pieces of equipment to improve its environmental performance, whose advanced technology was promoted in the construction guidelines as a way of attracting "sophisticated tenants" (Percio, 2004, p. 138). Its HVAC system is efficient, with high air renewal and without the use of chlorofluorocarbon (CFC), and the facades have double glazing. After unsuccessful attempts with the production of wind energy, electrochemical cells were installed inside the building, and photovoltaic cells were installed in place of glass plates on the envelope. However, the expected quantity of both cells were reduced, due to high costs. Although the energy produced by the building is sufficient to supply almost six (North American) residences, it only corresponds to 0.5% of its high consumption, so that its energy efficiency is not measured—or even disclosed—in absolute parameters, but relative ones.

Four Times Square does not redefine the typology of the office tower and does not show absolute efficiency gains, but it has become the replicated model of sustainable building typology, which would then be certified and legitimized by LEED®. Its high energy consumption typology due to vertical circulation, mechanical systems, deep slabs, and thermal exchanges allowed by the thin layer of glass that envelops it is essentially anti-environmental, but relatively more efficient than the standard office tower. If the project proceeded in this manner, it was to not contradict a fundamental principle of North American office architecture: efficiency—this time not of resource consumption, but of the ratio between net and gross areas, which corresponds to the potential financial return on the sale and rent of a building (Buchanan, 2007; Gonçalves & Umakoshi, 2010). The project therefore offered relative efficiency in the consumption of resources, without jeopardizing the absolute efficiency of the marketable area, which was what happened in the models of sustainable towers leading up to then, as in the projects of Foster + Partners in Europe. As stated by an anonymous entrepreneur for *Architectural Record*: "No one understood green design or what its advantages were. But after Four Times Square, everyone thought, 'We can do that too.' And LEED gave us a blueprint for understanding how to get there" (Glenn, 2003).

The building was indeed a model for other subsequent sustainable towers, in projects by Fox & Fowle architects, now disassociated. This is the case of One Bryant Park (2004–2009), next to Cook Fox's Four Times Square, the first building to be LEED® CS certified at the Platinum level, presenting extensive use of technological equipment to achieve resource efficiency (Figure 14.1). It was also the model for the new *The New York Times* headquarters (2000–2007), by Renzo Piano Building Workshop in collaboration with FXFowle (currently FXCollaborative), a project that abandoned the certification process due to the high costs involved. For both cases, the North American corporate architectural typology is maintained, to which the technological apparatus is added. As Nicolai Ouroussof, at the time an architecture columnist for *The New York Times*, says about the newspaper's new headquarters: "[t]he most contemporary

FIGURE 14.1 One Bryant Park, designed by COOKFOX Architects (2009).

features—the computerized louvers and blinds that regulate the flow of light into the interiors—are technological rather than architectural ones" (2007).

The contradiction between efficient technology and anti-environmental typology, observed in the context of New York, increases when the model is replicated globally—including in the tropics. Indeed, an important LEED® market is in Brazil, which in 2019 occupied the sixth place in the worldwide ranking of certificate use, with a high concentration in the cities of Rio de Janeiro and São Paulo. Certainly, it is not possible to state that Brazilian designers consciously replicate the solutions put forth in Four Times Square, but the good performance of some projects in the assessment made by LEED®, with similar design schemes, reinforces the role of legitimizing the certificate.

Take the Eldorado Business Tower building (EBT, 2002–2007), located near Marginal Pinheiros, an important expressway in São Paulo, between a train station and the mall that gives the tower its name (Figure 14.2). This project by aflalo/gasperini architecture office was once considered one of the most sustainable buildings in Latin America for having reached the maximum level of certification, Platinum, in the LEED® CS version 2 system. It did so while being one of the first certified buildings in Brazil, registering for evaluation when the local Green Building Council (GBC), the body responsible for the dissemination and management of LEED® systems in the country, was still coming into being. In fact, the building anticipated the founding of GBC Brasil by six months, as it was registered in mid-2006. The tower was part of the first group of large-scale certified developments in the country, in August 2009.

Contrary to the provisions of the LEED® system, the building was already under construction when it began to apply for certification. However, even though work started in 2004, it

FIGURE 14.2 Eldorado Business Tower, designed by aflalo/gasperini arquitetos (2007).

only gained momentum in 2006—the same year as the LEED® registration—with the entry of new investors in the project (Guerreiro, 2010, p. 180). This interval allowed the project to conform to the demands of certification, an adaptation that was facilitated by registering when version 2 of LEED® CS, which was less demanding, was still in effect.

The project acquired diverse efficiencies in its use of resources (always understood from a relative perspective). In terms of energy, the main architectural initiatives focused on the mechanization of the relation between user and space: a VRF (Variable Refrigerant Flow) air-conditioning system, which is energetically more efficient and has easier upkeep, was introduced; louvers were automatized,[3] responding to variations in light incidence on the inside; and the air-conditioning system in each area is automatically turned on at the moment when its occupant's car is admitted into the garage building (Guerreiro, 2010, p. 184).

The mechanization of the environment is associated with the envelope design. The spatial model is realized through a combination of these procedures. Thus, the EBT envelope is sealed, guaranteeing the efficiency of mechanical systems, respecting precisely the WWR favored by ASHRAE 90.1, with 60% opaque areas and 40% transparent areas. These proportions are distributed in the facade in a grid, a resource developed by aflalo/gasperini in the 1980s and 1990s, in which sunshade functions and structural expression overlap. The modern function of sunlight control and the postmodern function of the facade as communicative element are therefore combined. Although architects emphasize how much this design strategy is rooted in the history of the office (Serapião, 2011), it should be noted that in EBT the grid was flattened towards the surface of the building, and for this reason it lost its function of shading the facades. Furthermore, the structural grids found in older projects were replaced by a finishing grid, as the EBT grid does not follow the structural module (Guerreiro, 2010). There is also an additional illusion in the configuration of the facade: the building is entirely covered with glass, even in its opaque areas, where the coating is made of white glass with silkscreened ceramic painting (Paiva & Silva, 2008).

The building therefore foreshadows the entirely glass prisms that appeared a few years later in São Paulo's corporate architecture, mirroring in a tropical context the architectural forms widely present in global CBDs.

There is, therefore, in the EBT, a contradiction between the type of offices adopted and the project specifications necessary for them to be viable in the tropical context of São Paulo. Another case of the continuity of these forms is the São Paulo Corporate Towers group (SPCT, 2008–2015), with a project by Pelli Clarke Pelli in collaboration with aflalo/gasperini, a few blocks south of the EBT (Figure 14.3). The group of buildings also has high performance in LEED®, reaching the Platinum level in the CS version 3 system, and has, as of 2020, the highest score in the system in Latin America. As in previous projects, the high technology of environmental regulation and the glass envelope are still present. The latter, however, is now uniform in the facade envelope, which represents a serious thermal load problem. Again, there is a contradiction between the symbolic values of incorporation—the glass envelope that reproduces the North American typology, as required by customers—and functional needs—an appropriate internal temperature for the use of spaces. In this case, the total glazing solution in a tropical context was impossible to be sufficiently addressed by the air-conditioning technology and the glass specification. For this reason, the project inserts, to reduce thermal load, internal sills and external sunshades (Figure 14.4). Both are resolved in order to guarantee a uniform reading of the towers: the sills receive a shadow box solution as a way of not interfering with the color of the glass, when seen from the outside; the sunshades are shallow and applied uniformly to the facades, despite the specific incidence of sunlight on each face. The solutions appear, therefore, in order to guarantee adequate thermal performance, but for symbolic reasons they are not used to their full potential, namely:

FIGURE 14.3 São Paulo Corporate Towers, designed by Pelli Clarke Pelli and aflalo/gasperini arquitetos (2015).

the disposition of the sills directly on the external surface, creating opaque areas that would reduce thermal absorption, and sunshades adapted to the variation of insolation.

The architecture of the glass towers of the CBDs is relatively ordinary when compared to the formal spectacularization of the *star system* throughout the 1990s and 2000s. But they

FIGURE 14.4 Facade detail. São Paulo Corporate Towers, designed by Pelli Clarke Pelli and aflalo/gasperini arquitetos (2015).

reveal in themselves, and in the distinction offered by the certification, the contradictory spatial precepts to which they respond. Four Times Square was a model for LEED®, and the persistence of its architectural solutions in Brazilian projects reveals how the corporate model of environmental architecture spread, in its own dispositions of continuity of the previous model of the glazed tower, isolated in the lot, now legitimized by the certification distinction, and, above all, now made possible by the improvement of design strategies that transform the mechanized prism, in a contradictory manner, into a globally implemented environmental model.

LEED® is a tool of globalization. As such, it no longer produces the form, as traditional architectural codes, but manages its disposition. The system allows globally distributed buildings to be assessed by identical parameters, and as such homogenizes the way an architectural object is created, as these buildings are designed from the possible points—and not by the inherent characteristics of local climates. This process leads to the global transaction of uniform architectural forms, such as the North American corporate typology, which we have seen throughout this text. Thus, the fulfillment of points is not linked to the ecological turn, but to obtain the distinction of the certificate, which is an index considered in real estate assessments. A certified real estate asset has a quality assurance, at least from the point of view of the market, and the standardized architectural design corresponds to the transparency of its financial evaluation, contributing to its liquidity as an easily recognizable asset in global real estate funds transactions, which is why the presence of LEED® in corporate typologies is so prominent. If postmodernism is a condition, both cultural and economic (Harvey, 1989), in which information and globalization operate together, the management of the architectural disposition performed by LEED® is one of the tools of the technical apparatus of this historic period—at the same time offering a content of sustainability and guaranteeing the fluidity of spatial forms and investments.

Acknowledgments

I would like to thank those interviewed for this chapter, whose identities have been kept anonymous.

The preparation of this work stems from a doctoral thesis (Grazziano, 2019). I am grateful to my supervisor, Prof. Dr. Luiz Recaman, and to the support by CAPES (in Master and Doctorate modalities) and São Paulo Research Foundation (protocols n. 2016/21407-0 and 2017/16322-8).

Notes

1. Data sourced from the LEED® Project Directory and considered up to the end of 2018.
2. *ASHRAE Standard 90.1–2007 Energy Standard for Buildings—Except Low-Rise Residential Buildings* resulted from a collaboration between the American Society of Heating, Refrigerating and Air-conditioning Systems (ASHRAE), the American National Standards Institute (ANSI), and the Illuminating Engineering Society of North America (IESNA).
3. The mechanized solution inhibited occupants' autonomy to adjust the lighting as they preferred, so that the obstruction of the blinds, in an attempt to control them, became common, according to reports by architects.

References

Banham, R. (1969). *The Architecture of the Well-Tempered Environment*. London, UK: The Architectural Press; Chicago, IL: The University of Chicago Press.

Boschmann, E.E., & Gabriel, J.N. (2013). Urban Sustainability and the LEED Rating System: Case Studies on the Role of Regional Characteristics and Adaptive Reuse in Green Building in Denver and Boulder, Colorado. *The Geographical Journal, 179*(3), 221–233. https://doi.org/10.1111/j.1475-4959.2012.00493.x

Buchanan, P. (2007). The Tower: An Anachronism Awaiting Rebirth? *Harvard Design Magazine* (26, New Skyscrapers in Megacities on a Warming Globe). Retrieved from www.harvarddesignmagazine.org/issues/26/the-tower-an-anachronism-awaiting-rebirth

Cavalcante, R.C.D. (2010). *Simulação Energética para Análise da Arquitetura de Edifícios de Escritório além da Comprovação de Conformidade com Códigos de Desempenho*. Master's Thesis, University of São Paulo. Digital Library of Theses and Dissertations of the University of São Paulo. https://doi.org/10.11606/D.16.2010.tde-01062010-144907

Dwaikat, L.N., & Ali, K.N. (2015). Green Buildings Cost Premium: A Review of Empirical Evidence. *Energy and Buildings, 110*, 396–403. http://doi.org/10.1016/j.enbuild.2015.11.021

Easterling, K. (2007). *Enduring Innocence: Global Architecture and its Political Masquerades*. Cambridge, MA: The MIT Press.

Easterling, K. (2012). We Will Be Making Active Form. *Architectural Design, 82*, 58–63.

Easterling, K. (2014). *Extrastatecraft: The Power of Infrastructure Space*. New York, NY; London, UK: Verso.

Fernández-Galiano, L. (2005). ¡La Economía, Ecologistas!: La Construcción Sostenible ante la Crisis del Petróleo. *Arquitectura Viva*, (105, Etiquetas Verdes), 23–25.

Glenn, D.S. (2003, October 1). Green Grows Up ... And Up and Up and Up. *Architectural Record*. Retrieved from www.architecturalrecord.com/articles/12266-green-grows-up-and-up-and-up-and-up

Gonçalves, J.C.S., & Umakoshi, É.M. (2010). *The Environmental Performance of Tall Buildings*. London, UK; Washington, DC: Earthscan.

Gottfried, D. (2014). *Explosion Green: One Man's Journey to Green the World's Largest Industry* (Preface by Paul Hawken; Introduction by Rick Fedrizzi). New York, NY: Morgan James.

Grazziano, R. (2019). *Virtualidades e Contradições no Espaço sob Padrões Globais: LEED® e Arquitetura Corporativa em São Paulo* (Virtualities and Contradictions in the Space Under Global Patterns: LEED® and Corporate Architecture in São Paulo). Doctoral Dissertation, University of São Paulo. Digital Library of Theses and Dissertations of the University of São Paulo. https://doi.org/10.11606/T.16.2019.tde-11122019-122755

Guerreiro, I.A. (2010). *Arquitetura-Capital: A Funcionalidade dos Edifícios Corporativos Paulistas.* Master Thesis, University of São Paulo. Digital Library of Theses and Dissertations of the University of São Paulo. https://doi.org/10.11606/D.16.2010.tde-10112010-162120

Harvey, D. (1989). *The Condition of Post-Modernity: An Enquiry into the Origins of Cultural Change.* Cambridge, MA; Oxford, UK: Wiley-Blackwell.

Jameson, F. (2015). The Aesthetics of Singularity. *New Left Review*, (92), 101–132.

Ouroussoff, N. (2007, November 20). Pride and Nostalgia Mix in The Times's New Home. *The New York Times.* Retrieved from https://archive.nytimes.com/www.nytimes.com/learning/teachers/featured_articles/20071121wednesday.html

Paiva, C., & Silva, J. (2008, June). Vidros Vedam e Criam Estruturas. *Finestra*, 26–41.

Percio, S.T.D. (2004). The Skyscraper, Green Design, & The LEED Green Building Rating System: The Creation of Uniform Sustainable Standards for the 21st Century or the Perpetuation of an Architectural Fiction? *Environs: Environmental Law and Policy Journal*, *28*(1), 117–154.

Sassen, S. (1991). *The Global City: New York, London, Tokyo.* Princeton, NJ; Oxford, UK: Princeton University Press.

Serapião, F. (2011). *A Arquitetura de Croce, Aflalo e Gasperini*. São Paulo, Brazil: Editora Paralaxe.

Stephens, S. (2000, March). Fox & Fowle Creates a Collage in Four Times Square, Using Skyscrapers Past and Present and a Touch of "Green". *Architectural Record*, 90–97.

USGBC. (2011). *LEED 2009 for New Construction and Major Renovations with Alternative Compliance Paths for Projects Outside the US; V. 3 Reference Guide.* Washington, DC: United States Green Building Council.

Yudelson, J. (2016). *Reinventing Green Building: Why Certification Systems Aren't Working and What We Can Do About It.* Gabriola Island, Canada: New Society Publishers.

15
WHAT EVER HAPPENED TO SOCIAL HOUSING?

Sergio Martín Blas

The changing role of social housing architecture in the Latin American cities can be condensed in a short historical period: from its pre-eminence and international acclaim in the 1950s to its fall under the instrumental assimilation of corrosive theories against centralized housing production systems since the late 1960s. Influential contributions to this latter criticism arising from different positions and contexts, such as John Turner's or Michel de Certeau's, stressed the emancipatory potentials of a social production of space and domesticity, appropriation tactics working against, beyond, or disconnected from the strategies of modern social housing architecture and planning.

In Europe after 2007–2008, when the so-called global financial crisis unleashed a wave of cuts in welfare state policies, consistent with the neoliberal agenda since the 1980s, civic movements claiming for a more democratic and participatory society, for alternative spaces and processes, brought such promises to the fore again. "Urban social movements, riots and uprisings" from that recent period (Mayer, Thörn, & Thörn, 2016) shared a wide diversity of models, tactics, and inspirations, from self-managed cooperatives to squatting or do-it-yourself building, and fostered a diffuse new interest in the Latin American informal city—a city that is often contemplated from a distance, in a binary relationship with the formal, bureaucratized, regulated city. High-profile designs for interventions in *favelas*, *villas*, *pueblos jóvenes*, and other informal settlements have been repeatedly approached in architectural schools and magazines since then (Leguía, 2011), while terms such as "tactical urbanism" (Gadanho, 2014) or "urban acupuncture" became widely spread and operative, extending their influence beyond their early formulations. Spanish architect Manuel de Solà-Morales, who claimed the original use of the acupunctural analogy, was clear about the risks of its reduction to "minor actions for the suture of urban tissues or minimum-cost improvements." In his view, acupuncture "is not related to the small, minute or delicate, but to the strategic, systemic and interdependent," and so demands the observation of a wider urban-territorial picture (Solà-Morales, 2008). A picture in which the so-called informal city can be seen, again, as the bleak outcome of segregation strategies, related to what Italian urban designer Bernardo Secchi identified as a "new urban question": the increasing social and spatial inequality of contemporary cities (Secchi, 2013/2015).

Avoiding the naïve association between self-built city and democratic or participatory society, and the correlation of urban planning and official housing policies with corrupted bureaucracy and inefficiency, it is time to ask again about the fate of social housing and its architecture.

A Splendid Landscape

It is generally acknowledged that social housing, under its manifold associated forms and names (affordable housing, public housing, low-rent housing, etc.), has been a central issue for the development of great cities in Latin America at a not-so-distant period in history, an issue that demanded the strongest commitment from modern architects. Even a superficial survey like the one carried out by the historian Henry-Russell Hitchcock for the famous 1955 Museum of Modern Art (MoMA) exhibition "Latin American architecture since 1945" allowed to praise "how high [were] Latin American ambitions in the field of public building" at the time, especially regarding public housing (Hitchcock, 1955, p. 123). Commenting on an impressive photograph of the housing estates at Cerro Piloto in Caracas and the rather straightforward architecture by Carlos Raúl Villanueva and the Banco Obrero team (Figures 15.1 and 15.2), Hitchcock offered a hint about the adequate distance and state of mind to fully appreciate the potential of large public building complexes:

> The wooded mountains serve as a splendid background for the very tall blocks and the rising terrain on both sides of the valley has necessitated much variety in the grouping of the nearby identical blocks. . . . The scale and pace of the operation justify on the whole the lack of finish in the execution. The result seems almost equivalent of a complete city and the vision of these loose groups of blocks set against the splendid landscape seems to realize one of the recurrent dreams of twentieth century urbanism.
>
> *(Hitchcock, 1955, p. 137)*

FIGURE 15.1 *23 de Enero* housing estate in Caracas (originally *2 de Diciembre*), architects Carlos Raúl Villanueva, José Hoffmann and José Manuel Mijares, 1955–1957.

FIGURE 15.2 Aerial view of Caracas in 1958, with Cerro Piloto in the background.

The recurring dream was, of course, the dream of a modern city as formulated in the 1933 Athens Charter, plus some local "flavor": gladly colored facades, low cost and low-quality details, and the dramatic relation with a sublime landscape. By 1955, when Hitchcock wrote his comment, that dream seemed unattainable outside of America, especially in Europe, where most of the great modern housing ensembles where still to come. Moreover, the image of Cerro Piloto included some accidental details that supported its oneiric atmosphere, like the veil of thick clouds that covered the "splendid landscape" mentioned by Hitchcock, thus transfigured into a mysterious and intriguing presence.

More than 60 years later, the cloudy veil has disappeared to expose how the landscape of Cerro Piloto turned into something radically different, yet familiar: the landscape of the so-called informal city (Figure 15.3). Such is the background against which the monumental social housing blocks built in the 1950s are set against now, manifesting how reality overflowed the limits of modern dreams and imaginations, or maybe expressing how naïve those dreams ultimately were. The dream of social reform operated by architecture, more precisely by modelling the everyday life through its physical scenario, i.e., housing (Evans, 1997 [1978]), gave way to a rough awakening.

The transformation of Cerro Piloto illustrates the often-assumed dichotomy between the formal and the informal city, which has operated as a framework for urban debates in Latin America in the last decades. Ironically, many of the contemporary discourses that challenge the validity of the dichotomy tend to relate the formal city to the oppressive authority of architects, agents working for the hegemonic powers, whereas the informal city would be the free and democratic expression of "the people" shaping their environment. By doing so, such discourses reproduce the same schematic dichotomy they are trying to contest (Hernández, Kellet, & Allen, 2010).

Besides, the praise of the historically overlooked virtues of the informal or "free" city, the possibility of unveiling and understanding some of its hidden values and qualities, or the potential exploitation of its picturesque charm, are recurrently related to the same concept Hitchcock used in the 1950s to extol the poetics of mass social housing: the concept of landscape (Broudehoux, 2001, p. 274). The graphical contents on show at the "Uneven Growth" MoMA exhibition of 2014–2015 or the language used by influential scholars and practitioners such as Rahul

FIGURE 15.3 *Cerros de Caracas.* From the series "Caracas una quimera urbana," 1982.

Mehrotra illustrate the ambiguous connections between landscape and informality (Mehrotra, 2013; Lerner, 2015). The association is especially significant since the traditional definition of *landscape* implies a pictorial or picturesque situation given by the perception from a point of view, and points of view are usually conveniently distanced when dealing with the tough realities of the informal city. Detachment is, ultimately, the simplest prerequisite informing the taste for the sublime that stems from the explorations of Kant or Schopenhauer: the mix of pleasure and pain provided by the contemplation of a daunting landscape implies the necessity of framing mechanisms and conceptual stability (Wilson, 2017, p. 43). The dialectic between detachment and immersion arises, in fact, as one of the crucial issues to analyze the contemporary Latin American city.

Ethics, Aesthetics

Mass housing architecture following modern ideals was a primary target of harsh criticisms during the 1960s and 1970s, diverging from earlier and more cautious attempts to introduce corrections and instructive admonitions in the modern discourse. Rigidity, formalism, inhuman homologation, sheer dimension, cold machinism, and oppressive control were some of the problematic issues related to modern social housing ensembles. That was also the period in which Marxist critical materialism achieved its highest academic reputation, dominating what Peter Hall called "the city of theory" (Hall, 1988/1994, pp. 385–413). By the mid-1970s, the most popular works by Henri Lefebvre, Manuel Castells, or David Harvey converged with anarchist-inspired approaches to the city and housing, such as John Turner's or Colin Ward's, to attack the hegemonic powers governing the development of modern cities (Lefebvre, 1968, 1972; Castells, 1977; Harvey, 1973; Turner, 1963, 1977; Ward, 1976). The centralized production systems of modern social housing continued to be eroded in the following years under the effect of contributions stemming from different premises and methods, such as those of Brazilian architect Sérgio Ferro or French thinker Michel de Certeau (Ferro, 1979/2005; De Certeau, 1980/1988).

Assuming their diversity, all of these approaches shared the display of an ethical posture, rhetorically opposed to the aesthetic formalism and abstraction of modern architecture. The most typical design tools of Modernism were the instrumental premise of such formalism and contributed in a decisive way to its detachment from real life. Knowing the parallel processes of construction in Brasilia and the informal city built by the people who worked in its realization, Sérgio Ferro tried to uncover the way architectural drawing implied the oppression of the construction worker. The hegemonic role of drawing (expression of the architectural project) is the key to understanding the despotic system of building market production, according to Ferro:

> The fundamental function of drawing today is to enable the market form of the architectural object, which could not be realized without that drawing (if not under conditions of marginality). . . . Whether this drawing is, according to some of its features, depending on superior powers, whether it is already submitted to the capital since its creation or not, those are only restrictions that don't undermine its structural necessity: being an imperative part of the despotic direction. It is only as reason detached from concretion, effect of the breaking of production by violence, that drawing is what it is: an arrangement that, in order to be arranged, is dominated and passes top-down the forms of the force over which it appears, works and governs.
>
> (Ferro, 1979/2005, p. 23)

Drawing, as an agent of formal control and stable aesthetic value, prevents the fulfillment of the worker, its moral emancipation. In Ferro's work, as in other ruling critical discourses of the 1960s and 1970s, ethics and aesthetics were placed in an implicit dialectical confrontation: housing and architecture in general should stem from the first, with the latter being no more than a frivolous modern concern. Such schematic terms proved to conceal strong contradictions in the following decades, as the idea of a moral position devoid of aesthetics proved to be as naïve as the opposite (a formal language devoid of ideological and ethical connotations). In fact, some of the most rigorously ethical discourses derived into formal experimentation under the special conditions of academic ivory towers.

Today, the intricate interweaving of ethics and aesthetics in architecture cannot be overlooked or oversimplified, even if that is still an uncomfortable assumption in some contexts. Even the most referential and pioneering contributions to the ethical revolt against modern formalism, such as John Turner's, implied a tacit rethinking of aesthetic categories, too. Or is it just a coincidence that Umberto Eco's research and writings on the *Opera Aperta*, the open work of art (Eco, 1962), and Turner's claims from Peru about self-built housing as an open, ongoing process (Turner, 1963) were developed at the same time?

Turner and Ruskin

Working as an architect in the *barriadas* (informal settlements) of Arequipa and Lima since the late 1950s, John Turner was able to confirm the strong contrast between public housing policies, focused on the construction of big housing estates, and the reality of "huge areas of spontaneous dwelling that extend over the world," claiming "control for millions of autonomous builders" (Turner, 1976/1977, p. 164). According to Turner, workers, builders, "the people," must be free to build their own houses, while institutions should provide urban infrastructures and building materials. People were solving "the housing problem" by themselves, outside the public policies that failed *de facto* to provide adequate dwelling qualities and quantities, thus skipping the corrupt bureaucracies and inefficiencies of institutionalized systems. Individual freedom versus the highly inefficient centralized policies for housing production, those were the basic terms in Turner's narrative. The same visionary and emphatic tone promoted further, often contradictory, simplifications and instrumentalizations: for example, that "freedom to build" and "power for the user" implied no public investment or role for the institutions at all.

Anyway, it is interesting to remember that long before John Turner praised the virtues of the free builder or Sérgio Ferro claimed the emancipation of construction workers, 19th-century Romanticism codified the ethic and aesthetic contents of architectural freedom. "If there is perpetual change both in design and execution, the workman must have been set altogether free," wrote John Ruskin, a fellow countryman of John Turner, in the most quoted chapter of *The Stones of Venice*, the one devoted to "The Nature of Gothic" (Ruskin, 1853/1981, p. 122). The free participation of the builder in the ever-changing process of design and execution was, for Ruskin, a moral imperative and a way to achieve a higher level of rationality regarding the "practical needs" that arose in every building process. Such freedom made of Gothic not just the "only rational architecture," but also the fittest style for a nation of free men, a nation distinguished by the "habit of hard and rapid working," "the love of fact" against the love of design, the "strength of will," the "tendency to set the individual reason against authority," and the "intolerance to excessive control" (Ruskin, 1853/1981, p. 131).

Furthermore, practical necessity and freedom were, in Ruskin's view, sources of imperfection that complied with aesthetic demands, and more precisely with the implicitly romantic appreciation of the picturesque, the delights of difference and surprise:

> The architect . . . whom we will suppose capable of doing all in perfection, cannot execute the whole with his own hands, he must either make slaves of his workmen . . . and level his work to a slave's capacities, which is to degrade it; or else he must take his workmen as he finds them, and let them show their weakness together with their strength, which will involve . . . imperfection.
>
> Nothing that lives is, or can be, rigidly perfect. . . . And in all things that live there are certain irregularities and deficiencies which are not only signs of life, but sources of beauty. All admit irregularity as they imply change.
>
> *(Ruskin, 1853/1981, p. 121)*
>
> The variety . . . is the more healthy and beautiful, because in many cases it is entirely unstudied, and results, not from mere love of change, but from practical necessities.
>
> *(Ruskin, 1853/1981, p. 123)*

Of course, all of these aesthetic virtues are alien to classical architecture, and especially to formal control exercised through architectural drawing as codified during the Renaissance and assumed throughout the Modern Era. No surprise, then, if Ruskin claims that the proud moral nature of Gothic, expression of the strength of will of the tribes of the North, is opposed to the languid tribes of the South and their architecture—a racist overtone frequently skipped over by contemporary commentators on his work.

Back to John Turner and his followers, which seemed to multiply in recent years, the taste for variety and the irregular city is neither explicit nor directly related to their moral ideas about freedom and popular emancipation, but the link seems as unavoidable as the Romantic ascendance of such ideas. This and other socially committed discourses about an alternative architecture and city are no doubt prevailing again, after decades of relative disdain for any strong ethical position, while the aesthetic dimension of such approaches remains typically muted.

Great Expectations

A cloud of mystery similar to the one that wrapped the Cerro Piloto seems to conceal the so-called informal city in Latin America, in spite of the significant efforts of immersion, survey or visualization carried out in the last decades, even by architects. Little certainties can be asserted today regarding its reality, still largely covered by myths, common places, and a general lack of direct knowledge.

However, at least two recurrent conditions can be settled as premises to understand the current nature of informal urbanization. First, it is evident that most of the informal settlements today are far from the emancipatory ideals envisaged by John Turner and others since the 1960s. In fact, most evidences show that they are often the result of highly controlled and centralized procedures, not informal but simply illegal, that fit within harder segregation processes and tend to consolidate inequality (Davis, 2006). Second, discourses claiming the freedom to build and the need to dismantle the centralized production of public housing have been instrumental to the neoliberal turn, not only in Latin America. In this regard Peru is, again, the champion, with the economist Hernando de Soto as the guru of the unregulated city and the miraculous "conversion" of poor squatters into real estate entrepreneurs (Golda-Pongratz, 2018).

Looking at the other side of John Turner's medal, the problems derived from the highly centralized production of social housing should not be forgotten either. For what can be worse than the inhuman rigidity and homogeneity of mass housing? Well, we probably have seen worse spread in the pages of architectural magazines during the last years: worse than the absolute lack of variety is the fake variety and difference produced by architects at the drawing table, regardless of real dwelling processes and the tendency towards deep homogenization fed by market and regulatory frameworks (Figure 15.4). Even Jane Jacobs, whose ideas have been blamed as an inspiration for the cozy sceneries of New Urbanism, realized the "unavoidable esthetic dilemma" posed by homogeneity in the early 1960s:

> Shall the homogeneity look as homogeneous as it is, and be frankly monotonous? Or shall it try not to look as homogenous as it is and go for eye-catching, but meaningless and chaotic differences?
>
> *(Jacobs, 1961/1992, p. 226)*

In Europe, the pursuit of difference and variety has become a pervading tendency related to collective housing, useful to evoke customization or spontaneity and thus to soften the realizations of large-scale (public or private) developers. Some of the referential images of social housing architecture in the last decades, from the Silodam building in Amsterdam (MVRDV, 2003) or the subtler Brunnenhofstrasse complex in Zurich (Gigon & Guyer, 2009) to the spectacular realizations promoted by EMVS in Madrid, like the buildings in Carabanchel by Dosmasunoarquitectos (2007) or by Amann, Cánovas, and Maruri (2009), are eloquent enough in this sense. In most cases, such variety was produced by a calculated composition, far from the genuine variations created by the diverging actions of different agents or by accumulative

FIGURE 15.4 Cerro San Cristóbal in Lima, 2015 (left), and Silodam housing building in Amsterdam, MVRDV, 2003 (right).

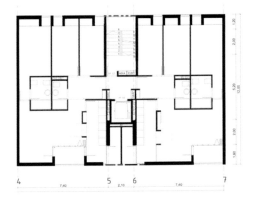 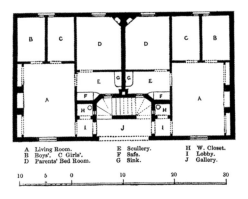

FIGURE 15.5 Social housing units for EMVS in Vallecas, Madrid, 2011 (left), and plan of Model House for Four Families, London, 1851 (right).

processes in time. Playful facade configurations have frequently concealed the reproduction of the same old internal spatialities for social housing, the ones codified in the 1920s that Robin Evans implicitly related to the mid-19th-century ideas of social reform through "decent" housing architecture: separation of family apartments, separation of family members and activities inside the apartment, reduction of communal space to a minimum, enabling circulation and access, and the more general principle of "specifying movement and distinguishing spaces" (Evans, 1978/1997, p. 107) (Figure 15.5).

In some more interesting and consistent cases, the search for variety in housing ambitioned to be actually related to tailor-made production, real customization, or the implementation of participatory processes involving the inhabitants. The personalized solutions in the context of new cooperative and building community housing—like the famous Kalkbreite complex in Zurich (2014) or other smaller-scale cases in Berlin (R50, 2013; Spreefeld, 2014), Hamburg

(Neue Hamburg Terrassen, 2013), Vienna (Krakauer Strasse, 2013), and Barcelona (La Borda, 2018), the individual adaptation and transformation of open frameworks and spaces, as in the Tila building in Helsinki (2009–2011) or in the influential housing proposals by the French architects Lacaton & Vassal, or the several do-it-yourself and customized housing experiences in the Netherlands and the UK—are expressive examples of that pursuit. Of course, variety and difference could be the result of a real process, not only of a nice composition in the architect's mind. And that's where the increasing interest for Latin American informal housing practices can play an instrumental role, together with the re-discovery of the old question of incremental housing, from the most notorious historical achievements, such as PREVI-Lima, to the recent proposals of Alejandro Aravena.

Memory is, however, selective. Pioneering experiences in incremental housing since the 1950s in Argentina, Colombia, Mexico, Brazil, and other countries have been somehow "forgotten" in favor of Aravena's "originality," acknowledged with a Pritzker Prize in 2016. A year before that recognition was granted, MoMA hosted the exhibition *Latin America in Construction: Architecture 1955–1980*, resuming Henry-Russell Hitchcock's historical overview. Even if housing assumed a significant part of the new exhibition's discourse, the boldness of large public housing estates such as Nonoalco-Tlatelolco in Mexico City or the 23 de Enero complex in Caracas was somehow downplayed in favor of other, alternative approaches to housing like, again, PREVI. The prize awarded to Aravena, allegedly related to "his commitment to social housing" (Breyer, 2016) in projects like the notorious Quinta Monroy in Iquique (2004), and the motto for the 2016 Venice Biennale curated by himself, "Reporting from the Front," helped to glimpse an unavoidable shift in the culture of architects. Apparently, these and other events pointed to a renewed social engagement and supported the hope that low-cost housing or social housing could become a central issue for architects again, with Latin America leading the shift. Social housing architecture in Latin America was necessarily back, one could say in 2015–2016, when such great expectations contrasted with the consequences of the global financial crisis, especially in Europe.

Participation Society

The European context before 2015 was sharply outlined and criticized by the Italian scholar Bernardo Secchi in his last book, originally published in 2013 and translated into Spanish and other languages since 2015 (Secchi, 2013/2015). Standing at the top of his international recognition as an urban planner and researcher, Secchi was bold enough to avoid the euphemisms of political correctness, starting from a striking title: *The city of the rich and the city of the poor*. The book is, in fact, one of the most accurate and relevant contributions to the understanding of cities after the recent crisis. A point to keep in mind is that *The city of the rich and the city of the poor* is mainly about European cities. According to Secchi's analysis, rising social inequality is one of the fundamental traits of a "new urban question" (the expression implicitly refers to Manuel Castell's work of 1972) that challenges the "European tradition," which he identifies with the modern techniques for social inclusion:

> some of the legal, institutional, procedural, and spatial devices put forward by European architects and urban planners of the XXth century seem much more sophisticated if compared to what later practices would show; they stand as the attempt to ensure that the material conditions in which rich and poor people choose, are induced or forced to live, are less distant than their respective incomes and properties.
>
> *(Secchi, 2013/2015, pp. 78–79)*

This tradition would be clearly distinguishable from the urban developments in Latin America or the US, where history often led to "separation, alienation and social exclusion, instead of inclusion" (Secchi, 2013/2015, p. 77). Now, the European city, under "the ideology of market and the rhetoric of security" (Secchi, 2013/2015, p. 86), has finally turned, since the last decades of the 20th century, into a space of rising inequality, modelled by several forces: "rich people's greed, the gradual dismantling of the welfare state and the degradation of life standards of the poorest social groups" (Secchi, 2013/2015, p. 84).

Secchi appeals, in an apparently outdated fashion, to the responsibility of urban planners and other technicians who deal with formal and spatial control. A claim that was in clear contrast with the now popular mistrust for the specialists and call for citizen participation as the only path towards urban equality and true democracy. It is not unlikely, still, that Secchi's long experience allowed for an easy prediction: ironically, the call for a more participatory society in Europe has been quickly instrumentalized by the discourses that surreptitiously support the dismantling of welfare state policies, including public housing policies, or what was left of such policies in the early 21st century. The speech from the throne of the Dutch King Willem-Alexander on September 17, 2013 has remained a milestone in this regard:

> It is an undeniable reality that in today's network and information society people are both more assertive and more independent than in the past. This, combined with the need to reduce the budget deficit, means that the classical welfare state is slowly but surely evolving into a participation society. Everyone who is able will be asked to take responsibility for their own lives and immediate surroundings. . . . [T]he classical post-war welfare state produced schemes that are unsustainable in their present form and which no longer meet people's expectations. In today's world, people want to be able to make their own choices, manage their own lives and take care of one another.
> *(Royal House of The Netherlands, 2013)*

The classical welfare state of the second half of the 20th century was declared obsolete and had to be replaced by a "participation society" for the sake of sustainability and "mutual engagement." Participation, sustainability, engagement . . . words generically associated with counter-hegemonic discourses that have recurrently proved to be useful for hegemonic goals. In this sense, "participation society" could be easily translated into a do-it-yourself society, or a try-to-get-by society, also in the field of housing, definitely burying the idea of public housing. Such is surely a distant prospect in a country like the Netherlands, but the tendency to dissolve public intervention and planning is clear in a broader European scene.

This is the context in which the claims for a free unregulated housing market and for an informal or free housing production involving citizen participation tend to converge into one of the most dangerous oversimplifications of our time: thinking that individual freedom and free private initiative will lead to a more democratic city and environment. Such simplification is somehow like thinking that democracy can be reduced to voting, ignoring the need to articulate public, group, and individual interests through legal frameworks. Can the common social interest implied in cities be fulfilled by "free" housing construction?

A parallel and similarly naïve oversimplification is assuming that public housing policies and public housing architecture are by nature oppressive, non-democratic, or dissociated from popular interests anyhow. Discourses that stem from this kind of premise tend to forget how housing and other public policies contributed to the reduction of inequalities in recent history.

Acknowledging the paradoxes of a welfare state, in which equal distribution can imply the cancellation of diversity and difference, and the broad influence of the criticism of everyday life since the 1980s, Bernardo Secchi concludes:

> The critical rage in the last decades of the XXth century against public housing programs, urban planning and urban design, or the construction of a welfare state through housing, public facilities, green areas and infrastructures, has probably led to underestimate the contributions of European urban policies in this regard.
>
> (Secchi, 2013/2015, p. 68)

In fact, critical rage and underestimation have been followed by a physical rage too, a rage against the traces of public housing policies. The "global rage to eliminate the evidence of the post-war period of architecture as a social project," in Rem Koolhaas' words (Koolhaas, 2010), found one of its main targets in social housing architecture, and extended even to its most iconic vestiges, such as the recently demolished Robin Hood Gardens housing estate in London (Martín Blas, 2018).

What Ever Happened?

Bernardo Secchi's remarks about the role of public housing and urban planning policies in relation to the "new urban question" of inequality are highly relevant, also in Latin America. The narrative that identifies great Latin American cities with extreme social inequality has been supported in the last years by iconic images such as Tuca Vieira's all-pervading photograph of the border between the affluent district of Morumbi and the favela of Paraisópolis in São Paulo, included in the 2007 exhibition "Global Cities" at the Tate Modern in London, or the less notorious but equally expressive *Panorámicas* of Lima (2011) by photographer Roberto Huarcaya. Such striking urban images promoted a supposedly new awareness and prepared the ground for the discourses that claimed a return to the housing problem by architects and planners, and the leading role Latin American experiences could play in that regard, as mentioned earlier (Figure 15.6).

However, it's time to consider the actual impact of those discourses, its relation to practice and policies, and wonder what really happened to social housing architecture in Latin American cities. The first thing to be noticed in this sense is that, in many cases, social housing has been weakened in qualitative terms, but not in quantitative ones. State programs such as *Mivivienda* in Peru, *Minha Casa Minha Vida* in Brazil, or *Procrear* in Argentina seem to prove that public investments in new housing construction have been significant in the last decades, but housing architecture or the opportunity to promote inclusive forms of urbanity through spatial planning were somehow taken out of the equation, or subordinated to other interests, with few exceptions. Indeed, the names of these and other public programs (my house, my house—my life, procreate) point to deeply atavistic urges like the possession of the house as a life purpose, or biological reproduction related to house ownership, which implicitly deny any articulation of social demands or their evolution through housing and urban design. Quite the contrary, they seem to retreat to the simple provision of housing units for traditional families.

However, the significant public investments that deal with the transformation of the informal city have often attained the provision of urban services and qualities, but induced little or no impact on housing architecture. The resulting dichotomy of public housing policies has been

FIGURE 15.6 The so-called wall of shame in Lima, defining the border between the informal housing at Pamplona Alta and the affluent neighborhood of Casuarinas, 2015.

sharply formulated by Anahí Ballent and Francisco Liernur, commenting on the Argentinian experience:

> the "right to the city" quite appropriately rivals with the "right to the house." Practical experience shows us that, in the specific products that result from public policies, both terms can be mutually excluded: we find houses with no urbanity, designs for decent housing units with a weak relation to the city and its benefits; or urban benefits with no housing, mainly in the cases of consolidation of popular settlements located in sectors with a high provision of urban services, but containing units that frequently lack any spatial, constructive or structural qualities.
>
> *(Ballent & Liernur, 2014, p. 14)*

As for the role of the architect, little or no changes can be identified regarding the disciplinary dislocations from housing architecture since the 1970s in Latin America. Many of those who considered the "housing problem" to be the main priority migrated to other disciplinary fields (social, political, economic), discarding, sometimes with disdain, architecture and its specific tools like drawing or design. Conversely, most of those that stood up for Architecture with a capital "A" abandoned the complexities and compromises of low-cost, affordable or social housing, in favor of more profiting and photogenic issues, despite Aravena's ambiguous contributions and other exceptional cases.[1]

Finally, what happened to social housing architecture in the Latin American city is that it became a preferred subject for historians and critics such as the aforementioned Liernur or the Spanish Carlos Sambricio (Sambricio, 2012), both related to a Tafurian ascendance that can be grouped together with other resurrected Marxist-inspired readings about the city, such as the ones of Henri Lefebvre or David Harvey. Apparently, our cities must be once more understood as a manifestation or testimony of a broader political, economic, and social context. As a result, one could wonder if social housing architecture is now, in the current political context, nothing more than a has-been, a grotesque and intriguing shadow with a glorious past, such as Henry Farrell's Baby Jane. There's little doubt that hegemonic powers are comfortable with such a view. And it should be equally obvious, then, that the critical categories that were used to corrode public housing architecture between the 1960s and 1980s cannot be fully operative in the current context, when tactics of appropriation and immediate actions seem to be perfectly compatible with hegemonic powers, and spatial planning strategies and programs (including social housing programs) have long become residual.

Anyway, the possibility that social housing contributes to a city in which the public and collective dimensions are not lost, in which inequality is contested by specific techniques, is still there. It implies, as a premise, putting architecture back into the housing problem in Latin America, acknowledging the spatial, formal, and material components inherent to social dynamics, but also reactivating the impact of public policies and institutions in the promotion of common interests. Disabling the rhetorical confrontation between public sector and private interests, and the sneaky "third way" solutions, either populistic or surreptitiously neoliberal, would be a valuable contribution from the academy—a task that seems as urgent as reconstructing the bridges between critical, historical discourses on social housing and the architect's drawing table.

Note

1. The case of the Pelli brothers epitomizes in an unparalleled, almost Dickensian way this second dichotomy, with César Pelli as one of the most renowned architects of the global star-system and his brother Víctor Pelli working on the social production of habitat for the poorest regions of the Argentinian North.

References

Ballent, A., & Liernur, J.F. (2014). *La Casa y la Multitud: Vivienda, Política y Cultura en la Argentina Moderna*. Buenos Aires, Argentina: Fondo de Cultura Económica.
Breyer, S., Ho Chang, Y., Feireiss, K., Murcutt, G. et al. (2016). *The Pritzker Architecture Prize 2016 Jury Citation*. Retrieved on April 1, 2019 from www.pritzkerprize.com/jury-citation-ale-jan-dro-ara-ve-na
Broudehoux, A. (2001). Image Making, City Marketing and the Aesthetization of Social Inequality in Rio de Janeiro. In N. Alsayaad (Ed.), *Consuming Tradition/Manufacturing Heritage: Global Norms and Urban Forms in an Age of Tourism* (pp. 273–297). London, UK: Routledge.
Castells, M. (1977). *The Urban Question: A Marxist Approach*. London, UK: Edward Arnold (Original work published 1972).
Davis, M. (2006). *Planet of Slums*. London, UK: Verso.
De Certeau, M. (1988). *The Practice of Everyday Life*. Berkeley, Los Angeles, CA: University of California Press. (Original work published 1980).
Eco, U. (1962). *Opera Aperta: Forma e Indeterminazione delle Poetiche Contemporanee*. Milan, Italy: Bompiani.
Evans, R. (1997). Rookeries and Model Dwellings: English Housing Reform and the Moralities of Private Space. In *Translations from Drawing to Building and Other Essays* (pp. 93–117). London, UK: Architectural Association (Original work published 1978).
Ferro, S. (2005). *Dessin/Chantier*. Paris, France: Eds. de La Villette (Original work published 1979).
Gadanho, P. (2014). *Uneven Growth: Tactical Urbanisms for Expanding Megacities*. New York, NY: The Museum of Modern Art.
Golda-Pongratz, K. (2018). Lecturas contemporáneas de las barriadas turnerianas: nuevas identidades y nuevos retos de la Lima emergente. In K. Golda-Pongratz, J.L. Oyón, & V. Zimmermann (Eds.), *John

F. C. Turner, *Autoconstrucción: por una autonomía del habitar* (pp. 257–292). Logroño, Spain: Pepitas de Calabaza.
Hall, P. (1994). *Cities of Tomorrow.* Oxford, UK; Cambridge, MA: Blackwell. (Original work published 1988).
Harvey, D. (1973). *Social Justice and the City.* London, UK: Edward Arnold.
Hernández, F., Kellet, P., & Allen, L.K. (2010). *Rethinking the Informal City: Critical Perspectives from Latin America.* Oxford, UK; New York, NY: Berghahn Books.
Hitchcock, H. (1955). *Latin American Architecture since 1945.* New York, NY: The Museum of Modern Art.
Jacobs, J. (1992). *The Death and Life of Great American Cities.* New York, NY: Vintage Books. (Original work published 1961).
Koolhaas, R. (2010). *Venice Biennale 2010: Cronocaos.* Introductory text retrieved on March 2019 from https://oma.eu/projects/venice-biennale-2010-cronocaos.
Lefebvre, H. (1968). *Le droit à la ville.* Paris, France: Éditions Anthropos.
Lefebvre, H. (1972). *Espace et politique: Le droit à la ville II.* Paris, France: Éditions Anthropos.
Leguía, M. (Ed.). (2011). Latin America at the Crossroads. *Architectural Design, 81*(3).
Lerner, J. (2015). Growing Pains. *Landscape Architecture Magazine, 105*(1), 110–119.
Martín Blas, S. (2018). Robin Hood Gardens: Casa e Monumento. *Rassegna di Architettura e Urbanistica, 155,* 46–54.
Mayer, M., Thörn, C., & Thörn, H. (Eds.). (2016). *Urban Uprisings: Challenging Neoliberal Urbanism in Europe.* London, UK: Palgrave Macmillan.
Mehrotra, R. (2013). Re-Thinking the Informal City. *Area, 128*(May–June), 6–11.
Royal House of The Netherlands. (2013). *Speech from the Throne 2013.* Retrieved on March 2019 from www.royal-house.nl/documents/speeches/2013/09/17/speech-from-the-throne-2013
Ruskin, J. (1981). *The Stones of Venice.* London, UK: Faber and Faber. (Original work published 1853).
Sambricio, C. (Ed.). (2012). *Ciudad y Vivienda en América Latina 1930–1960.* Madrid, Spain: Lampreave.
Secchi, B. (2015). *La Ciudad de los Ricos y la Ciudad de los Pobres.* Madrid, Spain: Los libros de la Catarata. (Original work published in Italian in 2013).
Solà-Morales, M. (2008). De Cosas Urbanas. In M. Solà-Morales (Ed.), *De Cosas Urbanas* (pp. 17–30). Barcelona: Gustavo Gili.
Turner, J.F.C. (1963). Village Artisan's Self-Built House. *Architectural Design, 33,* 361–362.
Turner, J.F.C. (1977). *Vivienda: Todo el Poder para los Usuarios.* Madrid, Spain: Blume. (Original work published 1976).
Ward, C. (1976). *Housing: An Anarchist Approach.* London, UK: Freedom Press.
Wilson, S. (2017). The Aesthetics of Immersion and Detachment in the British Natural Sublime: A Historical Perspective. *Environment, Space, Place, 9*(1), 43–62. Retrieved from www.jstor.org/stable/10.5749/envispacplac.9.1.0043

16

FIVE FRONTS FOR ONE SINGLE POSITION

Critical Strategies for Contemporary Pedagogy in the Subject of Architectural Design

Carmen Espegel Alonso and Daniel Movilla Vega

This chapter should be understood as a work in process dedicated to the elaboration of a teaching operative system for the field of architecture that corresponds to some of the main questions posed to the discipline in the first decades of the 21st century. These are ideas arising from practical activities, in the field of design and teaching, presented as a system that is open, changeable, and ongoing. In parallel to the text, a recent experience of a social housing project located in the central region of Madrid will be exposed. The leitmotiv of this text, *"what is necessary,"* is relevant in order to express what we understand is the basic theme of teaching design: *"what is possible."* To learn how to design is possible, and if it can also be done from an ethical stance, then it becomes more than just feasible, it is a must. In this context, it is important not to confuse what is necessary with what is a contingency or with what is probable. Far from this, the meaning of necessity that interests us, refers to a method of explanation of a cause of action. To verbalize is to think, to rationalize certain genuine intuitions in order to communicate them.

Five fronts and a single position inform the structure that explains a necessary approach faced with teaching design. These five points constitute the warp that weaves all aspects of this document together. They synthesize an ideological framework:

1. The first, the *architect with criteria*, refers to the ultimate goal of our teaching, which is none other than to train people to think independently and understand the role they will play in the society of their time.
2. *Feminine scenarios* is a call for the need to apprehend—in the sense of appropriation—mechanisms that have been traditionally used by women with positive and transformative purposes.
3. *More autonomy, more collectivity* stresses the importance of the development of students as individuals without losing sight of the social component.
4. *Shared thoughts* focuses on the form of education, which is based on a "collective professor" or group of professors instead of the classical single view and path seen in a classical master-student relationship.
5. Lastly, the key issue that structures this text is that by means of two components, *research* and *critique*, students can gradually enhance their own talent.

Our goal is to articulate a pedagogy that is historically determined and has a practical finality, based on theoretical research with applied knowledge and on the capacity to analyze, think, and produce an operative critique in relationship with instrumental dexterities. And all of this is within a changeable context regarding both theoretical principles and the specific practice of architecture, since the latter is also based on self-knowledge.

While outlining this position with respect to teaching architectural design, we would like to recall the belligerent stance taken by Igor Stravinsky during the six master classes he gave about the Poetics of Music when he delivered the Charles Eliot Norton Lectures at Harvard in 1939:

> . . . this shady collusion of "ignorance . . . and malice" . . . justifies a rebuttal, a loyal and vigorous defense. . . . So I am obliged to be polemical.
>
> *(Stravinsky, 1947)*

This is also our stance. The following is an explanation of our motives and arguments, and based on them, we can begin a debate.

First Front: The Architect With Criteria

Curator, art critic, developer, professor, movie set or theater stage designer, consultant, participatory manager, researcher, politician—from councilperson to mayor . . . of all of these professionals, who are we training? We think that an architect is no longer someone who actually studies architecture, but somebody who is capable of acting efficiently and involved in all matters of architecture.

Most architecture schools still contemplate a dated model in which the role of the architect remains almost the same as it was 50 years ago. Since then, the practice has changed dramatically. The role of the professional has evolved. It has become more multi-functional, with practices that do not fall within the traditional definition of the architect as builder, such as the design and programming of digital environments, the production of moving images, the participation in editorial projects, the management of cultural initiatives or digital fabrication, among others.

What is the common denominator of all of these practices? We could call it *criteria*, in the full definition of the term. That is, knowledge of a set of standards that provide a base for a decision and the ability to make judgments that lead to this decision.

The students of today, as the architects of the future, need to be involved in their profession from a critical standpoint, one that is resilient, proactive, and committed. Their interests must focus on the dynamic processes of architecture and landscape, and incorporate collaborations among the different disciplines that plan and define the city.

The reevaluation of urban identity, the transfer of public space to enable its sustainable recovery, territorial mobility, and more permeable metropolitan environments, or a more efficient management of participation are themes that show the criticality of a student.

In sum, the idea is to help the future architect to acquire a critical stance in order to straddle pairs of opposing views: between what is institutionally sanctioned and what has not been consigned, between art and context, between what is explicit and what is implicit, and between what is temporary and what is permanent. That is, to give the student tools to find her way in a society in which the economic and professional models have been exhausted, in which there are hardly any certainties, all in order to try to mitigate, as best as possible, the devastating interpretation of our world made by the economist Thomas Piketty, when he states: "capitalism automatically generates arbitrary and unsustainable inequalities that radically undermine the meritocratic values on which democratic societies are based" (Piketty, 2014, p. 15).

Second Front: Feminine Scenarios

> I received an email telling me it was over. I didn't know how to respond. It was almost as if it hadn't been meant for me. It ended with the words, "Take care of yourself." And so I did. I asked 107 women (including two made from wood and one with feathers), chosen for their profession or skills, to interpret this letter. To analyze it, comment on it, dance it, sing it. Dissect it. Exhaust it. Understand it for me. Answer for me. It was a way of taking the time to break up. A way of taking care of myself.
>
> *(Calle, 2008)*

We also claim a new attitude regarding the specific ways in which women are contributing to Western society. The idea is to understand the value provided by the light, egalitarian, and caring tools that have derived from the methodologies promoted by the feminist movements of the 1970s. This would entail advancing and highlighting the contexts that, up until then, had belonged to the realm of women: domesticity, the experience of everyday life versus grand discourses, shared intimacy. To this, we must add the importance of small things (Roy, 1997), the symbolic processes of the body, emotional flows, or the un-codified introduction of affectivity, all of which will become part of the teaching program. These minor topics contribute greatly to an architecture that strives to build horizontal affectivities or feelings, according to Agnes Heller (1979) or emotions by Cheshire Calhoun and Robert C. Solomon (1984), one that is probably less hierarchical, bodiless, and perhaps contrary and estranged from the logic of over-abundance that has characterized the profession.

We strongly believe that it is within the feminine world where the celebration of life takes place, with an emphasis in the present and leaving behind few traces. As architects, our role is to dignify the multi-functional capability that women have traditionally within the routine of domestic space. In this sense, for us, architecture, simply put, will be life itself. If, in the beginning, the goal was to improve the conditions of women, with the passing of time what has come about is "a corpus of thought and action in which emancipation has prefigured the entire set of cultural practices that explore the autonomous conditions of the self, constituting useful tools for any realm of thought and life" (Nieto Fernández, 2012, p. 246, translated into English).

Certain cultural prejudices regarding gender, such as invisibility, identity, self-limitations, stereotypes, and social routines, must be overcome in order to truly value other cultures that are almost definitely more adaptive and versatile, innovative, propositional, and transformational, but are doubtlessly necessary in our society.

Third Front: More Individuality, More Collectivity

The great debate of the 20th century around the goals of education revolved around two very different approaches that were considered mutually exclusive. For the first, the main objective of all education was the development of the conscience and the social reciprocity of the individual, whereas for the second, the idea was to promote her uniqueness as a person. Now, in the 21st century, we understand with Herbert Read that education must be simultaneously a process of individualization and one of social integration—that is, of reconciliation between the uniqueness of the individual and social unity (Read, 1958). Therefore, our position is that education needs to densify the social network without diminishing the autonomy of the individual.

The truth is the truth, whether Agamemnon or his swineherd says it.

> *Agamemnon:* I agree.
> *The swineherd:* I am not convinced.
>
> *(Machado, 1936, p. 1, translated into English)*

Our challenge is to teach students to learn by themselves by means of a critical training. This is the only way to raise the citizens that advanced democracies need, much like the opinionated swineherd who is not convinced by the existence of a single truth.

Muñoz Molina accurately reflects upon this issue, when he states that:

> Democracy needs to be taught, because it is not natural, because it runs against the grain of inclinations deeply rooted in humanity. What is natural is not equality, but the domination of the strong over the weak. What is natural is the family clan and the tribe, blood ties, mistrust towards foreigners, attachment to what we know, rejection of those who speak another language or have different hair or skin color. . . . What is natural is to demand limits for others and not accept them for oneself. . . . Prejudice is a lot more natural than an honest will to know. What is natural is barbarity, not civilization; yelling and punching, not persuasive argumentation; immediate fruition, not effort or the long term. . . . What is natural is ignorance: there is no form of learning that does not require effort and take time to show results. And if democracy is not taught with patience and dedication and is not learned as an everyday practice, its great principles will remain void or serve as a screen for corruption and demagoguery.
>
> *(Muñoz Molina, 2013, translated into English)*

To make this possible, in his essay *Education and Democracy*, Ignacio Sotelo considers the differences between socialization, instruction, and education, something crucial for pedagogues to distinguish. The broadest concept is socialization, which encompasses the transmission of principles that are widely accepted by a society. On the other hand, instruction has to do, firstly, with providing the general essential knowledge needed to manage oneself within a community, and secondly, with the specific knowledge that enables practical training towards getting a job. Finally, education is a more complex social process, the aim of which is to produce free human beings (Sotelo, 1995), as the educator Paulo Freire asserts:

> In problem-posing education, people develop their power to perceive critically *the way they exist* in the world *with which* and *in which* they find themselves; they come to see the world not as a static reality, but as a reality in process, in transformation.
>
> *(Freire, 1970, p. 83)*

Faced with this task, we share what the philosopher Martha Nussbaum, a specialist in ethics and humanities, has to say in her analysis of the "silent crisis" of education, lucidly expressed in her book *Not for Profit*:

> Indeed, what we might call the humanistic aspects of science and social science—the imaginative, creative aspect, and the aspect of rigorous critical thought—are also losing ground as nations prefer to pursue short-term profit by the cultivation of the useful and highly applied skills suited to profit-making.
>
> *(Nussbaum, 2010, p. 2)*

We should not prepare students for a predetermined future because by the time they reach it, the intellectual baggage provided will have become obsolete. This text proposes education as a tool to make students think, because only then will the future be in their hands and they will be able to construct it. Recently, reading the re-edition of Emilio Lledó's much-needed work *Filosofía y Lenguaje*, he reminded us of the following, basing his discourse on the ideas of the father of modern philosophy:

> Descartes stated that that which truly belonged to us, that which is in our power, is our thoughts. But thoughts deteriorate when we are not moved by intelligence. A shapeless amalgamation of interests, pittances, obfuscations and blind sightedness muddle the river and the flow of human life.
>
> *(Lledó, 1970, p. 57)*

Instead of a consumerist conception of education, we claim a type of learning that must be both collective and individual, as well as free, open, and horizontal. In this sense, we follow Epicurus' premises when he defends the role of sages not for what they teach, but mostly, for showing their disciples to have a critical attitude in order to free themselves even of the teachings of the masters and their imposed precepts. Hence, we propose reciprocity between the university and society based on cultivating a critical spirit that is constantly attentive and revising objectives in order to produce individuals who are autonomous thinkers.

Fourth Front: Shared Thoughts

> I know good writers who are half dumb and very smart people who don't know how to write. The main characteristic of a good writer is his role as a medium: someone who allows language to speak for itself, developing, establishing dialectics, transubstantiating, and surpassing itself.
>
> *(Pániker, 1990, p. 115, translated into English)*

María Zambrano has taught us that truth is nothing, neither current nor active, if it is not a shared truth. Only by reciprocal verbalization can an authentic pedagogy be created. But the problem with our mass and consumerist society is that it is neither interested in thinking nor does it allow time to think, therefore cancelling out and destroying the space needed for critical thinking.

Learning can be an act carried out autonomously by each subject independently, while teaching is an inevitably social act. The former will last much longer than the timing established for the latter. Three great thinkers summarize this to perfection. As the Spanish philosopher Fernando Savater maintains in his essay on the values of pedagogy: "True education does not consist only in showing how to think, but also in learning how to think about what one thinks" (Savater, 2003, p. 31, translated into English). Complementarily, the French writer and philosopher Gaston Bachelard added that: "The teaching we receive is, psychologically speaking, a kind of empiricism; the teaching we give is, psychologically speaking, a kind of rationalism" (Bachelard, 2002, p. 243). And lastly, the Spanish philosopher Emilio Lledó stresses the importance of dialogue: "The point is not only to be able to speak, to express oneself, but to be able to think, to learn to know how to think in order to, indeed, be able to have something to say" (Lledó, 2009, p. 56, translated into English).

Therefore, the scope of dialogue in our society and our teaching is crucial (Bauman, 2017). Knowledge is essentially and irreducibly a matter of dialogue (Felman, 1982), because most of our thinking comes from our collective background. For Plato, dialogue was the most anti-dogmatic form of thought. Dialogue means teamwork, and it activates what Gramsci described as the intellectual collective, promoting cooperation instead of competition.

Against this background, we propose to replace the single professor by the teaching group or the "collective educator," which will allow for complementarity, questioning, and contradiction to become part of the teaching process. The group of professors, which has long been a particularity of architectural design courses and has been exported as a methodology to other areas of knowledge, is a good example. It produces, with its critical consonance, a form of collective comprehension that, at the same time, defines judgments within students by stimulating their personal criteria. The group, not the individual, produces a set of horizontal relationships in the decision-making process in the manner of dialogue, but at the same time contributes substantially to the construction of autonomous thinking within each student.

It is our duty to undo the preacher-like voice of the professor. It needs to be replaced by a polyphone group of pedagogues. All acts of teaching must tend towards situations that require the collaborative participation of students, in order to avoid classes from turning into a routine and one-directional act, because just as Humberto Maturana tells us, "the listener understands only if he is prepared to understand" (Maturana & Varela, 1980, p. 5).

Just as it is essential for us as educators to expand our own horizons and question our own convictions, it is equally crucial and stimulating to collaborate and learn from our students. We need to know how to interpret and theorize the work of our students to turn it into an object of thought and learning. We understand that, as professors, we do not transmit contents, but the form and the way in which we approach the subject matter. As educators we do not teach to learn, but we teach learning proper. In this way, university education entails, once again, awakening the curiosity of students and maintaining their attention. The idea is to unlearn rules and behaviors that are based on prejudices and social conventions.

To provoke defiance, to stimulate controversy, to initiate debate, to say "work with me," place professors and students on the same side of things, pointing the way towards the unknown for us all. In this way, we propose starting out with a set of unorthodox premises in order to produce a certain attitude that leads to the action of designing and the immersion of students into the practice of architecture, while also transmitting excitement, enthusiasm, and our own interest in the subject that we teach.

Of all the tools that we work with, we shall pay special attention to two: passion and perseverance. This means energetically caring about the discipline we teach, because, to quote French philosopher Gilles Deleuze: "one must find the matter one studies and uses exciting" (Deleuze & Parnet, 1996, translated into English). We propose to make the most of the exaltation and momentum of the learner, the "amateur" who has an innocent, literal, surreal, and often agitated approach. Recalling Teresa de Jesús,[1] irrefutable patience and determination are the only essential tools one needs to transmit any effort.

Fifth Front: Research and Critique

In her *Propaedeutic Contribution to the Teaching of Architecture Theory*, architect Lina Bo Bardi points out that:

> We performed hitherto a sort of tour throughout time and throughout the "theories" of architecture, dwelling upon one of the aspects and modes of interpretation: the critical aspect. But the experience of teaching has led us to assume, among students, a certain impatience. This impatience we know very well: it means that we no longer feel the sap flowing from the past, that we have almost constitutionally "cut the roots," that the natural habit of a calm and methodical study no longer exists, despite the consciousness of an acquired cultural heritage. It is the impatience of those who no longer want to know things that do not produce a result soon, of things that do not serve solutions to the problems of immediate life.
> *(Bardi, 2013, p. 45)*

In order to correctly teach architecture, the educational program that we outline is based on our conviction that both research and critique are fundamental values. The American writer Zora Neale Hurston believed that research is "formalized curiosity, that is it poking and prying with a purpose" (Hurston, 1942, p. 182). Students work on the basis of a reality from which they will obtain relevant data and discover relationships and interactions among different social variables. We agree, understanding research as an operation that leads to obtaining new knowledge. It is a complex process that is not satisfied by mere description, but instead it consists of establishing a comparison of variables between the matters of study and defining a hypothesis that students must test and validate. Besides this, it builds on the ability to discern and solve situations, needs, or problems in a specific context.

After reading Charles Darwin's autobiography and his research methods, we have discovered and verified that most of the work of students should be dedicated to phenomenology: the meticulous, laborious, honest, and thoughtful observation of reality. This should allow them to discover the data that informs a design and the relationship between this data and the full picture. To draw either inventing or interpreting a totality made of fragments could be understood as the principal research work carried out by all design students. Therefore, we must show our students our conviction that designing is actually a form of learning and unlearning research process and that, consequently, it must be broad, gradual, exacting, and careful.

The definition of architectural elements, as Robert Venturi reminded us in the preface to *Complexity and Contradiction*,[2] does not solve the problem of creation, but it does have the virtue of pointing to the key aspects of the creative process, which is characterized by the intellectual quality, that is, the synthesis of the operation. To do this, we need to resort to active critique, enabling us to discern, bring together, and delve into the essence of the object of study through different stages, applying the method used in linguistics by the philosopher and historian Tzvetan Todorov, such as description, analysis, interpretation, and lastly, architectural critique (Todorov, 1981, 1984).

Indeed, any student can become a good architect if she develops, simultaneously, a great capacity for observation and self-critical research and, to achieve this, she will only need large doses of humility and determination. We know that design is not only construction, nor is it simple research or mere theory. The combination of all of these qualities should be the backbone of the educational program, because an informational system, or investigation, accumulates, analyzes, and interprets while a cognitive system selects through critique.

Therefore, the combination of both, *research* and *criticism*, constitutes, in our opinion, the act of designing. Actually, teaching design is understood as a form of personal research by the student in which a set of guidelines and conducts are defined, or she is stimulated by a series of previously established suggestions or principles. In this sense, it is quite similar to scientific experimentation, since it is based on references, comparisons, hypotheses, and verifications before reaching the intellectual construct of a proposal.

Our approach is to orient students towards a methodological doubt, towards distant skepticism, but not regarding the dogmas of the past but those relative to the group itself, set paths, trends, and even the ideology of the school. All in all, the idea is to push the student towards insecurities regarding what is known in order to enable her to form a critical judgment. We are referring to the sense of skepticism defined by Diderot: to think for oneself, to have hyperbolical or universal doubts, to critically negate everything regarding accepted knowledge, to be anti-dogmatic and immersed in a permanent revolution.

In this way, the classroom becomes a research and exploration space where new problems will be detected, innovative solutions will be proposed, and students' way of communicating them will be trained.

Therefore, we propose a didactic strategy that is closer to that of a laboratory than a design studio. The French philosopher Bruno Latour, with his forceful cry "give me a laboratory and I will raise the word," will help us explain this point. He distinguishes between three operations: "the dissolution of the inside/outside boundary; the inversion of scales and levels; and, finally, the process of inscription" (Latour, 1983, p. 163).

To learn architecture, first we need to situate ourselves in an aseptic space, the lab, that enables us to isolate an issue from reality and assess it without restrictions, to later exploit it to the last consequences without forgetting that the final goal is to return it back to society.

Afterwards, the obligation is to understand the territorial (macro) scale and the (micro) scale of architecture and make them interact by zooming in and out. The observation of the territory, of the landscape and of the body, oscillating and repeating sequences between its different scales, will provide us with the ability to detect the complexity of the new nature, which we are working with.

Lastly, there is the registering that takes place in a lab or research center. There, tests and instruments are organized, and systematic analysis and rigor are a must. Hence, registering and inscribing prospectively will prepare us, as Latour says, to make visible the invisible.

In this chapter, we consider that architecture stands on two basic principles that work dialectically together: applied research through structured information (philosophy, sociology, psychology, music, politics, history, etc.) and operative critique (structure, installations, constructions, physics, geometry, etc.). The design will result from the dialectic and synthetic union of both or, in other words, from the double negation of the academy and the polytechnic school, the union of theory and practice. What we call *praxis*.

We could describe the research work of any student in the same words used by Darwin:

> During some part of the day I wrote my Journal, and took much pains in describing carefully and vividly all that I had seen; and this was good practice. . . . Everything about which I thought or read was made to bear directly on what I had seen or was likely to see; and this habit of mind was continued during the five years of the voyage. I feel sure that it was this training which has enabled me to do whatever I have done in science. . . . Therefore my success as a man of science, whatever this may have amounted to, has been determined, as far as I can judge, by complex and diversified mental qualities and conditions.
>
> *(Darwin, 1993, pp. 43–44, 87–88)*

As Darwin thought of himself, anyone, or any student, with a high level of patience, diligence, observation, and some inventiveness would be able to investigate in any field.

Research enables us to know, hence the statement of Austrian philosopher Ludwig Wittgenstein that "the limits of my language mean the limits of my world" (Wittgenstein, 2001, p. 6). This implies that the limit of thought is language and, therefore, that we think with the words that are available to us. To research would involve adding new lexicon to out intellect, and therefore we raise the possibilities of generating a new terminology and, consequently, articulating new concepts.

Summarizing, as does Lledó, we understand that:

> language always takes us back to the essential and substantial structures of human beings. The ability to communicate, to have intelligence, to interpret and also to hide and manipulate continues to be, as it was in the time of the sophists "the issue of our time." Because human beings have never had it easier to communicate and understand each other as they

do today. Nevertheless, and in spite of the noise of the media, they may still stand in the middle of the immense desert of silence and oblivion.

(Lledó, 1970, p. 6, translated into English)

As for operative critique or design theory, we are referring to what Plato called *tekne*, or the art of building, which ends up coinciding with the term *poiesis*, that is, to make evident what is invisible. This concept develops later into the Latin term *veritas*, that is, the revelation of truth. During antiquity, everything was artifice and architecture, since the concepts of art, nature, and industry were all put on the same level. The hoe, the canoe, the wheel, the oar, the ax, or the piece of furniture were all simultaneous facts that depended on the *Firmitas*, the *Utilitas*, and the *Venustas*.

Centuries later, Picasso thought that "the best artist was always an interpreter because he does not copy directly," and he spoke ironically when he said that "bad artists copy, while good artists steal." Deriving from the word *criterion*, we understand critique as the action of discerning that determines the truth by evidencing previous fallacies and errors. Hence, research opens the diaphragm towards a large field of interests, while critique closes it, by finding out the internal reason of things, in a continuous iterative and self-reflexive process.

Conclusion: One Single Position

These five points are constituted as an ideological framework for action, an open nautical chart that can only be completed with the exercise of architectural practice. The project "Social housing in Lavapiés" serves as an applied example of these methodological premises. Embajadores' case has been chosen because it bears witness to the change of an era, not as a rupture but as continuity, as it is proposed as a connecting hinge between the experiences of the 20th century and those of the 21st century.

Architect With Criteria

When talking about social housing for rehousing, we refer to the lowest construction budget of all state-supported housing in Spain. For this reason, in the building at Embajadores 52 Street, what we could define as infrastructure (structure, the materialization of the facade, etc.) was awarded in contrast to the infill or finishing materials. Thus, the highest quality was taken to what was not seen, the support in Habraken's words, while the finishes were chosen taking into account that their useful life was shorter and that they were subject to the taste of the users.

Feminine Scenarios

In this work, the protagonist is living in those small places that serve as an expansion to the house. Thus, the gallery becomes a living place where to extract something of the interior existence of the habitat. The haven areas, the elevated courtyards that open the veranda to the city, the shared roof terrace, and the shaded garden are transformed into a new space in the house, where the resident can dream of an undetermined function. The quotidian, customary, and the usual—the world of women—take the reins of the project to transform themselves into extraordinary acts.

More Autonomy, More Collectivity

This project takes into account what rehousing is. We did not know the final users, but they were a group who lived precariously in the Lavapiés neighborhood, with their intense associationism,

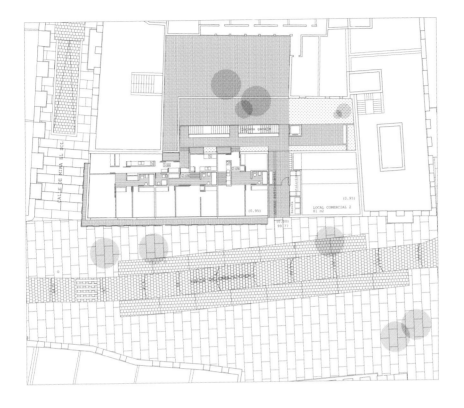

FIGURE 16.1 Ground floor plan.

with their knowledge of the old outdoor corridors of the working-class housing that, even though they were sub-housing, had constituted them as people because they had developed a high level of sociability in their poverty. We understood that, in a contemporary key, we had to reinterpret the domesticity to which they were accustomed; we had an obligation to defend that communal intimacy that they had developed over generations.

Shared Thoughts

At the turn of the 21st century, participatory projects were not yet a widely used formula in Spain. Instead, the administration considered an initially unknown community. Being a small community with only 24 homes, a project that allows dialogue was proposed to carry out the many collective and communal spaces of social friction that were suggested. The shared spaces were from the beginning the DNA of the project, with its self-management, use, and community maintenance. In this way, the neighbors could have it all, from the most private to the most collective: house with a roof terrace, patio, and orchard; houses oriented to all suns; even, they could revel in the bustling street and at the same time be absorbed in the shady garden—a luxury.

276 Carmen Espegel Alonso and Daniel Movilla Vega

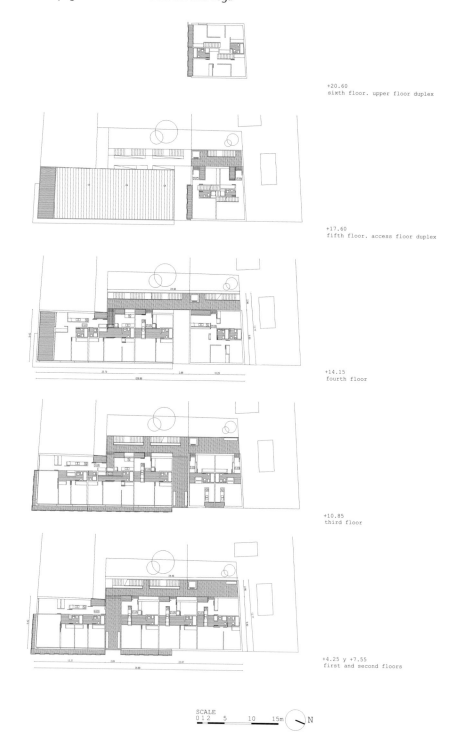

FIGURE 16.2 First to fifth floors.

FIGURE 16.3 View from Embajadores Street.

FIGURE 16.4 View of the living room towards Embajadores and Mira el Sol Streets with the expanded metal lattices open.

FIGURE 16.5 View of the living room towards Embajadores and Mira el Sol Streets with the expanded metal lattices closed.

Five Fronts for One Single Position 279

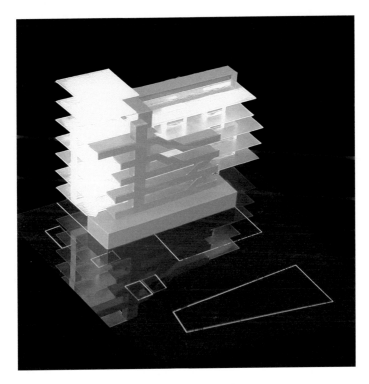

FIGURE 16.6 Model showing shared collective spaces in red.

FIGURE 16.7 View of the gallery with the stairs and the elevator in the background.

FIGURE 16.8 Longitudinal section from the courtyard to Embajadores Street.

Research and Critique

The research was fundamentally sociological in nature as it focused on unraveling the way of life in the neighborhood, while the critics selected to what extent past, present, and future should dialogue. Thus, Embajadores 52 is an absent interpretation of manners of a genuine neighborhood like Lavapiés, whose traditional elements, the patio and the outdoor corridor, are reflected in a sober construction: the facade has a modern vocation; the patio is a wooded interior plaza; and the access gallery is distanced from the facade for the sake of greater privacy.

All in all, the project built for social housing as rehousing, what we have called "action," emerges as the inescapable link between the proposed project pedagogy and the transformation of society.

Notes

1. Regarding the difficult search for an adequate language for her illiterate nuns, Teresa de Jesús maintained that what was needed was "a huge and determined determination to not to stop until the goal is reached, whatever may come, whatever may happen, whatever the work, whatever the rumors, even if I die along the way and even if the world ends in the process" (Jesús, 1583/2017, p. 75).
2. "Analysis includes the breaking up of architecture into elements, a technique I frequently use even though it is the opposite of the integration which is the final goal of art. However paradoxical it appears, and despite the suspicions of many Modern architects, such disintegration is a process present in all creation, and it is essential to understanding" (Venturi, 1966, p. 13).

FIGURE 16.9 View of the gallery and stairs from the backyard.

FIGURE 16.10 Contextual elevation of Embajadores Street.

Five Fronts for One Single Position **283**

FIGURE 16.11 View of the residential building in its context from Embajadores Street.

References

Bachelard, G. (2002). *The Formation of the Scientific Mind*. Manchester, UK: Clinamen Press.
Bardi, L.B. (2013). Propaedeutic Contribution to the Teaching of Architecture Theory (1957). In C. Veikos (Ed.), *Lina Bo Bardi: The Theory of Architectural Practice*. New York, NY: Routledge.
Bauman, Z. (2017). *Retrotopia*. Malden, MA: Polity Press.
Calhoun, C., & Solomon, R.C. (1984). *What is an Emotion?* Oxford, UK: Oxford University Press.
Calle, S. (2008). *Prenez Soin de Vous*. Retrieved from www.slow-words.com/take-care-of-yourself/
Darwin, C. (1993). *Autobiografía*. Madrid, Spain: Alianza Editorial.
Deleuze, G., & Parnet, C. (1996). *P de Profesor. El Abecedario de Gilles Deleuze*. Ed. Pierre-André Boutang, French Television Program.
Felman, S. (1982). Psychoanalysis and Education: Teaching Terminable and Interminable. *Yale French Studies. The Pedagogical Imperative: Teaching as Literary Genre*, *63*, 21–44.
Freire, P. (1970). *Pedagogy of the Oppressed*. New York, NY: Herder and Herder.
Heller, A. (1979). *Theory of Feelings*. Assen, The Netherlands: Van Gorcum Pub.
Hurston, Z.N. (1942). *Dust Tracks on a Road*. Philadelphia, PA; London, UK; New York, NY: J.B. Lippincott Company.
Jesús, T. (2017). *Camino de Perfección*. Buenos Aires, Argentina: Ed. El Aleph. (Original work published 1583).
Latour, B. (1983). Give Me a Laboratory and I Will Raise the World. In K.D. Knorr-Cetina & M. Mulkay (Eds.), *Science Observed: Perspectives on the Social Study of Science* (pp. 141–170). London, UK; Beverly Hills, CA; New Delhi, India: Sage Pub.
Lledó, E. (1970). *Filosofía y Lenguaje* (Prologue to the edition from 2015). Barcelona, Spain: Ed. Austral.
Lledó, E. (2009). Educación e Igualdad. In *Ser Quien Eres: Ensayos para una Educación Democrática* (pp. 51–62). Zaragoza, Spain: Prensas Universitarias de Zaragoza.
Machado, A. (1936). *Juan de Mairena*. Madrid, Spain: Editorial España Calpe.
Maturana, H.R., & Varela, F.J. (1980). *Autopoiesis and Cognition: The Realization of the Living*. Dordrecht, The Netherlands: Reidel Pub.
Muñoz Molina, A. (2013). *Todo lo que era Sólido*. Barcelona, Spain: Ed. Seix Barral.
Nieto Fernández, E. (2012). *¡ . . . PRESCINDIBLE ORGANIZADO!: Agenda Docente para una Formulación Afectiva y Disidente del Proyecto Arquitectónico*. Doctoral thesis. Alicante, Spain: Universidad de Alicante.
Nussbaum, M.C. (2010). *Not For Profit: Why Democracy Needs Humanities*. Princeton, NJ: Princeton University Press.
Pániker, S. (1990). *Primer Testamento*. Barcelona, Spain: Ed. Seix Barral.
Piketty, T. (2014). *Capital in the Twenty-first Century*. Cambridge, MA: The Belknap Press of Harvard University Press.
Read, H. (1958). *Education through Art*. London, UK: Faber & Faber Ltd.
Roy, A. (1997). *The God of Small Things*. London, UK: Flamingo Pub.
Savater, F. (2003). *El Valor de Educar*. Barcelona, Spain: Ed. Ariel.
Sotelo, I. (1995). Educación y Democracia. In *Volver a Pensar la Educación* (Vol. 1, pp. 34–59). A Coruña, Spain: Fundación Paideia.
Stravinsky, I. (1947). *Poetics on Music in the Form of Six Lessons*. Cambridge, MA: Harvard University Press.
Todorov, T. (1981). *Introduction to Poetics*. Minneapolis, MN: University of Minnesota Press.
Todorov, T. (1984). *Critique de la Critique*. Paris, France: Ed. du Seuil.
Venturi, R. (1966). *Complexity and Contradiction in Architecture*. New York, NY: The Museum of Modern Art.
Wittgenstein, L. (2001). *Tractatus Logico-Philosophicus* (1922). London, UK; New York, NY: Routledge.

IMAGE CREDITS

Cover Image: São Silvestre road race, São Paulo. Photo: Tuca Vieira
Figure 1.1   Tomaz Silva/Agência Brasil/Creative Commons.
Figure 1.2   Ville de Vélizy/Creative Commons.
Figure 1.3   Vitor Oliveira/Creative Commons (Left) and Mariana Wilderom (Right).
Figure 1.4   Drawn and engraved by F. Bate. Published by "The Association of all Classes of all Nations," at their institution, 69, Great Queen Street. Lincoln's Inn Fields, London, 1838/Creative Commons.
Figure 1.5   Alhzeiia/Creative Commons.
Figure 1.6   Ana Paula Hirama/Creative Commons.
Figure 1.7   PxHere.
Figure 2.1   Javcollao/Creative Commons.
Figure 2.2   Zhiqiang/Creative Commons.
Figure 2.3   Alejandro Islas Photograph AC/Creative Commons.
Figure 2.4   Mariana Wilderom.
Figure 2.5   Nelson Kon.
Figure 2.6   Cristiano Mascaro.
Figure 2.7   Cristiano Mascaro.
Figure 3.1   Boston Public Library/Creative Commons.
Figure 3.2   Pline/Creative Commons.
Figure 3.3   ETH Library.
Figure 3.4   ETH Library.
Figure 3.5   National Library of Scotland.
Figure 3.6   University of Strathclyde Archives.
Figure 3.7   Nelson Kon.
Figure 3.8   Claudia Kim Kim.
Figure 3.9   Claudia Kim Kim.
Figure 3.10 Mariana Wilderom.
Figure 7.1   Tim Adams/Creative Commons (7.1A) and A. Savin/Creative Commons (7.1B).
Figure 7.2   David Pendery/Creative Commons.
Figure 7.3   Charles Merville/Brown University Collection/Creative Commons.
Figure 7.4   Brooklyn Museum/Creative Commons.

Image Credits

Figure 7.5	Samuel Herman Gottscho Collection, Library of Congress/Creative Commons.
Figure 7.6	Morio/Creative Commons.
Figure 7.7	Piotr Zarobkiewicz/Creative Commons.
Figure 7.8	Jeffmock/Creative Commons (Left) and Robert J. Fish/Creative Commons (Right).
Figure 8.1	César Simoni Santos.
Figure 8.2	César Simoni Santos.
Figure 8.3	César Simoni Santos.
Figure 8.4	César Simoni Santos.
Figure 8.5	César Simoni Santos.
Figure 9.1	Nelson Kon.
Figure 9.2	© Instituto Bardi/Casa de Vidro.
Figure 9.3	Nelson Kon.
Figure 9.4	© Instituto Bardi/Casa de Vidro.
Figure 9.5	Nelson Kon.
Figure 10.1	Scheme redrawn by Nelson Mota.
Figure 10.2	Drawings by Noelle Dooper, supervised by Nelson Mota.
Figure 10.3	Drawings by Freya Crijns.
Figure 10.4	Drawings by Bas Hoevenaars, supervised by Nelson Mota.
Figure 10.5	Drawings by Roza Derakhshan Alavijeh, supervised and adapted by Nelson Mota.
Figure 10.6	Drawing by Roza Derakhshan Alavijeh, supervised by Nelson Mota.
Figure 10.7	Nelson Mota.
Figure 11.1	Victor Gruen Papers, American Heritage Center, University of Wyoming.
Figure 11.2	White Arkitekter/Creative Commons.
Figure 11.3	From Nishihara, 1968, p. 108.
Figure 11.4	From Granfelt, 1968, pp. 7, 9. Courtesy of Arkitektur Förlag.
Figure 11.5	From Frederick, 1913, p. 51.
Figure 11.6	From Gruen, 1973, pp. 87, 88.
Figure 11.7	Chicago Area Transportation Study (1959), p. 9.
Figure 11.8	Meyer & Miller, 1984, pp. 245, 247.
Figure 11.9	Figure by Legeby from Legeby, Koch, & Miranda, 2019, p. 15.
Figure 11.10	From Kallstenius & Fredlund, 2001, from supplementary map and p. 63 (typologies).
Figure 12.1	Marta Caldeira.
Figure 12.2	Marta Caldeira.
Figure 12.3	In *Studi per una Operante Storia Urbana di Venezia* (1959).
Figure 12.4	In *Origini e Sviluppo della Città Moderna* (1965).
Figure 12.5	In *Las Formas de Crecimiento Urbano* (1997) and *Lotus International 19* (1978). @ Laboratori d'Urbanisme de Barcelona.
Figure 12.6	In *Bologna: Politica e Metodologia del Restauro nei Centri Storici* (1973).
Figure 12.7	In *Lotus International 13* (1976).
Figure 12.8	In *Arees de Nova Centralitat* (1987).
Figure 14.1	Courtesy of COOKFOX Architects.
Figure 14.2	Raphael Grazziano.
Figure 14.3	Raphael Grazziano.
Figure 14.4	Raphael Grazziano.
Figure 15.1	Photograph by Hugo Segawa ©Hugo Segawa.

Image Credits

Figure 15.2   Archivo de Fotografía de Caracas, Despacho del Cronista (Public Domain).
Figure 15.3   Photograph by Ramón Paolini ©ArchivoFotografíaUrbana.
Figure 15.4   Photographs by the author ©Sergio Martín Blas.
Figure 15.5   Original image by the author based on material from www.ruedapizarro.es and *The Dwellings of the Labouring Classes*, Henry Roberts, 1851. ©Sergio Martín Blas.
Figure 15.6   Photograph by Pablo Tosco ©Oxfam Intermón.
Figure 16.1   Courtesy of Carmen Espegel.
Figure 16.2   Courtesy of Carmen Espegel.
Figure 16.3   Courtesy of photographer Angel Baltanás.
Figure 16.4   Courtesy of photographer Angel Baltanás.
Figure 16.5   Courtesy of photographer Angel Baltanás.
Figure 16.6   Courtesy of Carmen Espegel.
Figure 16.7   Courtesy of photographer Angel Baltanás.
Figure 16.8   Courtesy of Carmen Espegel.
Figure 16.9   Courtesy of photographer Angel Baltanás.
Figure 16.10   Courtesy of Carmen Espegel.
Figure 16.11   Courtesy of photographer Angel Baltanás.

Creative Commons images may have been edited.

INDEX

Note: Only authors discussed at length are included in this index. Figures in *italics* denote illustrations.

23 de Enero housing estate *253*, 260
2 de Diciembre housing estate *see 23 de Enero* housing estate

ABC City 183, 203n2
Abrams, Charles 164, 178
activism 34, 42, 47–49, 54, 157
Adorno, Theodor 95–96, 101, 114, 123n2
aflalo/gasperini arquitetos 246–249
Africa 112, 148, 152, 156, 158n15
Agamben, Giorgio 20, 51n14
Ahlsén, Erik 186
Ahlsén, Tore 186
Alexander, Christopher 87, 170
alienation 15–16, 26, 28, 40, 48–49, 96, 120, 125n21, 130, 135, 166, 261
Allen, Stan 35
Alphand, Jean-Charles Adolphe 59, *64*
Amann Cánovas Maruri *258*
Amaral, Tarsila do 147, 157n5, 157n6
Amazonia 153
American National Standards Institute (ANSI) 250n2
American Society of Heating, Refrigerating and Air-Conditioning Engineers (ASHRAE) 240–241, 247, 250n2
Amsterdam 258, *259*
Anderlecht 231–232
Anderson, Perry 41
Andrade, Mario de 157n5
Andrade, Oswald de 147, 157n5
Andujar, Claudia 153
Ant Farm 34
anthropophagy 5, 147–157
Appleyard, Donald 87
appropriation 14, 28, 135, 147, 169, 266; tactics of 13, 252, 264; *see also* right to the city

Aragon, Louis 113, 123n5
Arantes, Otília 4, 30n3, 37–38, 40, 52n18, 106–126
Arantes, Pedro Fiori 51n16, 176
Aranya 166
Aravena, Alejandro 176, 260, 263
Arbery, Ahmaud 86
Arc® 243
Archigram 34
Arens, William 147, 157n3
Arequipa 256
Argentina 38, 260, 262–263, 264n1
Aronsson, Albert 186–187
Arquitetura Nova 34, 42, 48, 49, 51n17; *see also* Ferro, Sérgio; Império, Flávio; Lefèvre, Rodrigo
Arrhenius, Thordis 203n5
Årsta Centrum 186
Artigas, João Batista Vilanova 38, 47–50, 51n15
artistic avant-gardes 14–15, 17, 20, 97, 99–100, 102, 147–148, 158n11; *see also* modernism
Asia 19, 115, 120, 123n1, 124n21
ATBAT-Afrique 169
Atelier Jean Nouvel 233n1
Athens Charter (1933) 254
Atomium 228
Augoyard, Jean-François 204
Aureli, Pier Vittorio 51n10, 103n1
Austria 25, 55, 149, 183, 273
autonomy: in aesthetics 41–42, 103; in architecture 1, 3, 17, 19, 21, 34, 36, 41–44, 46–47, 50, 51n10, 157, 191, 241; in capital 24, 26; in the construction site 30n2, 178, 257; in education 266, 268, 270–271, 274; in politics 12; in society 14, 63, 268
Avermaete, Tom 1–7, 51n13, 54–72, 169, 232

Aymonino, Carlo 36, 217–219, 221, 225n5, 226n9, 226n11, 226n17
Azerbaijan 124n21

Bachelard, Gaston 83n12, 270
Bahia 148, 158n11
Baird, George 35
Ballard, J.G. 233
Ballent, Anahí 263
Baltimore 184
Banham, Reyner 239
Barcelona 23, 221, 224, 226n12, 226n16, 260
Bardi, Lina Bo 5, *68*, 147–158, 271
Barker, Roger 80, 83n11
Baroque 21, 23, 110, 112, 123n6
Barthes, Roland 102
Basualdo, Carlos 158n13
Baudelaire, Charles 111–112, 123n2
Baudrillard, Jean 38, 204n15
Bauhaus 15, 25–26, 99, 143
Bauman, Zygmunt 204n18, 270
Bauwens, Michel 56
Becker, Gary S. 86–93
Beddington, Nadine 194, 203n4
Beijing *36*, 45, 112, 117, 122
Belapur 166
Belaúnde, Fernando 170
Belgium 228–232
Benjamin, Walter 4, 83n12, 92, 95, 101–102, 104n11; Arcades Project 106–108, 110–114, 120–121, 123
Bennet, Jane 65
Berlage, Hendrik 24
Berlin 158, 162, 259
Berlin Wall 34, 107
Bertoud, Alain 167
Besix 229
Bettelheim, Charles 226n11
Bing, Wang 109, 112
Biraghi, Marco 98, 103n3, 103n5
Bishop, Claire 196, 204n18
Black Lives Matter 86–87
Blas, Sérgio 6–7, 252–265
Bloch, Ernst 41–42, 49, 226n11
Blokland, Talja 187, 196, 204n18
Blumer, Herbert 81
Boal, Ian 125n25
Boano, Camillo 178
body 4–5, 79, 81, 83n7, 98, 130, 134, 144, 148–150, 153, 157n9, 158n10, 158n18, 268, 273
Boeing, Geoff 204n16
Bo, Lina *see* Bardi, Lina Bo
Bollier, David 54, 64–65
Bologna 221, *222*, 224, 226n14
Bombay Metropolitan Region Development Authority (BMRDA) 167
Boston common 56–58
Botti, Alberto 241
Botti & Rubin 241
Bourdieu, Pierre 83n5, 196

Boym, Svetlana 123n7
Bracops, René 231
Brasília 142, 256
Bratton, William 89, 92–93
Brazil 3, 5, 12, 21, *29*, 29n1, 30n2, 30n3, 30n5, 37–38, *46*, 47, *48–50*, 51, 52n18, 68, 77, 83n9, 147–154, 157–158, 161, 176, 214, 225n3, 237, 241, 246, 249, 256, 260, 262
Brazil Builds (MoMA exhibition) 34, 37–38, 51n5
Brazilian Communist Party 47
Brecht, Bertolt 41, 104, 148
Brenner, Neil 161, 225n6, 225n7
Breton, André 113
Brewer, Gale 211
Brienon-sur-Armançon 58
Broadacre City 97
Bronx 92
Brown, Denise Scott 16, 45
Browne, Enrique 38
Brown, Michael 86
Brunnenhofstrasse complex 258
Brussels 228–233
Brussels World Expo (1958) 228
Bruyère, Louis 59
Buber, Martin 106
Buck-Morss, Susan 106–110, 112–113, 120, 123n3, 124n11, 124n12
Budapest 122
Burgess, Ernest W. 83n10
Burj Dubai *121*
Burns, Carol 35
Burns, Wilfred 203n4, 204n7
Busquets, Joan *224*, 226n16
Butler, Judith 187
Butte des Moulins *113*

Cacciari, Massimo 51n1
Cairo 122
Caldeira, Marta 211–227
Calhoun, Cheshire 268
California 39, 122, 183
Caminos, Horacio 166–167
Candilis, Georges 169–170
capital: accumulation of 12–13, 17–18, 24, 27, 32, 34, 114, 116, 120, 125n21, 131, 133
capitalism: commercial 19; contemporary 2, 15, 107, 110, 114, 116; financial 19, 26; industrial 2, 14, 19, 26, 43, 120; late 14, 18, 32, 34–35, 37–43, 45, 50, 216; liberal 23, 25; neoliberal 34–35, 87, 229; post-industrial 14, 216
Carabanchel 258
Caracas 253, *254–255*, 260
Carlo, Giancarlo de 226
Carmona, Matthew 184
Carvalho, Laura 51n14
Cascaldi, Carlos *49–50*
Castells, Manuel 47–48, 196, 255
Castrillón, Natalia E. 5, 147–159
Castro, Amílcar de 157
Casuarinas *263*

Cavalcante, Rodrigo 240–241
Central Business District (CBD) 2, 235
Cerdà, Ildefons 16, 23
Cerdà plan 23
Cerro Piloto 253–254, 258
Cerro San Cristóbal 259
Certeau, Michel de 45, 252, 256
certification systems 6, 235–250
Cervellati, Pier Luigi 221, *222*, 226n14
Cézanne, Paul 111
CFE 229
Chambers Improvement Act 65
Chan, Sau Lai 164, *165*
Chapin, F. Stuart 187, 193
Charkop 167, *168*, 176–178, *179*
Châtelet, Gilles 200, 204n10
Chernobyl 110
Chicago 77, 83, 114
Chicago School of sociology 77–79, 216
Chigirinsky, Shalva 110
Chile *33*, 176
China 36, 45, 112, 122, 124n21
China Central Television (CCTV) 36, 45, 117
Chomsky, Noam 14, 32
Christaller, Walter 190
Christiaanse, Kees 233n1
Chrysler Building 124n18
Cia. Bartolomeu de Depoimentos 123n6
Cinema Novo 148
city: 21st century 160, 180, 233; big 26, 186; bourgeois 219; capitalist 19, 43, 47; contemporary 68, 219, 236, 252; existing 65, 225; garden 97; global 120, 262; historical 24, 226n10; ideal 143; industrial 21, 51n1, 216–217, 219; inequality in the 225; informal 252, 254–256, 258, 262; large 12, 18–19, 21; liberal 22; medieval 43; modern 5, 43, 107, 112, 216–217, 225, 226n11, 254–255; post-industrial 34; post-global 92; post-modern 26; smart 203; socialist 25; subaltern 219, 221; traditional 1, 14, 16, 23, 43, 186; utopian 47; world 120; *see also* metropolis
Clark, Lygia 157n8
Clark, T.J. 110–111, 121–122, 125n25
Club of Rome 232
Cold War 34, 229, 232
Colombia 260
commodity 12, 17–18, 34, 38, 40, 43, 55, 58, 106–107, 112–114, 123n2, 138, 141, 178
commodification 6, 11, 17, 162, 178, 233; *see also* reification
commons 3, 13–14, 54–72, 196
communication: language and 16–17, 21, 78–80; technology 11, 15, 19, 27, 34, 51n2
conceived space 44; *see also* Lefebvrian trialectics; lived space; perceived space
Coney Island 114–116, 124n16
Congrès Internationaux d'Architecture Moderne (CIAM) 25, 169, 177
Congress for the New Urbanism (CNU) 87, 219, 258

Constructions et Entreprises Industrielles (CEI) 230
consumerism 45, 204n15, 233, 270; *see also* consumer society
consumer society 12, 37, 45, 270; *see also* consumerism
COOKFOX Architects 244, *245*
Copan *24*
corporations 18, 26, 37, 46, 114, 236, 239
Corps des Ponts et Chaussées 59
Correa, Charles 166–167
Costa, Lúcio 37
counter-hegemonic 3, 12, 14, 28, 178, 261; *see also* hegemonic
covid-19 pandemic 7, 11–13, 27, 29n1, 32, 46, 51n14
Crane, Jacob L. 164, 178
critical theory 20, 35, 95, 101, 103, 145, 215, 226n11; *see also* Frankfurt School
cultural turn 18
culture: architectural 15, 17, 260; Brazilian 5, 148–149, 152, 158n15; capitalist 103; consumer 148, 203; industry 34, 37, 114; mass 16, 39, 107, 110, 123n4; popular 5, 15–16

daily life 11, 13, 28, 82, 130, 143, 235; *see also* everyday
Dal Co, Francesco 97
Dalí, Salvador 114, 124n18
Dardot, Pierre 26
Darwin, Charles 272–273
Dávila, Sérgio 124n21
Davis, Mike 122–123, 124n19, 258
Day, Charles 192
De Blasio, Bill 211
Deleuze, Gilles 37, 271
Del Picchia, Menotti 157n5
Dergalin, Igor 186
Derrida, Jacques 37
Descartes, René 143, 270
design methods movement 35
De Soto, Hernando 178, 258
Devimo 231
Diallo, Amadou 86, 92–93
Diderot, Denis 272
Diller Scofidio + Renfro 211, *212–213*
disciplinary strategies of architecture and urbanism 2–3, 5–7, 13–14, 16–18, 20, 27–28, 32, 34–35, 37, 40, 42, 49–50, 51n4, 178, 263
disenchantment 96, 104n7, 107, 109
division of labor 16, 18, 30n2, 102, 219
Donati, Vitaliano 188
Doshi, B.V. 166–167
dosmasunoarquitectos 258
Dreamland *115*, 116–117, 124n17
Drummond, Carlos 124n19
Dubai *121*, 122
Dubrovnik 169
Durkheim, Émile 75–76, 78, 81, 204

Eagleton, Terry 34
Easterling, Keller 235–236
Eckstein, Barbara 204n14
Ecochard, Michel 169
economic rationality 5–6, 91, 93, 161
Eco, Umberto 256
Ecuador 160
Edinburgh 65, 83n6
education 91–92, 140, 200, 266, 268–272; *see also* pedagogy
efficiency: energetical 6, 238–239, 241, 244, 246–247; financial 117; mobility 184, 187, 192–193, 195, 202; productive 161, 166, 177, 192, 252, 257
Egypt 30n2
Eisenman, Peter 36, 51n9
Eldorado Business Tower (EBT) 246–247
Elemental 176, 178
Elza Berquó house 47, *48*, 51n15
emancipation 5, 14–15, 19, 28, 37, 41, 120, 123, 130, 132, 147, 162, 166, 252, 256–258, 268
Emery Roth & Sons *122*
Emmons, Paul 188, 192
Empire State Building 116, 124n18
EMVS 258, *259*
enclave 4, 6, 110, 124n21
Energy Plus 241
Engels, Friedrich 21, 104n8, 214, 218–219, 226n11
England 21, 166, 169
Engström, Fredrik 203
Enlightenment 2, 20–21, 32, 37, 41, 96, 99, 107, 233
Epicurus 270
Erskine, Ralph 42
Escola Paulista 47, 156
Espegel, Carmen 7, 266–284
Europe 2, 6, 20–22, 24–26, 32, 36, 42–43, 45, 51n5, 51n12, 57, 107, 112, 116–117, 124n13, 135, 147–149, 151, 156–157, 157n2, 162–163, 166, 185, 191, 216, 221, 228–229, 232, 244, 252, 254, 258, 260–262
Evans, Robin 192, 254, *259*
everyday 1, 4–7, 14–16, 26–28, 35, 37–38, 40–45, 54, 74–75, 81, 98, 142, 144–145, 186, 254, 262, 268–269; *see also* daily life
exchange value 16, 18, 43, 138, 140, 161; *see also* use value
exploitation 19, 23, 110, 121, 132, 134, 214, 217, 254
explosion of the cities 1, 6, 14, 225n7
Expressionism 41–42
Eyck, Aldo van 170, *171*

Faculty of Architecture and Urbanism of the University of São Paulo (FAUUSP) 37, 47, *49–50*
Farrell, Henry 264
Fathy, Hassan 30n2
favela 12, *29*, 91, 252, 262; *see also* slum
Featherstone, Mike 38
Feher, Michel 93n4
Ferguson 86
Fernandes, Florestan 83n4
Ferraz, Marcelo 149
Ferro, Sérgio 30n2, 48, 51n17, 256–257; *see also* Arquitetura Nova
fetishism 38, 40
financial crisis: 1929 Great Depression 24, 97, 99, 117, 120; 2008 subprime mortgage crisis 6, 11, 17, 27, 32, 124n10, 252, 260
financialization 1, 17, 28, 32
Fiori, José Luís 51
Flint 109
Floyd, George 86
Foundation for Architects Research (SAR) 169
Ford Foundation 164
Fordism-Taylorism 2, 14, 20, 25–26, 107
Fort Worth 183–185, 191
Fosse de Dione *58*
Foster, Norman 110; *see also* Foster + Partners
Foster + Partners 244; *see also* Foster, Norman
Foucault, Michel 38, 45, 58–59, 87–88, 90–93, 100–101, 104n10, 188–189, 203n6
Fourier, Charles 30n5
Four Times Square Building 244, 246, 249
Fox & Fowle 244
France *15*, 57, *58*, 92, *111*, 138, 143, 169, 226n12
Frankfurt School 34–36, 101; *see also* critical theory
Frederick, Christine 192
free market 20, 35, 38; *see also* neoliberalism
Frehse, Fraya 4, 73–85
Freire, Paulo 269
Fresno 183
Freud, Sigmund 187, 194, 201
Friedman, Yona 169
Fuller, Buckminster 34
Fulton Mall 183, *184*
FXCollaborative 244
FXFowle 244

Galerie Vivienne *111*
Gallardi+Hellsten 203n4
Garnier, Tony 225n4
Garvin, Alexander 87
Gazprom 110
Geddes, Patrick 65–67, 72n5, 178
Gehl, Jan 184
Gehry, Frank 39
Genk 229–232
Gensler 184
Georgia 86
Germany 25, 154, 162
Gessen, Masha 110, 124n13
Giddens, Anthony 187
Giedion, Sigfried 104n9, 107
Gigon & Guyer 258
Ginzburg, Carlo 98
Giuliani, Rudolph 89, 93
Glaeser, Edward 88–92

Glasgow *218*
global commercial district *see* Central Business District (CBD)
globalization 2, 12, 14, 17–19, 32, 34, 37, 86, 235, 249
Global North 32, 37
Global South 32, 34, 46
global warming 32, 43
Glynn County 86
Goethe, Johann W. 106
Goethert, Reinhard 166–167
Goffman, Erving 4, 73–82
Gonçalves, Eros Martim 148
Goodwin, Philip 51n5
Gorelik, Adrián 124n20
Gosseye, Janina 6, 228–234
Gottsunda *197*, 200
Goulart, João 157n7
Gourna 30n2
Graham, Stephen 110
Granfelt, Bertel 190
Grazziano, Raphael 6, 235–251
Great Depression *see* 1929 financial crisis
Green Business Certification Inc. (GBCI) 243
Green New Deal 14
Gregotti, Vittorio 36, 226n9
Gruen Associates 183–185; *see also* Gruen, Victor
Gruen, Victor 183–186, 191–192, 203, 203n1, 204n12; *see also* Gruen Associates
Guerreiro, Isadora 241, 247
Guggenheim Museum Bilbao 40, 215
Gullar, Ferreira 157n8, 157n9

Habermas, Jürgen 11, 16, 18, 28, 37
habitat: Lefebvrian concept 141–142
Habitat III United Nations Conference 160
habiting *see* inhabiting
Habraken, Nicolaas John 42, 169, 274
Hall, Edward T. 83n11, 87
Hall, Peter 255
Hamburg 259
Hansen, Oscar 169–170
Hanson, Julienne 187, 192, 204n13, 204n17
Harcourt, Bernard E. 93
Harris, Richard 162–163, 178
Harvey, David 29, 32, 38, 45, 93n2, 216, 218, 225n8, 235, 249, 255, 264
Haussmann, Georges-Eugène 22, 112, 120, 143, 216
Hays, Michael 35–36, 40, 51n8, 104n7
Hegel, Georg 20, 41, 101, 104n10, 129–145
hegemonic 3, 5–6, 12, 14, 18–19, 25, 29, 34, 41–42, 131, 150, 161, 177, 179, 235, 254–256, 261, 264; *see also* counter-hegemonic
Heidegger, Martin 45, 92, 95–96, 104n10, 136, 142, 149
Hejduk, John 36, 42
Helfrich, Silke 54–55
Heller, Agnes 268
Helsinki 260

heterogeneity 19, 40, 153, 196; *see also* homogeneity
Heynen, Hilde 97, 103n4
Heysel Plateau 228
High Line *213*
Hightower, Henry C. 187, 193
Hilberseimer, Ludwig 25, 225n4
Hillier, Bill 187–188, 204n13, 204n17, 204n19
historian thought 130, 132–133, 136, *137*, 140, 145n1; *see also* historical thought
historical materialism 98, 106, 110, 214–219, 221, 224–225
historical project 4, 99, 102
historical thought 145n1; *see also* historian thought
Hitchcock, Henry-Russell 253–254, 260
Hoffmann, José *253*
homogeneity 5, 14, 25–26, 28, 142, 196, 215, 221, 226n17, 258; *see also* heterogeneity, segregation
homo oeconomicus 86–88, 91–93
Horkheimer, Max 96, 114
Howard, Ebenezer 225n4
housing: incremental 5, 160–180, 260; informal 256, 260–261, *263*; large-scale 25–26, 166, 169, 173, 177, 230, 254–256, 258; participatory process in 30n2, 161, 259–260; policy 25, 161–162, 164, 179, 214, 221, 225n3, 252, 261–262, 264; social 5–7, *15*, 25–26, 28, 30n2, 34, 42, 51n13, 142, 160–180, 211, 214, 221, 252–264, 266, 274, *276–280*; units 13, 25, 173, 221, *222*, 232, *259*, 263
Huarcaya, Roberto 262
Hudson Yards 211, *212–213*, 215, 225
Huet, Bernard 36
Hurston, Zora N. 272
Huyssen, Andreas 38
Hvattum, Mari 173

iconic architecture 13, 42, 215, 219, 225n4; *see also* spectacle
idiom 79, 81–82
Illich, Ivan 55–56, 63–64
Illuminating Engineering Society of North America (IESNA) 250n2
Império, Flávio 48; *see also* Arquitetura Nova
India 72n4, 157n6, 161, 166, 175, 177
Indiana 21, *22*
Indonesia 173
industrial city 21, 216, 217, 219
industrialization 2, 24–25, 37, 65, 107, 154, 216; *see also* industrial city; Industrial Revolution
Industrial Revolution 14, 32, 154, 179; *see also* industrialization
inequality 1, 12, 16, 20, 24, 29n1, 32, 47, 161–162, 211–216, 224–225, 225n1, 225n6, 252, 258, 260–262, 264; *see also* poverty
inhabiting: Lefebvrian concept 141–142
International Organization for Standardization (ISO) 236
International Style 26, 36
Internet bubble 32

Iquique 176, 260
Istituto Lombardo per gli Studi Economici e Sociali (ILSES) 226n9
Istituto Nazionale di Urbanistica (INU) 226n9
Istituto Universitario di Architettura di Venezia (IUAV) 36, 215–217, 225n5, 226n10, 226n12
Italy 4, 16, 20, 103n1, 148, 157n4, 217, 221, 226n9, 230, 252, 260

Jacob, Max 157n6
Jacobs, Jane 87, 90, 184–186, 191, 203n3, 204n12, 258
Jameson, Fredric 17–18, 26, 38–40, 120, 125n23, 235
Japan 188–189
Jardim, Reynaldo 157n8
Jesús, Teresa de 271, 280n1
Johannesburg 122
Johnson, Boris 211
Joseph, Isaac 79, 83n9
Josic, Alexis 169–170
Judt, Tony 51n12

Kalkbreite complex 259
Kant, Immanuel 101, 104n10, 255
Katyal, Neal K. 87
Kazakhstan 124n21
KCAP Architects & Planners 233n1
Kelling, George L. 86–87, 89–90, 92–93
Kentucky 86
Kimmelman, Michael 211, 225n2
Kipnis, Jeffrey 35
Kiruna 203n4
Koch, Daniel 5, 183–208
Koetter, Fred 38
Königsberger Vannucchi Arquitetos Associados 71
Koolhaas, Rem 35, 36, 40, 45, 113–117, 124n16, 124n17, 124n18, 124n20, 185, 262
Kopp, Anatole 34
Kos, Anton 72n1
Kowarick, Lúcio 48
Krenak, Ailton 32
Krishnamurti, Jiddu 157n6
Kropotkin, Pyotr 178
Kuala Lampur 117, 119
Kubitschek, Juscelino 157n7

Laboratori d'Urbanisme de Barcelona 216
Lacan, Jacques 36, 98, 104n7, 124n18
Lacaton & Vassal 260
Lacayo, Richard 124n21
Land, Peter 170
Lapa 149
Las Vegas 45, 77
Latin America 7, 37–39, 50, 216, 246–247, 252–255, 258, 260–264
Latour, Bruno 32, 51n14, 273
Laugier, abbot Marc-Antoine 21–22, 24, 96, 99
Laurence, Peter L. 204n12
Laval, Christian 26

Lavin, Sylvia 35
lavoir 56–58
Leadership in Energy and Environmental Design (LEED®) 6, 235–250
Leça da Palmeira *16*
Le Corbusier 25, 143, 154, 185, 203n5, 225n4
Lefebvre, Henri 1, 3–6, 26–27, 42–45, 48, 73, 83n13, 129–146, 186, 200, 202, 225n7, 255, 264
Lefebvrian trialectics 43–44; *see also* conceived space; lived space; perceived space
Lefèvre, Rodrigo 48, 51n17; *see also* Arquitetura Nova
Legeby, Ann 196–197, 204n22
Le Muet, Pierre 59–61
Lenin, Vladimir 226n11
León, González de 38
lex communis 55, 58–60, 67–68, 72; *see also* commons; praxis communis; res communis
liberalism 14, 20–25, 27–28, 49, 86–87, 124n21, 232; *see also* neoliberalism
Liernur, Francisco 38, 263
lifeworld: Habermas' concept 15–16
Lima 169–170, *171*, *179*, 256, *259*, 260, 262, *263*
Linköping 203n4
Linnaeus, Carl von 188
Lipovetsky, Gilles 38
Lisbon 214
lived space 19, 44, 142; *see also* conceived space; Lefebvrian trialectics; perceived space
Livingstone, Rodney 41
Lledó, Emilio 269–270, 273–274
logic: dialectical 2, 4–5, 17–20, 36, 42, 44, 82, 83n13, 95–97, 99, 101–102, 108, 111, 121, 123n2, 129–146, 152, 195, 216–217, 219, 255–256, 270, 273; formal 131, 137–146
London 21, *22*, 211, 214, *218*, *259*, 262
Loos, Adolf 162
Los Angeles 201, 214
Louisiana 30n5
Louisville 86
Luhmann, Niklas 42
Lukács, György 41–42, 49, 120
Luna Park 115, 117
Lund, Nils-Ole 173
Lynch, Kevin 87
Lyotard, Jean-François 18, 38

Macarthur, John 191
Madrid 7, 258, *259*, 266
Maki, Fumihiko 170
Malfatti, Anita 157
Mallarmé, Stéphane 111
Mall of Europe 228–229, 232; *see also* Neo
Manet, Édouard 111
Manhattan 26, 113–114, 116–117, 124n16, 124n18, 124n19, 200, 211
Martin, Reinhold 4, 52n18, 86–94, 212, 225
Marvin, Simon 110
Marxism 34–36, 38–39, 41, 47–48, 97–98, 102, 129–138, 145, 215, 255, 264

Marx, Karl 95–96, 99, 101, 104n8, 129, 131–138, 141, 144–145, 219, 226n11
Marx, Roberto Burle 153
Massey, Dorey 45
materialist critique *see* historical materialism
Matta-Clark, Gordon 34
Matthews, Joseph 125n25
Maturana, Humberto 271
McCarty, Willard 204n24
McMorrough, John 186, 191, 203n3
Medellin 122, 221
Medrano, Leandro 1–7, 32–53
meent 56–58, 72n1
Mehrotra, Raúl 255
Meller, Helen E. 72n5
Merleau-Ponty, Maurice 148–149, 151, 157n9, 158n10, 158n18
metropolis 18–21, 24–25, 32, 47, 112–113, 120, 148, 162, 177
Mexico 260
Mexico City *39*, 260
Meyer, Michael D. 193
Middle Ages 18, 23, 43, 56, 114
Migge, Leberecht 162, *163*, 178
Mijares, José Manuel 253
Million Program 183; *see also* housing policy
Minha Casa Minha Vida (housing program) 225n3, 262; *see also* housing policy
Minneapolis 86
Minnesota 86
Minoru Yamasaki Associates *122*
Missouri 86
Mivivienda (housing program) 262; *see also* housing policy
mixed-use planning 195, 200, 232, 242
MMBB Arquitetos *69–70*
modernism 2, 5, 14–17, 20, 25–26, 28, 34–35, 37–39, 41, 43, 47, 51n5, 51n15, 68, 95–98, 100, 102, 103n5, 104n12, 120, 125n21, 147, 154, 156, 183–184, 186–189, 191, 202, 224, 247, 252–256, 280n2; *see also* artistic avant-gardes
Mongs, L. 203n4
Monk, Daniel 122–123
Montaner, Josep Maria 51n4
Moore, Michael 109
Morocco 169
Morumbi 262
Moscow 106–108, *108–109*, 112–113, 122, 123n7, 124n21
Mota, Nelson 5, 160–182
Moulis, Antony 191
Movilla, Daniel 7, 266–284
Mulhern, Francis 41
Mumbai 167, *168*
Mumford, Lewis 117, 204n8
Muñoz Molina, Antonio 269
Muratori, Saverio 216–217, 226n10
Museu de Arte Moderna (MAM) 148
Museum of Art of São Paulo (MASP) 156

Museum of Modern Art (MoMA) 37, 91, 253–254, 260
MVRDV 258, *259*

Neo 6, 228–229, 232, 233n1
neoliberalism 1–6, 11, 13, 18–19, 26–27, 32, 34–36, 38–40, 42, 45–46, 50–51, 54, 86–88, 91–93, 93n2, 93n4, 93n8, 125n26, 161, 178–179, 229, 232–233, 252, 258, 264; *see also* free market; privatization
Netherlands 56, 161, 166, 169, 260–261
Nevada 77
New Deal 117
New Harmony Community 21, *22*, 30n5
Newman, Oscar 87, 90
New Urbanism *see* Congress for the New Urbanism
New York 4, 23–24, 26, 37, 45, 86, 88–92, 113–114, 116–117, *118*, *122*, 124n18, 124n20, 185, 201, 211, *212*, 214, 236, 246
Niemeyer, Oscar *24*, 37
Nietzsche, Friedrich 45, 90, 95, 99, 104n8, 129–136, *137*, 142, 144–145, 145n2
Nieuwenhuys, Constant 169
Nishihara, Kiyoyuki 188–189
nongovernmental organizations (NGO) 6, 42
Nonoalco-Tlatelolco 260
Northland Mall 191
Norway 173
Nussbaum, Martha 269

Obama, Barack 87
okidoki 203n4
Ocasio-Cortez, Alexandria 14
Ockman, Joan 51n10
Oehler, Dolf 124n15
oeuvre: Lefebvrian concept 18, 42–43, 48; *see also produit*
Office for Metropolitan Architecture (OMA) *36*
Oiticica, Hélio 5, 34, 148, 153, 158n16
Okhta Tower 110
Oliveira, Francisco de 48
Oliveira, Olivia de 152, 158n27
Olivetti, Adrianno 226n9
Olympics: 2008 games 117, 122; 2016 games *13*
One Bryant Park 244, *245*
Openshaw, Stan 196
Oslo 173
Ostrom, Elinor 54–55
otherness 147, 149, 151
Ouroussof, Nicolai 244
Owen, Robert *22*, 30n5

Pamplona Alta *263*
Pape, Lygia 157n8
Paraisópolis 262
Parc Monceau 59
Parent, Claude 169–170
Paris 22, 59–60, *64*, 83n12, 110–114, 120, 157n6, 185

Park, Robert E. 77, 83n10
participatory process 16, 30n2, 49, 54, 160, 176–177, 252, 257, 259–261, 275; *see also* appropriation; popular organization; self-management; social movement
Patel, Shirish B. 175–176
Paulista Architecture *see* Escola Paulista
Paulista School *see* Escola Paulista
pedagogy 7, 106, 123n3, 266–280; *see also* education
Pedrosa, Mário 37, 157n8
Pelli, Cesar *119*, 264; *see also* Pelli Clarke Pelli
Pelli Clarke Pelli 247, *248–249*; *see also* Pelli, Cesar
Pelli, Víctor 264
perceived space 44; *see also* conceived space; Lefebvrian trialectics; lived space
Perry, Clarence A. 190, 204n8
Peru 30n2, 170, 175, 178, 256, 258, 262
Perucich, Francisco V. 178
Petronas Towers 117, *119*
Phatak, Vidyadhar 167
phenomenology 5, 37, 41, 43, 104n10, 147–149, 151, 157n1, 157n9, 272
Philadelphia 77
physical space 4, 73–82; *see also* social space
Picasso, Pablo 274
Piccinato, Luigi 226n9
Piketty, Thomas 267
Piranesi, Giovanni B. 98
Piscina das Marés *16*
Place du Carrousel 112
Plato 270, 274
Plumier, J.M. 230
Poland 230
Polanyi, Michael 51n4
pollution 1, 32, 154, 183, 186, 237
poor door 6, 211–215, 225
popular organization 13; *see also* participatory process; self-management; social movement
Porto 221, *223*
Porto Maravilha Urban Operation *13*
Portugal 221, *223*
post-colonialism 34, 47, 147, 151
post-critical 3, 35, 37, 39, 41–42, 44–45, 51n3, 51n4; *see also* pragmatism
postmodernism 5, 17, 35–37, 39–40, 45, 109, 123n7, 235, 249
poverty 2, 32, 48, 117, 121, 275; *see also* inequality
Praça Mauá *13*
Prada 45
pragmatism 3–4, 7, 13, 23, 26, 35, 39–40, 45–46, 48, 51n4, 116–117, 163, 167, 173; *see also* post-critical
praxis communis 55, 62, 65, 67, 69, 72; *see also* commons; lex communis; res communis
PREVI-Lima 169, 260
Price, Cedric 169
Pritzker Prize 176, 260

privatization 18, 42, 51n12, 112; *see also* neoliberalism
Procrear (housing program) 262; *see also* housing policy
produit: Lefebvrian concept 18; *see also* oeuvre
Public-private partnership (PPP) 229, 231–233
public space 6, 40, 59, 78, 151, 164, 184–187, 190–191, 196, 201, 203, 203n5, 229, 232–233, 267
Putin, Vladimir 110

Quadros, Jânio 157n7
Quaroni, Ludovico 226n9
Quetglas, Josep 36, 40
Quinta Monroy 176, 178, *179*, 260
Quito 160

Radcliffe-Brown, Alfred R. 75, 81
Ragon, Michel 169
Rapoport, Amos 87
rationality: architectural 5–7, 15–16, 24–25, 27, 38, 117, 148, 161, 236, 257; economic 4, 6, 12–14, 18, 25, 86, 88, 91, 93, 103n1, 161, 232; social 12–15, 19–20, 24–25, 35, 43, 89, 107, 130–131, 135–136, 138, 140, 142, 144, 145n4, 187, 194, 201, 233, 270; spatial 5, 15, 24, 26–29, 116, 142–143, 193–194, 204n9, 204n13
Read, Herbert 268
Reagan, Ronald 232
Recaman, Luiz 1–7, 11–31, 47, 51n6
refugee crisis 32, 43
reification 5, 19, 97, 120; *see also* commodification
Remick, Christian 57
Renaissance 22, 97, 103n5, 257
Renzo Piano Building Workshop 244
representational space 44
representations of space 44
res communis 55, 67–68, 72; *see also* commons; lex communis; praxis communis
Reynolds, William H. 116
rhythm 5, 142, 200–201
Rice, Charles 204n11
right to the city 6, 19, 28, 43, 48, 50, 161, 221, 263; *see also* appropriation
Rio de Janeiro *13*, 91, 148, 153, 246
Risério, Antonio 158n11
ritual 54, 62, 75, 79, 147, 152–153, 201
RMJM 110
Robin Hood Gardens 262
Rocha, Glauber 148
Rocha, Paulo Mendes da *69–70*
Rockefeller Center 117, *118*
Roddier, Mireille 72n3
Rohe, Ludwig Mies van der 26, 42
Rolnik, Raquel 51n13
Romanticism 257
Rossi, Aldo 16, 36, 103n3, 226n18
Ross, Stephen M. 211, 225n2
Rouanet, Sérgio Paulo 37

Rowe, Colin 38
Ruskin, John 256–257
Russia 107, 110, 112

Safir, William 93
Saint Petersburg 112, 124n21
Saí phalanstère 21, 30n5
Salmona, Rogelio 38
Salvador 148, 158n11
Sambricio, Carlos 263
San Giminiano 114
Santa Catarina 21, 30n5
Santa Monica 39
Santiago *33*
Santos, César S. 5, 129–146
Santos, Milton 1, 48
São Paulo *24*, 30n2, 46–47, *48–50*, 123n6, 148–149, *150*, 246–247, 262
São Paulo Corporate Towers 247, *248–249*
São Victor 221, 226n15
Sartre, Jean-Paul 96
Savater, Fernando 270
SCAFT 183
Scannavini, Roberto 226n14
Schein, Ionel 169
Schmid, Christian 44, 161, 225n6
Schneider, Tatjana 162
Schopenhauer, Arthur 255
Schultz, Theodor W. 93n4
Scotland 65
Scott, Felicity 52n18
Seagram Building 26
Sears, Roebuck & Co. 231
Secchi, Bernardo 252, 260–262
segregation 1, 5–6, 11–12, 14, 28, 40, 43, 92, 120, 143, 186, 196, 201, 211, 214–215, 252, 258
Segura, Matías *33*
self-management 7, 16, 28, 252, 275; *see also* participatory process, popular organization, social movement
Sennett, Richard 54
September 11 terrorist attacks 32, *122*, 124n19
Serviço Ambulatório de Apoio Local housing program (SAAL) 221, 226n15; *see also* housing policy
Serviço Social do Comércio (SESC) 5, 68; 24 de Maio *69–70*; Paulista *71*; Pompeia *68*, 147–158
Seurat, Georges 111
Shenyang 109
Shetland Islands 77
Shklovsky, Viktor 103
Siedlung 15, 25, 162, *163*, 179
Silodam housing 258, *259*
Silvestri, Graciela 38
Simmel, Georg 12, 74–76, 78, 83n5, 92, 95, 120, 125n22
Singh, Neera M. 72n4
Skjetten Town 173, *174–175*, 179

skyscraper 23–24, 26, 114, 116–117, 124n18, 124n19, 244
slum 30n1, 48, 123, 167; *see also* favela
Smith, Adam 22
Smith, Neil 219, 225, 225n1, 226n13
Smithson, Alison 16
Smithson, Peter 16
social democracy 6, 14–15, 25, 27
Social Housing Lavapiés 7, 274–280
social movement 7, 12, 252; *see also* popular organization
social space 4, 12, 44, 75–78, 81, 140–141, 144, 164, 170; *see also* physical space
society: consumer 12, 37, 45, 270; global 12; industrial 12, 16, 20–21, 34, 142; urban 11–12, 19–21, 50, 214–215, 221, 225, 225n7
Socrates 135
Söderstaden-Hovet *185*
Soja, Edward 11, 45, 215–216, 225n8
Solà-Morales, Ignasi de 36, 40
Solà-Morales, Manuel de 216, 218, *220*, 252
solidarity 4, 12, 50, 204n17
Solomon, Robert C. 268
Solzhenitsyn, Aleksandr 112
Somol, Robert 35
Sontag, Susan 124n19
Sorokin, Pitirim 83n5
Sotelo, Ignacio 269
South Africa 110, 161
South America 32, 115
Soviet Union 107, 113, 138, 163
Spain 274–275
Spanudis, Theon 157n8
spatial practice 3, 44, 140, 143, 164, 169, 180, 235
spatial turn 4–5, 14, 44
Speaks, Michael 35, 51n3
spectacle: architecture of 3, 19, 34, 40, 42, 45–46; society of 2, 14, 110, 113; *see also* iconic architecture
Stäck, Josef 186
Staden, Hans 147, 157n2
Stakhanovism 110
Stalin, Josef 108, 138, 145n4, 226n11
Stenungsund 184
Stephens, Suzanne 244
Stirling, James 170
Stockholm 163, 184, *185*, 186, *190*, 197, *198*
Stockholms Byggnadsordning 197, *198*
Stoppani, Teresa 103
strategic urbanism 34, 224; *see also* tactical urbanism
Strategisk Arkitektur 184
Stravinsky, Igor 267
Strommen 173
suburb 2, 12, 16, 39, 43, 91, 183–184, 186, 191–192, *193*, 204, 231
superstructure 18, 20, 28, 101
Superstudio 34
surrealism 107, 114, 123n5, 124n18

sustainable development 6, 56, 160–161, 179, 184, 187, 196, 214, 228, 236–239, 243–244, 246, 250, 261, 267; United Nations Sustainable Development Goals 160–161, 186
Sweden 162, 183, 186, 190, 196, *197*, 200
Swenarton, Mark 51n13

tactical urbanism 42, 252; *see also* strategic urbanism
Tafuri, Manfredo 3–4, 14, 20–22, 25, 28, 34, 36, 41, 52n18, 95–104, 114, 117, 124n20, 215, 226n9, 263
Tate Modern 262
Taut, Bruno 97
Taylor, Breonna 86
Taylor, Robert 35
Team 10 177
Testa, Clorindo 38
Texas 183
Teyssot, Georges 93
Thatcher, Margareth 26, 232
The New York Times headquarters 244
Thompson, Frederic 115–116
Throgmorton, James 204
Tiananmen Square 112
Tiexi 109
Tila building 260
Todorov, Tzvetan 272
Tonnerre *58*
Tönnies, Ferdinand 97
Tournikiotis, Panayotis 104n12
transduction 144
Trelleborg 184
Treviño, A.J. 77, 83n8
Trigg, Dylan 149–152
Tropicália 148
Tschumi, Bernard 35–36
Turkey 230
Turner, John 30n2, 161, 164, 178, 252, 255–258
typology 6, 16, 21, 23, 40, 42, 47, 58, 60–61, 114, 153–154, 162, 199, 215–216, *217*, 219, *220*, 221, *222*, 226n10, 235–236, 239, 244, 246, 249

Ukraine 230
Ungers, Oswald Mathias 45
Unibail-Rodamco 229
United Arab Emirates 122
United Kingdom 16, 260
United States Agency for International Development (USAID) 164
United States Green Building Council (USGBC) 236–238, 242–243
United States of America 12, *22*, 30n5, 51n5, 86–87, 103n3, 114, 117, 183, 214, 237, 261
Universidade Federal da Bahia 148
Uppsala *197*, 200
urban acupuncture 221, 252

urban design 3–5, 55, 59, 67, 72–75, 82, 120, 160, 167, 170, 177–180, 184–188, 191, 201, 233, 252, 262
urban fabric 1, 6, 12, 23, 38, 61, 186, 214, 216, 221, *222*, 230
urban form 4, 6, 18, 21, 26, 48, 54, 97, 120, 123, 214–219, 221, 224–225, 226n10
urbanization 5, 11–12, 14, 32, 51n1, 57, 90–91, 107, 123n1, 160, 166, 180, 214–216, 218, 221, 225, 225n7, 228, 231, 258; planetary 2, 161, 180
urban revolution 11, 19, 43, 129, 225n7
Uruguayan Housing Cooperatives 42
use value 16, 19, 43, 161–162; *see also* exchange value
utopia 12–14, 17, 21, 26–27, 32, 34–35, 38–40, 44, 47, 49, 97–98, 102–103, 107–110, 112–113, 121–123, 132, 134, 136, 143–144, 203n6, 214, 217

Vainer, André 149
Valery, Paul 45
Vallastaden 203n4
Vallecas *259*
Vällingby Centrum 186–187
Van der Linden, Jan 166
Vélizy-Villacoublay *15*
Veloso, Caetano 148
Venice 217, 226n10
Venice Biennale: 1980 edition 18; 2016 edition 260
Venice School *see* Istituto Universitario di Architettura di Venezia (IUAV)
Venturi, Robert 16, 45, 272, 280n2
Vergara, Camilo 123
Vieira, Álvaro Siza *16*, 221, *223*, 226n15
Vieira, Tuca 262
Vienna 162–163, 260
Villanueva, Carlos Raúl 253
Ville radieuse 185, 225n4
Virilio, Paul 45, 51n2
virtuality: Lefebvrian concept 12, 19, 27, 44, 50, 138
Vitruvius 22
Von Thünen, Johann Heinrich 90
Vriesendorp, Madelon 124n18

Wagner, Martin 162
Waisman, Marina 38–40
Wales 166
Wall, Alex 191, 203n1, 204n12
Wallenstein, Sven-Olov 4, 52n18, 95–105
Wallerstein, Immanuel 125
Walts, Michael 125n25
Ward, Colin 255
Waterschei 230
Weber, Max 11, 43, 95–96, 107, 122
Weimar Republic 25
Weissmann, Franz 157
welfare state 2, 35, 42–43, 51n13, 54, 232, 252, 261–262

Wester + Elsner 203n4
Westland 231–232
White Arkitekter AB 184, *185*
Whiting, Sarah 35
Wiese, Leopold von 83n5
Willem-Alexander (King of the Netherlands) 261
Wilson, Elizabeth 187, 204n9
Wilson, James Q. 86–87, 89–90, 92
Winterslag 230
Wisnik, Guilherme 158n16
Wittgenstein, Ludwig 273
Woluwe 231–232
Woods, Shadrach 169–170
World Bank 164, 166–167, 177
World Trade Center 32, *122*
World Wars: First 25, 110, 163; Second 15–16, 19, 25, 112, 148, 177, 232

Wright, Frank Lloyd 97
Wright, Herbert 80
Wunderlich, Filipa 184

Xinyu, Lü 124n9

Yonne 58
Yudelson, Jerry 237, 240, 243

Zabludovsky, Abraham 38
Zambrano, María 270
Zedong, Mao 226n11
Zevi, Bruno 226n9
Zhang-ke, Jia 124n13
Zizek, Slavoj 51n14
Zook, Julie 201
Zurich 258–259
Zwartberg 230